CHANGING STAGES

The première of the
first part of Tony
Kushner's **Angels in
America:
Millennium
Approaches**.
RNT 1992.

CHANGING STAGES

A VIEW OF BRITISH AND
AMERICAN THEATRE
IN THE TWENTIETH CENTURY

RICHARD EYRE

AND

NICHOLAS WRIGHT

ALFRED A. KNOPF
NEW YORK
2001

THIS IS A BORZOI BOOK
PUBLISHED BY ALFRED A. KNOPF

Copyright © 2000 by Richard Eyre and Nicholas Wright

All rights reserved under International and Pan-American Copyright Conventions.
Published in the United States by Alfred A. Knopf, a division of Random House, Inc.,
New York. Distributed by Random House, Inc., New York.
www.aaknopf.com

Knopf, Borzoi Books, and the colophon are registered trademarks of Random House, Inc.

Originally published in Great Britain by Bloomsbury Publishing Plc, London, in 2000.

By arrangement with BBC Worldwide Limited
in association with the BBC TV series *Changing Stages*.

The BBC wordmark is a trademark of the British
Broadcasting Corporation and is used under licence.

Translations of Brecht excerpts are by Steve Gooch,
John Willett, Hugh Rorrison and Derek Bowman.

Words from 'Adelaide's Lament' quoted by kind
permission of the Loesser Estate

ISBN 0-375-41203-4

Manufactured in Great Britain
First American Edition

Contents

Foreword

Ostensibly, this is the book of the TV series called *Changing Stages*. In fact, the reverse is true.

In 1997 I was asked if I would take part in a 'Millennium Project': writing and presenting a series of programs about the history of twentieth-century theatre for television. I knew little of how these sort of programs are put together but enough to know that I couldn't do it off the top of my head; I needed to write the book before the series in order to find out what I thought and what I didn't know. I was confirmed in my instinct by talking to Robert Hughes, whose TV series and book, *American Visions*, I admire unreservedly. He told me that I should write the book before the series if I didn't want a nervous breakdown.

I asked Nicholas Wright, who is an old friend and had been an indispensable associate director during the whole time of my directorship of the National Theatre, if he would join me in writing the book. We have spent most of our working lives in theatres, and we have tried to distil some of the fruits of two professional lifetimes into this book.

This is our view of British theatre in the twentieth century. Since our work has been primarily in Britain, *Changing Stages* is primarily about British theatre. It's one of the virtues of our theatre, however, that over the last hundred years it has been eclectic, pragmatic and thoroughly opportunistic. Any account of 'British' theatre therefore includes many North American actors, writers, composers and directors – as well as the Irish, Germans, French, Russians and Norwegians who have enriched all theatres of the English-speaking world.

Although *Changing Stages* makes no claims to be comprehensive or exhaustive, even personal views can have a consistent basis. Theatre, for us, is a figurative art, one which cannot excite or thrill or even entertain for more than a minute or two unless it's about people, and unless the audience experiences those people as being real. Every worthwhile revolution in modern theatre has sprung from a desire to make that reality more profound, more complex, more like life as it really is, as opposed to how it's supposed to be.

We were tempted towards providing a sort of unified field theory that would fit the wires together and 'explain' the theatre of our century, but conceded that it is better to tell the story than to seek for neatness in its meaning. Or as David Mamet puts it at the end of his essential book on the theatre, *True and False*: 'It is not a sign of ignorance not to know the answers. But there is great merit in facing the questions.' Facing the questions did not train us to act as fortune-tellers: we have made no attempt to spot the stars of tomorrow.

This is a partial, personal, unscholarly view of the century's theatre written from the perspective of practitioners. Consequently, you will look for footnotes or a bibliography in vain. What is more, playing 'Spot the Author' will be a fruitless game: this was a true collaboration.

In our account of the century's theatre we have, of course, leaned on a variety of different sources. The one writer we have returned to frequently – not to borrow his opinions but to corroborate our own – is Kenneth Tynan, who died in 1980 at the age of fifty-three. Tynan is irresistibly quotable, not because he was always right, but because he never wrote diffidently or without engagement about the theatre. For many years (during the 1950s and '60s) he was the theatre critic for the *Observer*, and his weekly copy was always alive, opinionated and provocative. He was unashamedly infatuated with stars, but he responded to the right sort of life in theatre: he made it seem as if it mattered.

Tynan's contemporary, Harold Hobson, who wrote for the *Sunday Times*, was as passionately concerned, even if he was as perverse and opaque as Tynan was rigorous and lucid. From today's perspective, it's sadly enviable that their weekly reports from the theatrical front line were eagerly looked forward to, not only by those who worked in the theatre, but by everyone who wanted to know what was important in the current culture. Hobson said this a few years ago: 'The trouble with our successors is that nothing seems at stake for them.'

What is at stake today is the survival of the theatre itself. We float in a muddy pool of relativism where everything in our culture is seen as having as much weight as everything else: advertising, television sitcoms, body-piercing jewellery, Hollywood movies, Polaroid photography, bodice-ripping novels, punk music, hip-hop, house, rap, acid and this season's fashions all press for our attention, and the theatre, frail and mutable, fights to keep its head above water. This book argues that the announcement of its death has been premature. In short, we are optimists.

'Oh for Christ's sake, one doesn't *study* poets!' said Philip Larkin. 'You read them and think, that's marvellous, how is it done, could I do it? First and foremost, writing poems should be a pleasure. So should reading them, by God.' The same goes for plays: but their point is that you have to see them. The theatre resists theory even more than poetry: whatever you think, feel or say about it, its only test is in performance. When the dancer Pavlova was asked what she meant when she was dancing, she said, 'If I could tell you, I wouldn't dance it.'

Making television programs about the theatre is as quaint a folly as putting ventriloquists on the radio: the essence of the marvel is impossible to display. Perhaps because I come from a generation which happily listened week after week to a program called *Educating Archie* in which Peter Brough did radio sketches with an inert dummy, I lean towards believing that the effort is worthwhile. Every theatre production – and TV program – is sustained by the virtues of faith, hope and charity: faith that what you are doing is worth doing, hope that your opinion is shared by the audience and charity – in the sense of friendship – for those who are doing it with you.

Nick and I would not have written this book, and I would not have made the TV programs, had it not been for the enthusiasm and persistence of Andrea Miller. When she approached me, I was trying to plan my life after ten years as the Director of the National Theatre. I was torn between yearning for the stability of a large long-term project and welcoming the fecklessness of the freelance life. She provided the long-term project; an attritional spell on an unmade film filled the other spot.

Andrea's quixotic mission to put theatre history on television was supported unhesitatingly by Kim Evans, then Head of the BBC's Classical Music and Arts Department, Mark Thompson, then Controller of BBC2, and Alan Yentob, then Head of Television.

The TV series was made by one executive producer: Andrea Miller; four directors: Roger Parsons, Mary Downes, Chris Granlund and Jamie Muir; four cameramen: Luke Cardiff, Patrick Duval, Fred Fabre and Spike Geilinger, and their assistants: Philip Eason, Derrick Little and Mike Sarah; four sound recordists: Simon Firsht, Godfrey Kirby, Andrew Todd and Cormac Tohill; two researchers: Robin Dashwood and Celia Bargh; one production manager: Jo Hatley; four film editors: Colin Minchen, Dave Kitson, Joyce Gentle and Guy Crossman; and three production assistants: Suzanne North, Jane Rundle and Charlie MacCormack. I thank them all for their enthusiasm, their skill, their faith in the project and their charity for an often exasperating presenter.

In writing the book, Nick and I were grateful for Robin Dashwood's research, for advice from Lyn Haill, for Mary Tomlinson's expert editing and for Liz Calder's constant enthusiasm.

RICHARD EYRE
July 2000

Introduction

1

After a rare snowfall in Florence, Piero de Medici is alleged to have commissioned Michelangelo to make a sculpture in snow. It was said to have been his greatest work, but you had to have been there to have seen it – it was as frail and as ephemeral as a theatre performance, living on only in the memory.

In this century war has acquired a cosmic barbarity, economies have become bulimic, sex has become public wallpaper, and tyranny has been the best-rehearsed political system. The virus of sloganry and demagoguery has infected every cell of our minds, and mass has distorted proportion by eliminating human scale in entertainment, buildings, industry, weapons, armies, death, poverty and disease. Giants stalk the globe – corporations, political leaders, showbiz icons – and we frail humans crawl dwarfed beneath them, surrounded by a Babel of communication.

In the age of the computer, knowledge is everlasting, nothing is destroyed. Our date of birth, our nationality, our health, our schooling, our home, our work, our money, our tastes, our crimes, our deaths are recorded in binary digits, invisible and inextinguishable as God. We swim in oceans of information, surrounded by continents of recorded images and sounds. We barely breathe above the ever-deepening incoming tide.

In this context what we hold in our heads – our memory, our feelings, our sense of our own history – becomes more to be valued, more to be cherished. What is human can't be digitised. The art of the theatre is an expression of that humanness: it is an art that can never dissolve its reliance on the scale of the human figure, the sound of the human voice, and the disposition of mankind to tell each other stories. A theatre performance cannot be stored or recorded: it is live and it is unrepeatable, ephemeral even at its very greatest, melting away after the event like a snowman in the sun.

To like the theatre you have to like its transience and its immediacy: it happens in the present tense and it's fallible. There's a sense of occasion in any theatre performance and of participation in a communal act: you go into a theatre an individual and you emerge an audience.

Theatre thrives on metaphor: a room becomes a world, a group of characters becomes a whole society. If you're attracted to theatre it will be on account of its 'theatreness' – those unique properties that make it distinct from any other medium: its humane proportions, its potential for poetry, its insistence on the present tense, its use of space, of time, of light, of speech, of music, and of story-telling.

When the theatre's there it's there, when it's gone it's gone, and you'll never be able to describe a memorable moment in the theatre accurately, because the essential element of context – real time and real space – will never be there in the description. You can conjure a musical performance in your head from looking at the score; a play text denies that realisation, even to the most skilful and practised reader.

The novelist John Updike wrote: 'I've never much enjoyed going to plays. The unreality of painted people standing on a platform saying things they've said to each other for months is more than I can overlook.' This is missing the point. It's the re-creation that animates the art and makes it unique. All art forms are unreal in some sense: they have their formal rules, their conventions, their partiality, novels as much as paintings. A woman said to Matisse, 'Surely the arm of this woman is too long?' To which Matisse replied, 'It's not an arm, Madame, it's a picture.' That's the answer to someone who observes that theatre is an unreal medium: of course the theatre is 'unreal' but it doesn't stop it being truthful.

Believing in the power of the theatre is like believing in religion: you have to experience its effect in order to understand the attraction of it.

2

A collaborator once told Brecht of an English play called **The Beggar's Opera** that combined music, speech, and moral satire. 'Ah,' said Brecht, 'that smells of theatre.'

There is something about Britain that smells of the theatre, which has spread to every country where theatre exists, with the possible, and characteristic, exception of France, in spite of the best efforts of Victor Hugo and Berlioz to infect their countrymen with their passionate adoration of Shakespeare. The British theatre has inspired Pushkin and Goethe, Chekhov and Schiller, Ibsen, Eugene O'Neill, Mamet, Stanislavsky and Brecht – as well as legions of visitors to the country who cite the theatre as one of the principal reasons for coming to Britain.

Of course one of the reasons for the pre-eminence of British theatre is that there's been so much of it. Sporadic seismic cultural movements at several periods in Britain have thrown up extraordinary riches – from the late 1580s for thirty years, the Restoration era for nearly fifty years, the late eighteenth century for thirty years, the late nineteenth for forty-odd years, and from 1956 for – well, it would be invidious to say. These eruptions have interrupted long periods of torpor and seem to have coincided with periods of economic growth and national self-confidence.

'Can one talk about nations as though they were individuals?' Orwell asked. Is there something in the British character – if there is such a thing – that lends itself to an enthusiasm and a talent for making theatre? The British love gardens and animals, are tolerant, broad-minded, politically moderate, and have a well-developed suspicion of dogma and ideology. Many of the characteristics of theatre coincide with those of the British nation: our love of ritual, processions, ceremonies, hieratic behaviour and dressing up. And our parliamentary and legal systems depend, as does theatre, on adversarial conflict. And theatre is concerned with role-playing, which is, of course, second nature to a nation obsessed with the signs and behaviour of class distinction and inured to the necessity of pretending to be what you aren't.

It's a common claim that the British have the finest theatre in the world; the same thing is often said of our television, our judiciary, and our parliamentary system, so we should be cautious of accepting it. But we can recite a litany of names of great British actors, actor-managers and directors, and we inherit the traditions of the mystery plays, of Marlowe, Shakespeare, Jonson, Webster, Middleton, D.H. Lawrence, Coward, Rattigan, Osborne, Pinter, Stoppard – not to mention a procession of glittering Irishmen who have enriched the British theatre over 300 years: Congreve, Farquhar, Goldsmith, Sheridan, Boucicault, Wilde, Shaw, Synge, O'Casey, Beckett and Friel.

British theatre – at least until the twentieth century – has always been insular and insulated from what would have been described in the eighteenth century (and until quite recently) as 'foreign' drama. With the British knack for turning a blind eye to the uglier parts of their history, for the purposes of theatrical history the 'foreignness' of the Irish playwrights has been ignored: they have always been claimed as honorary Englishmen.

Britain – or at least England – lost much in the Reformation, not just many of its abbeys and churches. A tradition of painting and sculpture was broken, and the loss of a potent visual imagery forcibly produced in the English a keen attraction to the verbal. The shadowy pragmatic equivocations of the Church of England replaced the tangible certainties of Catholic dogma, which in Ireland remained a fertile provocation for writers – even the Protestant ones.

The Irish have always had a strong verbal culture, a natural gift for story-telling born out of myth-making and of illiteracy, both created or exacerbated by colonial rule. The English of the conquerors came to be used in an idiosyncratic way, ghosting and mimicking in its form and its idioms the Gaelic language which it had forcibly replaced. It became a weapon of wit, and Irish English acquired the force and allure of a ghetto language, like black or gay argot: inventive, witty, vivid and essentially satirical. Their Irishness has defined their perspective of Britain and amplified their desire to succeed in a milieu that regarded them as second-rate Englishmen.

In the American theatre the Jews have played the role of the Irish in Britain, injecting their theatre with energy, high artistic purpose, and social consciousness. In the musical theatre, they have been largely responsible for transforming an anaemic form of operetta into one of the great dramatic forms of this or any century: the book musical.

In the 1940s and '50s Britain borrowed from American theatre – musicals and plays – energy, a voracious appetite for passionate language used with unembarrassed enthusiasm, and an ambition to make theatre worth bothering about. For all the commercialism of Broadway, the British theatre gained something that seemed to have been lost: the New World gave life to the Old.

The one great natural asset that the British theatre has shared with the Irish and the American is the English language, a language ideally suited for drama: it's spoken differently from the way it is written, it's supple, highly imagistic, highly idiomatic, has simple if casual rules of grammar and – most importantly – an extensive range of tone. A German philologist said in 1852, 'Of all modern languages, not one has acquired such great strength and vigour as the English ... it may justly be called THE LANGUAGE OF THE WORLD.'

This is not to make a point about political supremacy or to observe that there are many millions of people who have not welcomed (and still don't) the (often forcible) introduction of English into their countries. It is also a fact that much of the life of that language has been stimulated by the theatre, which depends on the distillation and stylisation of colloquial speech.

3

A steam engine lashed by torrential rain rushes towards you across a new brick bridge built over a river. A panic-stricken hare runs ahead of the train. In a second the train will cleave through the wind-driven rain, overtake the hare and leave a blurred image frozen on your retinas for eternity. You are looking at Turner's *Rain, Steam and Speed*. You can marvel at the virtuosity and the beauty, but to a creature of the early twenty-first century it has nothing to teach you about the sensation of speed.

The child born a hundred years ago who went to school in a horse-drawn tram under an open sky would not be surrounded by a world in which the only things that have not changed utterly are the clouds scudding above the lofty buildings and the fragility of the human body. The changes of the physical world and the advances in technology have altered our perceptions. No artist today could treat the subject of speed in paint, and the only speed that impresses us now is the speed of light. It's still possible, however, to watch a production of **Othello** and be exasperated and moved by a catastrophe precipitated by a lost handkerchief: jealousy is immutable.

The evolution in the theatre is, irrespective of technological advances, more an evolution of content than form. Changes are not forced by the pressure of history or the avalanche of technology, but the luck of genius. 'Art is in love with luck, and luck with art,' said Aristotle, and of no art form is it more true than the theatre.

The writers of genius are the ones who write what couldn't be written before: they license their successors to open the doors of their imagination. Shakespeare spilled out plays in blank verse with a volcanic prodigality that displayed no limits of invention or subject matter, setting the golden rule for his successors: that there are no rules. Within the century of his death Jonson catalogued the follies of ambition, Webster made plays about violence and preferment, Congreve made theatre out of sex.

Chekhov performed alchemy on the leaden minutiae of daily life in the Russian provinces, while Ibsen demonstrated that theatre could concern itself with social issues at the same time as anatomising individual pain. Shaw made theatre of debate, Brecht of politics. Osborne shouted in the ear of a soporific society, while Beckett disturbed it with stillness and despair. Pinter conjured plays about silence, cruelty and nervous breakdown, while Stoppard juggled with chance, chaos theory and quantum mechanics. Rodgers and Hammerstein showed that wife-beating, racism and masturbation could be set to popular music, Hare that you could examine the state of Britain through Church of England vicars in South London, while Tony Kushner examined the state of America through Mormons, McCarthy lawyers, homosexual couples and angels.

Anything is possible to imagine, and anything can be staged. Here is a stage direction from Sheridan's **The Critic**:

> *Scene changes to the sea – the fleets engage – the musick plays 'Britons strike home'. – Spanish fleet destroyed by fire ships, &c. – English fleet advances – musick plays 'Rule Britannia'. – The procession of all the English rivers and their tributaries with their emblems, &c. begins with Handel's water musick – ends with a chorus, to the march of Judas Maccabaeus.*

And here, famously, is Shakespeare in **The Winter's Tale**: *Exit, pursued by a bear.*

No art form remains consistently healthy. From the late nineteenth century all the visual arts faced problems induced by technological advances. The development of means of reproduction – founding, stamping, copying, woodcuts, engraving, etching, lithography – had culminated in a discovery that had captured a place of its own among the artistic processes: photography. Representational art was confronted by the challenge of a medium that appeared to be able to do its job quicker, better and by any trained operative. It became possible to imagine that a painting or a sculpture – an artefact defined in part by its unique presence in time and space – could be replicated and distributed. For the first time a work of art could become accessible to anyone. Would this be the death of art? With the invention of the moving photograph – film – the same threat was made to the theatre.

Apocalyptic predictions were made for the effect of film: 'I can no longer think what I want to think,' said the French playwright George Duhamel in 1924. 'My thoughts have been replaced by moving images.' It was predicted that film would be *the* art of the twentieth century, the synthesis of all arts, the end of progress: 'Shakespeare, Beethoven will make films ... all legends, all mythologies and all myths, all founders of religion, and the very religious ... await their exposed resurrection, and the heroes crowd each other at the gate,' said the film director, Abel Gance, who in his silent films with their dazzling if undiscriminating technical ingenuity, anticipated most of the cinema of the next fifty years.

Perhaps the 'heroes' do crowd each other at the gate – if you can count Leonardo DiCaprio and Jennifer Lopez as heroes. Film has produced icons but, by the beginning of the new century, seems to have exhausted its imagination. Economic considerations – with rare exceptions – now dominate the content. Movies have become a spectacle that requires no concentration and presupposes no intelligence, which kindles no light in the heart and awakens no hope other than the one of someday becoming a star in Los Angeles; the medium awaits another transforming genius. Within our century, from being the medium that would make all other forms of dramatic expression redundant, film has become accepted as just another way of telling stories and of looking at the world, no more or less potent in its essence than the theatre.

Far from the visual arts being destroyed by photography, or the theatre being drowned by the movies, the period from the turn of the century up to 1930 was one of great inventiveness in all the arts, a dizzying roundabout of revolution and counter-revolution. It was as if all art forms – aware of the challenge of mass reproduction in art and industry and the threat of mass engineering of human souls in politics – were determined to express the might of the individual voice and vision. The Norwegian painter Edvard Munch provided the rallying cry for the twentieth century: 'The camera cannot compete with brush and palette – as long as it cannot be used in hell or heaven.'

In the theatre the response produced a flight from naturalism, a voyage into the forbidden parts of the imagination as well as of society. In the face of a century of systematic cruelty, mass barbarity and suffering, the secular religions of faith in science or political Utopias dissolved. The theatre was forced to examine what appeared to millions of people in 1945 as the absurdity of a life without jobs, homes, or countries, a world without hope, religion or sense.

There were two distinct approaches to this according to Kenneth Tynan, writing in 1961:

> On the one side there are the playwrights who believe that the key to a man's soul is his social and political environment, and on the other, those who believe that the key to his social and political environment is to be found through his soul. The former group is predominantly leftist, concerned with social change and the necessity of communicating with the many as well as the few ... The opposition group is anarchic and in the main pessimistic; uninterested in social change, rejecting all possible solutions, it concentrates on exploring individual *malaise* in a world where communication between human beings has become (it contends) a virtual impossibility.

15

The godfather of the first group – if not its father – is Bertolt Brecht, and of the second, Samuel Beckett. Brecht's children are numerous and varied, many of whom rejected his politics if not his influence; Beckett's progeny are no less numerous but less obviously definable. Let us settle for a distinction between those who explore the landscape of society – the philosophers, and those who explore the landscape of the soul – the poets. Later in the book we will examine their work and their respective legacies.

4

In writing this book, the task we set ourselves was to find out how we got here: to identify the people, the plays, the ideas that had come together over the last hundred years or so to bring about the flowering that we see today. It felt like paging through a photograph album, working through from turn-of-the-century sepia to 1950s black-and-white and ending up with an armful of colourful Polaroids.

As always, the story the album told was at odds with the myth. Just like those so-called respectable ancestors who on close inspection are obvious reprobates, or the old money which turns out to have been amassed through bootlegging, so the age-old traditions of British theatre are a great deal newer than they're often claimed to be, and a lot less British. We offer no apologies for our forays into Europe, across the Atlantic or over the Irish Sea: the modern British theatre, far from being a deeply rooted, heritage affair, was assembled in free-booting spirit from a variety of sources over little more than a century.

One of the pleasures of putting this book together was the discovery of half-hidden genealogies. To trace the way in which an influence spreads from age to age, and from country to country, is to uncover a line of power. To see, for example, how the Shakespearian tradition was restored to the land of its birth by the German Brecht was to gain an insight into the radical British theatre of the 1970s that we lacked at the time, close to it though we were in our different ways.

Another insight was how often these genealogies – 'stories', you could call them – underlined the role of the outsider: the artist who is somehow out of key with his or her surroundings. European ghetto song-writers, transplanted to New York, created a genuine American art form, the Broadway musical. It was an Anglo-Irishman who cleared the path for British political theatre, another who founded the theatre of coded self-expression, which in turn would be taken up by gay men. Theatre, it seemed, was never, and could never become, a medium for the socially complacent. It's an uphill road towards ever-elusive self-identity: a bastards' art.

The argument of this book will depend on charting the history of the British theatre of the twentieth century through the work of writers, actors and those directors who have transformed the art of direction or who have blurred the edges of definition of authorship, not so much by usurping the power of the writer, but by combining all the elements of theatre into a seamless whole.

This is a book about change, which is why it gives so much of its attention to play-wrights: it is they, on the whole, who have changed the theatre, the demands of their content obliging those who stage the plays – and musicals – to seek new modes of presentation. In the last century the writers who have most significantly transformed the theatre are Chekhov, Ibsen, Beckett, Brecht, Rodgers and Hammerstein.

We've written at length about Laurence Olivier and John Gielgud since both, as actor-managers, were able to make a structural change to the theatre of their day, but many great actors – both famous and less known – have gone unmentioned. This, in a curious way, is a mark of respect. It is actors who provide the theatre, not with change, but with its continuity. It's thanks to them that, whatever winds of fashion have blown across the British theatre, its subject has remained the human form and the human mind.

British theatre is set on a seam of Shakespeare, like a land that sits over a massive mineral deposit. Along with our landscape and our climate, Shakespeare is our greatest national asset. He's our miraculous accident, writing in a language that's a stew of neologisms, foreign importations, Latin, dialect and courtly speech. The English language, the Irish genius, the American vitality – and a reasonably benign funding attitude – have all conspired to keep the British theatre alive: without Shakespeare the body would have long been buried.

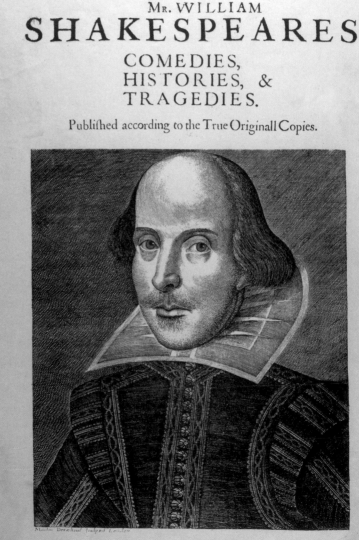

Shakespeare: Frontispiece of The First Folio.

Shakespeare

'The remarkable thing about Shakespeare is that he really is very good – in spite of all the people who say he's very good.'
ROBERT GRAVES

1

At the end of a 1991 performance of **King Lear** by the Royal National Theatre in Bucharest a man walked up to Brian Cox, who was playing Lear, and handed him a note and a bouquet. The note read: 'Nobody can play Sir William Shakespeare's plays better than his English people. I've seen with your remarkable help that somewhere in England Sir William Shakespeare is still alive. Thank you. Signed: A Simple Man.'

Sir William Shakespeare's plays are alive in Japanese, German, Mandarin, French, Finnish, Yoruba, Arabic, Esperanto, pidgin English – and every other language in which any sort of theatre performance is given. You can hear him described as 'our national play-wright' in Poland, Russia, Ghana, in the United States and in South Africa. Shakespeare's plays are quoted by politicians in India, cited in lawcourts in Sarawak, studied as set texts in Bulgaria and Bradford.

In Britain Shakespeare is our icon, our emblem, our logo, our talisman, our secular saint, our patriarch, our sage, our national poet, our Bard of Britannia, our Man of the Millennium, the heart of Great Britain plc. He is invariably conscripted to inflate any commonplace assertion about almost any subject from public speaking to space travel, or to provide ballast to stabilise our rocky national morale.

He has been claimed for their own by Marxists, Buddhists, Catholics, Lutherans, monarchists, feminists, animists, agnostics and absurdists. He speaks across centuries, across race and class and creed.

Who is he? Mercifully we know little of Shakespeare's life. It saves us from making fatuously mechanistic equations between the life and work. What we do know about Shakespeare is no more or less remarkable than the bare biography of any other playwright who has left their mark on the British theatre in the last 400 years: he was born in Stratford-upon-Avon on 23 April 1564 and died there in April 1616; his father was a glove-maker, businessman and bailiff, he grew up in a small town in beautiful countryside; he went to the local grammar school where, if we are to believe his fellow playwright Ben Jonson, he learned 'small Latin and less Greek'; he married (possibly in haste) a woman eight years older than him, and had three children – one of whom, his only son, died at the age of eleven. He owned property in London and Stratford and died a rich man.

It's possible that he may have started as a schoolmaster, it's probable that he became an actor, and it's certain that he wrote thirty-nine of the best plays ever, with an extraordinary fluency: 'His mind and hand went together.'

What can we learn about Shakespeare from his plays?

He was not a religious man – at least in the sense of showing any passion for organised religion. However hard you try, you cannot conscript Shakespeare to the body of any church. Certainly there are priests in the plays, but they are generally officials who carry little more weight than the vicars in Ealing comedies. The workings of Christian grace are often ambiguous and the theology is often vague – sometimes suggesting Catholicism, the old, proscribed religion, but more often an unassertive pragmatism. The Bible is frequently referred to – explicitly and implicitly – largely because it was the only published literature available to many of his audience.

Shaw, who went out of his way to find reasons for diminishing 'Shakspear's' (*sic*) reputation, observed that he was 'not overtly religious or without religion'. Tolstoy, who thought Shakespeare a much overrated writer (but had only read him in poor translations) bemoaned his lack of 'religious consciousness'. While there is an awareness in the plays of the presence of the supernatural in human affairs, doubt is always acknowledged. This is the world of the Renaissance, the age of Galileo, the age, as John Donne put it, of the 'new philosophy which calls all in doubt'. In Hamlet's last words: 'The rest is silence,' it's not hard to infer that he fears that there is nothing after death but a blank white wall.

Shakespeare is fascinated by politics, charting the world of secular power with an avid curiosity, showing a very highly developed sense of the workings of the machinery of bureaucracy and power. No one who has brushed against the world of *realpolitik* in any government of any colour could fail to recognise Polonius, and Elsinore will be immediately identifiable to anyone who visited or lived in Eastern Europe under Communism. The world of bugged hotel rooms, the ever-present secret police, the smug strutting arrogance of the Party's apparatchiks, the friends who lower their voices and look about them before speaking, the fear of prison, the familiarity with those who have experienced it, the swaggering display of the privileges of the nomenklatura, these all belong to the world that Hamlet finds so 'out of joint'.

Students of politics, keen to study the anatomy of opportunism, moral ambiguity, expediency, and hypocrisy could take as their primer The History Plays and The Roman Plays, and for advanced study **Troilus and Cressida** and **Measure for Measure**. **Richard III** would serve as a practical handbook for a would-be tyrant. You could say it already has: the narrative of Hitler's coup mimics Shakespeare's play with uncanny accuracy. And you can read **The Tempest** as a play about colonialism without any distortion – which is not to deny that it is about other things: fathers, daughters, power and magic.

19

Shakespeare certainly believes that without order chaos reigns. He sees the need for society to be a microcosm of the cosmic design, a mimicry of nature, but recognises the capriciousness of nature as well as its harmony. Precisely for that reason – in **King Lear**, for instance – we see suffering that has no order, sense, meaning, or redemption:

> As flies to wanton boys are we to the gods,
> They kill us for their sport.

At the end of that play, as Edgar speaks surrounded by the legacy of a domestic holocaust – a heap of corpses – it's hard to salvage much comfort from this:

> The weight of this sad time we must obey,
> Speak what we feel, not what we ought to say.
> The oldest hath borne most; we that are young
> Shall never see so much, nor live so long.

We can say with conviction that Shakespeare was knowledgeable and even obsessed by the subject of soldiering: most of his protagonists are soldiers – Othello, Antony, Lear, Macbeth, Troilus, Julius Caesar, Coriolanus, Benedick, Prince Hal, Richard III, Bolingbroke, and the formidable off-stage character of old Hamlet, and many of his plays have war as their subject, but we can't infer from that evidence that Shakespeare spent even a short period as a soldier.

Shakespeare was a writer of fiction and he did what all writers of fiction should do: he used his ears, his eyes and his imagination. He exemplifies the axiom of Henry James: A young lady novelist of talent and imagination should be able to look through the window of a guards barracks and write a perfectly reasonable novel about the life of a guardsman.

Of Shakespeare's sex-life there is no end to speculation. By which we mean: was he gay? He writes about homosexual love in The Sonnets in the one medium – personal poetry – where it *is* fair to look for some association between his life and his work, where he is not concerned with writing in character and where we would expect the author's voice to be transparent.

This is Sonnet 20, probably written to the Earl of Southampton:

> A woman's face with Nature's own hand painted
> Hast thou the master-mistress of my passion;
> A woman's gentle heart, but not acquainted
> With shifting change, as if false woman's fashion;
> An eye more bright than theirs, less false in rolling,
> Gilding the object whereupon it gazeth;
> A man in hue, all hews in his controlling,

Which steals men's eyes and women's souls amazeth.
And for a woman wert thou first created,
Till Nature as she wrought thee fell a-doting,
And by addition thee of me defeated,
By adding one thing to my purpose nothing.
But since she prick'd thee out for women's pleasure,
Mine be thy love, and thy love's use their treasure.

'I must be at pains to stress,' said a recent Shakespeare scholar, 'that there is no evidence to support the myth that William Shakespeare and the Earl of Southampton were homosexual lovers.' The prejudices of a Victorian critic in 1840 were perhaps more honest: 'I could heartily wish that Shakespeare had never written it.' Many commentators put a fog of sophistry round the matter or resolve their problem by changing the sex of the object of the author's passion. From the perspective of our times, when homosexual love is no longer a crime or cause for social opprobrium, we must concede that it appears that Shakespeare was an untroubled bisexual.

We are left, like bumbling detectives, to construct a 'personality profile' from a huge mass of available information. If he has what we might describe as an 'obsession', it is this: the indissoluble human bond between parents and children. This is the most clearly identifiable DNA strain in the plays – which is simply to say that he was 'obsessed' with the human-ness of being human.

We can say only this with absolute confidence: here is a man who is unquestionably humane, who believes in the redeeming power of compassion and the transforming – if not always benign – power of love: sexual love, fraternal love, maternal love, paternal love, love of parent, love of war, love of nation, love of ambition – all love except love of God. He affirms the infinite ambiguity of people and of nature and takes upon himself the 'mystery of things' as if he were God's spy.

What Shakespeare *believed* is the sum of his plays: to misunderstand that is to misunderstand the role of a playwright. Playwrights don't have a 'set of beliefs'; they're not theologians. Who could construe from **The Homecoming, The Caretaker** and **The Birthday Party** that the author was a passionate socialist, or that the author of **Waiting for Godot** was an active member of the French Resistance?

The playwright's job is to be able to imagine and describe characters of wildly opposed sensibilities: to be able to invent Rosalind as fully as Jacques, Desdemona as fully as Iago, and the actor's job is to inhabit and animate those characters impartially: they must approach a character with a child's heart, innocent of judgement.

Plays are about the spaces in between the spoken word as much as about speech itself, about how people *react* as much as how they *act*. The playwright has to balance revelation against concealment, has to animate character through action rather than

21

description, has to juggle relationships, plot, entrances and exits by sleight of hand, and above all has to engage the attention of the audience consistently at the instant of performance.

However much we admire Shakespeare we're foolish if we treat the creator of the plays as a sort of holy fool or a messianic seer. He was a playwright, a producer, and an actor, and most actors – the good ones – are resourceful, pragmatic, witty, humane, generous, irreverent and courageous. It is precisely his contact with the practicalities of his chosen medium that makes his work so effective.

2

To stage a Shakespeare play is to begin to trifle with an indivisible part of our cultural heritage, to toy with our genetic make-up. When you approach a new play as a director or an actor, you carry no baggage, you are free of opinion. With a Shakespeare play you arrive with pantechnicons: you cross continents of critical prose.

Surprisingly few commentators, however – all convinced of the greatness of the work on the page – are prepared to concede, or perhaps even to understand, the singularity of Shakespeare's genius. Shakespeare was writing plays not for publication or reflective analysis, but for a medium that only exists in the present tense, a medium which depends for its success – at the moment of performance – on the skill of the actors and the imagination of a willing audience.

Shakespeare is often patronised by being referred to as a poet of variable abilities – as if to call him a playwright or an actor is to risk some sort of intellectual infection. Dr Johnson was a keen theatregoer but he said that 'Shakespeare never had six lines together without a fault', and Johnson's successors are all around us – many of them holding distinguished positions in English-speaking universities.

We can only understand or appreciate Shakespeare's extraordinary achievement if we are prepared not only to concede that he was not writing poetry for the library or the bedroom, but that he had actually chosen to write for the theatre – writing, *in character*, narrative revealed by what people say and do. He was demonstrably not interested in publication – a fact as alien to the present-day playwright as a horse-drawn cart would be to the owner of a Ferrari.

Poetry is applied to Shakespeare's plays not, as Dr Johnson seemed to think, like a sort of decorative paint, but as an expressive tool that gives a greater pulse, momentum, and distillation of thought and feeling than prose; but it's no less a medium for delineating individual character. If Shakespeare had wanted to write his plays in prose he would have been more than capable of it – as a glance at the 'Willow' scene in **Othello** will confirm. To appreciate Shakespeare thoroughly is to believe in him as a writer who wrote for the theatre in verse as a matter of choice. The wonder of Shakespeare lies not only in his profundity but in his accessibility.

The life of his plays is in the language, not alongside it or underneath it. Feelings and thoughts are released at the moment of speech. An Elizabethan audience would have responded to the pulse, the rhythms, the shapes, sounds, and meanings within the consistent ten-syllable, five-stress lines of blank verse. Above all, they were an audience who listened.

To a large extent we've lost that priority; nowadays we see before we hear. Verse drama places demands on the audience, but a greater demand still on the actors, habituated to naturalistic speech, and to private, introspective emotional displays. The meaning must be felt as much as understood. 'You should be able to feel the language,' says the poet Tony Harrison. 'To taste it, to conscript the whole body as well as the mind and the mouth to savour it.'

Picasso once told a friend that Giacometti's work was becoming increasingly monotonous and repetitive. The friend defended Giacometti, talking of his intense desire to find 'a new solution to the problem of figuration'. 'There isn't a solution,' said Picasso. 'There never is a solution. That's as it should be.'

Picasso's casual assurance has been one of the curses for artists in his shadow, daunted and diminished by his omnivorous genius. It has been one of the 'problems' for art in the twentieth century, and Shakespeare might well have had the same effect in the theatre. His response would certainly have been that there wasn't a problem, there never is a problem, and that's how it should be.

His contemporaries – Heywood, Middleton, Jonson, Webster, Tourneur – do not seem to have been intimidated by writing plays alongside a man who was inventing and re-inventing the art of the theatre with every play that he wrote. Every 'ism' in the theatre – naturalism, expressionism, absurdism, Brechtianism – can be found, latent or full-blown, in the plays of Shakespeare. He has had no imitators, and his successors seem universally to have regarded his work as an inspiration rather than an inhibition. His presence, hovering over the British theatre for 400 years, has been a blessing. 'Shakespeare, c'est le drame,' said Victor Hugo: Shakespeare is theatre.

Theatre is a paradox – the art of the present tense is also the art of repetition. Samuel Butler's aphorism: 'The history of art is the history of revivals,' is never truer than of the theatre. Plays that survive from a previous era are like leaf-mould, acting as a compost for succeeding generations, fertilising the work of theatres which continue to perform them. **King Lear** can play contentedly in repertoire alongside Patrick Marber's **Closer**; they both belong to the same continuum.

What is the nature of Shakespeare's originality?

His originality does not lie in his plots, nearly all of which – except for **The Tempest** and **A Midsummer Night's Dream** – are lifted from novels, historical accounts or other plays. But that shouldn't surprise us, educated as we are by the movies, where films created from original material are as rare as hens' teeth. Most films are reworked from plays, novels, journalism or other films. The success of their transformation lies in the manner of their reworking, and what is original in Shakespeare is what he did with his material. To know that he followed Plutarch's *The Life of Mark Antony* almost word for word for **Antony and Cleopatra** is not to diminish his achievement or our enjoyment of the play.

Of course the particularity of Shakespeare's genius lies in his humanity, his virtuoso skills with language, his wit, and his imagination, but beyond all that in his astonishing control both of the grand structure and the minute detail; he is able to play God and play Man at the same time. In **King Lear**, for instance, look at the themes: parenthood, authority, evil, nature, love – family love, patriarchal love, parental love, brotherly love, sisterly love, sexual love, love flouted, love refused, love suppressed, love unrequited. This symphonic construction arches over the play like the roof of a Gothic cathedral, but almost the last words that Lear speaks before he dies are these: 'Pray you, undo this button.' Edgar – probably – does this. 'Thank you, sir,' says Lear. A king blind to the existence of servants and the suffering of his subjects has been educated in humanity, the simplest of words of gratitude acknowledging the simplest gesture of help: the architect of the great cathedral has also carved the face of an angel on a choir stall.

Shakespeare is responsible for the invention of distinct – and largely inimitable – forms of play for which compound words should have been minted; we'll have to make do with *Shakespearian comedy*, *Shakespearian epic*, and *Shakespearian tragedy – Master William Shakespeare's Comedies, Histories and Tragedies*, as the editors of the First Folio billed the book that they published in 1623.

The Comedies are comedies in that they are not tragedies; they have happy endings, but most of them are marinated in melancholy, and some of them – **As You Like it**, for instance – are not even particularly funny.

You can recognise the landscape of The Comedies as you can Watteau's, Piero della Francesca's or Cézanne's: it is something like the world you know, but more like the painter's own imagination. In Shakespeare's landscape the natural world is very strongly evident and not always benign – the sea, the wind, the rain, woods, forests, parkland, mossy banks. It is not always sunny: much of it lies in shadow, not the cool shade of an English oak where lovers take refuge from the sun, but the shadow of tragedy: expulsion from court, shipwreck, war, and death.

You can't help noticing that the landscape is peopled by quite narcissistic young men and strikingly feisty young women, who have a prominence and authority unusual even by the standards of the twenty-first century. The women have frank and realistic attitudes to sex, and are often the cause of sexual competition between male friends. Sex is never achieved without suffering, pleasure is never pure.

The epigraph for The Comedies could be this – it's Rosalind, old beyond her years, speaking to the man who is in love with her and she with him:

> Love is merely a madness, and I tell you, deserves as well a dark house and a whip as madmen do: and the reason why they are not so punished and cured is that the lunacy is so ordinary that the whippers are in love too.

The pulse of the plays is derived not from courtly love – formal and constrained – but real sexual love, a turbulent force that is as much a curse as a blessing. Sex is ever present: flirtation, courtship, pursuit, cross-dressing, gender-games, rivalry, jealousy, resolving in the end, invariably, into the harmony of marriage.

These plays balance the need for companionship with the desire to be alone; except in the earliest comedies nothing ever ends unequivocally – for all the glowing romantic hope there is always at least a hint of bitter scepticism. And we are moved as much by the lovers who have found happiness and each other as by the certain knowledge that their love is not everlasting. From **As You Like it**:

ROSALIND: Now tell me, how long you would have her
after you have possessed her?
ORLANDO: For ever and a day.
ROSALIND: Say a day without the ever. No, no,
Orlando; men are April when they woo,
December when they wed. Maids are May
when they are maids, but the sky changes
when they are wives.

If there is another writer who sets the passion, torment and optimism of youth against the presence of life's melancholy, who blends laughter with tears, it is Chekhov – which is perhaps why the British theatre has colonised Chekhov as the Russians have Shakespeare.

Shakespeare's comedies belong with a clutch of works of art that embody the pleasure principle – Mozart's **The Marriage of Figaro**, Howard Hawks' film *Bringing Up Baby*, Matisse's paper cut-outs – works that combine insight, wit, joy and generosity of heart in an irresistible and wholly accessible fashion.

In The Histories Shakespeare developed an existing genre – the history play – into something that we now call 'epic theatre', which derived currency in the twentieth century largely, but not exclusively, from Brecht's work and from his successors'. Epic theatre exploits the power of the theatrical medium for metaphor, showing a whole society in a microcosm: kings and commoners, the rulers and the ruled.

By epic theatre we mean a play that concerns itself with public events and private lives and the way in which the two impact on each other. In Shakespeare's epics intimate domestic behaviour co-exists with the mobilisation of armies and the fate of nations. Our sympathies follow a twisting course of affiliations: no one is without blame or guilt, all are morally ambiguous. Shakespeare takes familiar historical events in the reigns of **Richard II, Henry IV, Henry V, Richard III** and **Henry VI** or known events from the classical world in **Julius Caesar, Antony and Cleopatra, Coriolanus,** and makes them vehicles for exploring power, war, politics, families, fatherhood, morality, tradition – and even social justice.

These plays are dominated – you might almost say infected – by the malest of male occupations: war. It's not with the hindsight of history that we can observe that all The Histories, in a way that might seem prescient in the post-feminist era, show the miseries visited on women by the male appetite for power. The women are educated by the experience of grief – even the ones who have exhorted and conspired with their men. The dead are always some mother's son.

> Demand me nothing; what you know, you know.
> From this time forth I never will speak word,

says Iago at the end of **Othello,** and he is as good as his word – leaving audiences baffled, frustrated and horrified by being unable to resolve his motives. This is like life: we are confronted by a mass murderer like Frederick West, we stumble through a thicket of indignation, sickened horror and moral outrage, and emerge able only to describe something that we find hard to give a name to if we cannot call it 'evil'.

Shakespeare does not offer us solutions or moral instruction in The Tragedies. He does not, as some academic critics would love to believe, present themed dramatic essays. We can say that **Macbeth** is *about* overweening ambition, **Romeo and Juliet** *about* sectarianism, **Othello** sexual jealousy, **Lear** family love, **Hamlet** growing up, but in doing so we describe no more of the universe of each play than to describe London as a large city on the Thames.

Shakespeare's tragedies do not conform to any rules of drama, philosophy or religion. Blind fate, the pagan gods, the Christian God, nature itself, all take the blame from time to time for the catastrophe of the lives of the protagonists, but in the end the responsibility for their misfortunes is their own.

If there is a lesson to be learned from The Tragedies it is this: our fate lies in ourselves. To pretend otherwise is, as the supreme realist Edmund says in **King Lear:**

> The excellent foppery of the world, that when we are sick
> in fortune – often the surfeits of our own behaviour – we
> make guilty of our disasters the sun, the moon, and the stars,
> as if we were villains by necessity.

What are the tragedies *about*? Being alive and becoming dead: the smell of mortality.

3

Those familiar with Shakespeare's **Richard II** might be surprised to see a scene set in the streets of London ('skilfully acted out by competent performers' according to a contemporary witness) in which Bolingbroke led a procession preceded by leaping jesters, followed by multitudes of supporters, watched from balconies and housetops. 'This,' a contemporary critic opined, 'is one of the most gorgeous and effective scenes that we ever witnessed on the stage.' If you went to see a Shakespeare production in the 1890s you would be surprised to be presented with anything less: the signing of the Magna Carta in **King John**, the christening of Elizabeth in **Henry VIII**, live sheep in **As You Like It**.

At the turn of the century the British theatre was dominated – as it had been for two centuries – by actor-managers, who managed the theatres, produced the plays, directed them and starred in them. Plays were tailored to fit the prejudices of the actor-manager and the design of the scenery, and immense care (and cost) was lavished on the historical accuracy of the sets and costumes.

Shakespeare's plays offered the actor-manager a banquet of columns and pillars from Ancient Greece and Rome, piazzas from Renaissance Italy, oak-woods from England, heather-clad hills from Scotland, castles, tournaments, ceremonies, pageants, heraldry, crowds, live rabbits and sheep, all garnished with lavish orchestral music. The production of Shakespeare's plays foreshadowed the Hollywood biblical epic – all they lacked was Charlton Heston. His absence was more than made up for by titans like Sir Henry Irving and Herbert Beerbohm Tree – who rode Shakespeare's plays like the charioteers in **Ben Hur** (staged at the Theatre Royal, Drury Lane in 1894 with real horses) and, as Shaw said, 'positively acted Shakespeare off the stage'.

It's not hard to infer that the acting was highly exaggerated, even ritualised – much as the acting of many opera singers today. The verse was probably spoken in a style which to our ears would be mannered, slow, arhythmic, and overstretched. The characterisation would often be founded on caricature or convention. 'When you had to play a Shakespearian part that was strange to you,' said the actor-manager Frank Benson (who pioneered repertory seasons at Stratford), 'you could and did go to any one of a score of small-part actors in the company, and ask him how it was done. He knew, every actor knew, the traditions that had grown up about the playing of eighty, a hundred, or even more characters. And if you told him that you intended to do something different, he would answer flatly, "You can't do that, it's wrong."'

'Style' in acting is induced by the spirit of the ear as much as observation of eternal truths about human behaviour; film acting has made us much more conscious of the mirror being held up to nature. We have been educated by film to expect naturalness in theatre acting, and we should not be too hasty to condemn actors and audiences whose standards of theatrical plausibility were bound by different parameters. Since Shakespeare's age there have been those who have copied the stage-business and bad-acting habits of the previous generation, and at the same time there have been those who have been iconoclastic, and have introduced a new – and shocking – realism to the stage; David Garrick was one of these in the eighteenth century, Edmund Kean was in the early nineteenth century, Henry Irving in the late nineteenth century and Laurence Olivier in the mid-twentieth century.

All theatre has a tendency to decline to the condition of the superficial and silly. Every now and then someone comes along, shakes it up and demonstrates that it's an art to be fought for and to be unembarrassed about taking seriously. At the beginning of the twentieth century in Britain it was someone whose influence, if not whose name, has resonated throughout the entire century: Harley Granville-Barker. He possessed a passionate certainty about the importance of the theatre and the need to revise its form, its content, and the way that it was managed. He ushered in a style of production that still – ninety years later – approximates to our ideas of the best in contemporary Shakespearian production.

Harley Granville-Barker, the first modern British director.

Granville-Barker was born without the hyphen in 1877. His mother was an entertainer who did bird imitations; his father a dilettante architect/property developer. He had no or little formal education. He started performing at the age of thirteen, and at the age of fourteen he went to a stage-school in Margate; he was a playwright by the age of seventeen, was running a theatre by the age of twenty-seven, and had retired by the time he was forty. He is Chekhov with an English accent, the real founder of the National Theatre, and the first modern British director.

'Roughly, one might say,' said Harcourt Williams, an actor at the Court who later directed Shakespeare at the Old Vic, 'that he worked from the inside to the outside. He had an exceptional interest in what was theatrically effective, but never got it by theatrical means. It had to be won by mental clarity and emotional truth – in fact the very opposite to the method of most producers.' Granville-Barker knew the burrs and nettles of the actor's life, and he knew the sensitivity they engendered. If a piece of direction didn't work, he'd change it over and over again till 'out of the subconscious, if you will' would emerge the right way of doing it.

Granville-Barker left a manifesto and a record of what he had tried to achieve – *The Prefaces to Shakespeare*, a practical primer for directors and actors working on the plays of Shakespeare. 'I want to see Shakespeare made fully effective on the English stage. That is the best sort of help I can lend.' Barker despised the bombast and the scenery-encrusted productions that he had seen when he was growing up in the last years of the century: 'If Shakespeare had had our modern scenic resources,' he wrote caustically in 1910, 'he would have been only too thankful to arrange his plays to fit them. Unfortunately the poor chap is dead, so we must do it for him.'

What Barker argued in *The Prefaces* (and achieved in his productions) was that for the theatre to be expressive it must be, above all, simple and unaffected: a distillation of language, of gesture, of action, of design, where meaning is the essence. The meaning must be felt as much as understood. 'They don't have to understand with their ears, just with their guts.'

He aimed at re-establishing the relationship between actor and audience that had existed in Shakespeare's theatre. He abolished footlights and the proscenium arch, building out an apron over the orchestra pit which Shaw said 'apparently trebled the spaciousness of the stage … To the imagination it looked as if he had invented a new heaven and a new earth'.

His answers to staging Shakespeare were similar to Brecht's for his plays and, in some senses, to Chekhov's for his. He wanted scenery to be expressive and metaphorical, not to be decorative and literal. It had to be specific and real, while being minimal and iconographic: the cart in **Mother Courage**, the nursery in **The Cherry Orchard**, and the large dining table – the heartland of the upper-middle-class family – in his own play **The Voysey Inheritance**. 'To create a new hieroglyphic language of scenery. That, in a phrase, is the problem. If the designer finds himself competing with the actors, the sole interpreters Shakespeare has licensed, then it is he that is the intruder and must retire.'

What you have is yourself and the text, only that, that's the lesson of Granville-Barker: 'We have the text to guide us, half a dozen stage directions, and that is all. I abide by the text and the demands of the text and beyond that I claim freedom.'

He argued too something that invariably becomes apparent to directors who attempt to understand the demands that a Shakespeare text makes on the staging of it: that the physical relationships of the acting areas should reproduce the essential relationships of the stage for which that particular play was written, whether the Globe or the Blackfriars or one or other of the great private halls of Elizabethan and Jacobean times. In practical terms, that means entrances at both sides of the stage, some sort of equivalent of the curtained inner stage, and some sort of balcony or higher level.

Barker argued for a fluency of staging unbroken by scene changes – and one wishes he were still listened to. It's a current commonplace to observe that Shakespeare has a 'filmic' style. However, only by providing a staging that allows a seamless cut from the end of one scene to the beginning of another can we begin to experience it: the pulse of the verse and the action is allowed to beat unbroken. In most Shakespeare plays the vertiginous speed and the breathlessness at which events develop are a crucial element of the descent into disaster – and the plausibility of it. We have all sat down to a family meal that has declined from geniality to savagery before the pudding's been put on the table.

Likewise Barker argued that the verse should be spoken fast: 'Character in action, not sound like the voice beautiful from the lectern … ' BE SWIFT, BE SWIFT, BE NOT POETICAL, he wrote on the dressing-room mirror of Cathleen Nesbitt when she played Perdita. Within the speed, however, detailed reality: meaning above all.

Barker was not unique in Europe in wanting to conscript all the elements of production, acting, staging, design and lighting, to make a production in which the sum of the parts was integrated into a whole. In the 1860s the Duke of Saxe-Meiningen – the ruler of an obscure German principality – set up his own theatre company with that precise aim: that a performance should be an organic whole, a complex combination of acting and movement, orchestrated to achieve a symphonic synthesis.

The Duke delegated the job of running the company and rehearsals to a long-suffering deputy, who translated his instructions into action while the Duke presided, like God, over the proceedings.

The Duke of Saxe-Meiningen (1826–1914) was the first modern director, the father of what we now recognise as a craft. It is often said that the function of directors is as recent as their title – which is a twentieth-century American coinage – but no one who has ever watched a Shakespeare play could doubt that someone has to sort out the flow of traffic across the stage, the exits and entrances, and the staging of the often bewilderingly confused codas to the comedies when the stage becomes crammed with couples all declaring that they are related to long-lost fathers, mothers, cousins or children.

Shakespeare and Molière were undoubtedly directors in all but name, just as much as composers were *de facto* conductors, but directing as a full-time occupation is the invention of the Duke of Saxe-Meiningen. His legacy was to inspire people to pursue the craft in Britain, France, and Russia.

In the summer of 1897 Stanislavsky met the novelist and playwright Vladimir Nemirovich Danchenko for lunch in a private room in a restaurant in Moscow and stayed until breakfast the next day. By the following dawn they had drawn up the principles for a new theatre company.

> Overall policy and organisation will be determined by the needs of the text and the actors.

> Each production will have specially designed sets, props and costumes.

The performance will be an artistic experience, not a social occasion; entrance and exit rounds will be discouraged.

Their company became the Moscow Art Theatre.

Konstantin Stanislavsky (1863–1938) was an actor and director of experience, Nemirovich was not. The one tall, aristocratic, ascetic; the other short, middle class, a gambler and bon viveur. Their differences, however, were more than superficial, and over the years it became apparent that they were irreconcilable. Nemirovich saw the theatre as the servant of the text, Stanislavsky was an *auteur*. He saw performance as an autonomous art, a medium combining acting, design, music, the text merely part of the whole symphonic structure.

Both were directors of undoubted talent, but Stanislavsky was something more. He was big-hearted and humane, in spite of being egotistical and overbearing, arrogant and self-important – but that's not an uncommon combination in the theatre. 'He has one huge and unpleasant shortcoming,' said an actor, 'the way he thrusts his interpretation of a part at you.' He infuriated Chekhov by his preoccupation with sound, lighting and scenic effects at the expense of the meaning in the text. 'I am ready to vouch that Alekseyev (Stanislavsky) hasn't read **The Cherry Orchard** through carefully even once,' Chekhov complained to his wife, the actress Olga Knipper. Stanislavsky pursued his ideas (what became ossified as the 'Method') with a dogged ruthlessness that was in many ways a precursor of the rather more pernicious political system that was introduced in the 1917 Revolution.

Chekhov reads **The Seagull** to the company of the Moscow Art Theatre.

Although Stanislavsky had a taste for the engineering of the human soul, his fascination with the art of acting, his curiosity about human behaviour and his scientific obsession with emotional detail has provided a theoretical basis for successive generations of actors – whether they are aware of it or not. Most of what we now take for granted as the rehearsal 'process', and much of what actors actually achieve in rehearsal, owes some debt not only to Stanislavsky but to his determination to run a theatre which took itself and the art of acting seriously. It was not called the 'Art' theatre for nothing.

Stanislavsky offered a pseudo-scientific dissection of the art of acting which resembles Freud on the mechanism of the joke: solemn, earnest, well-meaning, but lacking a sense of humour. Stanislavsky's great contribution was twofold: he demanded that actors observe human behaviour, and that they respect both their craft and the writers they serve. He provided some sort of formal discipline within which both aims could be realised. He was trying to give shape to an inchoate process. His so-called System is a vast concordance of common sense; the fact that few, if any, good actors invoke his work is not to say that they don't recognise and follow most of his pragmatic principles.

If the Duke of Saxe-Meiningen was the archetype of the director as maestro or magus, and Stanislavsky of the 'actor's director', André Antoine was the model for the 'playwright's director'. As an amateur actor and employee of the Gas Company he set up the Théâtre Libre to present unperformed plays. He introduced the *quart d'heure* – brief, intimate, slice-of-life plays which focused on character and encouraged a style of natural acting. He progressed to larger theatres, naturalistic design and lighting effects, but still pursued what we would now label a 'new-play policy': discovering, nurturing and developing new playwrights. In seven years he presented 111 plays – most of them previously unknown in France.

The success of the Théâtre Libre led to the formation of independent theatre groups elsewhere in Europe – Strindberg founded his own company in Copenhagen in order to produce his own plays in 1889, the Freie Buhne opened in Berlin in the same year, and in London the Independent Theatre was opened by Jacob Thomas Grein in 1891, giving the first performance of the first play of a precocious Irish writer called George Bernard Shaw.

In Britain, Granville-Barker drew on the ideas of two men: William Poel and Edward Gordon Craig. Like most of the nineteenth-century theatre revolutionaries, William Poel (1852–1934) was an amateur enthusiast, a businessman who abandoned his office for the theatre. He had a passionate hatred of the commercial theatre – its long runs, its lack of rehearsal time, its superficiality – and a passionate love of Shakespeare. In an age of scenic excess and decoration, re-writing, bowdlerisation and indiscriminate cutting, he embarked on a mission to return Shakespeare to his original text and to the bare Elizabethan stage.

He escaped the era's obsession with realism – 'exhausting and enervating in its effect' – by refusing to conform to the dogged orthodoxy of period costume or the plodding literalism of geographically 'accurate' settings. Costume was there to express character, not to decorate the actors: in his production of **Coriolanus** the hero wore a leopardskin, Volumnia a Gainsborough dress with a plumed hat, Virgilia a Pre-Raphaelite smock, and the citizens – the militant proletariat – were turned out as French railway porters.

Poel was an innovative, if wayward, director. He cast women in men's parts, no matter how unsuitable the role or the actress, but he was not a natural director, more an exponent of theatrical archaeology than theatrical art. Barker learned from him the importance of verse-speaking and respect for what Shakespeare wrote, and he saw the lure of an open stage that extended into the auditorium and of lighting that evoked the open air.

From Edward Gordon Craig, Barker learned this:

> The Art of the Theatre is neither acting nor the play, it is not scene nor dance, but it consists of all the elements of which these things are composed: action, which is the very spirit of acting; words, which are the body of the play; line and colour, which are the very heart of the scene; rhythm, which is the very essence of the dance.

This appeared in *The Art of the Theatre*, a catechism for the rebirth of the theatre under the presiding genius of a director. Craig was incapable of realising his articles of faith: he had no patience or inclination for what he regarded as the compromise of rehearsals and the capriciousness of actors, preferring puppets to people. And he could never reconcile himself to the tedium of accommodating financial limitations or meeting deadlines.

Craig was born in 1872. His mother was John Gielgud's great-aunt, the actress Ellen Terry, and his father was an architect and a highly original theatre designer. He had a precocious theatrical upbringing, starting as an actor at the age of six, and playing his first speaking part at the age of thirteen on tour in American with Henry Irving and Ellen Terry. He stayed eight years with Irving, eventually playing Hamlet and Romeo, but became increasingly interested in the visual arts, and increasingly determined to fuse theatre with their new expressiveness.

He was responsible for only a few productions, the most successful being operas such as **Acis and Galatea, Masque of Love** and **Dido and Aeneas** where he felt he could express abstract sensations, unencumbered by character and plot. He aspired to a fusion of poetry, performer, music, light, colour and movement. **Hamlet** for the Moscow Art Theatre, which used massive but intricate sliding panels, foundered on the rocks of technical inadequacy and excessive ambitiousness. Most of his productions existed only in his notebooks and sketchbooks.

Craig was the first designer to use light as an element in design rather than merely as a vehicle for lighting the actors' faces and providing atmosphere. He abolished overhead lighting battens and footlights, used concealed lighting bars, movable spots, colour changes, and double gauzes: in effect, he provided the twentieth-century lighting designer

Gordon Craig's **Hamlet** *for the Moscow Art Theatre.*

with his syntax. Many of the scenic principles that he espoused – getting rid of painted flats and backcloths, the expressive use of stage space and of moving scenery, the use of new materials – prefigured the kind of design that started to be seen in this country in opera and in the theatre in the 1960s.

Craig has never been truly honoured in this country, and he died in 1966 in exile, neglected and feeling deeply wronged. Peter Brook speaks passionately of him:

> I would say that the true influence, which we all carry today, whether we know it or not, comes from Gordon Craig. Craig was the person who went right back to the origin of the theatre, described how theatre had its roots in the temples, and wrote marvellous humorous but incisive pieces like his 'Advice to a Young Director', where he said, if you want to put on **Hamlet** the first thing that you have to recognise is that there is a ghost and there is the supernatural. If you're not prepared to accept the supernatural in Shakespeare, go home. Don't touch this author because you won't understand anything about it.

Actors in costume for Granville-Barker's **A Midsummer Night's Dream**.

All the best theatre productions of today bear the marks of Harley Granville-Barker and Edward Gordon Craig: the determination to maximise the power of the text through the actor, allied to the desire to make the staging as expressive as possible through the use of space, scenery, lighting, and costume: in short, to exploit the theatreness of theatre.

Barker's production of **A Midsummer Night's Dream** in 1914 embodied his ideas. 'Find a way of reaching the audience with that magic,' he said of the play, 'convince the onlookers of the *power* of the fairies, the natural dwellers in the misty twilight, and the play comes magically to life … ' His not-altogether-human fairies were slightly sinister adults rather than coy children, and they moved in a formally choreographed fashion against a forest of flowing people and green draperies. They were gold from head to foot, shimmering like oriental statues, and had a different way of speaking from the mortals – they were galaxies away from the traditional gauzy pantomime conventions of Victorian tradition.

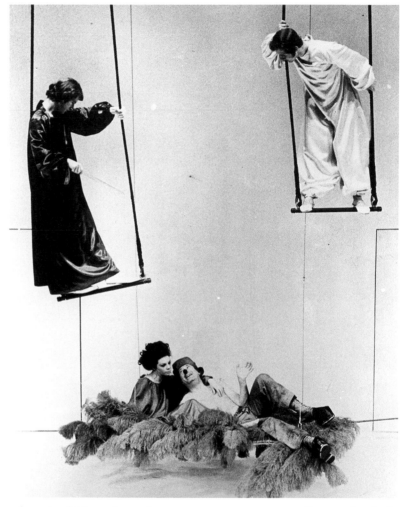

A year after his production Barker wrote this: 'These modern theatres with their electric lights, switchboards and revolving stages are all well enough but what is really needed is a great white box.' Peter Brook's production of the play in 1970 provided exactly that – a great white box with two doors and a balcony above with ladders leading to it. The fairies swung on trapezes, manipulating the action like casual and none too diligent stage hands. Like Barker's **Dream** there was nothing of pantomime, nothing of received ideas of the natural or supernatural, and nothing of received ideas about theatre.

There was a wild atavistic energy about the production, animating the axiom that there must be an element of 'play' in a play: 'Theatre becomes a deadly industry if a performer is not there to play.' Peter Brook could see that:

> A way existed of giving the invisible world its own plausible reality, and I had been particularly influenced by a performance of Chinese acrobats I had seen in Paris [who] did astonishing feats with such ease that they vanished into anonymity, leaving in their place an impression of pure speed, of pure lightness, of pure spirit.

'A great white box' – Peter Brook's production of A Midsummer Night's Dream.

Actors in costume for Granville-Barker's A Midsummer Night's Dream.

The production demanded the skills of conventional professional actors combined with conjuring and gymnastics in a way that Craig would have envied.

'The text of a play,' said Granville-Barker, 'is a score awaiting performance, and the performance and its preparation are, almost from the beginning, a work of collaboration. A producer may direct the preparation, certainly. But if he only knows how to give orders, he has mistaken his vocation; he had better be a drill sergeant.' With Shakespeare as with any other playwright the director's job is to make the play live, now, in the present tense. 'Spontaneous enjoyment is the life of the theatre,' said Granville-Barker. SHAKESPEARE ALIVE! said a review of his **A Midsummer Night's Dream**: it's the most, but should be the least, that a director must hope for.

4

It was not until the foundation of the Royal Shakespeare Company and the National Theatre that the kind of theatrical universe that Granville-Barker dreamt of and planned for was realised. Both companies were inspired by a desire to celebrate Shakespeare.

The first plan for a National Theatre in Britain was put forward in 1848 by a radical bookseller called Effingham Wilson, who had suggested a 'house for Shakespeare' where the works of the 'world's greatest moral teacher would be performed'.

William Archer, a critic and the first translator of Ibsen's plays into English, took up the banner in 1877, in an anonymous pamphlet attacking Henry Irving for having ruined his talent by greed, vanity and long runs. 'The only remedy,' he said, 'lies in a national theatre, with good endowment, good traditions, good government.' Barker joined him in his campaign and in 1904 the two of them produced a paper: 'The National Theatre: A Scheme and Estimates'. It covered everything from staff and repertoire to wages, royalties and pension funds. The company was to total sixty-six (forty-four men and twenty-two women), there would be between forty-five and fifty plays in the repertoire, seats would cost 1sh. to 7/6d – from £3 to £21 in today's money – and the entire scheme was expected to cost a third of a million pounds. A committee was formed to raise the necessary money; state aid was assumed to be out of the question.

It's seldom been accepted by British politicians that the theatre should be seen as an expression of national identity and a matter of public pride. A surprising exception was Churchill, that enduring icon of Englishness, who observed in 1906:

> I am one of those who hold that it is the duty of the state to be the generous but discriminating parent of the arts and sciences … Let us think with what excitement and interest we witness the construction and launching of a battleship. What a pity it is that some measure of that interest cannot be turned in the direction of the launching, say, of a National Theatre.

The opening date was set for 23 April 1916, the tercentenary of Shakespeare's birth, but the war intervened and it was another fifteen years before Granville-Barker managed to revive the campaign, suggesting two theatres under one roof and a site on the South Bank of the Thames. Paradoxically, it was the Second World War that succeeded in giving substance to Barker's dream: state funding for the arts was introduced in 1940, with the foundation of CEMA – the Council for the Encouragement of Music and the Arts – which, at the end of the war, became the Arts Council.

The urge to build the National Theatre on the model proposed by Barker was swept up in the rhetoric of the New Jerusalem of the post-war government, and in 1949, with the support of the Chancellor Stafford Cripps (of whom it used to be said, 'There but for the grace of God goes God') a bill was passed in Parliament to finance the theatre. The site was repeatedly changed, and the foundation stone, laid in 1951, was moved up and down the South Bank, leading the Queen Mother to say that it should be put on castors. Then in 1961 the Chancellor Selwyn Lloyd seemed to kill all hopes of a national theatre by stating publicly that the required money couldn't be found.

This attempted assassination revived popular support: the theatrical profession joined forces with the Arts Council to protest the government's evasion of its legal responsibilities, and the London County Council offered to pay part of the cost of construction and provide a rent-free site. A board was established and it was decided that, rather than wait for the new building to be built, a national theatre company would be set up under the leadership of Laurence Olivier.

The critic Kenneth Tynan mourns the failure to build the National Theatre.

39

No theatre grows out of government legislation or civic decree, even if they are fuelled by nationalist manifestos or cultural self-esteem; it grows out of the obsessions and stubbornness of gifted and persistent individuals. The National Theatre exists largely because of people like Effingham Wilson, Harley Granville-Barker and a quixotic cockney busybody, Lilian Baylis, who managed the Old Vic from 1912 to 1937. With her determined populism and her genuinely unaffected desire to give people of all classes access to theatre, she laid the foundation for the National Theatre that Laurence Olivier took on in 1964.

In 1914 Shakespeare visited a woman in a dream. 'Why have you allowed my beautiful words to be so murdered?' asked Shakespeare. 'If they have been slaughtered,' she replied, 'the fault is not mine but the actors'.' 'You must run the plays yourself,' said Shakespeare. And for over twenty years she did.

Lilian Baylis (1874–1937), the object of Shakespeare's attentions (God also paid visits), was the niece of a temperance reformer, who had bought a music-hall – the Old Vic – and converted it into a concert-hall. Baylis took the theatre over from her aunt and, under the instruction of God and Shakespeare, devoted her life to producing his plays. She was a wonderfully eccentric woman given to doing her office work and cooking sausages on a primus stove in a box by the stage during rehearsals and performances, and inviting her actors to kneel to pray for success and for money, if not urging them to play at leper colonies on Sundays.

Her desire was to create a loyal local audience for a then unfashionable playwright, and accordingly she kept the seats cheap. By the end of the 1920s, when John Gielgud went there for

Lilian Baylis was visited in a dream by Shakespeare.

his first season, the Old Vic was established as Shakespeare's London home. Gielgud was not known prior to his Old Vic appearance as a Shakespearian actor; within a season it was hard for him to be known as anything else. With three weeks' rehearsal (and only thirteen performances) for each production, he played Romeo, Antonio in **The Merchant of Venice**, Richard II, Mark Antony, Orlando in **As You Like It**, topping the season off with Macbeth and Hamlet – all at the age of twenty-six. It became fashionable to play Hamlet, and Gielgud played the part in the West End, after the Old Vic; in 1934 (with a design influenced by Gordon Craig) for 155 performances; and on Broadway; and once again in the West End in 1944.

By 1935, when he had become Britain's leading Shakespearian performer, Gielgud invited Laurence Olivier to join him in his production of **Romeo and Juliet** – alternating the parts of Romeo and Mercutio. To invite the actor regarded as your closest rival to appear on the same stage is an act of great – and daring – generosity and self-confidence. It marked Gielgud out from generations of actor-managers who had clad the stage with inferior talents in order to illuminate their own.

Gielgud's production was suffused with the spirit of Granville-Barker. He was trying to make a successful marriage of language with mood and action, so that the complexities, as he said, 'became audible, visible and even physical as they must have been on Shakespeare's stage,' and he allowed Olivier the room to carve out his own territory.

Olivier saw Romeo as a rough adolescent and was criticised for defying the orthodoxy of the times – missing the poetry. 'What is the use of Shakespeare's writing such an image as "the white wonder of dear Juliet's hand" if Romeo is not himself blasted with the beauty of it?' said one critic. He was considered to be more successful as Mercutio, where his quick-silver dexterity and cool scepticism didn't disturb the prevailing romantic expectations. Olivier was, as he said later, 'trying to sell realism in Shakespeare', while Gielgud 'was paying attention – to the exclusion of the earth – to all that music, all that lyricism'.

Olivier – ironically perhaps for the son of a vicar – was ushering in the new world: defiantly unpatrician, muscular and anti-romantic, giving a hint of subversion of the class barriers that existed on British stages and screens until the late 1950s. His Hamlet at the Old Vic, directed by Tyrone Guthrie in 1937, bore both the strengths and the weaknesses of his Romeo – the verse-speaking was still rough-edged, with a tendency to rush the big speeches and reach for puzzling emphases. The passions again ruled the intellect; here was no scholar Hamlet, more the frustrated man of action with a flashing temper.

Tyrone Guthrie had taken over the running of the company after Lilian Baylis's death. He reduced the number of productions, making the actors less absurdly overstretched, and contracted them for shorter engagements. He assembled a company that included Edith Evans, Michael Redgrave, Alec Guinness, Ralph Richardson, Emlyn Williams, and the young Peggy Ashcroft – a starry line-up, but it was always a 'poor theatre', always

Gielgud, Olivier and Edith Evans in **Romeo and Juliet**.

depending on the actors' willingness to subsidise the theatre with their work. During Guthrie's regime the theatre started to acquire a new, younger generation, many of whom had never been to a theatre before.

Olivier's Hamlet and his Iago (to Richardson's Othello) in productions by Guthrie were both steeped in the contemporary enthusiasm for Freudian readings of the plays: Oedipal complex in **Hamlet**, suppressed homosexuality in **Othello**. Probably his finest performance was as **Coriolanus**, and as the King in **Henry V**, overcoming an initial contempt for the character, with his appetite for war and what Olivier described as 'his scoutmaster humour'. Gradually, he said, 'The words worked their own medicine.'

Their medicine was commandeered by the Ministry of Information in 1944 for a film of **Henry V** which Olivier starred in and directed. The film was intended as a piece of propaganda, but Olivier created something that, while it satisfied the jingoistic demands of the time, offered a more thoughtful and subversive subtext. His black-and-white film of **Hamlet** in 1947 had some visual bravura and successfully used the device of voice-over to translate Hamlet's soliloquies to the screen, but it was a reductive reading of the play, presenting Hamlet, in Olivier's voice-over during the credits, as a MAN WHO COULDN'T MAKE UP HIS MIND.

Nevertheless, the film was a great commercial success, running for six months in Leicester Square. The last of his Shakespeare films – **Richard III** – made in 1954, has become the stuff of legend: generations of schoolchildren have developed a relish for Olivier's gloriously witty and malign hunchback, and a sharp-voiced high-pitched 'Now is the winter of our discontent' is still an impersonation almost universally attempted by the most ill-equipped mimics. Olivier's films gave countless people of all ages access to Shakespeare, enfranchising whole swathes of the population who would otherwise have been excluded from theatres by Britain's obdurately embedded class system.

Gielgud was always diffident about the movies, seeming to regard them as something to be amused by, but not to take seriously, but his Cassius in Joseph L. Mankiewicz's film of **Julius Caesar** – with Marlon Brando as Mark Antony, James Mason as Brutus – is definitive. The film is still, with Orson Welles' adaptation of **Henry IV** and **V, Chimes at Midnight**, the best Shakespeare film in the English language.

Olivier became the first artistic director of the National Theatre in 1963. His performance in **Othello**, directed by John Dexter in the same season, seized the imagination of the public. His performance was the apotheosis of his acting process – working from the outside in, an act of mimicry from an actor in love with making up and dressing up: he blackened his skin, lowered his voice, curled his lip, rolled his eyes and prowled the stage like a giant cat. 'I had to *be* black. I had to feel black down to my soul. I had to look out from a black man's world. Not one of repression, for Othello would have felt superior to the white man. If I peeled my skin, underneath would be another level of black skin. I was to be beautiful. Quite beautiful.'

It was a performance that to many seemed a risible caricature of a black man, but he endowed Othello with a heroic power, oscillating between arrogance and self-abasement, and reducing Iago (played by Frank Finlay) to a pale near-cipher. It was a star performance: the triumph of the actor as tyro.

Throughout the careers of Olivier and Gielgud the public always wanted to talk up a rivalry between the two actors, latching on to their polarity: fire and ice, air and earth, poetry and prose, Manolete and Dominguin, John Lennon and Paul McCartney, chalk and cheese. Gielgud was characterised as the traditionalist, but this was true only in the sense that he worked within the radical tradition that Granville-Barker had strived to establish: truth to the text – verse-speaking that was reflective, poetic swift and musical. He was always half in love with his own voice, but it was a failing that he recognised and fought against. 'John still has the most beautiful voice, but I felt in those days he allowed it to dominate his performances and, if he was lost but for a moment, he would dive straight back into its honey,' said Olivier.

Gielgud could have stayed a 'West End actor' – wealthy, complacent and artistically unambitious – but he consistently took risks and accepted challenges. In 1950, leading the company at Stratford, he played Angelo in **Measure for Measure** with great success,

43

directed by the young and iconoclastic Peter Brook, in which he dared to be ascetic, unsympathetic and unromantic. He also championed the trio of young designers who called themselves 'Motley': the sisters Margaret and Sophie Harris, and Elizabeth Montgomery. They introduced a spare, ascetic and elegant approach to stage design in which meaning took precedence over decoration – a revolutionary approach in the British theatre of their day.

And no one could accuse him of timidity five years later, also at Stratford, when he acted in **King Lear**, designed by the Japanese sculptor Isamu Noguchi. Echoing Craig's moving screens, the abstract set aimed to portray a timeless world. 'His Japanese costumes killed all our efforts to act in them,' said Gielgud ruefully later. The production was not a success, but Peter Brook said that he would never have arrived at his production of **King Lear** with Paul Scofield in 1962 if Gielgud had not paved the way for him.

'I've always thought that we were the reverses of the same coin, perhaps,' said Olivier of Gielgud:

> The top half John, all spiritual, all spirituality, all beauty, all abstract things; and myself as all earth, blood, humanity; if you like, the baser part of humanity without the beauty. I've never been so interested in that side, though naturally I've had to develop something of it in order to be an actor at all. But I've always felt that John missed the lower half and that made me go for the other.

It might be tempting to take Olivier's judgement at face value. His Shakespeare performances had great glamour, bravura, energy, and virtuosity, but their brilliant luminosity should not be allowed to blind us to the intelligence, the detail, the humanity, the insight and the sheer beauty that Gielgud brought to Shakespeare. He established classical repertory companies in the West End with high aims and high achievements, and did more than anyone to create the situation that led to the foundation of the Royal Shakespeare Company and the Royal National Theatre. He made the Old Vic fashionable: neither Richardson nor Olivier would ever have gone there without him and the National Theatre would never have emerged from it.

People want greatness, glory, extremes. That's why they want to go to the theatre – they want it to be bigger, more daring, more physical than their own lives. Olivier always occupied a larger part of the public's mind than Gielgud. He was not necessarily *the* actor of our time, nor even the best or the wisest or any particular superlative – he simply satisfied a desire for actors to be larger than life and to be able to be seen to be acting at the same time as they are moving you to tears or to laughter. It's the desire to be knowingly seduced.

It's inconceivable that we'll see the like of Olivier and Gielgud again. The theatre has changed, the spirit of the age has changed, the taste of the times has changed. There's too much money, too much publicity and self-consciousness, too little time, too little care for the medium. The ecology – and the economy – of the theatre now resemble the country as whole, steeped in opportunism and restlessness. Olivier and Gielgud had a fierce loyalty and appetite for the theatre that – in spite of the lure of the movies (and Olivier was a hugely celebrated film-star) – remained constant throughout most of this century.

Olivier was once asked what his policy was for the National Theatre. 'To make the audience applaud,' he said. Applause was his life's music: 'Scratch an actor,' he said, 'and you find an actor.'

The National Theatre Company at the Old Vic gave its first performance in 1963. It was another twelve years before the National Theatre building on the South Bank opened its doors under the directorship of Peter Hall. It was conceived with three auditoria under one roof, each playing a rotating repertoire of three plays. This principle is at the heart of its activities – its source of artistic adventure. To have three theatres in one building is, to say the least, a noble project. It was the triumph of Olivier's will, his wilfulness, and his ambition. When the National Theatre was built, a 'dream made concrete' (a metaphor made literal), he was asked what he thought of it. He smiled wryly: 'It's an experiment.'

The National Theatre is defined by its building on the South Bank: designed by Denys Lasdun, it's stern, elegant, forceful, and ascetic, but even though in its intentions and its realisation it's classical, it betrays its period of origin as much as the frontlights on a Ford Cortina. It was conceived in an age in which the exponential expansion of public funding for the arts was virtually unchallenged, an age in which the 'art' theatre and the commercial theatre would *not* walk hand in hand – this, after all, was a building so certain of its purpose, its commercial chastity, and the respect of its audience, that it was built without any sign advertising its function. Like those great temples to mercantile expansionism – St George's Hall in Liverpool, for instance – it supposes a world whose needs and whose wealth would not be varied by the whim of individuals, the change of government, the capriciousness of fashion or, indeed, the imperatives of art.

By 1964, with the creation of the National Theatre and the Royal Shakespeare Company, the mould was cast for the shape of British theatre until the end of the century. The two major subsidised companies have loured over the country's theatre like two giant – and mutually hostile – brothers standing over their often intimidated and resentful family. The National Theatre – which clumsily metamorphosed into the oxymoron *Royal National* in 1988 – and the Royal Shakespeare Company are enduring, but not indelible, monuments to the 1960s.

5

The Royal Shakespeare Company was born out of beer. A philanthropic Midland brewer, Charles Fowler, put his passion for Shakespeare and his money into building the Shakespeare Memorial Theatre beside the river at Stratford-upon-Avon. It opened on Shakespeare's birthday in 1879.

It's easy from this distance to be diffident or dismissive about the work at the Memorial Theatre – in both its manifestations. It's easy to suppose that prior to the mutation of the Shakespeare Memorial Theatre into the Royal Shakespeare Company the theatre consistently lived down to its caricature of being somewhere an actor went for the summer to play cricket, and a tourist went to see pageant Shakespeare.

Flower had heard of the Meiningen Company and wanted to imitate the ensemble. He realised that a permanent company, protected from commercial pressures by subsidy, could effect a sort of revolution of quality. However, hampered by lack of an English Duke of Saxe-Meiningen and of subsidy, he relied from 1886 until 1919 on the actor-manager Frank Benson, whose productions, which invariably placed Benson and his wife at their centre, were Victorian spectacles with elaborate scenery, costume, ballets and processions.

It was not until Barry Jackson became Director in 1946 that the company started to achieve consistent artistic credibility. Jackson was a gifted – and wealthy – impresario and director, who was known as the 'Butter King' after the Birmingham Maypole Dairies from which he derived his income. He had designed and paid for the construction of the Birmingham Repertory Theatre in 1913, and he put on an adventurous mix of work including Chekhov, Ibsen, Strindberg, Synge, Shaw, Coward, Restoration, Shakespeare and forgotten Elizabethan and Jacobean plays. He had an excellent eye for talent, and was one of a small number of enlightened philanthropists, rare as ospreys, who wanted to use their money to make art accessible to all.

He wanted to produce Shakespeare as a contemporary playwright:

> The man in the street is robbed of the real experience of watching Shakespeare by the sublime unnaturalness of the blank verse, the strangeness of the costumes and the conventions of Shakespearian acting interposing a veil between him and the author's intention, and comes away with an increased feeling of almost superstitious awe but with no understanding that he has been witnessing a real conflict of real human beings.

In 1923 in his theatre in Birmingham he directed a modern-dress **Cymbeline**, and in 1925 a much-celebrated modern-dress **Hamlet** – the 'plus-fours' **Hamlet**.

'Every conceivable value was buried in deadly sentimentality and complacent worthiness – a traditionalism largely approved by town, scholar and press,' was Peter Brook's scathing perception of the Stratford that he and Jackson found in 1946. Jackson made a complete break with the past, refusing to employ anyone who had ever appeared at Stratford before. His protégé, the twenty-one-year-old Brook, directed a production of **Love's Labour's Lost**, which was the triumph of that first season.

Brook's production of **Love's Labour's Lost** was described as 'Watteau-esque'. It had visual echoes of Watteau, but none of the inert classicism that the description implies: it was an anarchic rag-bag, funny, fast, daring and eclectic. This was Brook's manifesto

– an echo of Barker: 'We must move the productions and the settings ... away from romance, away from fantasy, away from decoration ... Now we must look beyond an outer liveliness to an inner one ... Any time the Shakespearian meaning is caught, it is "real" and so contemporary.'

Anthony Quayle, the actor-director, took over from Jackson when he was retired forcibly by the Board in 1948. Quayle exploited the relative decline in the fortunes of the Old Vic, and within six years almost every major actor on the British stage – Olivier, Richardson, Gielgud, Ashcroft, and Redgrave – had played at least one Stratford season, working with most of the best British directors – Brook, Guthrie, Glen Byam Shaw, and George Devine.

Brook's production of **Titus Andronicus** was a watershed: violent, visceral and disturbing. He translated Shakespeare's least-known and least-admired (but invariably successful) play from a blood-steeped melodrama into an account of real pain and suffering. The production looked forward to a theatre that would be prepared to confront the reality of a world in which millions had recently died in war and in the camps. Theatre in Shakespeare's birthplace could no longer insulate itself from the horrors of the twentieth century.

Quayle resigned in 1957 to be succeeded briefly by Glen Byam Shaw, who invited the twenty-seven-year-old Peter Hall to direct at Stratford. The next year, while the company was on tour in Leningrad with Michael Redgrave's **Hamlet** and Peter Hall's production of **Twelfth Night,** the Chairman of the Trustees – Fordham, grandson of the first Flower – discussed the future of the theatre with Hall. Hall enticed Flower to share his dream of becoming a major European company, and of acquiring a London theatre where they could mount a season of their Stratford successes and a repertoire of classical revivals and new plays.

The newly christened Royal Shakespeare Company breathed the spirit of the 1960s: a young, ambitious, talented and iconoclastic director from a working-class background with a Cambridge English degree was at the epicentre of a meritocracy of actors, writers and directors, who approached Shakespeare not as a relic but as a contemporary.

If there was a handbook for the new Shakespearians it was not Barker's *Prefaces to Shakespeare* but the work of a Polish academic, Jan Kott: *Shakespeare Our Contemporary.* Shakespeare is the mirror of our own age, he argued, as he has been the mirror for every other – but we have to find new ways to express his contemporaneity. He invited the West to see the politics of the tragedies and the history plays in the totalitarianism of the Iron Curtain countries, to see Beckett's pessimism in **King Lear**, and dark sexual meanings in **A Midsummer Night's Dream**. The disaffected student Hamlet that David Warner played in Peter Hall's production in 1965 would have been at home passing samizdat literature round in the cafés of Warsaw – or three years later on the streets of Paris in the 1967 *événements*.

*Four **Hamlets**: David Warner; John Gielgud; Colin Keith-Johnston in Barry Jackson's **Hamlet**; Jonathan Pryce.*

Peter Hall had a messianic determination to follow the model of the great European companies. 'I was clear from the outset,' he said, 'that I could contribute little unless I could develop a company with a strong permanent nucleus.' Actors were recruited on three-year contracts to play at both theatres – often in Stratford in Shakespeare on one night, in London in a new play the next. Hall invited a university don, John Barton, to join him as Associate Director immediately after his own appointment, and in 1962 Michel Saint-Denis and Peter Brook joined the company as resident directors. Saint-Denis, a Frenchman, who had directed and taught at the Old Vic, founded a studio for research and training.

However infused by the climate of the age, Peter Hall's company was not driven by an aesthetic vision or ideological dogma. Its ideal was, as Peter Brook said, 'to do good things very well', its ethos underwritten, like the BBC and the Arts Council, by a belief in the pursuit of excellence for the collective good. The intellectual framework that lay over the company was derived from Cambridge University, where Peter Hall and John Barton had met. Hall, like Erasmus bringing humanist learning from Rome to England, brought to Stratford an approach influenced by the literary critic, F.R. Leavis, who pursued textual analysis and moral purpose with fundamentalist fervour.

*Paul Scofield in Brook's **Lear**.*

Hall and Barton brought a systematic approach to the rehearsal process: an emphasis on the construction of the verse and its speaking, an insistence that character could be grasped from within the text, not from specious speculation and received opinion.

To take two productions from this era:

Peter Brook's 1962 production of **King Lear** with Paul Scofield redefined the play for several generations. 'I think for me everything shifted around the time of **King Lear**,' said Peter Brook. 'Just before rehearsals were due to begin, I destroyed the set.' The production was 'the thing itself' – a bare stage, stripped of its pseudo-Celtic costumes and bric-à-brac, with a violently energetic Lear (Scofield was forty). The play was revealed in all its elemental force in a production that refused the audience the comfort of making judgements on the characters. Their universe was without moral absolutes, a permanent condition of fallibility, moral ambiguity and frailty: Shakespeare as Beckett's contemporary.

If Brook's production brought Shakespeare's philosophical view into the world of post-war nihilism, Peter Hall's production of **The Wars of the Roses** brought Shakespeare into the world of contemporary power-politics. 'We wanted to reveal the political ironies which are at the heart of any power-struggle at any time. Hypocrisy and cant were as common on the lips of politicians in Tudor England as they are on television during modern British elections.' John Barton condensed the **Henry VI** trilogy and **Richard III** into three plays. The productions were swift, graphic, unsentimental and brilliantly acted.

John Bury, the designer, developed an ascetic house style, a synthesis of the work of Brecht's Berliner Ensemble and his designer, Caspar Neher, with the raw populism of Joan Littlewood, with whom Bury worked for many years. His designs were harsh, used natural materials – iron, wood and stone – and clothes that were rough and lived-in.

Add to this fine productions of **Twelfth Night**, **The Comedy of Errors** and **As You Like It**, the premières of Harold Pinter's **The Homecoming**, David Rudkin's **Afore Night Come**, Dürrenmatt's **The Visit**, Peter Weiss's **Marat/Sade**, and Peter Brook's experiments with the 'Theatre of Cruelty', and it's not hard to see why the reputation and influence of this period has endured, acting as a benchmark and provocative inspiration to succeeding generations of actors and directors.

The Wars of the Roses.

It was inevitable – and healthy – that a rivalry developed between the Royal Shakespeare Company and the newly created National Theatre. The former was caricatured as a 'director's theatre', the latter as an 'actor's theatre'. It would be hard, however, to argue that a company that included Peggy Ashcroft, Paul Scofield, Vanessa Redgrave, Eileen Atkins, Irene Worth, Peter O'Toole, Judi Dench, Ian Holm, Diana Rigg, David Warner,

Patrick Stewart, Helen Mirren and Glenda Jackson comprised marionettes manipulated by autocratic directors, or that the National Theatre lacked authoritative directors in John Dexter, Bill Gaskill, Noël Coward, Franco Zeffirelli and Ingmar Bergman.

That there has always been a whiff of collegiate fervour about the Royal Shakespeare Company is true, whereas if there was a scent from the National Theatre – from Olivier's National Theatre at least – it was always more the smell of greasepaint. It is possible to have admired the work of both companies, to have felt blessed to have lived in a time of such extraordinary theatrical ferment; it is also possible to envy a time when allegiances and taste could be so passionately held, when, to paraphrase Auden, no treaty was negotiable between the 'Eden' of the National Theatre and the 'New Jerusalem' of the RSC.

When Peter Hall appointed a new associate in 1965 he might have been fairly accused of putting his *doppelgänger* in place: a twenty-six-year-old Cambridge graduate (and pupil of F.R. Leavis) called Trevor Nunn, from the same part of the country – East Anglia – and a similar background: Hall's father was a stationmaster, Nunn's a cabinet-maker. Hall showed both faith and prescience in his new recruit, who had a rocky start with several unsuccessful productions, but struck a seam of gold with a production of **The Revenger's Tragedy**.

The production was highly theatrical, highly stylised, non-naturalistic, monochromatic, with thematic costumes and schematic staging. It challenged the prevailing orthodoxy of the Brechtian neo-realism – cracked leather and mud on boots – and sparked off a row with John Barton, who found the stylisation of the production anathema. The row became known in Stratford as the 'Moss on the Tomb' incident: there was a tomb, said Barton, why was there no moss on it?

It was a clear difference of aesthetic principles and when Nunn became Hall's successor in 1968, Nunn's style replaced that of Hall and Barton – less realistic, more flamboyant. The company was still rich in remarkable actors – Peggy Ashcroft, Judi Dench, Ian Richardson, Donald Sinden, Janet Suzman, Helen Mirren and Alan Howard – and for a time was a true ensemble, leading actors playing small parts as a quid pro quo for the big ones.

Everything in the world obeys a wave pattern: sound, light, atomic particles. Theatre companies are no exception: their fortunes fluctuate. The collaboration of Stanislavsky and Nemirovich-Danchenko at the Moscow Art Theatre ostensibly lasted forty-one years, but only about seven of these years were unmarked by conflict. For over thirty years they didn't speak to each other and the work of the company calcified. The Royal Shakespeare Company's work has certainly undulated, but for many years they were riding on top of the wave with Peter Brook's production of **A Midsummer Night's Dream**, Terry Hands' exhilarating history cycle, Trevor Nunn's season of Roman plays, his quasi-musical **Comedy of Errors**, his chamber **Macbeth** and his elegiac **All's Well That Ends Well**.

From the early 1980s the successes of the company – significantly – were not with Shakespeare: John Barton's adaptation of ten plays culled from the Oresteia legend, **The Greeks**, Tom Stoppard's **Travesties**, Trevor Nunn and John Caird's production of David Edgar's eight-hour adaptation of **Nicholas Nickleby**, and the long-running musical **Les Misérables**, which entered the eighteenth year of its run with the coming of the Millennium.

The RSC expanded in the 1970s to mimic the size of the National, in the end becoming the victim of its own expansionist policies: the epicentre of the work of the company shifted away from its wellspring. The lure of a noble populism – the desire to make the good popular and the popular good – that underwrote the company from its inception in the early 1960s started to show signs of declining from a faith to a slogan: the musicals of **Carrie**, **A Clockwork Orange** and **Showboat** did not even have excellence or financial success to claim as a justification for putting them on. The company set up in order to celebrate the works of Shakespeare began to have to ask itself: what was it for?

The Shakespeare canon has been recycled and re-examined by the two national companies for the last thirty years. What started as an endeavour to reclaim a repertoire largely lost to us has become a spiral of repetition, and the spiral is a diminishing one: big theatres demand big audiences to preserve their financial ecology, and ever more frequent productions of the small number of always popular Shakespeare plays become a necessity for survival. Many productions have become reductive, exemplifying the Goldwynism: 'Let's find some new clichés.' The fabric has started to wear thin from over-use: the directors' and actors' imaginations have got stale, the audience's enthusiasm has dwindled.

At Stratford they have not been helped by a 1,500-seat theatre which always had problems from its opening in 1932. What the then director said at the time has a familiar ring to anyone who has struggled with a new auditorium in the twentieth century. 'What we eventually got when the architects, pressure-groups, quacks and empirics had finished with us was the theatre, of all theatres in England, in which it is hardest to make an audience laugh or cry.' There are plans to spend £45m to replace this theatre. The problem remains: what is it for?

The limbs of the body of British theatre were entirely rearranged in the 1970s and '80s: fringe theatre companies and small-scale touring groups now exercised their radical muscles and the two national companies often struggled to keep up. The big companies were obliged to become accessible to the periphery, to annex the territory of dissent, and by the 1990s the radicalism of the RSC had become institutionalised. The company that had fought the Establishment had become the Establishment – they had become, as it were, the people they had warned themselves against.

Adrian Noble's production of The History Plays – **The Plantagenets** – characterised the shift in the company's polarity. They were staged at the same time as Michael Bogdanov's

The new Globe Theatre. productions for the English Shakespeare Company. Where Noble's productions were elegantly staged, and richly symbolic, Bogdanov's were roughly mounted and often crudely abrasive, but they had a political urgency that echoed the confrontational approach of the RSC's **The Wars of the Roses** of the early 1960s.

Of course there continued to be successful productions at the RSC – Adrian Noble's **A Midsummer Night's Dream**, **Hamlet** and **Henry V** with Kenneth Branagh – which, to say the least, fertilised Branagh's films; Nick Hytner's **Measure for Measure** and **The Tempest** with John Wood as Prospero – and, at the National Theatre, Peter Hall's **Antony and Cleopatra** with Anthony Hopkins and Judi Dench, **Richard III** with Ian McKellen, Trevor Nunn's **Troilus and Cressida**. However, the unbroken continuum of Shakespeare productions of excellence in large theatres came to an end.

54

6

Each generation has to keep rediscovering ways of doing Shakespeare's plays. They don't have absolute meanings. There is no fixed, frozen way of doing them. Nobody can mine a Shakespeare play and discover a 'solution', and to pretend that style, fashion, and taste are fixed is to ignore history.

Many of the most illuminating productions of the last twenty years have come from outside the large companies, viewing Shakespeare through fresh prisms. Declan Donnellan's touring Cheek by Jowl company produced a series of light-footed productions characterised by economical story-telling and beguiling emphasis on ambiguity of gender, while Barry Rutter's company, Northern Broadsides, played Shakespeare in Yorkshire accents and defied the tyranny of 'received pronunciation' as successfully as the New York production of **Much Ado About Nothing** in Central Park.

The Globe Theatre – Sam Wanamaker's quixotic project for a replica of Shakespeare's theatre – opened in 1996 with Mark Rylance as Actor-Manager-Director. Rylance's evangelical zeal has carried many sceptics away by the sheer pressure of his enthusiasm and his own protean gifts as an actor, but recreating the Globe is a sort of aesthetic anaesthesia – it involves the audience in a fragile conspiracy to pretend that they are willing collaborators in a vain effort to turn the clock back. 'We shall not save our souls by being Elizabethan,' said Granville-Barker. Nevertheless, to be among an audience who are unquestionably moved by the sight, and above all, the *sound* of a Shakespeare play in broad daylight is to be obliged to recognise that it is folly to be proscriptive about the experience of theatre.

Foreign-language productions of Shakespeare's plays have forced us to see his work through new eyes, powerful staging ideas inspired by loyalty to Shakespeare's text: a seductively romantic **Macbeth** in Japanese, Cold War productions of **Hamlet** in Polish, Russian and Romanian, a demonic Georgian production of **Richard III**.

If there have been truly 'accessible' Shakespeare productions that have crossed class barriers and language barriers, in Britain at least – given the sense of apartheid that exists between those who benefit from the arts and those who feel excluded from them – those productions are more likely to have been on film: Olivier's **Richard III** and **Henry V**, Kozintsev's film of **Hamlet**, Kurosawa's film of **Macbeth** (*Throne of Blood*), **The Taming of the Shrew** and **Romeo and Juliet** of Franco Zeffirelli, the **Romeo + Juliet** of Baz Luhrman, the **Henry V** of Kenneth Branagh. They have all earned the headline: SHAKESPEARE ALIVE!

Clearly these films and the foreign-language stage productions are not dependent on Shakespeare's language – any more than Berlioz' or Prokofiev's **Romeo and Juliet** or Verdi's **Otello** or Britten's **A Midsummer Night's Dream** – but, paradoxically, they are not necessarily less 'Shakespearian'. They articulate characters, stories and themes that embody a spiritual, philosophical, and magical language that is instantly recognisable as belonging to the imaginative continent of Shakespeare.

*Shakespeare in small spaces: Ian McKellen and Judi Dench in Trevor Nunn's **Macbeth**; Sonia Ritter and Brian Cox in Deborah Warner's **Titus Andronicus**; Paul Rhys, Ian Holm and Anne-Marie Duff in Richard Eyre's **King Lear**; Adrian Lester and Simon Coates in Declan Donnellan's **As You Like It**.*

How do we continue to present the plays in the theatre in a way that is true to their own terms, and at the same time bring them alive for a contemporary audience?

The most successful performances of Shakespeare in recent years – the most alive, the truest to Shakespeare – have all taken place in small spaces, seating no more than a few hundred people at most, where the potency of the language hasn't been dissipated by the exigencies of voice projection, and the problems of presentation – finding a physical world for the play – have become negligible.

To talk of presenting Shakespeare's plays without 'stars' is to talk of cooking without olive oil. When people sneer at the idea of stars in Shakespeare, they assume a tyranny: egos strutting over a docile supporting cast. Most of Shakespeare's plays depend on the performance of at least one prodigiously gifted actor and/or actress with a marked presence and a number of other actors of considerable power. Without strong actors the force of the plays is bound to be diluted.

Shakespeare will continue to underwrite British theatre as its greatest capital asset, but it's time to consider how to conserve this asset. Perhaps the most constructive gesture that could be made on Shakespeare's behalf is this: a moratorium on public performances of his plays for two years. Let an appetite breed on starvation, and if his plays are taught in schools let a few simple precepts apply:

> Believe that the playwright knows what he is doing, and remember his plays were performed in the theatre to a not wholly literate audience who *must* have understood them at the time.

> Rely on the evidence of the text, not on speculation, and specious psychological theory.

> Trust your own knowledge of the world. Try to be simple; trust that the writer is trying to do the same, however eloquent and complex his intention is.

> Be specific: all good art is derived from specific observations, all bad art from generalisations.

No amount of propaganda, no amount of recitation of Shakespeare's qualities will make the case for him. Without vigorous, imaginative and gifted actors who are prepared to make the effort to enlist Shakespeare's verse as an asset not a hindrance, the reaction of future audiences will be like that of a schoolboy in Soweto: 'For us Shakespeare is dust.'

Audiences need to do their bit too: travel hopefully, expect everything. 'Shakespeare, coming on me unawares, struck me like a thunderbolt,' said Berlioz. 'The lightning flash of that discovery revealed to me at a stroke the whole heaven of art, illuminating it to its remotest corners. I recognised the meaning of grandeur, beauty, dramatic truth … I saw, I understood, I felt … that I was alive and that I must arise and walk.' And he didn't speak or understand a word of English at the time.

Ireland and England

''Tis Ireland gives England her soldiers, her generals, too.'
GEORGE MEREDITH

1

London theatre was the glory of the Elizabethan and Jacobean eras. Yet from the Civil War to a time so recent that it's almost within living memory, England produced not one native playwright of genius and only a handful of good ones. Byron, writing to a friend in 1822, described what he found when reading plays for Drury Lane:

> … the number of plays upon the shelves were about five hundred … I do not think that of those which I saw, there was one which could be conscientiously tolerated … The Scenes I had to go through! – the authors – and the authoresses – the Milliners – the people from Brighton – from Blackwell – from Chatham – from Cheltenham – from Dublin – from Dundee – who came in upon me! – to all of whom it was proper to give a civil answer – and a hearing – and a reading … Miss Emma Somebody with a play entitled the 'Bandit of Bohemia' – or some such title or production – Mr O'Higgins – He was a wild man of a savage appearance – As I am really a civil & polite person and *do* hate giving Pain – when it can be avoided – I sent them up to Douglas Kinnaird – who is a man of business – and sufficiently ready with a negative – and left them to settle with him …

English theatre was halfway through a two-and-a-half-century-long coma: a time so blank and unsettling that we prefer to forget all about it. But, as Dr Oliver Sacks, the author of that great study of coma, *Awakenings*, has pointed out, 'Such forgettings are as dangerous as they are mysterious, for they give us an unwarranted sense of security.'

So it's worth looking quickly at how and when the coma started. One date is irresistible, at least symbolically: 6 January 1642. Three great, interlocking themes are packed into that winter evening: theatre, Ireland and the state.

Twelfth Night was a traditional date for Royal Command Performances. The choice this year was a twenty-six-year-old romantic comedy by Beaumont and Fletcher, to be performed in the Cockpit Theatre at the Palace of Whitehall. The actors were the King's men, the direct descendants of Shakespeare's company; their patron was Charles I.

The show took place, but the two best seats in the house were empty. A few days later, the Master of the King's Revels, one Sir Henry Herbert, wrote the following entry in his daybook:

> On Twelfe Night ... the prince had a play called **The Scornful Lady** at the Cockpitt, but the kinge and queene were not there; and it was the only play acted at court in the whole Christmas.

Vast events were unfolding behind the scenes. Two months before, the Irish chieftains had rebelled against English rule. Terrifying reports had been rushed to London: Catholics were murdering Protestants in their beds, thousands were dead, the atrocities were unspeakable. The King proposed to raise an army. Parliament started raising one of its own. On 4 January two days before the show, the King led a posse of cavalry to Westminster in an attempt to arrest his five main enemies. But they'd gone missing. 'I see all the birds are flown,' he said before retreating in disgrace.

The King had lost control of London: it's no wonder he couldn't face the play. The following week he left London, not to return until his trial and execution seven years later. Years of Civil War had intervened. With the strange dramatic symmetry that haunts this story, he walked to the block on a specially constructed scaffolding built out of the first-floor window of Inigo Jones' Banquet Hall in the Palace of Whitehall, so that the site of the show he'd skipped was the last thing he saw on earth.

His flight from London left the King's Men facing ruin. Charles had given them money and status. They often played at Court, and the fees were high. When plague broke out, and public theatres were closed down as a safety measure, other troupes went bankrupt: they were compensated. By 1642, they reigned supreme.

The price was the loss of their popular audience. They had already, in the previous reign, raised the minimum entry-price from a penny to sixpence, the equivalent in modern terms of hiking the cheapest seats from five pounds to around thirty, with all the effect on the audience profile that you'd expect. The plays got blander. Out went the thrilling weirdnesses of Webster and Middleton; in came the tinsel delights of James Shirley and John Suckling. 'This comedy,' wrote Sir Henry, of Shirley's **The Young Admiral,** 'being free from oaths, profaneness or obsceneness, hath given me much delight in the reading ... When Mr Shirley hath read this approbation, I know it will encourage him to pursue this beneficial and cleanly way of poetry ...' No doubt it had the same effect on others.

With their patron gone, the actors had nowhere to turn. The ordinary Londoner had long been put off by their bumped-up prices and dumbed-down repertoire. Sales slumped. That April, the prologue of Shirley's comedy **The Sisters** addresses the remnants of the audience:

> ... if you leave us too, we cannot thrive.
> I'll promise neither Play nor Poet live
> Till ye come back ...

It was left to Parliament to stick the knife into the dying beast. In September, it decreed that:

> ... whereas the distressed state of Ireland, steeped in her own blood, and the distracted estate of England, threatened with a Cloud of Blood, by a Civil Warre, call for all possible meanes to appease and avert the Wrath of God appearing in these Judgements ... publike Stage-Playes shall cease and bee forborne.

And that was that. Some of the actors joined the army, all in the Royal cause, though, with the tactical alertness for which their profession is famed, several changed sides when they found that they'd backed the wrong horse.

In 1660, the monarchy was restored. The playhouses opened and Sir Henry Herbert got his job back – thereby becoming the direct ancestor of the Lord Chamberlain's office, which would control the theatre until the week of the opening night of **Hair** in 1968. But, for the English theatre, there was no real Restoration. Plays in the Elizabethan or the Jacobean sense, as serious forays into love, death, politics and whatever else makes life worth living, were a dead form.

Eighteen years of theatre closure were partly to blame. But much of the damage was self-inflicted. The compromises of the pre-war years had robbed the theatre of its heart: there was, in a sense, no theatre to restore.

From now, and for the next 250 years or so, most English playwrights would arrive from Ireland. If you detect a certain ambiguity in that phrase – why 'arrive from'? Why not 'Irish'? – it's intended. The ambiguity is what links them. Only one, from many, came from a native Irish background. None was a Catholic. All were privileged by birth and religion and none was prey to institutional persecution. These rescuers of the English theatre were the sons of England's first colonial adventure: its banished children, bringing home a memory of a time when theatre had meant something.

Their impulse to succeed in London was a complex one. For the colonial child, returning home, or 'home', has a left-out, almost heartbroken quality about it. Like the country cousin in some manor-house *divertissement* by Somerset Maugham, he or she slithers into polite English society only to live in terror of putting his bow-tie on the wrong way round, or twisting her seams or (worse) saying something boringly provincial. It's while fiddling helplessly with the kedgeree, or fumbling with mysterious forks beneath the stony stare of the butler, that the decision is made to be wittier and more clever than anyone else: that this is the only way to pass as English.

William Congreve (1670–1729) was at least born in England. He seems to have felt obliged to spell this out to people, so the fact cannot have been an obvious one and his accent was presumably Irish. He was taken to Ireland as a baby when his father, an army officer, landed the post of Commander of the English garrison at Youghal, near Cork, and he returned to England at the age of nineteen.

In London, he was given a helping hand by another Irish exile, Thomas Southerne – the adaptor of Aphra Benn's **Oroonoko** – and wrote his masterpieces, **Love for Love** and **The Way of the World,** by the time he was thirty. Then he joined the Establishment: very much the colonial syndrome. He received a generous income from no fewer than three dull public positions, one of them being Commissioner for Licensing Hackney Coaches, and it was, ironically, a coach which caused his death at the age of fifty-nine by turning over on the road from Bath. A sign of his social success is that when he died the Duchess of Marlborough had a full-sized Congreve-replica made which sat at her dinner-table at mealtimes and was so constructed as to nod when she spoke to it.

George Farquhar's life (1678–1707) shows what happened to those for whom the theatre was more than a stepping-stone. He was the son of a Church of Ireland clergyman who supposedly died of grief when his rectory was burned down by James II's army in the aftermath of the siege of Derry. As a child, young George fought at the Battle of the Boyne in support of William III (the King Billy who to this day appears in Northern Irish Protestant murals). Grown up, he became an actor in Dublin only to leave the acting profession – and Ireland – after accidentally wounding another actor on-stage.

In London he became a playwright. He was always poor – rather a mystery, since his plays were popular. He tried to better his position by marrying a wealthy widow, but her fortune turned out to be a fiction designed to get him to the altar. He took the job of recruiting officer for the Grenadiers in Shrewsbury and based **The Recruiting Officer** on that experience; he then died penniless at the age of twenty-nine, having just completed **The Beaux' Stratagem.**

Both of his two great plays have a natural, unforced quality which marks them out as something totally new. Paradoxically, given his staunch colonial-class credentials, the quality he brought to English comedy was exactly the one that people think of as most Irish: a buoyant elegance of speech. He's a realist – motive, status and power are baldly stated – but there's no gloating or giggling. 'It is Farquhar's great merit,' said the critic William Archer, comparing him with his predecessors, 'to have released comedy from this circle of malign enchantment.'

Richard Steele (1672–1729), from Dublin, pioneered the 'sentimental comedy'. More popular in her day was Susannah Centlivre (1667–1723) whose plays depart from formula by having spunkier heroines than most. She was herself a striking character from County Tyrone, who left Ireland at the age of sixteen. On the way to London she came across a young Cambridge undergraduate who installed her in his rooms in male disguise, passing her off to his friends as his cousin Jack. She made good use of her stay at Cambridge, learning logic, rhetoric, ethics and fencing. Two of her husbands were killed in duels and she was briefly Farquhar's mistress, before meeting and marrying a Mr Centlivre, who was head cook at the Palace of Windsor. Strangely, her life has not yet been turned into a musical.

Arthur Murphy (1727–1805), came from a well-off family of Dublin merchants, joined a London bank and left it for the stage. His best play, **The Way to Keep Him**, is strictly room-temperature. Oliver Goldsmith (1728–1774), from County Longford, the son of a Church of Ireland curate, combined the setting of **The Beaux' Stratagem** and a plot from Marivaux in England's most robust and undentable comedy to date: **She Stoops to Conquer**. The Dubliner John O'Keeffe (1747–1833) wrote an outright plagiary: **Tony Lumpkin in Town**. But his **Wild Oats** is a stunning romantic farce. Its rediscovery by Ronald Bryden at the RSC at a time when it seemed that there weren't any more lost classics left to rediscover was a milestone of the 1960s.

In Richard Brinsley Sheridan (1751–1816), Ireland produced a character so gifted, so baffling and so deeply fake as to defy analysis. Perhaps, as Yeats suggested of Oscar Wilde, he lived not in the actual England normal people live in, but a dream of England: one where fantasies become reality, as Sheridan's did, and are never exploded, as his always were.

He is the only classic Irish playwright to be Irish through and through: the Sheridan (O Sioradain) family stemmed from an ancient line of Gaelic-speaking chieftains. His father, Thomas Sheridan, ran the thriving Smock Alley Theatre in Dublin. In a celebrated incident of the 1740s, he rebuked a party of drunken Trinity students from the stage with the words, 'I am as good a gentleman as you are.' This unheard-of claim from a man who was not only an actor but a native Irishman caused a riot but made him a Dublin hero.

Like Congreve, Sheridan the younger wrote almost all his plays (and all the good ones) by the time he was thirty. He had also by now bought Drury Lane. His life thereafter was one of frenzy: swimming in alcohol, sucking up to royalty, juggling stupendous debts and delivering – in his preferred career as politician – speeches which lasted not just hours but days. Somewhere behind all this can be glimpsed an exaggerated version of his father, the 'gentleman' theatre-owner. **The School for Scandal** elevates family feeling to the status of sole and all-redeeming virtue and in the process becomes the only great masterpiece to be contemptuous of culture, art and learning. Shelley was the first to spot this. 'I see the purpose of this comedy,' he said. 'It is to associate virtue with bottles & glasses, & villainy with books.'

The first playwright from Ireland actually to *write* about the place was Dion Boucicault (1820–1890). He was a rampant plagiarist who earned a shady reputation early in life by taking his first wife – who was twice his age and rich – on their honeymoon to the Alps, where she fell to her death in the absence of witnesses. He wrote or adapted 142 plays, and their quality can't be guaranteed.

But at his best, he's amazing. Like a Victorian Andrew Lloyd Webber, he devoted his life to creating spectacular long-runners aimed at playing across the world, so their basis in day-to-day reality was necessarily slim. And the Ireland of his three best melodramas is strictly an Emerald Isle of the mind, full of tinkling fountains and apple-cheeked colleens.

What's fascinating about him is his ambiguity. Part hack, part Irish-patriot, he's endlessly sneaking in political messages and then hastily covering them up. It's striking how well the camouflage succeeded. His repeated butt is the feckless, rapscallion Paddy: Myles na Gopaleen or the Shaughraugn. London audiences found this stereotype hilarious, as you might expect. More strangely, so did Irish ones. In a reverse example: he staged benefit performances in London for Fenian prisoners and nobody minded a bit.

In **The Colleen Bawn** he gives full rein to his flair for myth. Young Hardress Cregan, penniless child of the Anglo-Irish Ascendancy, is secretly married to Eily, the native Gaelic maiden. Much is made of the fact that his matrimonial visits to her cottage require his sailing across a wide and mysterious lake: the purging ritual without which national reconciliation cannot take place. When her life is threatened, water is both the murder weapon and the source of her renaissance: thus the spirit of Ireland soars from its ancestral springs. Fantastic scenic spectacle and outrageous plotting ice the cake. The play ran for ever.

The English theatre had clung to life because of a handful of playwrights from Ireland. Meanwhile the playwrights from Ireland clung to life by having their plays produced in England. This classic cycle of dependence was challenged by the self-propelled arrival of three remarkable Irishmen: George Bernard Shaw, William Butler Yeats and – to give him the rich and evocative name he pronounced in the dock – Oscar Fingal O'Flahertie Wills Wilde.

All three were born into the Protestant Ascendancy. All were close in age and each was a Dubliner. All three were politically engaged: Yeats as Irish patriot, Shaw as Fabian socialist, Wilde, under cover of socialism, as the creator of something more subversive. All three were superb self-publicists and all spent most of their adult lives in fancy dress: Yeats flamboyantly attired as magus-cum-actor-laddie, Shaw in patent Jaeger woolwear, Wilde first in aesthetic breeches and ruffles, then in clothes so immaculately conventional as to be parodic, in the manner of Gilbert and George.

It's tempting to think of them as locked in troika – Greek conspirators in the heart of Rome. In fact, they were never close: their visions were too different. They made contact, though, at significant moments: in Wilde's crucial hours, both Yeats and Shaw appeared from nowhere to offer advice. It's as though the link between them sprang into life at points of crisis. Their writing for the theatre was unequal. What made them such an epoch-making force is that each had the guts to push a political insight.

It's to Shaw that we owe that mighty engine of twentieth-century drama, the theatre of daylight: one that assumes that plays are subject to the same laws of common sense and logic as any other field of human endeavour – driving a bus, let's say, or brain-surgery. Brecht caught this ball and ran with it.

Three remarkable Irishmen: Wilde, Shaw and Yeats.

Wilde created not just a single opposite, but a cluster of them: theatre of the self, art for the sake of art, sexual self-expression, the veiled confessional. In his hands they merged into something new and lasting: it was the Wildean vision that inspired the best of English theatre in the years between the wars, not to mention fuelling the 1960s.

Yeats was the father of an authentic Irish theatre. He dreamt it up, he protected it with tiger-like ferocity and he created a structure within which it could germinate and thrive – although the form of 'authenticity' that the Irish theatre chose was very unlike the one he'd imagined.

2

William Butler Yeats was born into an ancient Anglo-Irish family. 'Butler' refers to an actual butler to the English throne who was brought to Ireland by King John in 1165, given large tracts of land and upgraded to Duke of Ormond. Yeats was proud of his supposed connection, even to the point of sometimes claiming to be the rightful Duke himself. But whether this had any genealogical reality remains unclear.

He was born in 1865, the son of a barrister, John Butler Yeats, who left the bar on impulse. Oscar Wilde, whose family knew the Yeatses well, described the father coming down to breakfast and announcing, 'Children, I am tired of the law, and shall become a painter.' 'Could he paint?' Wilde was asked. 'Not in the least,' he answered, 'that was the beauty of it.'

Yeats's grandparents' home was in Sligo – their 'ancestral' home, place of magical family summers, enchanted woods and the occasional never-to-be-forgotten sighting of a ghost. Like Wilde and Shaw, he was encouraged to show off his cleverness as soon as he could talk. 'In Ireland,' he wrote, 'a bright boy becomes the family confidant, learning all about the family necessities ... He is full of intellectual curiosity, so much conversation keeping it alive ... He is at once sceptical and credulous but, provided his opinions are expressed gaily and frankly, no one minds.'

He never learned to spell and was till the end of his life incapable of learning a foreign language. But he read voraciously, devoured the work of every poet he could find and determined to be one himself. As a career? But careers were not an issue. 'My father brought me up,' he wrote, 'never when at school to think of the future or of any practical result. I have even known him to say, "When I was young, the definition of a gentleman was a man not wholly occupied in getting on."'

He went to art school in Dublin and soon discovered seances, occultisms and Eastern Holy Men: a slightly embarrassing passion which would last for the rest of his life. He heard a lecture by Oscar Wilde, and met the Irish Nationalist John O'Leary, who persuaded him to turn his back on foreign, i.e. English, themes. The family lifestyle had till now been funded by income from land. When, in 1885, native Irish tenants were granted the right to buy their holdings, this income vanished and the Yeatses moved to London, there to survive on Father's meagre earnings as a painter.

Nostalgia trips you up when you least expect it. Yeats was twenty-three when, walking down the Strand, he found himself gazing into a shop window. On display was a pretty but pointless trick: a little water-jet with a wooden ball bouncing on the summit, never quite falling off. He stared at the ball's unnatural poise. He heard the trickle of running water. And his mind shot back to the streams and cataracts of Sligo. This, he later wrote, was when he discovered his voice as a poet. He rushed back to the family home in Bedford Park – a cheapish middle-class artists' quarter halfway between Chiswick and Hammersmith – with a poem taking shape in his head: it would be his most immediately successful, rather a bane in later years. As a grand old man, he hated being asked to quote it.

At home were his sisters Lolly and Lily; one was painting, the other quietly sewing. 'Willy burst in,' Lily reported, 'having just written, or not even written but having just brought forth "Innisfree" … I felt a thrill all through me and saw Sligo beauty, heard lake water lapping …' They put down their work and listened while he declaimed:

> I will arise and go now, for always night and day
> I hear lake water lapping with low sounds by the shore;
> While I stand on the roadway, or on the pavements grey,
> I hear it in the deep heart's core.

This is the image of Yeats's life: the brilliant brother, never off-stage, loved and indulged by an intimate circle of women. He was already a figure in the literary-party world. He wrote poems. He developed a taste for hashish, which he found worked best when eaten. He fell in love with the inspirational Maud Gonne – a star of the Republican circuit and an awesome beauty – and sharpened up his politics to suit. Oscar Wilde asked him to his exquisite Chelsea house under the impression that Yeats was alone in London. Yeats felt awkward there: his shoes were too yellow – or so he felt when Oscar gazed thoughtfully at them – and when he was invited to tell one of Wilde's small sons a bedtime fairy-tale, he'd hardly got past the first few words before the little boy shrieked with terror.

Most of all, he felt a sense of unreality. Wilde, in coming to terms with England, had turned it into a place of his own imagination, a place where social class was a pantomime beanstalk and the aristocracy was a crowd of richly dressed theatrical supers. Nothing was real: not England, nor even Wilde himself, the principal actor in his own charade.

Meeting his famous fellow-Dubliner taught Yeats something he would never forget: that the reality of England was unattainable to an outsider. The colonial boy, returning home to storm the castle, is aiming his cannons at a piece of scenery, something held together by struts and wobbling canvas. Only home is real.

He got involved in theatre in a roundabout way, through the partly erotic help of two fellow-members of a London occult group. One was Annie Horniman, the spinster heiress to a tea fortune. She smoked in public, rode a bicycle in slacks and, when she first met Bernard Shaw, startled him by sporting a black eye. Much will be heard of her activities later,

67

both in Dublin and Manchester, but for the present her contribution rests on her offer of a large sum of money to a fellow-occultist, Florence Farr, for the purpose of putting on plays.

Farr was an enterprising young actress who believed in daily sexual intercourse as a tonic for the system, the current beneficiary of this healthy practice being Bernard Shaw. Yeats tried hard to get her into bed, but she refused. (Things worked out in Dublin ten years later.) His consolation prize was a commission to write a short play with a cracking good part for her niece. The result was the first of Yeats's twenty-six plays to be produced on stage: **The Land of Heart's Desire.**

It's set in Sligo 'at a remote time'. Young Mary stands in the doorway reading a book that she's discovered in the attic. It's a family heirloom well known for its supernatural propensities, so husband, mother-in-law and priest unite in imploring her to leave the wretched thing alone. But on she reads … and under the influence of this ancient tome, fairies ('faeries') of various shapes and hues steal forth from the wood: a little queer old woman dressed in green, a child. Mary dies, thereby escaping a world of household drudgery. In a stage direction which must have had the stage-management scratching its head: *Outside there are dancing figures, and it may be a white bird and many voices singing.*

The second half of the bill was Shaw's **Arms and the Man**: a thunderous hit. The curtain-raiser was soundly eclipsed. Yeats watched his rival's play in deepening gloom. He hated it. It seemed mechanical, cold, inhuman, 'I had a nightmare that I was haunted by a sewing-machine, that clicked and shone, but the incredible thing was that the machine smiled, smiled perpetually.'

It's at moments like this that playwrights want a theatre of their own. Yeats was lucky. Barely a week had passed before he found himself scooped up at a party by Lady Augusta Gregory: forty-two, an Anglo-Irish grandee, widow of a former Governor of Ceylon. 'Very calculating, dutiful, courageous, purposeful,' said an acquaintance, 'and all built upon a bedrock sense of humour and love of fun and a bitter sarcasm with a vein of simple coarseness of thought and simple inherited Protestantism.' Yeats and Lady Gregory met regularly for the next few years, often on her estate at Coole in Galway. Here stood the historic oak, on the trunk of which artistic visitors were invited to carve their names. And it was here, in 1897, that Yeats and Gregory hatched their plan for an Irish theatre. Their manifesto was historic:

> We propose to have performed in Dublin in the spring of every year certain Celtic and Irish plays, which whatever their degree of excellence, will be written with a high ambition … and so to build up a Celtic and Irish dramatic school … We hope to find in Ireland an uncorrupted and imaginative audience trained to listen by its passion for oratory, & believe that our desire to bring upon the stage the deeper thoughts and emotions of Ireland will ensure for us a tolerant welcome, & that freedom to experiment which is not found in the theatres of England, and without which no new movement in art or literature can succeed …

This was the birth of the Irish Literary Theatre. One of its prime purposes (not to be too cynical about it) was to present the plays of Yeats himself; next in line was Lady Gregory, who now discovered a new lease of life as a competent playwright. Other like-minded writers were welcome on board, provided they conformed to the moody and misty aesthetic. Racy story-tellers – Shaw, Boucicault – were barred from the lifeboat. A few years later Yeats commissioned a play from Shaw – **John Bull's Other Island** – but he rejected it on slender grounds ('Our actors just wouldn't be good enough') and it never occurred to him, for all his delvings into Irish culture, to welcome Farquhar, Congreve, Sheridan, Wilde or Goldsmith back to the land they sprang from.

In 1904, Violet Horniman bought the Abbey Theatre, gave it to the Movement and promised to underwrite it. From this point on, its rise was unstoppable. It was also acrimonious, as was inevitable.

'Very calculating, dutiful, courageous, purposeful': Lady Gregory.

A theatre that tries to mean something will have its reward: it *will* mean something. It will also get its punishment, which is that every one of its supporters will have a different notion of what that 'something' ought to be. The results are always the same: disillusion, accusations of betrayal and screaming-matches.

The Coole manifesto had led Irish Nationalists to expect, quite reasonably when you come to think of it, that Yeats and Gregory had a down-to-earth political aim. 'Let Mr Yeats give us a play which will rouse this sleeping land,' was one response. 'There is a herd of Saxon and other swine fattening on us. They must be swept into the sea along with the pestilent crowd of West-Britons with which we are troubled, or they will sweep us there.'

But Yeats ignored this call and all the others like it. Art was 'art': too high a form to mix with propaganda. And he couldn't be a truly political playwright – like D.H. Lawrence, Sean O'Casey or Synge – because his talent wasn't up to it. He was blessed with two quite separate brands of genius – one as man of the theatre, the other as poet. But they didn't connect. When his characters address each other, nothing happens. They're inert.

69

Irish Republicanism, then as now, had a strongly puritanical streak, so there was plenty to object to in Yeats's and Gregory's choice of play. Prudery came wrapped in patriotic colours: anything that defamed the Irish nation was a comfort to the enemy. Portrayals of loose morals, drunkenness or disrespect to the Catholic faith were all deplored. These issues paled beside the portrayal of women. The one great theme of the Edwardian theatre was a woman's right to make her mind up, and from the Nationalist perspective, this was the next worst thing to whorishness, so the rows continued. 'Going, going, gone! An Irish wife – an unchaste Irish wife – secured for hell for a hundred crowns!' raged a critic after Yeats's **The Countess Cathleen**, going on to accuse the play of presenting the Irish race 'just like a sordid tribe of black devil-worshippers on the Congo or the Niger'. All this came to a head with the arrival of John Millington Synge.

John Millington Synge.

Synge (1871–1909) was six years younger than Yeats. He too came from a middle-class Protestant family and, like Yeats, he'd chosen the bohemian life at an early age. But Synge was educated and a linguist. The two men met for the first time in 1896 in Paris, where they saw the first performance of Jarry's **Ubu Roi**, and it was here that Yeats told the younger man to go to the Aran Islands: the windswept, desolate archipelago off the West of Ireland. 'Live there as if you were one of the people themselves; express a life that has never found expression.'

This was on the face of it an odd command, certainly not one Yeats ever thought of following himself. But it was clever. Synge stayed on the Aran Islands for four summers running. Life there was poor and backward. He lived, not quite like one of the local inhabitants – unlike them he could always escape – but genuinely among them: it was 'participant observation', as anthropologists call it. His journals capture precisely the mix of remoteness and closeness that all anthropologists feel. 'There is hardly an hour I am with them that I do not feel the shock of some inconceivable idea, and then again the shock of some vague emotion that is familiar to them and to me.' It's the 'familiar' that jolts the writer: the way in which an exotic surrounding isolates common human emotions, so that you feel you're seeing them for the first time.

His first play, **In the Shadow of the Glen**, was delivered to Yeats in 1903. It's written in dialect of a sort: a mix of English-Irish and Gaelic-in-translation, thick with ornament. 'I got more than any learning could have given me,' Synge wrote later, 'from a chink in the floor in the old Wicklow house where I was staying, that let me hear what was being said by the servant girls in the kitchen.'

In a funny way the play is a rewrite of Yeats's **The Land of Heart's Desire**. Again the scene is rural Ireland, scene of beguiling supernatural forces only a few paces outside the cottage door. And again a young wife escapes the prison of marriage. But instead of the fairies, there's a tramp, part ingratiating, part sinister: 'He lights his pipe, so that there is a sharp light beneath his haggard face.'

When Ibsen's Nora left her doll's house, she banged the door behind her. Synge's Nora is modest by comparison. But this was Dublin, 1903. Yeats arranged a private reading, always the first resort of a nervous producer. There was bitter opposition; Maud Gonne didn't even have to read it to announce that it sounded 'horrid'. She resigned. So did other associates, including one Arthur Griffiths, later to found Sinn Fein.

Yeats's speeches from the stage, berating the audience for its dimness and bad behaviour, would become major Abbey attractions, and the one he delivered on the first night of **In the Shadow of the Glen** – claiming the artist's right 'to show life, instead of the desire which every political party would substitute for life' – was one of his best. The reviews were savage. Arthur Griffiths, with his inside knowledge of Synge's Parisian background, blamed 'the decadent cynicism that passes current in the Latin Quarter', and Maud Gonne dealt her ex-lover what must have been a bruising rap on the knuckles: 'Mr Yeats asks for freedom for the theatre ... I would ask for freedom from one thing more deadly than all else – freedom from the insidious and destructive tyranny of foreign influence.'

Synge took the whole thing with saturnine equilibrium: all he'd done, he said, was put back the sex that normally got cut out, and the audience was so surprised to see it that they couldn't see anything else. He was made a director of the Abbey and his next play – the flawless pocket tragedy **Riders to the Sea** – was respectfully received. Fury broke in 1907, over **The Playboy of the Western World**.

Plays about peasant life struggle against two big disadvantages. The first is a lowering of expectations on the playwright's part: a refusal to believe that the characters are capable of complex emotion. The handful of playwrights to have transcended this inhibition makes an interesting list: Verga, in his harsh portrait of Sicilian life, **La Lupa**, Daudet writing about the Languedoc

Yeats berates.

The Poet addressed the Audience.

71

peasantry in **L'Arlesienne**, the Czech Gabriela Preissova in **Her Foster-daughter**, Lorca many times: all, like Synge, asserting the values of a marginal community and making rather a point of this, and all placing a woman at the centre of the canvas.

But if playwrights are slow to take peasant life seriously, the public is slower still. **The Playboy of the Western World** is rare in being so popular. One reason is the story: a fable with 'timeless' printed through it like a stick of rock. Synge's dialogue is as rich and salty as before, but suppler: it no longer feels like a gown so richly sewn with gems that it can stand up stiff even when there's no one inside it. And it's full of surprises: not twists of plot so much as the surprises that come from lives lived close to so many edges: the edge of hunger, the edge of the law, the edge of the world.

In the West of Ireland, Synge wrote, there exists a universal impulse to protect the criminal:

> It seems partly due to association between justice and the hated English jurisdiction, but more directly to the primitive feeling of these people, who are never criminals yet always capable of crime, that a man will not do wrong unless he is under the influence of a passion which is irresponsible as a storm of the sea.

Playboy melds this situation with that of another great folk-tale play, Gogol's **The Government Inspector**. Christy Mahon arrives in a small village in Mayo announcing that he's hit his father over the head with a spade and killed him. He's a meek, insignificant fellow to start with, but the news of his crime turns him into a local hero and before the day is out two women are competing for his hand – the Widow Quin and a young girl of twenty, Pegeen Mike. Illusions crash to the ground when Christy's father appears, bloody but whole. But the fiction has done its work: Christy has become a man. A fraud no longer, he turns his back on the treacherous people of Mayo and on Pegeen. Alone, she utters her celebrated curtain-line, one which in the hands of certain Irish leading ladies has been known to take several minutes: 'Oh, my grief, I've lost him surely. I've lost the only Playboy of the Western World.'

'We were almost bewildered by its abundance and fantasy,' remembered Lady Gregory. 'But we felt, and Mr Yeats said plainly, that there was far too much "bad language".' Yeats was surely being tactful to his jealous fellow-playwright: he can only have felt delight. Ten years before, he'd launched a manifesto for an 'Irish Theatre' for which there existed no real basis whatsoever. One of his prime cultural inspirations, a Hebridean chronicler of myth and faery by the name of Fiona Macleod, had turned out to be a red-faced Englishman called William Sharp. His own plays, with the help of Lady Gregory's dilettantiste pot-boilers, had kept the business ticking over. Time was running out. And here – thanks to his own discovery of a writer, and his weirdly intuitive piece of advice – was a copper-bottomed Irish classic in the line of **The School for Scandal** and **She Stoops to Conquer**, but with its roots in Irish soil.

On the night of the first performance, Yeats was in Aberdeen. He was woken by the arrival of a telegram from Lady Gregory: AUDIENCE BROKE UP IN DISORDER AT THE WORD SHIFT.

She was understating it. The immodest reference to a petticoat had indeed caused an uproar, but this had been well prepared for by boos, hisses and cries of, 'Where is the author? Bring him out and we will deal with him.' Yeats sped back to Dublin for the second night. Forty Griffithites were spotted in the audience, objecting from start to finish. Sinn Fein was on the warpath in defence of Irish honour. No Irishman would hit his father on the head with a spade, still less be thought a hero for doing so, least of all by a pure-bred Irish maiden – and no Irish patriot would suggest the opposite.

At the third performance, the police were called. Yeats got the blame for this, though in truth these agents of the oppressor had arrived more or less spontaneously to dampen the spirits of a gang of Anglo-Protestant Trinity students who were demonstrating in *support* of the play by singing 'God Save the King' in drunken chorus, very unfortunately led by Lady Gregory's nephew. The week rolled on and the press went wild. Yeats was bounding on to and off the stage like a yo-yo, delivering some of his finest harangues. Griffiths attacked the play as 'a vile and inhuman story told in the foulest language we have ever listened to from a public platform'. Synge declared he didn't care a rap. Yeats held a public meeting. His father popped up in the body of the hall to speak in his son's support, but his satirical reference to 'plaster saints' outraged the Catholics in the audience. 'Kill *your* father,' somebody called to Yeats the younger, in witty reference to the plot of the play. But the Abbey had made its point. 'We have won a complete victory over the organised disturbers,' wrote an associate. 'Sinn Fein men to a great extent.'

Synge died two years later, of Hodgkin's disease – a rare, slow-acting cancer – at the age of thirty-eight. An unfinished play survived: **Deirdre of the Sorrows**. He remains the playwright's playwright. Lorca spoke of his debt to him and so did D.H. Lawrence. **The Widowing of Mrs Holroyd** is drawn from **Riders to the Sea**, and Brecht's **Senora Carrar's Rifles** is an adaptation of it, while Beckett acknowledged the influence of no other playwright at all.

Miss Horniman had had enough. She'd poured a fortune into the Abbey, and got little back. She disapproved of Home Rule and didn't like the Irish, a feeling that was heartily reciprocated. She was also suspected of banning plays on political grounds. (The truth was that she'd tried but mostly failed.) Yeats was good at banking cheques but bad at returning calls. True, he'd let her design the costumes for his play **The King's Threshold**. 'Do you realise that you have given me the right to call myself "artist"?' she wrote. 'How I do thank you!' But respect was bafflingly withheld. She cancelled her subsidy and packed her bags: her next endeavour would be the founding of the English Repertory movement.

3

Yeats and the Republican movement were at odds over most artistic matters, but they shared a common belief: that the soul of Ireland had its home in the countryside, probably in the West, certainly somewhere remote and undeveloped. There, amid the humble cottages and glowing hearths, was the wellspring: the source of language, myth and nationhood.

This belief was challenged by Sean O'Casey (1880–1964). In his three best plays, the Irish soul is found in Dublin: a raucous, acrimonious gossipy place of tenements, pawn shops and picture-houses, a city so sensuously imagined that the smell of frying and the racket of public houses seems to emanate from the stage.

O'Casey's Dublin is a Catholic city, and a working-class one, though he was neither of these things by birth. He was born into a Protestant, lower-middle-class family in Dorset Street, a few doors down from Sheridan's birth-place. The family name was Casey and he was christened John. His father died when he was six, his family declined into genteel poverty and he took up a variety of hard manual jobs: work on the docks, breaking stones. He learned Irish, joined the labour movement, took an active part in the 1913 strike of the Irish Transport and General Workers' Union and was secretary of the Citizens' Army: the force put together to defend the strikers.

He became a playwright late in life – he was forty-three when his first play was produced – and was fond of claiming that he'd taught himself to write plays, helped only by reading

Sean O'Casey.

them, seeing them and occasionally acting in them. (But what better teachers are there?) Shaw's **John Bull's Other Island** was a decisive influence: it shook him out of what he called 'the romantic cult of Nationalism'.

Each of his first three plays has a topical subject, and placed in order they form a dissenting patriot's history of the birth of the Irish Free State. **The Plough and the Stars,** the last to be written, is set at the time of the Easter Rising of 1916, when a Republican force of something over a thousand men, led by Patrick Pearse and an old associate of O'Casey's from the Citizens' Army, John Connolly, occupied a number of key buildings in Dublin – notably the post office – and declared an Irish Republic. Dubliners were dumbfounded by this move, nobody backed it and the insurgents were defeated. But the way in which the British army put the rising down was so atrocious that Sinn Fein gained nationwide support.

The Shadow of a Gunman is set four years later, at the height of the independence struggle. By now, the IRA ruled hearts and minds. Particular hatred was reserved for the British Auxiliaries, the notorious Black and Tans. **Juno and the Paycock** is set just after the signing of peace, a mere three years before the play was written. The Treaty enshrined the Free State, but conceded the loss of six counties (present-day Northern Ireland): this caused a split in the IRA and much shedding of blood.

O'Casey worked hard to cultivate his working-class image, and one of the results of this was that he got severely patronised by the Abbey elite. ('Why does W.B.Y. treat O'Casey as a baby?' Shaw asked Lady Gregory.) But not all the advice he got was bad. Lady Gregory urged him to 'develop his peculiar gift for character-drawing'. In **The Shadow of a Gunman**, O'Casey fined down the plot so ruthlessly that it's like a line of hooks on which comfy, capacious character-sketches can be hung like coats.

Donal McCann and John Kavanagh in **Juno and the Paycock**.

Donal Davoren, a young proletarian poet, lives in a tenement room. When the other residents get it into their heads that he's an IRA gunman, he's happy to play along, especially since it so impresses young Minnie Powell. But Minnie's off-stage death (none too convincing) at the hands of the Black and Tans exposes him as the posturing fantasist he is.

What gives the play its life is dialogue packed with idiom, richly musical, closely patterned on music-hall crosstalk. Here's the gag of the word tossed back and forth like a smoking bomb which neither the comic nor the straight man wants to be left holding:

> MAGUIRE: Keep your hair on; I just blew in to tell you that I couldn't go today at all. I have to go to Knocksedan.
>
> SEUMAS: Knocksedan! An' what, in the name o'God, is bringin' you to Knocksedan?
>
> MAGUIRE: Business, business. I'm going out to catch butterflies.
>
> SEUMAS: If you want to make a cod of anybody, make a cod of somebody else, an' don't be tryin' to make a cod o' me. Here I've had everything packed an' ready for hours; you were to be here at nine, an' you wait till just one o'clock to come in rushin' like a mad bull to say you've got to go to Knocksedan! Can't you leave Knocksedan until tomorrow?

Maguire departs a moment later, leaving this bag behind. It's full of bombs. This vital and delightful character has a mere three speeches: this is what's meant by 'lightly plotted'. More knockabout in the shape of jiggery-pokery with the props:

> SEUMAS: (*counting the spoons*) There's a dozen of each in these parcels – three, six, nine – damn it, there's only eleven in this one … Now I suppose I'll have to go through the whole bloody lot of them, for I'd never be easy in my mind thinkin' there'd be more than a dozen in some o' them. And still we're looking for freedom – ye gods, it's a glorious country! (*He lets one fall, which he stoops to pick up.*) Oh, my God, there's the braces after breakin'.

And a groanful pun:

> MRS GALLAGHER: Oh, Mrs Henderson, that's a parrotox.
>
> MRS HENDERSON: It may be what a parrot talks, or a blackbird, or for the matter of that, a lark.

The gags may make us laugh (well, most of them) but that isn't their aim. They're there to undercut a culture rotten with false heroics.

If there are better twentieth-century plays than **Juno and the Paycock**, it's because they exceed it in mystery. No play is more accessible. It takes the one-set, three-act family drama and handles it with brilliance. The jokes never fail, the tragedy always stops the heart, not a line of dialogue goes wasted and the way in which the various denouements are squeezed into Act Three without squeaking or shouting 'Help!' is a lesson for every playwright.

The plot is an urban myth, a tale you might hear in a pub and laugh at, glad that it didn't happen to you. A will is so badly drafted that the intended beneficiary ends up getting nothing at all – by which time, of course, he's spent the money. But, as in **Gunman,** the plot's just there to give the characters something to do.

Juno, the careworn tenement housewife, struggles to keep the family afloat. Her drunken husband, 'Captain' Boyle, lives on a cloud of fantasy. His boozing pal Joxer Daly is a sort of half-tamed household devil: he makes our flesh creep. Boyle's fantasies are tolerable enough when we first come across them: by the end of the play, we're longing for Juno to up sticks and leave him, which she does. Her world has collapsed: the family is ruined, her son has been 'executed' by the self-righteous Diehards and her daughter is pregnant.

In **The Plough and the Stars**, young Jack Clitheroe escapes the cloying enchantments of marriage to play his part in the Easter Rising. Act Two shows Patrick Pearse, in silhouette, exhorting his troops in messianic terms. The war in France, we hear, provides a glorious example to all loyal Irishmen. 'The old heart of the earth needed to be warmed with the red wine of the battlefields.' O'Casey particularly disliked this kind of blood-sacrificial nonsense: inside the pub, we see the ebb and flow of working-class life in all its healthy incoherence.

The rising is crushed and Jack is killed. Bessie Burgess, his raucous Protestant neighbour, takes on the role of earth-mother by stopping an English bullet while rescuing Nora. But there's welcome realism in her dying words: 'You bitch!' she snaps.

The common wisdom about O'Casey is that he wrote three great plays and entered decline with the fourth. In fact, the third is ominous. Perhaps Yeats's endless fussing about what plays ought to be like – New forms? What about masks? Or chanting? Or is it better in Japan? – had begun to sap O'Casey's confidence in what he did best.

The subverting influence is film. It's almost as though O'Casey had a camera slung on his shoulder, one which recorded that momentous Easter everywhere he went, even when he popped into the pub for a drink. But his stagecraft couldn't stretch that far (whose could?) so the result is clumsy. The Man of Destiny declaiming in silhouette comes out of early Soviet cinema, and so does the cutting to and from his exhortations: on stage it doesn't work at all. Tragic Nora is pure D.W. Griffith, and her truly frightful dialogue reads like the captions from a silent weepie: 'Send him away and stay with your little red-lipp'd Nora.'

The first night of **The Plough and the Stars** at the Abbey in 1926 went quietly enough. But a few nights later, the auditorium erupted into riot. The play made fun of the Easter Rising, it showed the Citizens' Army flag being disrespectfully brought into a pub, it even made the preposterous claim that there were prostitutes in Dublin. Yeats fought back as hard as in the day of **Playboy**. His speech survives: he'd sensibly put it out as a press release:

> You have disgraced yourselves again! Is this to be an ever-recurring celebration of the arrival of Irish genius? Synge first and then O'Casey. The news of the happenings

of the past few minutes will go from country to country. Dublin has once more rocked the cradle of genius. From such a scene in this theatre went forth the genius of Synge. Equally the fame of O'Casey is born here tonight.

Scandals are always more hurtful to playwrights than they let on. O'Casey was invited to England, to boost the publicity for a West End production of **Juno**. He went and stayed: **The Silver Tassie** was sent from London in 1928. It's a difficult play, made or marred by an expressionist second act: before an array of Great War icons – a tilted crucifixion, a stained-glass window, barbed wire, a gunwheel with a soldier tied to it – a pageant of atrocity passes.

Yeats's rejection letter struck a bogus note. 'Dramatic action is a fire that must burn up everything except itself.' The play was finally done in London, where it flopped. Lady Gregory saw it there and said (rightly) that the Abbey should have done it, flaws and all: an early example of the Royal Court doctrine of the right to fail.

The wound stayed open. O'Casey remained in England, married, had three children and lived in Devon – as far as he could from streets and tenements. He had little to do with English theatre, but he kept on writing. In 1958, **The Drums of Father Ned** was scheduled for the Dublin Festival and then abandoned under clerical pressure. Furious, O'Casey banned performances of all of his plays in Ireland.

Criticising a theatre for wrongly turning down a play is a dangerous game, since the truth is that everyone's done it. Yeats got off lightly with **The Silver Tassie**, since the only loser was the playwright. The next mistake resulted in hot-making embarrassment.

One year after the **Tassie** débâcle, Denis Johnston (1901–1984), a Dublin lawyer, sent the Abbey a play called **Shadowdance**. It started with a spoof romantic episode, based on nineteenth-century melodrama and using the dialogue from as many corny old hits as Johnston could cram in. After a few pages, one of the actors was accidentally concussed, a doctor was called up from the audience, Pirandello-style, and the rest of the play – the real play, as it were – depicted the actor's hallucinatory wanderings through contemporary Dublin.

The play was rejected, with the reason carelessly scribbled on the envelope: 'The old lady says no.' The 'old lady', of course, was Lady Gregory, who turned out, when Johnston challenged her, to have got the wrong end of the stick entirely: 'We liked the little play it starts with very much,' she said kindly, 'but later on we thought it got a bit common.' Yeats backed her up. 'If we put on your play,' he explained, 'we will alienate our audience and lose £50. We don't mind losing the £50, but we don't want to alienate our audience.'

Mícheál MacLiammóir as Don Juan.

All this would have been just one of those minor unhappinesses that never leak out, if it weren't for the fact that the play was promptly snapped up by the newly formed Gate Theatre Studio Company, produced with vast success and revived year after year, under

a title which everyone except for Lady Gregory and her friends found quite hilariously funny: **The Old Lady Says No!**. The play launched Johnston as a major Irish playwright, the Gate as a significant rival to the Abbey and the leading man – Micheál MacLíammóir (1899–1978) – as a great and durable Irish star.

MacLíammóir was born, according to his memoirs, in Cork. He was in fact born Alfred Willmore, in Kensal Green, London NW10. His parents were from Kent and his earliest Irish connection seems to have been as a child actor, playing Michael Darling in a tour of **Peter Pan** which passed through Dublin. Noël Coward played Slightly, and the two thirteen-year-olds vied fiercely in sophistication. 'It really is unbelievably difficult to act like a moron when one isn't a moron,' Noël complained to Alfred. 'And I have very little sympathy with morons. Rather like you, darling, in your absent moments.'

Quite why or when he decided to transform himself into an Irishman is unknown: he may have been inspired by the avant-garde techniques and twilight mood of the Abbey Theatre on its visits to London. Having started, he did it to the hilt: he learned the Irish language, studied Irish myth and buried himself in Irish history. In 1927, he was playing in Enniscorthy, Wexford in a company led by his brother-in-law, the great Irish Shakespearian Anew McMaster. When an English actor, Hilton Edwards, joined the company, their lifelong partnership began.

MacLíammóir and Edwards founded the Gate the following year and continued to put on plays – first in an adjunct to the Abbey, then in a theatre of their own, then in premises toe-holdingly clung-on-to, and often on tour, until old age and death brought down the curtain. Both acted, Edwards staunchly, MacLíammóir with an eagle eye for effect. Edwards directed; MacLíammóir wrote and designed as well. He had studied art at the Slade and drew very well, in a Rackham-esque, kitschy way: one of the great differences between the Gate and the Abbey was that where the Abbey gave you nothing to look at – just a string of old-fashioned flats cleated together – productions at the Gate, on a tuppenny budget, were theatrically flamboyant. It's here that Orson Welles, who hustled his way into the Gate at the age of sixteen, first saw experimental staging in the European style: fierce back-lighting, dizzying angles, chiaroscuro. MacLíammóir's adventurous visual style extended famously to his own appearance: his made-up face and boot-black toupee were as startling as a three-eyed Picasso.

Oscar Wilde was an enduring inspiration. **Salomé** was one of their first shows, **The Importance of Being Oscar** the one-man warhorse which MacLíammóir put together in old age and played until his dying days. Simon Callow, as a student, dressed him on tour in Belfast, and in *Being an Actor* he gives a superb vignette of the frail, blind maestro braving himself to play:

> He reached out for my hand. 'Lead me,' he said. 'I can't see, d'you see.' Down the pitch-dark corridor we went, his fingernails digging ruts into my palms, while with his free hand he crossed himself again and again. 'Jesus, Mary and Joseph. Jesus

protect me. Jesus.' We reached the stage. I said, 'There are three stairs now.' 'Where? Where?' I helped him up, one, two, three. He fumbled with the black cotton drape, pushed it aside, and was on stage. In the pitch black, the light dazzled, but I heard big, solid, welcoming applause, and then Micheál's voice, rock-steady, as if he'd been on for hours: 'To drift with every passion till my soul ...'

'Sodom and Begorrah' went the joke: the Gate looking out towards chic, sophisticated Europe, the Abbey relying ever more on weary studies of a rural heartland. Yeats's defiance over **The Plough and the Stars** had been a last hurrah. No longer was the Abbey a centre of dissent in an occupied land: it was a central cultural pillar of the Irish establishment. It had a government grant (the first theatre in the English-speaking world to get one) and government nominees sat on the Board. The pressures to conform were stronger and more insidious. As the Irish State became more puritanical and inward-looking, so the Abbey's repertoire grew duller. It became an axiom, and remained one for many decades, that a play of historic importance would be rejected by the Abbey as a rite of passage.

Yeats died in 1939. Late in life, he wrote his finest work for the stage: Sophocles' two Oedipus plays, freely translated into English. The protagonists speak in swift, lean prose, the choruses are incandescent verse. That these aren't the standard versions is a mystery.

He was a great producer, lacking only one gift: the ability, like the magical puppet-master of a folk-tale, to tiptoe out of the shop at midnight and let the dolls take over. Reading Synge's last play, so Celtic and crepuscular, or O'Casey's foray into botched experimentalism, it's hard to avoid the feeling that neither writer could really escape the great man's influence. Yeats was both father and son: the marvellous paterfamilias of his youth, who let the children do as they pleased, and the brilliant show-off schoolboy who could never stop talking.

Playboy was his triumph. O'Casey's plays were different: Yeats had never intended anything quite so modern, harsh or working class. But without him, they would never have existed. He'd wanted to found an Irish school of drama, and he'd succeeded. That it would, by the time he died, have succumbed to the national mood of stagnation was something he hadn't foreseen – but neither had anyone else.

The New Drama

'Every play, every preface I write conveys a message.
I am the messenger boy of the new age.'
BERNARD SHAW

1

Bernard Shaw (1856–1950) was prophet and leading playwright of the New Drama and its father-figure.

As prophet he was inspired: only Kenneth Tynan wrote about the theatre with equal zest. Like Tynan, Shaw was a stage-struck fan with an almost adolescent weakness for star performances. Also like Tynan, he saw the link between the theatre and the politics of his day. The difference is that Shaw was immune to fashion. His politics were never chic in the 1960s style: they were weathered and honed by day-to-day political agitation, the sort of thing that gets tomatoes thrown at you. So his prose is swifter and more hilarious. With Shaw the playwright, paradox creeps in. His themes were modern, but the form of his best and earliest plays is unashamedly old-hat, packed with thrilling reversals, shock-entrances and ringing curtain-lines, all pulled out of the Boucicault bag.

His study of Ibsen was rewarding. Chekhov was a different matter. Even when writing his Chekhov-*hommage*, **Heartbreak House**, Shaw learned nothing from his Russian contemporary: not his studied amorality, nor his weaving of talk with silence, nor his illustrative use of time and space. Most foreign to Shaw was the Chekhovian technique of sub-text: doing or saying one thing while thinking or feeling another. In Shaw, everything's on the surface: start worrying about the depths below and the boat will sink.

He was born into a long-established Protestant line. The paradox of Anglo-Irishness was one he felt very at home with:

> When I say that I am an Irishman, I mean that I was born in Ireland, and that my native language is the English of Swift and not the unspeakable jargon of the mid-XIX century London newspapers. My extraction is the extraction of most Englishmen: that is, I have no trace in me of the commercially imported North Spanish strain which passes for aboriginal Irish; I am a genuine typical Irishman of the Danish, Norman, Cromwellian, and (of course) Scotch invasions. I am violently and arrogantly Protestant by family tradition; but let no English Government therefore

count on my allegiance: I am English enough to be an inveterate Republican and
Home Ruler …

A Captain William Shaw from Hampshire had fought at the Battle of the Boyne in 1689
and been rewarded with large tracts of land in Kilkenny; a Robert Shaw was made a
baronet in 1821. But the family weakness for the bottle made deep inroads into its wealth
and status and by 1856 the Shaws were merely shabby-genteel. Oscar Wilde's birth-place,
only a few streets away from the modest two-up, two-down where Shaw was born, was
aeons away in terms of class. These things rankle: later in life, Shaw described Wilde as
'a snob to his marrow, having been brought up in Merrion Square'.

His father was a drunk, his mother an accomplished mezzo-soprano who, when Shaw
was ten years old, took the unusual step of moving her music teacher into the house as
lodger and (it was generally assumed) her lover. He was a handsome, piratical figure by
the name of George Vandeleur Lee. Shaw's father's name was also George, which must
have caused some confusion: when Shaw grew up, he flatly rejected the name. 'Don't
George me,' he would growl.

Mother and lodger filled the house with music: a lasting influence on the son. Lee ate
brown bread and slept with the window open: habits Shaw was never to drop. Was Lee
the father of Shaw the son? They certainly looked alike. 'Quite amazingly,' said Beatrice
Webb years later, having studied the music teacher's photograph with interest. Shaw
senior sank into depression and stepped up the drinking. In 1873, Lee left for London
and Shaw's mother followed. 'We did not realise, nor did she, that she was never coming
back,' young Shaw wrote later.

He stayed in Dublin. Money was tight, so Trinity was out of the question. He worked
as an office junior, taught himself the piano, thought about girls, though he hadn't the nerve
to approach them, paced the National Gallery and went to Dublin's rickety and romantic
theatres. He saw the plays of Boucicault, and he watched the vintage barnstormer Barry
Sullivan – an actor he'd recall throughout his life with the rapt adoration Tynan felt for
Olivier. Two years later, he came to London.

There followed twenty years of relentless, unrewarded, self-improvement. He was
teetotal and a vegetarian – a great eccentricity then. He imposed fierce working guidelines
on himself but, to his misery, sometimes flunked them: slept through the alarm, nodded
off in the British Museum. He lost his virginity (he claimed) at the age of twenty-nine to
Jenny Patterson: first of a line of handsome, tempestuous women.

He also joined the Fabian Society: a small and select socialist grouping. One reason
was that he wanted to learn to speak in public: the speed and ease with which his words
cascaded on to paper for the rest of his life suggests that anyone aiming to be a professional
writer ought to drop the creative-writing course and start addressing public meetings.
Brain-to-mouth and brain-to-pen aren't all that different. 'If only I could write as fast as
I can think,' he'd say.

The least predictable thing he did was start to write plays. He was a socialist intellectual, and theatre was mostly mindless. There were pockets of enterprise here and there: Stage Society matinées, 'readings' from the European avant-garde, the plays of Ibsen. But the major attraction of the stage was actresses. Shaw was mad about actresses: even after his companionable marriage, he couldn't leave them alone. (The best-kept secret about the theatre is the number of people who've joined it largely for sexual reasons. 'I went on the stage to meet boys': Sir Ian McKellen.)

In 1883, the critic William Archer was studying in the Reading Room of the British Museum when he saw what he took to be a badly wrapped brown-paper parcel on the seat next to him. This was Shaw in his foxy-coloured Jaeger suit reading either *Das Kapital* or a full orchestral score of **Tristan and Isolde**: Shaw read both, obsessively, day after day.

The two men struck up a friendship. Dismayed by Shaw's horrible diet, which he ascribed to poverty, Archer wangled him a job as book reviewer. He then suggested that they collaborate on a play. The title would be **Rheingold**. Two acts were drafted, then the play was dropped.

Time passed. Shaw had a thousand other things to think about: political activism, journalism, sex. In 1889 he was 'suddenly magnetised, irradiated, transported, fired, rejuvenated, bewitched' by the twenty-five-year-old Janet Achurch, who had just scored a huge success as Ibsen's Nora. A passionate affair followed, broken only when she left on a two-year tour of Australia. 'My next effort in fiction – if I ever have time to make one,' he wrote in his diary, 'will be a play.'

Instead, he wrote a lecture about a playwright: 'The Quintessence of Ibsenism'. It remains an excellent crib to the plots of Ibsen's lesser-known plays. (Shaw didn't know them either: Archer helped him out.) Major attention is given to Ibsen the stern destroyer of false ideals. Ibsen the mystic doesn't fit into the Shavian scheme so he gets left out along with Ibsen the hater of socialists, Ibsen the crosspatch, Ibsen the satyr, etc. etc.

Then Shaw met Florence Farr, fell in love and returned to **Rheingold**. He'd twiddled with it over the years, but had never been able to solve the final act. He'd got this far: the upright hero, young Harry Trench, has discovered that his fiancée's wealth derives from the rental of slum properties. He rejects her money and the engagement is broken off. The problem was how to contrive a happy ending – boy gets girl – without making Harry abandon his principles. (Never mind Shaw's principles.)

Marx and Ibsen helped him out. From Marx, Shaw learned that it was no use sneering at the vulgar landlord: what about the unseen aristocrat who owns the freehold? What he learned from Ibsen was to cut the sentiment: to analyse a domestic scene with all the breadth and realism that you'd aim at when describing a war. From **A Doll's House**:

TORVALD: Nora, I'd gladly work night and day for you, and endure poverty and sorrow for your sake. But no man would sacrifice his honour for the one he loves.

NORA: Thousands of women have.

The iris widens: we see a class, a sex, a system. Nora's reply, which still electrifies an audience, took Ibsen three rewrites to achieve. It took Shaw eight years to finish **Rheingold** – now rechristened **Widower's Houses** – and he had to write a book about Ibsen first. But it was worth it.

Harry drops his principles soon enough when his own decidedly unearned income is put at risk. The heroine shows a vile and tyrannical nature. 'Let me go, Miss Blanche,' squeaks the maid when her mistress yanks her about by her hair. 'Remember how dreadfully my head was cut last time.' The slum-racketeer, now much the most intelligent man in the play, defends his corner sanely: 'If we made the houses any better, the rents would have to be raised so much that the poor people would be unable to pay, and would be thrown homeless on the streets.' Who could argue, given the way things are? Brecht said much the same in **The Good Person of Setzuan**: wouldn't it be nice to have a blanket large enough to shelter every homeless person in the city?

Florence Farr played Blanche: this piece of casting had its Pirandellian side, given that her character's screams and physical assaults were based on Jenny Patterson's reaction when she discovered what Farr and Shaw were getting up to. Shaw filled the newspapers with articles by himself, interviews with himself (some conducted by himself) and reviews of his own reviews. By the time the fuss was over, 'I had not achieved a success,' he wrote, 'but I had provoked an uproar; and the sensation was so agreeable that I resolved to try again.'

He would always have a down on **Widower's Houses**. 'My first and worst', he called it. Wilde was more acute: 'I admire the horrible flesh and blood of your creatures,' he wrote to Shaw, thus putting his finger on it. 'Flesh and blood', horrible or not, aren't qualities you associate with characters in plays by Shaw. But the biliousness of **Widower's Houses** is a life-giving force: it's like the bolt of lightning in *Frankenstein* that turns the monster into a moving, sentient being – even a poignant one.

Early Shaw is undersold, just as most of the later, self-important plays are overrated. **The Philanderer** and **Mrs Warren's Profession**, which closely followed, are terrific, especially acute on the clownish nature of close relationships. **Arms and the Man** is tiresome, but **You Never Can Tell** is an excellent stab at writing a play about nothing at all. The curious thing about the plays he wrote between **Widower's Houses** and the first Court season in 1904 – and there were many – is that none of them had a proper run in London. None of the obvious reasons hold up. He got some bad reviews, but plenty of good ones, and all were 'selling notices', or so you'd think if you read them now. He wasn't a shy young writer who could safely be ignored: he was a sparkling, middle-aged celebrity. His first nights were lively coterie occasions, his audiences were never bored and often laughed like anything. What went wrong?

Commercial managers resist new trends. That was one thing. Acting style was another. Shaw wrote plays for old-school players. 'Keep your worms for your own plays,' he told

Granville-Barker, 'and leave me the drunken, stagey, brassbowelled barnstormers my plays are written for.' You can see what he meant in a photograph that hung for many years on the stairs leading up to the Theatre Upstairs at the Royal Court. It shows Shaw in rehearsals of **Androcles and the Lion**. Barker had directed it; Shaw, seeing a run-through, was dismayed by what he considered to be feeble underplaying. Legs astride, sword held swaggeringly aloft, he's twice as large as life and then some.

Shaw in rehearsal: 'Twice as large as life and then some'.

But his plays also call for quick-thinking volatility: something the old-school boomers weren't very good at. 'What you have always wanted for a leading actor,' said Granville-Barker, 'is a Barry Sullivan with brains. But do the two things ever go together?'

Shaw hoped they might. For years he begged, bullied and cajoled the brassbowelled stars of the day to act in his plays. They always passed. He read aloud **The Devil's Disciple** to the matinée idol William Terriss, but the actor fell asleep. Irving turned down **The Man of Destiny**. He felt it 'wasn't for him' and he was probably right: he came from a different culture. **You Never Can Tell** was set up for the Haymarket, but never got past the first reading: two of the actors walked out, one saying witheringly, 'No laughs and no exits!' Shaw needed actors who understood his plays. He needed a theatre. And a director.

The first recorded connection between Shaw and Granville-Barker is the Stage Society performance of **Candida** in 1900, in which Barker played Marchbanks: an innocent, ardent suitor, supposedly based on Yeats. Shaw didn't approve the casting. 'I have often

seen Granville-Barker act and I cannot remember him in the least,' he wrote. He'd later say, 'I withdrew my observations concerning G.B., whom I certainly never saw before.' Spot the discrepancy. Were they father and son? Rumour said they were; they looked alike, each was a red-head and the dates add up. Shaw gave the younger man 'the tender interest and straight-from-the-shoulder-dealing of a son,' said a friend. Barker, as Jack Tanner in **Man and Superman**, made himself up as Shaw, complete with beard and swept-back hair: he looks so like the playwright that it seems a coded signal.

At the age of twenty-two, he had written a play of fantastic vision and precocity: **The Marrying of Ann Leete**. Till then, dialogue in English plays was clean and linear. Maurice Maeterlinck – a favourite of the turn-of-the-century *avant-garde* – had shown that something different could be tried: a feathery, hushed, fragmented tone. Barker took the hint, but used as his tools the debris of ordinary speech: interruptions, overlaps, repetitions, non sequiturs, pauses. His method is still alive and well.

It's a summer night. Over a game of whist, a bet was placed that Ann – a girl of twenty – could venture to the bottom of the garden without uttering a scream. Lord John kissed her and the bet was lost. The talk is circular and ambiguous; then a dreamy, sensuous note is heard:

*Mia Farrow in the RSC revival of **The Marrying of Ann Leete***.

LORD JOHN: Miss Leete trod on a toad.
TATTON: I barred toads ... here.

LORD JOHN:	I don't think it.
TATTON:	I barred toads. Did I forget to? Well … it's better to be a sportsman.
SARAH:	And whereabouts is she?
ANN:	(*from the corner she has shrunk to*) Here I am, Sally.
TATTON:	Miss Ann, I forgive you. I'm smiling, I assure you, I'm smiling.
SARAH:	We all laughed when we heard you.
TATTON:	Which reminds me, young George Leete, had you the ace?
GEORGE:	King … knave … here are the cards, but I can't see.
TATTON:	I had the king.
ANN:	(*quietly to her sister*) He kissed me.
SARAH:	A man would.
GEORGE:	What were trumps?
MR TATTON:	What were we playing … cricket?
ANN:	(*as quietly again*) D'you think I'm blushing?
SARAH:	It's probable.
ANN:	I am by the feel of me.

Aged twenty-six, Barker wrote to William Archer:

> Do you think there is anything in this idea? To take the Court Theatre for six months or a year and to run there a stock season of the uncommercial drama: Hauptmann – Sudermann – Ibsen – Maeterlinck – Schnitzler – Shaw – Brieux etc. Not necessarily plays untried in England. A fresh production every fortnight. Not necessarily a stock company. The highest price five or six shillings. To be worked mainly as a subscription theatre. One would require a guarantee of £5,000 – if possible fifty people putting down £100 each. I would stake everything on plays and acting – not attempt 'productions'.

One year later, a businessman by the name of Leigh, who'd rented the Court Theatre in Sloane Square as a showcase for his wife, found he needed a director. Archer suggested Barker, who accepted on condition that he could revive **Candida** (not starring Mrs Leigh) for six matinées. J.E. Vedrenne, the manager of the Court, took charge of the administration, and thus, through the familiar theatrical mix of chutzpah, sex and the old-boy-network, the Vedrenne-Barker seasons were born.

The Court was ideal. It was off the West End map (which made it cheap to rent) but perfectly placed between artistic Chelsea and grand Belgravia and easy to reach by tube. The number of seats, then in the mid-600s (thanks to dense packing and a gallery which in those days was enormous) was about right for experimental work. More to the point: the jobbing architect who'd slung the building together had quite by chance hit on the perfect frame for new plays. The classicism of the building gave authority to the new and unproved; its intimacy made it thrilling to be inside. The tall proscenium arch gave epic size to the smallest domestic scene; the narrow stage, when skilfully used, suggested space, but never at the expense of the human figure. The acoustics were good but not a pushover: actors' energy was required. There was one small problem: only a small triangle of stage was visible from all the seats. Edwardian audiences were tolerant of impeded views: no one complained and the fault was only corrected when the theatre was rebuilt at the end of the twentieth century.

The continuity between Barker's Court and the Royal Court Theatre of today is strangely unremarked. But to remark it overmuch might kill the spirit. How and when the 'Royal' attached itself to the theatre's name is no doubt documented somewhere, but it's a mystery to the present writers. It's never stuck: people working there still call it 'the Court', as though nothing had changed since Granville-Barker's day. But whether they do so for historical reasons or republican ones is hard to say.

The second production of the season – the Abbey reject, **John Bull's Other Island** – hit the button. The play is about Home Rule, so Beatrice Webb brought the Prime Minister, who liked it so much that he came back four more times. This sensational mark of favour led to a special performance for King Edward VII, who laughed so much that he broke his chair. Not for the last time, the Court had staged a radical work, only to see it become a smart success.

In the three Vedrenne-Barker seasons, just under a thousand performances were presented. The writers included Ibsen, Maeterlinck, Galsworthy, Masefield, Yeats and Hauptmann. Euripides had three productions at the Court: his quirky scepticism and feminist perspective were very much New Drama. But the star was Shaw: no fewer than 701 performances were of plays from his bursting portfolio of unperformed and under-exploited titles.

From his privileged niche, he treated Barker to a stream of advice and exhortations, just as annoying fathers have done since the dawn of time. He directed his plays himself, though he refused to be credited and his notion of directing was a primitive one. Rehearsals started with his reading the play aloud; this done, the cast would try to repeat his timings and inflections, though not his accent. For a man so wrapped in ego, he was surprisingly good at gauging what to say to actor A, as opposed to actor B who required some other approach. Gwen Ffrangcon-Davies, who played Eve in **Back to Methuselah** at the Birmingham Rep years later, recalled him popping into the dressing-room after the dress-rehearsal. 'Not bad,' he said to Edith Evans. She glared at him in fury. Shaw continued 'Not bad at all. But you realise, don't you, that Frances Doble is acting you off the stage?' She could barely restrain herself until he'd gone. Then she exploded. 'Frances Doble? Frances Doble? *I'll show him!*' 'And that,' said Ffrangcon-Davies, 'was *just* what Edith needed.'

Barker's **The Voysey Inheritance** played in the second season: it's his most accessible play. Edward Voysey's inheritance is the fact that his father's law firm has been systematically

Jeremy Northam and David Burke in the RNT revival of **The Voysey Inheritance**.

swindling its clients. They get their interest on the dot, but God forbid they ask for their capital back: it's long been spent. Edward's father lets him into the secret, just as his own father had done before him. Then, unexpectedly, he dies. Edward must now decide whether or not to keep up the fraud.

You can spot the Hamlet echo, in the paternal challenge from the grave. And the psychological self-portrait: Edward follows the footsteps of a thrilling but irresponsible father. But in plays by Shaw, there are no mysteries. Barker can hardly write a line without suggesting nameless secrets. The lights burn bright in the Voyseys' Chislehurst mansion: this is English suburbia at its most secure. But it's all a little over-normal, like the fake American town in **The Truman Show**.

'There is a certain strangeness in the air, a lack of nitrogen, a disconcerting quality of dream,' said one perceptive review:

If that hat of Mr Voysey's suddenly began quietly turning somersaults on its little red-curtained shelf, we would not feel tremendously surprised. For in the accentuated realism of these rooms, there is something oddly like the bright veracity of the streets of shops in harlequinade; and although the characters all apparently behave with the most absolute naturalness, we watch them as though they were figures moving in a void ... these rooms are haunted. There is a skeleton in that sideboard. The characters are under a spell ... The true Voysey inheritance is something far more fateful than the black bequest that burdens Edward.

2

The years at the Court set a standard of vision and excellence which remains mandatory in serious theatre. They also set in motion two great streams of energy. One was the work of woman playwrights; the other was the regional repertory movement.

The 'women's issue' was as inseparable from the New Drama as 'Irishness' was from Yeats's and Lady Gregory's crusade in Dublin. Any new form of realism must reassess the role of women: there's no other place to begin. Besides, too many women were backing plays and starring in them for their concerns to be neglected.

The decisive moment was the 'bang' when Ibsen's Nora slammed the door on domesticity. Shaw took the note. He could hardly have ignored it: all the women in his political life, let alone his sexual life, had been extraordinary. His women on stage, from the point that Vivie appears in **Mrs Warren's Profession**, are clever and confident. Oscar Wilde, in his own peculiar way, contributed by turning the outcast fallen woman of 1890s melodrama into the triumphant queen bee, precursor of an unstoppable line of camp icons.

Plays by women, as opposed to plays about them, got a new sharp profile with one of the Court's most unexpected hits: Elizabeth Robins's **Votes for Woman** in 1907. Robins was an American actress who came to England after her actor-husband committed suicide in Boston by walking into the Charles River wearing a full suit of stage armour. She was the first person to play Hedda Gabler in London and by all accounts she was sensational. Shaw made a pass at her but fled when she pulled a gun on him.

Her play takes the conventional fallen-woman drama and turns it on its head. Women discuss the things that matter, women decide and women agitate. The play subverts its form but never escapes it. No one could call it a very good play unless they saw it when the issue really mattered to them. Then they'd think it not just good but wonderful. A polemical piece like this can sometimes make mincemeat of the accepted truths about theatre being a higher form than propaganda.

Votes for Women drew crowds of highly motivated sympathisers, and did the Court the enormous service of identifying it with a political cause, in much the same way that the Royal Court would be linked with CND in the 1950s. It also inspired a host of followers.

Cicely Hamilton's **Diana of Dobson's**, written in 1908, exposes marriage as a commercial takeover; Elizabeth Baker's **Chains** contrasts dependence in the home with exploitation in the workplace. If you can choose between the two (her play suggests) you should take

*Bob Peck and Tom Mannion in the RNT revival of **Rutherford and Son**.*

the job: at least you can give it up later, a theme taken up by James Barrie, the author of **Peter Pan**, in his miniature (and only) masterpiece **The Twelve-Pound Look**.

The best feminist play of the New Drama followed in 1912. Githa Sowerby (1876–1970) was an author of children's books until she searched her own middle-class, manufacturing-family history for a stunning synthesis of feminism and Marxist analysis: **Rutherford and Son**.

It's set in the North, where inherited old-money – the keynote of **Widower's Houses** – is so remote as to be irrelevant. Wealth in this part of the country is seldom more than two generations old: the second generation, newly respectable, puts it into gilts while the third fritters it away. 'Clogs to clogs in three generations.' Rutherford senior has heaved himself out of the clog-wearing classes by dour application of capitalist ethics. His firm is a devouring Moloch: first cousin to the biome-chanical Gorgon of Fritz Lang's *Metropolis*. The Red revolutionary Emma Goldman was delighted by this side of the play: 'The Rutherfords are bound by time, by the external forces of change. Their influence on human life is indeed terrible. Notwithstanding it all, however, they are fighting a losing game.'

When old Rutherford discovers his daughter's affair, he orders her out of the house. In a scene of blazing rage, she answers him back:

> Who are you? Who are you? A man – a man that's taken power to himself, power to gather to him and use them as he wills – a man that'd take the blood of life itself and put it into the works – into Rutherford's. And what ha' you got by it – what? You've got Dick, that you've bullied till he's a fool – John, that's waiting for the time when he can sell what you've done – and you got me – me to take your boots off at night – to well-nigh wish you dead when I had to touch you … Now! Now you know!

Sowerby became a celebrity, though not for long. 'The most virile work we have seen for some years,' said the *English Review*: high praise indeed. The *Westminster Gazette* struck a personal note, describing the thirty-five-year-old author as 'young, modest and charming'. The waters closed over her and the play was forgotten until a number of fringe productions in the 1980s and a first-rate revival at the National Theatre in 1994.

It comes as a jolt to realise that 'rep' – that cheerful bottom drawer of theatrical history, immortalised in phrases such as 'weekly rep', 'seaside rep' and 'reppy' (i.e. dreadful), stems from Barker's lofty vision of 'repertory': a rolling, ever-changing cycle of plays performed by a crack ensemble. But this is the case, and the early years of the repertory movement had no connection at all with Agatha Christie, tea-matinées or long speeches taped to the furniture.

This is the point where Annie Horniman rejoins the story. She had, as she saw it, been exploited, patronised and snubbed in Ireland and the example of the Court was all she needed. Its success ruled London out, but Manchester was perfect: a rich and powerful city with a robust tradition of theatre-going and a newspaper whose reviews carried as much weight as any in London. "There is no place which can match its union of intellectual vigour, artistic perceptiveness and political sagacity,' wrote Arnold Bennett in 1907.

Once again, Miss Horniman bought a theatre: the Manchester Gaiety. She opened in 1908 with two Court hits – **Candida** and St John Hankin's **The Return of the Prodigal** – along with **Measure for Measure** directed by William Poel. The public came, the season took off and she herself became a popular local landmark.

'We must not imitate the Celtic temper nor Mr Shaw's paradoxes,' said a Manchester critic, 'but tragedy and comedy may be found in Lancashire life as well as in the West of Ireland or London.' Miss Horniman agreed: she issued a call for scripts by local writers and promised to read them all herself. The result was the Manchester School: a group of playwrights who wrote for the North about the North, who wrote from time to time in dialect and who all created strong and independent women.

'I started to write expressly and absolutely for you,' wrote Stanley Houghton to Miss Horniman: a welcome contrast to the brushoffs she'd been getting across the water. 'Had the Gaiety not been there, I wouldn't have written a line. I can assure you that I shall never forget it, and if ever I can do you and the Gaiety a good turn you have only to command me.'

Houghton (1881–1913) was twenty-seven when his one-act-play **The Dear Departed** was chosen as a curtain-raiser to **Widower's Houses**. After this, he wrote like a fiend: in 1911 he finished five new plays, reviewed both plays and novels and kept his full-time job at the Cotton Exchange. He was gay and generally thought of as a witty sophisticate in the Wilde tradition; his enduring hit was **Hindle Wakes**.

Fanny, a shop-floor girl, has spent the weekend in Llandudno with Alan, the son and heir of the richest man in Hindle. When the scandal breaks, outraged morality requires the guilty pair to marry. But Fanny refuses: a loveless marriage doesn't attract her:

Look at old Mrs Eastwood – hers was a case like ours. Old Joe Eastwood's father made them wed. And she's been separated from him these thirty years, living all alone in that big house at Valley Edge. Got any amount of brass she has, but she's so lonesome-like she does her own housework for the sake of something to occupy her time. The tradesfolk catch her washing the front steps. You don't find me making a mess of my life like that.

Alan is stunned: didn't she ever love him, he asks? Her answer is what made the play sensational:

Love you? Good heavens, of course not! Why on earth should I love you? You were just someone to have a bit of fun with. You were an amusement – a lark.

Alan's appalled: 'I never thought of a girl looking on a chap just like that!' Nor had several million other Alans. **Hindle Wakes**, in every historical sense an heir to Shaw and Granville-Barker, reads like vintage Rattigan. Women's sexuality is on the one hand an unknowable mystery; on the other, it's as down-to-earth and up-for-grabs as that of any gay man.

Houghton's other plays are well-dug territory for literary managers looking for lost gold. None has half the impact, so writing five plays in a year may not be such a good idea after all. Perhaps when the pace had slowed, something marvellous would have happened. We'll never know: he fell ill on holiday in Venice, was rushed to hospital, was operated on without anaesthetic and died shortly afterwards at the age of thirty-two.

Harold Brighouse (1882–1958) was a cotton-salesman. **The Price of Coal** is tough and powerful. But his enduring hit was **Hobson's Choice**, a play which for many years held a firm place in the Lancashire psyche along with Mendelssohn's **Elijah** and Gracie Fields.

Hobson's Choice is set in the shoe-trade. Hobson, pickled in drink, is stuck in a bygone era; his daughter Maggie escapes his tyrannical sway to marry his best workman, timid Willie Mossop, and together she and Willie start a business. Hobson's business is eclipsed. The 1964 National Theatre revival of this marvellous play was a reclamation from cliché: it was as though 'The Laughing Cavalier' turned out to be a lost Rembrandt.

When war broke out, Miss Horniman found herself in trouble. More than a quarter of her audience was Jewish, and from 1914 onwards people with Hunnish-sounding names were better advised to stay indoors. In 1917, the company closed. The amiability and left-ish views of the Manchester School lived on, in dilute form, in the plays of J.B. Priestley, Keith Waterhouse and Willis Hall and (bringing us almost up to the present time) Bill Naughton, the author of **All in Good Time** and **Alfie**.

Other reps survived. Bristol, Liverpool and Glasgow remained alive and well, while Birmingham took on the mantle of national status under Barry Jackson. It's no coincidence that both he and Miss Horniman were born rich: money, or the lack of it, was what would scupper the vision of a National Theatre.

Barker's seasons at the Court were a small-scale tryout. In 1907, he upped the stakes with a move to the much larger Savoy Theatre in the West End. But the expansion didn't work. The cutting-edge had gone, and the audience noticed. 'I learn with disgust and horror,' wrote Shaw, 'that you played the National Anthem and made the audience stand up on Monday … Have you any notion of the extent to which your sworn supporters are republicans or aristocratic souls with a loathing for public demonstrations?' The theatre's capacity was too large; money grew tight; the management split; worst of all, Barker's new play, **Waste**, intended as the season's centrepiece, was banned by the Lord Chamberlain.

So the dream remained elusive. In 1915, Barker fell in love, in the Italian manner, as Shaw said churlishly, with an American heiress, married and left the working theatre. This was seen in the theatre as a great betrayal. Much fun was made of his majestic lifestyle and the hyphen that he added to his name. Shaw thought he had buried himself alive: communications stopped completely until decades later, when they wrote to each other on the occasion of the death of Shaw's wife. 'I did not know I could be so moved by anything,' wrote Shaw.

He blamed Barker's exile on the heiress-wife – who disliked theatre and detested Shaw – but the truth was that Barker had decided to withdraw from the theatre years before. 'On the personal count I made up my mind … to give up acting when I was thirty and producing when I was forty.' He was weary with management, with artistic compromise and with the lack of a context in which to work seriously.

His blueprint for the National Theatre had a fatal flaw. Theatre of quality – as he often pointed out – must have a subsidy. But in Edwardian England, not one penny could be expected from the government. He pinned his hopes on private sponsors, but few came forward. He went on fund-raising trips to America, only to come back empty-handed. Not till the end of the Second World War, when the argument for public subsidy had been fought and won, could a National Theatre exist.

As the vision faded, the New Drama itself dispersed. It may be that, if it had lasted a few years longer, its finest playwright, D.H. Lawrence (1885–1930), would have had the recognition he deserved. But probably not.

The first thing to realise about Lawrence's best and earliest plays is that they aren't novelist's offcuts: they're skilled, instinctive. He wrote them early in life convinced, not that he was joining a movement, but that he was starting one. 'We have to hate our immediate predecessors to get free from their authority.' Most of all, he distanced himself from the Court elite:

> I believe that, just as an audience was found in Russia for Chekhov, so an audience might be found in England for some of my stuff, if there were a man to whip 'em in.

Judy Parfitt and Michael Coles in the Royal Court revival of **The Widowing of Mrs Holroyd**.

It's the producer that is lacking, not the audience. I am sure we are sick of the rather bony, bloodless drama we get nowadays – it is time for a reaction against Shaw and Galsworthy and Barker and Irishy (except Synge) people – the rule and measure mathematical folk.

A Collier's Friday Night is a sensuous exploration of the themes that would evolve into *Sons and Lovers*. **The Widowing of Mrs Holroyd** is a short, packed tragedy of working life: it owes a lot to **Riders to the Sea** but has an added sexual ambiguity. 'I wish I could write such dialogue,' said Shaw when he read it. 'With mine I always hear the sound of the typewriter.'

The Daughter-in-law is a blinding masterpiece. Minnie, the daughter-in-law, has ideas above her station: a relic of her years 'in service'. But Lawrence never sneers at her pretensions in the way that a middle-class writer would: they're lovingly drawn. When it's revealed that her husband has made a local girl pregnant, neither Minnie nor anyone else pretends to be shocked: they're too grown-up.

What follows is a meditation on themes of sex, dependence and freedom. Minnie is affronted by what the episode reveals about her husband's moral laziness: only his mother (he feels) deserves the best of him, and that's the trouble. Joe, his brother, is the family joker: now he reveals a sense of tragic incompleteness. Brought up under his mother's wing, adored and dominated, he's doomed to eternal adolescence. The mother – a daughter, wife and mother of miners – is challenging, wily, articulate.

The natural heir to D.H. Lawrence is David Storey (1933–) whose plays – performed, like his, at the Royal Court – have everything in common with Lawrence's: 'Their poetry, their realism uncluttered by naturalism, their elegance "without extravagance", their seriousness and their laughter, their vision of society uncluttered by propaganda.' So spoke their director, Lindsay Anderson.

David Storey was born in Wakefield, like Lawrence, the son of a miner, and like Lawrence, he studied at art school and became a painter as well as a prolific novelist. Both writers have a concern in their plays that is rare in playwrights: the love of the physical, the way that men and women use their bodies to work, or wash, or eat, or touch or avoid each other.

The Contractor and **The Changing Room** are 'work' plays: in the former, a group of workers erect and dismantle a marquee during the course of the play; in the latter we see a Rugby League (the working-class version of the sport) team before, during and after a match in 'the changing room where people "changed"', and in turn a place that was 'changed by the people in it', as Storey said. Both plays are ideal illustrations of the metaphorical power of theatre: a room, or a tent, becomes a world, containing an entire society, layered and nuanced with the gracenotes of the English class system.

*David Storey's **The Changing Room**.*

Both plays deal with a tribal life of loyalties, bonds, affections, and community, before that was a politicians' buzz-word. Lindsay Anderson's brilliant productions garlanded the rugby players with his adoration for male beauty and the 'working man', for the North, for the honest combat of sport, and for the nobility of manual labour – an attitude that now seems as distant as the pre-Raphaelite movement. A consistent theme of Storey's is the nostalgia of the son for an occupation that employs the body rather than the mind, that has something palpable to show for a day's work, and the guilt (and relief) induced by turning his back on it. In **In Celebration** the son who has left a working-class home to 'better' himself shows the wounds of alienation from his family, and in a seismic reunion the family display confused pride, love, envy and anger, engendered by his detachment. As with Lawrence's plays, powerful emotions are always mined in a social context: love is the seam, class is the fault line. There was a sequel to **In Celebration** in 1992: **The March on Russia**. It wasn't nostalgic; it was all about loss – of youth, of way of life, of community, of hope.

Possibly his best-known play – it starred Ralph Richardson and John Gielgud – is **Home**. It came about in a painterly fashion, 'starting with a blank page and seeing what would happen'. The play was a Beckett-like meditation on old age and sanity: 'Half-way through the play I discovered it was taking place in a lunatic asylum' – as did the audience. Like all David Storey's work it had a sort of solidity and beauty, like a Henry Moore sculpture.

Lawrence wrote for a National Theatre that was more national, more regional and less middle class than even Barker or Shaw had imagined. The grandness of the characters' emotions and the nuance of what happens between them is expressed in dialect. It's supple, strong and beautiful: Brighouse or Houghton look phoney beside it. But it means that the plays fall foul of the first law of English aesthetics, which is that working-class life is a low form, art is a high one and the two don't mix. So Lawrence had to wait until 1968 – 38 years after his death – for his reputation as a playwright to be made, when a season of his plays was presented at the Royal Court, flawlessly directed by Peter Gill.

Shaw the playwright entered many decades of decline. There's much arid fantasy, along with a testy impatience with human nature. Two plays are worth a mention. **Pygmalion** is a late farewell to his best and earliest phase: a work of charm and vitality, as well as a penetrating insight into dysfunctional adulthood.

Saint Joan was received with awe and delight: at last the jester had laid his motley aside to tell a story of simple faith. It's his most exasperating play. Who, or what, is Joan exactly? What's her inspiration? If not God, why not? If not, then what? Shaw had succeeded in writing a play so muddled ('even-handed') that practically anyone could find their own beliefs reflected in it. For this, the world forgave him all his sins.

From now on, he was a celebrity; every schoolchild recognised him, his *bons mots* were quoted across the globe, when he toured the Dominions crowds turned out as though for a Papal visit. He lived so long that you don't even have to be particularly old to have read about it when he died: to remember – as though some peculiar time-slip had occurred – the death of a man who, over lunch at the Café Royal, had begged his compatriot Oscar Wilde to drop his lawsuit.

Sybil Thorndike in
St Joan.

Wilde and After

'I took the drama, the most objective form known to art, and made it as personal a mode of expression as the lyric or the sonnet.'
OSCAR WILDE: De Profundis

1

Wilde's influence was as radical as Yeats's or Shaw's and in a way more deeply rooted. It dominated the inter-war years, it's still pervasive and it's hard to imagine a theatre of the future being unaffected by it. It came about in a dramatic way, one which Wilde himself could not have predicted, still less hoped for.

Both Shaw and Yeats built for the future. Each underpinned his writing with a real-life institutional basis, Yeats by founding a theatre, Shaw by helping his younger self to set one up. Each put down a marker on the next generation: they spotted talented younger writers, they encouraged them and to a greater or lesser degree they moulded them. Each defined himself in the public eye by a series of political battles and generally ended up, if not always victorious, then at least looking creditably bashed and bloody. Yeats ended his life a statesman, Shaw a national treasure.

Wilde was perfectly happy with the theatre as he found it. Subversion, in his plays, is hidden, while the surface is all delight: that's his style, he hits it off without any sense of compromise and the result is that – except in the immediate aftermath of his arrest and trial – his plays have always done good business. The progressive audience that Granville-Barker would be so keen to foster didn't have any attraction for Wilde, given the much greater size of the audience that flocked to see his plays at the St James's or the Haymarket; he certainly didn't need a made-to-order theatre of his own. As for the younger generation: the writers he chose to encourage were pretty but untalented, so no Wildean school of any value was to be expected. Public issues tended to evade him: he was a socialist and an Irish Republican and made no secret of this, but his tone was so flirtatious and benign that nobody could object. He hated rows.

What stamps him so indelibly on our consciousness is the same thing that so appalled the public at the time of his trial. It's the contrast between his style – that exquisite, allusive construct – and the reality of sex. Behind the dark and tantalising hints there lurked, not darker and more tantalising hints, but the chambermaid of a West End hotel complaining about the Vaseline stains on the sheets.

Wilde is unique in being a Victorian writer of genius whose sex-life is known in clinical detail. It's worth remembering that this might never have happened. We're quick to suppose that homosexuality, in the London of the 1890s, was a kamikaze activity, doomed to be stamped out the moment it reared its head. Of course this wasn't the case, any more than it was in almost every other period of repression. There were occasional embarrassments in St James's Park, though not enough to stop young guardsmen from viewing its conversational opportunities and abundant ground cover as a means of supplementing their army pay. No two males, of course, could have a mature relationship. But casual sex between a middle- or upper-class man and somebody lower on the social scale was easy and safe to arrange. This attitude lingered: as late as the 1940s, Auden – in New York – was dwelling wistfully on the feudal traditions of Europe. 'I feel if I ask a member of the lower classes there to go to bed, it's his duty to do so.'

To be charged with homosexual offences committed in private was in fact quite difficult to achieve. It's remarkable that Wilde succeeded, since he wasn't on the whole very good at organising his life. His trials and imprisonment are now too much of a showbiz myth to be worth repeating, but it's perhaps worth saying that the entire disaster was due to the Oedipal madhouse jointly built by Lord Alfred Douglas ('Bosie') and his father. Bosie wanted to see his father thrown into jail. A successful prosecution for criminal libel would do the trick, assuming that it succeeded. If it failed, Wilde would go to jail instead. Either way, Bosie would get what he wanted: a father-figure humiliated and destroyed.

Wilde was entirely lacking in malice, so he never quite grasped the complexity of Bosie's scheme. Their sexual relationship seems not to have gone on for very long or been very important. But the world of male prostitution which Bosie introduced him to was very important indeed, thanks to Wilde's gift for fantasy. Perfectly ordinary rentboys were transformed in his imagination into fevered monsters. 'Feasting with panthers' was his irresistibly comic phrase for what in reality amounted to little more than a few wanks in Soho. Most of the boys, no doubt, were simply earning the odd five bob on the back of their natural sexual inclinations; none of them sounds remotely feral. One of them made a feeble attempt to blackmail Wilde, but he didn't ask much. Most were admirably discreet. Criminal evidence would emerge, when it was called for, not from Wilde's prostitutes, but from his actors.

We only know about his Soho nights because he made the bizarre mistake of suing Bosie's father. If he hadn't – if he'd followed the advice of Shaw, Yeats and all his other sensible friends – Oscar Wilde would to this day be one of those Victorian celebrities, like Rhodes, Kitchener, Henry James or Florence Nightingale, about whom much may be suspected but nothing has ever been proved. Gay historians would point to his fulsome prose and the warmth of his relationships with younger men. Conservative ones would point to a loving and beautiful wife, two strapping sons and a total and utter lack of evidence. The jury would be out and it would stay out. Instead, it's Oscar Wilde who's out. Thanks to a single, ghastly blunder, he's the twentieth-century's arch-definer of the homosexual style.

He was born in Dublin on 16 October 1864. 'Oscar' and 'Fingal' were nods to Irish legend. 'O'Flahertie' was a homage to the O'Flaithbherartaigh line: pre-Norman kings in Galway. Oscar's mother was an Irish Nationalist who wrote prolifically under the name 'Speranza'. His father, Sir William Wilde, was a leading oculist. The Wildes were renowned for their eighteenth-century style, i.e. their aristocratic raffishness. A popular Dublin story had Speranza crossly asking a servant, 'Why are you putting the plates on the coal-scuttle? What do you think the chairs are meant for?' Sir William once removed a patient's eyes and put them on a plate, intending to replace them as soon as his work was done. But the family cat caught sight of the eyes and ate them. Yeats told this story to a cat-lover, who said thoughtfully, 'Cats love eyes.'

The paradox is that, though Bosie was one of the nastiest little time-wasters ever known, Wilde wrote more and better in the four years between meeting him and going on trial than at any other time in his life. Perhaps Bosie was an inspiration, though it seems unlikely; perhaps Wilde was forced to pull the stops out to support the younger man's extravagant tastes. We'll never know.

Lady Windermere's Fan is a high-society drama about the shape-shifting nature of good and evil as conventionally defined. **A Woman of No Importance** is generally thought less sympathetic; several of the old plot devices are trotted around the course once more, looking at little bit tired and dejected this time round. The talk is brilliant: more to the point is the disjunction between what's said and what is meant. Serene artifice masks turbulent restraint or the highest of high camp, depending on how you look at it. **An Ideal Husband** is a warmer play, partly because the homosexual subtext leaps so startlingly to the fore. 'I remember so well,' says Lord Chiltern of a former friend, 'how, with a strange smile on his pale curved lips, he led me through his wonderful picture gallery, showed me his tapestries, his enamels, his jewels …' Much else besides: it's no wonder the noble lord is looking shifty. The blackmailing Mrs Cheveley doesn't mince her words. 'Yours is a very nasty scandal. You couldn't survive it.' Years ago, Lord Chiltern peddled government secrets – is that what she's referring to? Some complicated tale about the Suez Canal? Well, maybe. When **An Ideal Husband** opened, the critics weren't impressed. By now, wit and sparkle were only to be expected in a play by Wilde: he'd made it look too easy. Shaw sprang to his defence: 'As far as I can ascertain, I am the only person in London who cannot sit down and write an Oscar Wilde play at will.'

The Importance of Being Earnest is in a different class; one of the greatest English comedies of all time, arguably the greatest, and a profound enigma. The plot is neatly filched from two other plays: the lovers' quadrille and the fearsome aunt can be found in a minor farce by Boucicault, **A Lover by Proxy**; the abandoned baby, identified in adult life by the container he was found in, comes from Euripides' **Ion**.

The Importance is an Arcadian play: love conquers all, grace and beauty belong to the young. Like all Arcadias, this one contains a death's-head: age. But even this, it seems, can be indefinitely postponed: London is full of women who have remained thirty-five for years and it will be a hundred and fifty years or so before Gwendolen turns into her mother. That other great reminder of the body – sex – doesn't exist at all. You will search in vain for the slightest hint of an erotic charge between Jack and Gwendolen or Algy and Cecily, and if you imagine that this is the cue to go looking for signs of hanky-panky between Algy and Jack, you can forget it.

Lady Bracknell, an ageless oracle, is the voice either of total anarchy or deep-dyed conservatism. Does she know how funny she is? There's the sliver of a possibility that she does: that her entire existence is a parodic impersonation of herself, that she's daring the pathetic creatures who surround her to shout, 'Oh, come off it!' If this is the case, she never lets on. There's a curious artistic slither in Act Three, when she actually cracks a joke. She's had twenty-four hours to think about it so it's rather a good one: 'Until yesterday I had no idea that there were any families or persons whose origin was a Terminus.' But the audience seldom laughs: for her to *share* a joke is out of character.

*Edith Evans as Lady Bracknell in **The Importance of Being Earnest**.*

No play has had a greater influence. There's its musicality: something which underlines every considerable prose stylist of the century from Coward to Mamet to Caryl Churchill. Pace, inflection, tempo are embedded in the scoring: there's only one way to say any line. Auden called it 'the only pure verbal opera in English'. Wilde is building here on the work of earlier playwrights: Congreve, Farquhar, Boucicault. What's new and radical is his use of code.

The more you see or read this play, the more you realise that it cannot begin and end in its own perfection. Beneath the impeccable surface, there are secrets. The clues are plenty. A double life? Wilde's is mirrored in Jack's and Algy's. The absence of eroticism is all very well, but what about the food? Few plays boast such orgies of what psychoanalysts call 'anal activity': muffins are shoved down throats, cucumber sandwiches are devoured even before the guests arrive, sugar and cake are forced on the unwilling rival. Is this a code for sex? Or surrogate for it? Some of the clues are in-jokes for the cognoscenti. (Wilde bought fifty seats to the first night and goodness knows who sat in them.) 'Earnest' was Victorian slang for gay; 'Cecily' was a popular trade-name for rentboys, silver cigarette-cases Wilde's tactful means of paying them off. Bosie's mother lived at Bracknell; Lady Bloxham, 'a lady considerably advanced in years', recalls Jack Bloxham, the undergraduate editor of a homosexual magazine; his friend George Ives, homosexual activist, lived at the Albany (E4) as does Jack Worthing (B4). Algy's suggestion that he and Jack might 'trot round to the Empire at ten' would lead them directly to a notorious hookers' hangout; 'Bunbury' is loaded with louche associations and so, come to think of it, is the cloakroom at Victoria Station. Some passages are pure autobiography. Here are Jack and Algy:

JACK:	Well, I can't dine at the Savoy. I owe them about £700. They are always getting judgements and things against me. They bother my life out.
ALGERNON:	Why on earth don't you pay them? You have got heaps of money.
JACK:	Yes, but Ernest hasn't, and I must keep up Ernest's reputation. Ernest is one of those chaps who never pays a bill. He gets writted about once a week.
ALGERNON:	Well, let us dine at Willis's.

Years later, in **De Profundis**, Wilde described what it was like to try to write a play while sharing one's life with a flibbertigibbet: farce is repeated in the form of tragedy:

At twelve o'clock, you drove up and stayed smoking cigarettes and chattering until one-thirty when I had to take you out to luncheon at the Café Royal or the Berkeley. Luncheon with its liqueurs lasted usually till three-thirty. For an hour you retired to White's. At tea-time you appeared again and stayed till it was time for me to dress for dinner. You dined with me either at the Savoy or at Tite Street ...

He dwells on Bosie's gift for guzzling food and drink at Wilde's expense:

The Savoy dinners ... the suppers at Willis's, the special *cuvée* of Perrier-Jouet reserved always for us, the wonderful pâtés procured directly from Strasbourg, the marvellous fine champagne ...

Jack, in **The Importance**, had made precisely the same complaint:

JACK: I suspect him of being untruthful … Under an assumed name he drank, I've just been informed by my butler, an entire pint bottle of my Perrier-Jouet, Brut '89; a wine I was specially reserving for myself.

It's frustrating at first to find that none of the clues add up. These two young men aren't really lovers. Bosie certainly tortured Oscar, but Algy isn't torturing Jack: this is a comedy, for God's sake. Neither has ever met a rentboy, nor have they read a homosexual magazine. Directors trying to squeeze suggestions of this nature into the play will swiftly find their arms nipped off by the whirring wheels of farce mechanics.

That's the point. The clues don't tell you anything about the characters or the story: they're not meant to. They're there to convey, in coded form, the sensibility of the playwright. If you want to know quite what that sensibility is, the answer is, 'You've not been watching. Look at the play. Try harder.' There's no simpler way of putting it. Impressionistically, allusively, with jokes for the in-the-know, mysterious hints for the ordinary punter, the message is: 'I wrote this and this is what I'm like. Work it out.'

It's hard to convey how radical this invention was, or how completely, utterly new. It's now accepted, like the weather. 'I enjoyed your play,' write literary managers to the authors of submitted scripts. 'Could we meet?' As though the personality, once known and disentangled, will illuminate the work of art. Or the other way round. As it does. This was Wilde's invention and he knew it. 'I took the drama,' he wrote in **De Profundis**, 'the most objective form known to art, and made it as personal a mode of expression as the lyric or the sonnet …'

During his brief, productive life as a first-rate playwright, Wilde was considered merely a wit. After his trial, he was an unspeakable. But when the New Drama of Shaw and Barker collapsed, the Wildean style rose triumphant. For centuries, Anglo-Irish writers had sustained the English theatre. Now that Ireland had an idiom of its own, colonial *arrivistes* were replaced by sexual ones. Gay men took over, writing – just like an Anglo-Irishman of the eighteenth century – from the position of semi-outsider.

All the Wildean icons took root. Oscar's green carnation became the Green Hat of the racy 1920s. Every playwright of any consequence staked his claim for decadent sophistication. All of them wrote about the English upper classes, and did so with a truly Wildean ambivalence. All chain-smoked, most sported long cigarette-holders and many wore dressing-gowns of some-or-another sumptuous fabric. Somerset Maugham sharpened his ungenerous wit; Noël Coward pretended to lounge about in bed all day; Terence Rattigan disguised himself as Brylcreem man; Ivor Novello turned his profile to the camera; Rodney Ackland stuffed the bills under the sofa and Binkie Beaumont reigned supreme.

2

Allusions, hints and coded sensibilities would now proliferate – and this wasn't just Wilde's example. Theatre had started to deal with real-life issues. The Lord Chamberlain's Office, which had dozed undisturbed throughout the nineteenth century, now sprang to life.

People old enough to have steered a play through the licensing process speak mostly of the sheer dotty incongruity of it. Even at the height of the so-called swinging '60s, a work of art was obliged by law to be sent to a palace to be read by an official of the Queen's Household. You had to pinch yourself to believe it.

Back the script would come with a list of cuts and provisos, beautifully typed on crested paper, the very touch of which breathed privilege. When negotiations stalled, the censor could occasionally be met *in situ*: a sombre, poky room in St James's Palace. The censor himself was enchantingly polite – a bit like a fashionable doctor of the old school, though his profession was that of soldier – and always willing to help.

A sticking-point in Edward Albee's **Who's Afraid of Virginia Woolf?** was George's reference to Martha as her father, the college president's, 'right ball'. Albee refused to yield. 'What about "right testicle"?' suggested the Chamberlain's man. Albee didn't like the rhythm. 'Right nut?' proposed the censor, ever helpful. At the last minute, Albee remembered the phrase 'a right bawl', meaning a good old cry in Southern argot. This was passed, though whether the censor was being naive or devious isn't known. He was an enigmatic figure. Much enjoyed were the giveaways when he found obscene intent in harmless lines: a mention of Peter O'*Toole*, for example, in Charles Wood's **Fill the Stage with Happy Hours**.

The Lord Chamberlain's involvement in the theatre dates back to the sixteenth century. His job was (and is) to run the royal household, arrange royal weddings and funerals, administer palaces and look after royal parties, pictures and, believe it or not, swans, so it was only natural in the reign of Henry VIII for his deputy – the Master of the Revels – to be put in charge of in-house entertainments: jesters, jugglers, things like that. Theatres followed as a matter of course.

In the reign of the Stuarts, Sir Henry Herbert was a more assiduous censor than Charles I himself. 'The King was pleased to call me into his withdrawing chamber to the window,' he confided in his daybook in 1634, 'where he went over all that I had crossed in Davenant's playbook, and allowing of "faith" and "slight" to be asseverations only and no oaths, allowed them to stand.' Forced to wave them through, Sir Henry placed his disagreement on record: 'But I conceive them to be oaths.'

In 1737 the Theatres Act, designed in order to curb attacks on the corrupt government of Sir Robert Walpole, devolved censorship directly on to the Lord Chamberlain. A loophole permitted 'private' performances of unlicensed plays. Or did it? The law was vague. In the 1880s, the Shelley Society was formed with the express intent of staging Shelley's play **The Cenci**, long banned because it featured incest. A private matinée was announced for 'visitors' to attend. The Shelleyites prepared themselves for prosecution: none took place.

A private performance of Ibsen's **Ghosts** was staged by the Independent Society in 1891: again the Chamberlain's Office held its fire. 'Club' performances soon became the rule for riskier work: Brieux's **Damaged Goods**; Tolstoy's **The Power of Darkness**; Maeterlinck's **Monna Vanna**. Nobody stopped these 'private' shows and it's easy to work out why. By letting a play be seen and reviewed, they eased the pressure for reform. But since the audience was limited to a small nucleus of dedicated theatre-lovers, there wasn't any danger of obscene and inflammatory notions leaking out to the nation at large, still less to the working classes. It's exactly the same principle as the objection to the paperback (i.e. cheap) edition of *Lady Chatterley's Lover* which caused all the fuss in the 1960s. 'Would you leave this book lying about for your wife or your servants to read?'

The censor was notoriously hard to second-guess. This, of course, is the most effective form of censorship: if rules are too precise, they quickly become a recipe for evasion. But there were certain concrete guidelines. 'Hands off royalty' was one: **Vickie**, an exceptionally inoffensive play dealing with the childhood of Queen Victoria, was banned in 1935; and as late as 1953 that notorious firebrand Anna Neagle was only allowed to play Victoria in **The Glorious Years** as long as the script made clear that her character was a totally unconnected young woman dreaming she was the Queen while in a state of concussion. Actresses in motion about were 'not to wear less than briefs and an opaque controlling brassière'. Nudes couldn't move at all: this was aimed at vaudeville theatres like the Windmill. Leaders of friendly states were not to be upset, hence the banning of **The Mikado** in 1907 on the occasion of the visit of the Emperor of Japan. In the troublesome 1930s the list grew longer. **Full Swing**, the Cambridge Footlights Revue of 1937, was obliged to drop the following passage:

> This wire from the Lord Chamberlain says we can't mention Hitler or Mussolini or Spain or Abyssinia or Anthony Eden. Take that moustache off, Mike! (*Somebody who has been dressed as Hitler wrenches off his moustache and swastika.*)

And it was in the same tradition, the following year, that Terence Rattigan's **Follow My Leader** bit the dust on the grounds of possible offence to Hitler.

Club performances took place throughout the 1950s, mostly of American plays on homosexual themes: Arthur Miller's **A View from the Bridge**, Tennessee Williams' **Cat on a Hot Tin Roof**. No matter that they'd both been hits on Broadway: London audiences were thought in need of protection. Even Robert Anderson's feeble **Tea and Sympathy** joined the queue.

In June 1965 the Royal Court became a 'club' – i.e. five bob on top of the normal ticket price – in order to show John Osborne's **A Patriot for Me**. Three whole scenes had been refused a license, including the indispensable drag ball. Osborne was a reliable draw and so was the movie-star Maximilian Schell, so the Court packed out. Later that year, when the Lord Chamberlain issued an extortionate list of cuts and changes to Edward Bond's **Saved**, it seemed only sensible to repeat the fiction. No one expected a commercial success along the lines of **Patriot**, but there was no other way to present the play in anything like an authentic form.

All hell broke loose. The play, if the press were to be believed, was not just badly written – the trawlings of some sociological reporter, waving his tape-recorder at the dregs of London's working class – but positively evil. The Lord Chamberlain sprang into action. William Gaskill (the Royal Court's Artistic Director), Greville Poke (its Secretary) and the lessee of the theatre, one Alfred Esdaile, were summonsed, found against and conditionally discharged.

The Court had lost the case but won a moral victory. All were delighted except for Esdaile who was furious to have found himself in the dock. (He was an ex-music-hall comedian who had pioneered the use of the revolving stage in vaudeville, thus getting around the 'naked ladies don't move' rule.) The irony was that by destroying the safety-valve that phoney clubs afforded, the Lord Chamberlain's Office had signed its own death-warrant. From now on, the choice was stark: it was either censorship right across the board, clubs included, or no censorship at all.

Two years later, the script of Bond's **Early Morning** was returned to the Royal Court with the shortest Lord Chamberlain's letter anyone there had ever seen. It said, 'This play may not be performed.' There could be no corrections, trims or rewrites. In its essence, **Early Morning** was incorrigible.

This wonderful play is often described as the one where Queen Victoria has a lesbian affair with Florence Nightingale. It's more than that: a dream, a political epic, a family romance, a periscope-view from the pram: one of the few truly visionary plays of modern times. But the lesbian affair is there all right ('Her legs are covered in shiny black hairs,' Florence complains) and the order to ban the play – so rumour had it – came right from the very top.

Disregarding the law, the press and his job-security, Gaskill staged the play for a semi-secret Sunday performance. Florence was played by Marianne Faithfull. The budget was so large for a Sunday one-off that when the Royal Court's Chairman saw it at a Board meeting he had a mild heart attack. Complex stratagems were devised to outwit Alfred Esdaile and the play's many other enemies within and without the Royal Court. The performance was announced for the evening but in fact took place in the afternoon, with the highly select audience being advised of the change of plan by a last-minute telephone call. Particular care was taken not to inform the box-office. How many artistic directors these days would go to such extremes simply to do a play? Tynan was there and scored a memorable own goal: 'If the production had been better, one would have seen how bad the play was.'

The police arrived at some or another point in the next few days but took no action.

The following year, the reign of the Lord Chamberlain over the British theatre was brought to an end and shortly after **Early Morning** got the showing it deserved. It all now seems as remote as the days of public executions.

The law against homosexual acts – largely abolished in 1967 – seems less remote. Were great plays lost – torn up, or never written – because of it? A few, no doubt, but not that many. Ackland would have chanced his arm. Coward or Rattigan surely not. Witty and unattached young men got their plays produced and were asked to parties. Rubbing the collective nose of heterosexual society in the physical details of your sex-life was a different matter entirely: cue for raised eyebrows, emptier diaries and smaller royalties.

The ambiguities were fruitful. The act of writing, for even the most respectable citizen, stems from two quite opposite urges: the urge to reveal oneself and the urge to conceal oneself. For the illegal gay – indulged on the one hand, suspected on the other – danger and concealment were the colours on his palette. When he wrote, the evasions flowered.

Edward Bond's
Early Morning:
'This play may not be performed.'

109

The Pink Room

*'Well, I've always, ever since I was a child, felt it was so "rude", so absolutely
unbelievable and sort of surrealist, for two people not of the same sex to have sex
together that I must say it does give me a really rather terrific and most horribly, I'm
afraid, perverted – kind of thrill.'*
RODNEY ACKLAND: **Absolute Hell**

1

Coward and Rattigan are the subjects of infinite study by students of this ambivalent era.
Somerset Maugham (1874–1965) is seldom included. He's a charmless writer but a skilled
one and he was in his day enormously popular. He trained and practised as a doctor, hence
the icy nature of his clinical observations, so we're told. But the same cannot be said of
other doctor-playwrights: Schnitzler, Chekhov or Bulgakov. **Our Betters** was banned and
if you ever see it you'll understand why – in what other play is a whole act so graphically
constructed around off-stage sexual intercourse? **The Constant Wife** is a lively feminist
vehicle: if your husband plays around, boot him out and get a sex-life. **For Services
Rendered** is a dark, sharp, cynical inquest into the death of First World War illusions.
The Circle is a sort of dramatic Gloomy Sunday: a celebration of the death of youthful
sexual attraction which really does leave you wanting to cut your throat. With all this
adult insight to hand, it's hard to say why his output isn't more inviting. Maugham must
have felt a similar impatience because his last play, **Sheppey**, is an amazing break from
style: the death-rite of a Jermyn Street barber who achieves an unexpected sainthood. In a
surrealistic scene, the prostitute whom he's befriended becomes the incarnation of Death.
The dialogue is so stunning that you want to cheer. This was the last thing he wrote for
the stage. The play was a flop and, much deterred, he retired to the South of France, there
to sulk in reptilian gloom. He still enjoyed being called 'The Master': a title wrested from
him late in life by Noël Coward.

Coward (1899–1973) stands firmly in the coded-gay tradition, but he had little time for
its founder. 'One of the silliest, most conceited and unattractive characters that ever existed,'
he said of Wilde. Wilde had committed the cardinal sin of getting caught. Coward conveyed
just enough decadence to tease, never enough to risk his neck. The conservative clothes,
the masterful wagging finger, even the famous vocal delivery (strange though this may seem)
were all contrived to put the public off the scent. The society photographer Cecil Beaton
never forgot the lesson he got from Coward in cutting out the camp. Coward 'studied his
own façade', he explained to Beaton; that's why his voice was 'definite, harsh, rugged'.

On matters of dress: 'Your sleeves are too tight, your voice is too high and too precise. You mustn't do it. It closes so many doors … It's hard, I know. One would like to indulge one's own taste. I myself dearly love a good match, yet I know it is overdoing it to wear tie, socks and handkerchief of the same colour.'

Coward was born in Teddington, the son of a piano salesman. The family was poor, and to this extent there's some truth in the notion of his having struggled up from grimy suburban deprivation. But the family connections included titles, coats of arms and even royalty at a stretch. High-ranking naval officers abounded, which adds another level to Coward's lifelong love of the fleet. His obsession with social class was fuelled by aristocratic cousins, much discussed but never in view.

He went on the stage at the age of eleven: bang went his London accent. Aged fourteen, he was introduced to a world of bohemian sophistication by a thirty-five-year-old painter, one Philip Streatfield – a fond depictor of naked youths on rocks. Streatfield quickly died: what did that mean to the child whom he'd befriended, probably more?

Further education came at the country house of a friend of Streatfield's, one Mrs Astley-Cooper. Streatfield, on his deathbed, had extracted a promise from her to look after his little protégé and she willingly obliged. She was kindly, rich and so enormously fat as to be unable to rise from a chair without assistance. Now this sharp, ambitious boy could study the upper classes at pinpoint range: Coward dressed for dinner, charmed and amused the guests and followed his hostess around with a little black book in which he noted her wittier *bons mots*: an indelible influence on his writing.

He earned his living as an actor, though his range was small: it really only extended to an early version of the Noël Coward impersonation that he was to give both on- and off-stage for the rest of his life. He edged his way into high society, showed off shamelessly and wrote like a madman: the habit of daily plugging away, whether the inspiration came or not, would never desert him. One of his earliest plays, **The Young Idea**, written in 1922, is partly stolen from **You Never Can Tell**. Nervously, Coward sent it to Shaw for his comments. It came back covered in thoughtful and generous notes – 'No you don't, young author' was one – together with an idea for the second act which saved the play. Coward never forgot this: he was generous to younger writers, even when piqued by their success.

In **The Vortex**, sensitive Nicky Lancaster loses his fiancée to his mother's dull but masculine young lover. Mother and son, unnaturally close even to the dimmest eye, hammer it out in the final act. Her sexuality is the major point at issue, followed closely by Nicky's disclosure of the coke-habit he picked up in Paris. Out of the window flies the little gold box in which he keeps the demon powder. 'Crash!' go mother's foolish aids to youth as Nicky sweeps jars, pots and bottles off her dressing-table. Down comes the curtain on this oh-so-modern couple as they find, together, just a glimmer of hope.

The play is shameless hokum but it's done with verve. The wit is hectic, the brand-names fly thick and fast, the catch-phrases are actually catchy: before the year was out, people who'd never been near the play were saying 'How perfectly marvellous', 'Too thrilling for words!', 'Divine!'.

The Vortex nearly didn't happen. No West End management wanted it, so Coward was driven far from his natural orbit to a dowdy fringe theatre: the Everyman in Hampstead, now the Everyman Hampstead Cinema. The backing collapsed. Then, one week before the opening, the leading lady walked out. Coward had barely talked the gracious star of tea-cup comedy Lilian Braithwaite into accepting the role of the lascivious matriarch before the Lord Chamberlain, one Lord Cromer, stepped in.

'This sort of play is unfortunately the inevitable sequence to a play like **Our Betters**, by which it is evidently inspired,' he wrote. 'To my mind the time has come to put a stop to the harmful influence of such pictures on the stage.' Coward met Lord Cromer at St James's Palace. He'd written, he carefully explained, a highly moral attack on depraved behaviour. Cromer relented and the play was licensed.

The irony is that Coward was telling the truth. The pleasures of **The Vortex** are louche and voyeuristic: you can enjoy every minute of these creatures' horrible doings and leave the theatre thanking God that you aren't like that yourself. Nicky (Coward wrote the part for himself) is drawn with care. His cocaine habit is smart and up-to-the-minute. But could anyone in the audience not have read it in terms of homosexual code? Dominant mothers, sat-upon fathers and excitable sons meant one thing and one thing only to a generation that was just discovering Freud. 'Is she pretty?' Florence asks when Nicky breaks the news of his engagement to young Bunty Mainwaring. Nicky's reply is reassuring, at least to her: 'I don't know – I haven't really noticed.' The truth, as we discover when Bunty arrives, is that she's 'more attractive than pretty in a boyish sort of way'. Oh, *that* explains it. Boring old Dad comes up with a startling but unintentional piece of camp argot. 'Is she musical?' he wonders.

Nicky finds his mother's boyfriend both a threat and an attraction. 'He dances beautifully,' says Florence. 'I shall never stop dancing with him,' Nicky answers pertly. It isn't surprising that the boyfriend smells a rat. 'It's funny your being in love with that sort of chap,' he remarks to Bunty. 'You know – up in the air – effeminate.'

Just to muddy the waters further, the cast-list features Pauncefoot Quentin(!), an 'elderly maiden gentleman' and despicable queen. If that's what queers are like – we're meant to think – then the basically decent Nicky must be straight as a die. Except he clearly isn't. Give up? That's what you're *meant* to do.

Coward's celebrity took different forms at different periods of his life. This early phase was daring and outrageous. In **Fallen Angels**, two women make a date with a lover they shared before they met the boring chaps they're married to now. He doesn't arrive and they both get sloshed. This play seems to have been written in about five minutes: it's short, camp and caused a scandal ('Slander on British womanhood').

Revue, in Coward's day, was both very camp indeed and mainstream. Coward's affinity with revue was total: the epigrammatic brevity of each item, the one-by-one

ticking-off of fashionable topics, their air of chic, all struck a deep and productive chord. The sketches he wrote are dust and ashes. His songs are another matter: some are masterpieces.

Hay Fever at the National Theatre in 1964.

Hay Fever was welcomed as a break from his decadent style. An impossible family – mother an actress, father a writer, daughter and son an insouciant duo – invite a quartet of conventional types for a country-house weekend and systematically torment them. This is the purest of Coward's plays: it has no subject other than its attitude to boring people; it has hardly any story and no link with life apart from the hints that the country-house style is newer to the Blisses than they're letting on. If Judith needs to wander the garden 'learning the names of the flowers by heart', she clearly lacks the aristocrat's inborn rapport with the herbaceous border. It's in the abstract nature of this play that Coward the playwright came closest to genius. The funniest lines are funny for no discernible reason. 'Go on.' 'No, there isn't, is there?' 'This haddock's disgusting.'

The 1964 revival at the National Theatre, directed by Coward himself, would restore him in the public mind as master-playwright. It also exposed his limited view of acting. **Hay Fever** calls for a grand comedienne in the classic style; the National offered Edith Evans, at seventy-six too old by several decades for the part but incontestably the

113

greatest actress of the English-speaking world. Coward had no experience of such a creature. His avoidance of great actors of his own generation was almost neurotic. He never worked with Ashcroft, Redgrave, Richardson or Guinness. The young Olivier had played the stooge in **Private Lives**; Gielgud, in a dip in his career, had been lured into **Nude with Violin** and the result was frightful. Vivien Leigh had played in **South Sea Bubble** when she was mad and in **Look After Lulu** when she was dulled by shock-therapy. Edith Evans baffled him. Why could the silly old bat not learn her lines? In vain she pleaded that she didn't work like that: that she built it up from … 'Oh, but I can't explain!' She ended up, at the out-of-town tryout, with the sheets pulled over her head in a Manchester hotel bedroom. 'I *won't* go on! Why *should* I? There's an *adequate* understudy!' (Maggie Smith, who in the role of Myra hit the style spot-on, had as a great concession agreed to cover.)

Buoyed by success, Coward came as clean as he was ever to do with **Semi-Monde**: an over-the-years account of sexual disappointment. Gay men and women feature in the mix without sensational comment. Production in Britain was a hopeless cause; Coward gave up on it. **Post-Mortem** was too harsh for comfort. Coward stuffed it in a drawer, **Private Lives** came to him in a sleepless night. It provoked the most interesting statement Coward was ever to make about writing, because the only one that allowed for intuition: 'The moment I turned out the lights, Gertie appeared in a white Molyneux dress and refused to go away until 4 a.m., by which time Private Lives, a title and all, had constructed itself.'

'Gertie' was Gertrude Lawrence. She and Coward had first met in 1913 when both were child actors. She grew up to be a limited actress, not much of a dancer, and if you play her recordings of musical comedy, you will be startled to find that she sang about as well as you or I do in the bath. (Anna's songs in **The King and I** were written to fit her narrow vocal range, which is why bathrooms across the world still echo to the sound of 'Hello, Young Lovers'.) She wasn't a beauty either. She was provocative, bold and ineffably stylish: a self-invented star. Coward adored her: he saw in her, perhaps, the brilliant, common counter-jumper that he was himself.

Private Lives is a paean to their impossible love. In form it's perfect: if there were any chance that Coward had read a play by Marivaux, or even heard of Marivaux, you'd think the influence was undeniable. It's also reminiscent of **The Vortex**: the destined pair, no longer mother and son but highly charged, incompatible adults, leave the boring world of conventional sex behind them. Ahead of them lies an alternative world of spiky, physical passion. It's a fantasy of what that-women-I-love-so-much would be to me, if only … It's the 'if only' that makes this play so sad and so accessible.

Invited to produce an enormous show for Drury Lane, Coward came up with **Cavalcade**, a jelly-boned giant of a play which charts the decline of British values largely in terms of the growing insubordination of the working classes. Coward appeared at the

curtain-call as bold as brass to proclaim, 'In spite of the troublous times we live in, it is still pretty exciting to be English.' The reign had begun of Coward the true-blue playwright laureate. What had happened to Coward the scourge of dull convention? The key lies somewhere back in Teddington, in grand relations who were never seen and in Mrs Astley-Cooper's country house where it was always summer.

He had one good play left in him. **Design for Living** was written for himself and the Lunts: the American theatre's bisexual royal couple. What it celebrates is not so much bisexual love as polymorphous perversity: the overwhelming sexuality of the whole of life as experienced at a certain stage of infancy. Most people grow out of it. 'Forty years ago,' Tynan was to write of Coward many years later, 'he was Slightly in Peter Pan, and you might say that he has been wholly in Peter Pan ever since.'

*Coward and Lawrence in **Private Lives**: 'a paean to their impossible romance'.*

115

Vanessa Redgrave in
Design for Living
in 1973.

The Second World War saw Coward throwing himself wholeheartedly into the patriotic cause. The film **In Which We Serve** depicted him in command of a destroyer. The notion of Coward in this butch and masterful role excited a certain amount of ridicule at the time: this took too little account of his natural toughness. **Blithe Spirit**, his clunking one-joke farce about the afterlife, was a huge success. **Present Laughter** is an autobiographical show-off: playwright Garry Essendine, society peacock, prances about in a dressing-gown. Predatory women are given short shrift and an over-earnest younger playwright gets shut in a cupboard. All deeply disagreeable.

After the war, Coward was beached. The Labour Government, supertax, the collapsing morale of the upper classes, the mood of egalitarianism all stood in hideous contrast to the construct of his life. He took this ill.

In fact, from a material point of view, he wasn't doing badly. A Las Vegas cabaret date made him a worldwide icon. He had his Jamaican tax-haven. **Relative Values** enjoyed a healthy West End run and so did **Nude with Violin**, which is even worse. None of these worldly gains gave him the slightest comfort. He'd lived by London fashion: now he was dying by it. Young writers whom he'd never heard of were getting disproportionate attention. The critics sniped at him. Tynan was having the greatest fun sending him up. This cut deep. Coward couldn't see that the star-struck Tynan was his most helpless fan: that he was *copying* him. Tynan was a *critic*. Critics weren't meant to have *fun*, they were meant to *write good reviews*. The pain that Coward suffered at the hands of Tynan was as acute and incongruous as the agony of an elephant with a mouse up its trunk. He went public: 'My age and experience entitle me,' he mused, 'to offer a little gentle advice to the young revolutionaries of today and also to those of our dramatic critics who have hailed their efforts with such hyperboles of praise.'

This was his preamble to three successive essays in the *Sunday Times* on the state of the modern theatre. They were disastrous. Wilde – that 'silly, conceited character' – couldn't put pen to paper without saying something illuminating. Coward, recording his deepest beliefs, had nothing to say. Most striking was his total lack of intellectual curiosity. He sounded dull.

It didn't help that his latest play, **Waiting in the Wings**, chose that particular moment to fold. 'The bridge of a sinking ship, one feels, is scarcely the ideal place ... to deliver a lecture on the technique of staying afloat,' crowed Tynan. Only John Osborne kept his head screwed on. 'Mr Coward, like Miss Dietrich, is his own invention and contribution to this century,' he wrote. 'Anyone who cannot see that should keep well away from the theatre.'

2

When Terence Rattigan (1911–1977) felt the chill, he too went public and the results were even worse. Coward at least could write. Rattigan's prose was as flat as Coward's Norfolk: 'I don't think that ideas, *per se*, social, political or moral, have a very important place in the theatre. They definitely take second place to character and narrative anyway ...' This credo – from a 1950 *New Statesman* essay – was widely mocked. But it isn't as glib as Rattigan makes it sound. If you advertise your theme (he's trying to say) you'll kill it. Let it emerge from the specifics of your story: it's truer that way.

What makes it sound so boring is Rattigan's humdrum use of language. All his prose is boring. You wonder how anyone who writes so lifelessly could catch the colour, the verve and the wit of drama. The answer is that for most of the time he couldn't. His comedies are hamstrung by his blindness to the comic possibilities of the English language. The only witticism that anyone remembers is in fractured French: '*Elle a des idées au-dessous de sa gare.*' Nor could he fit the grander notes required for costume drama: **Adventure Story**, based on the life of Alexander the Great, has a decided note of Biggles:

ALEXANDER: I've noticed the men have accumulated far too much baggage –
HEPHAESTON: Yes – I've spoken to the under-officers about it.

But when he writes about repressed emotions, his dullness is eloquent. Hidden feelings smoulder beneath the surface: the fact that they're being signalled by the tepid diction of the golf-club or the canasta party is what gives the plays their layered effect. And the metaphor is exact: just as the rules of middle-class life prevent the characters from owning up to their hidden lives, so Rattigan's prose deprives them of the means of doing so.

He was born in London into the purple of the upper middle classes. His father, a diplomat, was a rampant womaniser whose career was abruptly curtailed when he made the great mistake of having an affair with the Queen of Greece.

As a schoolboy, Rattigan developed three lasting passions: theatre, cricket and sex, the third of these culminating in a lengthy affair with the racing correspondent of the *Daily Express*. At Oxford he met a number of fellow-undergraduates who would figure in his life in later years: one of them, George Devine, would be rather a nemesis as Director of the Royal Court. Even at this early stage, he turned down Rattigan's plays.

First Episode is what it sounds. Rattigan's next play, **French Without Tears**, was slung on cheaply with a cast of then unknowns (Rex Harrison, Trevor Howard, Jessica Tandy), hailed all round as a delightful romp and ran for no fewer than 1,030 performances, though to see it now is to wonder at its misogyny. Its comic premise is the efforts made by a group of red-blooded young Englishmen – students in a language-crammer's in France – to avoid the attentions of the gorgeous, twenty-year-old Diana Lake. 'You must never, never leave me alone with that girl' stutters Alan to his chums. (He's 'twenty-three, dark and saturnine'.) 'You don't realise the appalling danger I'm in. If I'm left alone with her for a minute I shudder to think what might happen.' The play ends as Diana – all of whose other intended victims have wriggled free – prepares herself in bathing-dress and nonchalant pose for the arrival of the new student, one Lord Heybrook. In he comes and guess what? He's only fifteen! That'll show her! (The original script made the same point by portraying Lord Heybrook as a 'blond, swishy queer' with a borzoi dog at the end of a lead.)

It's startling, when you first discover it, to find the Act One curtain punchline echoed by David Mamet fifty years later. Both Jacqueline and Gould have won a bet about the person they fancy:

JACQUELINE: Five francs please, Alan.
                (**French Without Tears**)
GOULD: … and tell him he owes me five bucks.
                (**Speed-the-Plow**)

Rex Harrison, Jessica Tandy and Robert Flemyng in **French Without Tears**.

But master-painters study each other: why not master-playwrights? Rattigan's skill at the nuts and bolts of putting-a-play-together is justly famous. A star at twenty-five, he honed an image which only time and decrepitude could erode: the perfectly tailored matinée-idol, glass at his side, cigarette lightly poised. He was left-wing and a pacifist: his reputation as a moral lightweight was something he found bewildering and unfair. **After the Dance** is a bid for seriousness: a glimpse of the abyss that threatens ageing Bright Young Things. It flopped and, when **Follow My Leader** was

119

banned, Rattigan fell into a depression which lifted only on his entry into the RAF at the outbreak of war.

Attacked over the South Atlantic by a German Heinkel, he and the rest of the crew were forced to jettison all they had in order to maintain height. Rattigan was faced with a dilemma which few playwrights before or since have had to face: the first act of the play he was currently writing was in his jacket. He kept it. This was **Flare Path**, an upbeat account of lives and loves in the RAF which very much caught the public mood. It was also the first of his plays to be presented by Hugh Beaumont of H.M. Tennent Ltd.

Beaumont was born in Cardiff in 1908. When he was a baby, two unknown women peered into his pram and called him 'Binkie' – meaning black or grubby – and the diminutive stuck for life. After a few years in box-office work and company management, he persuaded one H.M. Tennent to form a production company with Binkie himself as the predominant force; when Tennent died, Binkie became dictator.

For the next two decades, 'Tennent's' was a byword for star-studded, impeccably mounted, middlebrow theatre. Its power was absolute. No writer, director, designer or actor could earn much of a living in London without Binkie's approval and those who displeased him were out in the cold till death. (Theirs or his.) His diplomatic skills were legendary. He imposed his taste on everything he produced: luckily he had an excellent eye. The Binkie myth was enhanced by the fact that he had no public profile: he never gave interviews, was seldom even photographed. A suave, immaculate figure, he ruled unseen from an eyrie at the top of the Globe Theatre, reached via a lift of minute dimensions: young actors, flattered when he offered to escort them down to the street, soon found themselves pressed to his torso as though in the Tokyo rush-hour.

During the war, he began to exploit a loophole in the law regarding entertainment tax, a long-vanished extortion which at that time stood at one-third of the box-office income. This tax was waived in the case of an educational production which made no profit. Binkie set up a second, 'educational' company: it added hugely to his lustre, and the fact that it seldom made any profit didn't stop him skimming off a healthy management fee.

The Binkie mixture of homosexual good taste and manipulativeness gave the rest of the theatre much to gossip about, and throughout the 1940s and 1950s Tennent's enjoyed a vivid greenroom notoriety as a nest of gay intrigue. One of the results of this was that, when the English Stage Company was set up at the Royal Court, it seemed not merely an aesthetic opposition to the Tennent's style but a moral one. The two, of course, were easily confused. When Devine said famously that there'd be no queers in his theatre he wasn't (as soon became obvious) referring to sexual propensities as you or I might know them: it was an anti-Binkie statement.

Flare Path was one of Binkie's earliest shows. 'It is a masterpiece of understatement,' said an approving Churchill to the cast. 'But we are rather good at that, aren't we?' Rattigan followed it up with the spiritless **While the Sun Shines**. **Love in Idleness** is no better. There's a fathomless gulf between Rattigan's bad plays and his good ones.

The Winslow Boy is the first of the second kind. He wanted, he said, to write a play in the line of Maugham and Galsworthy: an Edwardian domestic drama with a standing set and a powerful story. It's better than that: a subtle, ironic account of the price of justice, with two fabulous *coups de théâtre*.

The paradox about Rattigan, who chased the bright lights like a moth, is that he wrote best when the setting he'd chosen was drab and depressing. **The Browning Version** is the small-scale tragedy of a mediocre teacher at a none-too-brilliant public school. To enjoy this masterly account of a man who has failed in life, in work and in love, you must accept the fact that his wife is a destructive bitch and not ask too many questions about what turned her into one.

Who is Sylvia? is based on Rattigan's father's amorous adventures. It's so bad that nobody would accept the leading role. Finally it was offered to Robert Flemyng, a veteran of **French Without Tears**. Since then he'd fought at Montecassino so his fears of Binkie were less than most. Called in for a meeting, he explained in detail why the play didn't work and why he'd be utterly wrong for the part. 'Well, dear,' said Binkie, 'that's all very interesting and I'll see you at rehearsal at ten o'clock on Monday morning.' The play was a flop and Flemyng got blamed. 'If *only* we hadn't had Bobbie!'

Three days before the opening of **Adventure Story**, Rattigan's ex-lover Kenneth Morgan killed himself: he'd moved in with another young actor a month before. 'Terry was quite simply stunned,' said Flemyng, years later. He added: 'I remember thinking, I bet a play will come out of this.' It did: **The Deep Blue Sea** is Rattigan's masterpiece, the play in which he most fully expressed the battle between the disorder of the senses and the order of what's allowed.

Hester Collyer is in her thirties, the wife of a judge whom she's left less than a year ago for Freddie, a young ex-RAF pilot. He's idle and dim but he satisfies her sexually. When her husband asks her what the attraction is, she replies in code. But her meaning is clear:

HESTER:	Perhaps the answer could be put in a single word.
COLLYER:	We might disagree on the choice of that word.
HESTER:	I don't expect so. There are polite words and impolite words. They all add up to the same emotion.

But Hester's world, the world of the Southern-English middle classes, is one where men think sex is unimportant. Either they drown it in respectability or – like Freddie – they're happy enough to give it a try but, when the chips are down, would rather be having a drink with their pals. Philip, a newly wed young husband, has made up his mind on the subject. 'The physical side is really awfully unimportant,' he explains to Hester in a scene of great irony.

Hester begins the play unconscious in front of the gas fire. She'd tried to gas herself, but the meter had run out of shillings. The play ends symmetrically: given the faith to go on living by a fellow-outcast (false note) she once again turns on the gas, but this time lights it.

*Peggy Ashcroft and Kenneth More in **The Deep Blue Sea**.*

What distinguishes **The Deep Blue Sea** from other great plays of the century is its air of artifice. What makes it great is that the artifice is so painful. This was the year in which Rattigan, on a holiday cruise, wrote to his mother:

> I'm being chased by a highly predatory female ... the lady in question is extremely decorative, but – as I only learned to my cost when it was too late – has just dumped a husband and is very firmly on the lookout for another ... So

I'm making the excuse that you're joining me at Cannes – incidentally I wish you were – and am skipping the boat the day after tomorrow.

His life was a lie. But a lie, if worked upon intensely enough, will result in a truth of an unexpected kind. Rumours abound of an earlier version featuring one Hector Collyer, identical to Kenneth Morgan. Frith Banbury, who directed the play, is certain it never existed. But what if it did? Would **The Deep Blue Sea** be better or worse?

The truth is that gender is irrelevant. To stress it is, in the words of Wilde, 'to assign to the mere accident of sex what properly belongs to imaginative insight and creative energy'. The playwright gives to a character whatever comes: it could be ballsiness, it could be damp submission. Motive matters. So does the way in which that motive is pursued: bullishly, deviously, passively, negatively, hopelessly. None is specific to any one sex. They're in our common reservoir.

And Rattigan, spokesman of middle-class repression, is as much alive in Hester Collyer as he is in Hester's sporty lover and her decent, bewildered husband – not to mention the struck-off doctor living upstairs.

The play was a triumph. But the clouds were gathering. **The Sleeping Prince**, intended as Coronation froth, was postponed into the Coronation's hangover, where it looked as stupid as it is. **Separate Tables** was Rattigan's last great flowering. The New York production marked a significant stage in his decline.

The play uses the setting and characters of a seaside boarding-house to tell two unrelated stories. One is about a bogus major caught in a sexual misdemeanour. Rattigan's first impulse was to make the Major a homosexual cruiser. Knowing that this would never get past the Lord Chamberlain, he made his vice the more acceptable one of molesting women in cinemas. The play was passed and thus it was played in London with success.

On Broadway, censorship didn't apply. Rattigan longed to restore the truth. He did a rewrite and pestered the director to include it. 'An English audience,' he explained, 'knew my problem and accepted that I had to skirt round it.' Now that Broadway beckoned, couldn't he spell it out, just this once? But the actor involved, the homosexual Eric Portman, had his reputation to consider. The rewrite was discarded, not to reappear until a small-scale revival in 1999 when, small as it was, it made an enormous difference. Rattigan didn't like the climb-down, but he bought it, thus losing his final chance to escape his carapace of pretence.

Variation on a Theme not only flopped but brought an added humiliation: when the young and unknown Shelagh Delaney saw it on tour, she was so outraged by what she called 'its ridiculous attitude to homosexuality' that she went home and promptly wrote the Theatre Workshop hit **A Taste of Honey**. Rattigan pinned his final hopes on **Man and Boy**. It's about a rogue financier who uses his handsome young son as bait to ensnare a homosexual rival: a cheesy embarrassment.

Rattigan had lost his audience and was too fixed in a role to find a new one. Unlike Coward, he couldn't act or sing in cabaret: instead, he wrote preposterous screenplays and earned vast quantities of dollars. Nothing made up for the disdain that he endured at home.

Like Coward, he had a particular reason for finding it so unfair. If your career as a playwright has been built on advertising the unacceptable side of your life in a coded form, and you've been richly rewarded for doing so, it produces a false sense of invulnerability. The public *knew*, rages the furious author. Of course they *knew*. I never spelled it out exactly but they jolly well *knew*. And if they could forgive me *that*, why can't they forgive me for **Variation on a Theme**? It *doesn't make sense*!

When he died in 1977, he was convinced that the times had passed him by. In fact, he'd simply been accepted, though at less than his occasional worth. He could never quite take this in.

3

From time to time, throughout the long, ambiguous summer, playwrights appeared who weren't mere boulevardiers but who didn't fit into the mould of gay poseur: some had a distinctive voice, others a searching mind. But their creative lives were short. A strikingly grown-up voice, Ronald Mackenzie, blew the royalties of his first play **Musical Chairs** on a holiday in the South of France. A tyre burst, his car turned over and he was killed at the age of twenty-three. More than any other playwright of his time, he caught the stern, staccato mindset of an age of disillusion. **The Maitlands** survived him and is equally fine.

Dodie Smith (1896–1990) had wit and fearlessness: she was the terror of her directors. She rose from the shopfloor at Heal's, running a dress-designing outfit on the side: 'Quaint Clothes for Queer Customers'. Memorable is her conversational opener to Mr Ambrose Heal, once she'd decided to seduce him. 'How long,' she murmured, eyeing a VENDU sticker, 'is one supposed to hold goods for customers who don't take delivery?' But neither **Autumn Crocus** nor **Dear Octopus** is half as smart: her claim to fame is the novel **101 Dalmatians**.

Bridget Boland's excellent **Cockpit** depicts the chaos of Britain's excellent collapsing empire; Denis Cannan's **Captain Carvallo** is a fresh, unstuffy comedy. (Cannan reappeared in the 1960s as the author of Peter Brook's **US**, when few remembered Cannan's plays of the pre-**Look Back** era.)

John Whiting (1917–1963) was an intellectually ambitious writer, far removed from matinée culture. His mock-pastoral **A Penny for a Song** is just about bearable. **Marching Song** is grim. His most successful play was **The Devils**, though in the wake of the Brecht/Littlewood/Osborne revolution its mad nuns and existential angst seemed vaguely pointless. Whiting was an excellent polemicist and his attack on Sloane Square playwrights, a sensation at the time, still sounds a thoughtful note. 'Their hearts are in the right place. It's their tiny little heads I'm worried about.'

J.B. (Jack) Priestley (1894–1984) was a more provocative and enduring playwright. His best-known play, **An Inspector Calls**, appeared in 1946, hard on the heels of Attlee's socialist government. Uniquely for the West End theatre of its times it showed its audience a political face, even if its political agenda only amounted to an assertion of the importance of charity and compassion. The action takes place in an unnamed Yorkshire town, during a family celebration in the home of factory owner Arthur Birling, to celebrate his impending knighthood and his daughter Sheila's engagement. The party is interrupted by an Inspector Goul, apparently investigating the suicide of a poor young woman. All, it turns out are guilty, but 'society' is the real culprit.

An Inspector Calls – *Stephen Daldry's RNT revival.*

J.B. Priestley was also a journalist, novelist, essayist, critic, political commentator, travel writer, and professional Yorkshireman. His output was vast and varied – over 100 novels, plays, and essays. His early successes were melodramas and comedies – **Dangerous Corner**, a psychological melodrama; **Laburnum Grove**, a comedy of suburban life; **Eden End**, a comedy of backstage life in a provincial theatre – the same ground that he covered in his hugely popular novel, **The Good Companions.**

His most serious plays are his 'time' plays: **Time and the Conways** – hopes for the future contrasted with the reality of twenty years on; **I Have Been Here Before**, patterns of life established in previous incarnations; and **An Inspector Calls** – a play which subverts the conventions of time, place and reality.

His most successful play is a really funny, brilliantly characterised domestic comedy called **When We Are Married**; with Gogol's **The Government Inspector** it's the best account of provincial society in the thrall of snobbery that exists.

The case of verse drama is a curious one. In the pre-Restoration theatre, the words 'poet' and 'playwright' were used interchangeably. It was simply assumed that anyone who wrote a play would do so largely in verse except where there was some good reason for doing otherwise. After the Restoration, this changed. Verse was used for elevated sentiments but, to convey the lives of human beings as you or I might know them, the medium of default was prose. It was as though drama had gone into a profound sulk: from now on, it would stay out of fancy dress and appear, whenever it could, in working clothes.

So verse, which for Shakespeare, Middleton or Webster was the means of making reality more intense, became for their successors a way of blurring it. This continued for centuries. T.S. Eliot's **Sweeney Agonistes** is one of the most exasperating false theatrical dawns in living memory. Only a fragment, it draws some of its inspiration from Yeats's Noh-theatre experiments but at once advances into a wholly different area: baleful, colloquial, jazzy. It evokes the Jacobeans to better effect than any poet had done since the Civil War; it also prefigures the angular rhythms of Beckett and Pinter. Here two good-time girls receive a telephone call. Pereira, who will remain unseen, is a quintessential Pinter off-stage presence along the lines of Casey in **Betrayal**.

TELEPHONE:	Ting a ling ling
	Ting a ling ling
DUSTY:	That's Pereira
DORIS:	Yes that's Pereira
DUSTY:	Well what are you
	going to do?
TELEPHONE:	Ting a ling ling
	Ting a ling ling
DUSTY:	That's Pereira
DORIS:	Well can't you stop that horrible noise?
	Pick up the receiver
DUSTY:	What'll I say?
DORIS:	Say what you like: say I'm ill,
	Say I broke my leg on the stairs
	Say we've had a fire
DUSTY:	Hello Hello are you there?
	Yes this is Miss Dorrance's *flat* –
	Oh Mr Pereira is that you? How do you do?

The small invited audience that saw **Sweeney Agonistes** on 16 December 1934 included not only Yeats but Bertolt Brecht, who thought it was 'by far the best thing in London'. It is pleasing to imagine a fantasy scenario in which Yeats buttonholed Eliot after the show and dynamised him just as, years before, he had dynamised Synge, or one in which Brecht hustled him over to Europe for a course in sex and politics.

But Eliot chose drama of the spirit as seen through the prism of the Anglican Church, viz. **Murder in the Cathedral**. Christian martyrdom and Sweeney-ish pastiche seem an odd mix on the face of it, like a 1960s art-school show turning serious every so often. But in the 1993 RSC production it seemed true and moving. **The Family Reunion** inserts an episode from the Oresteia into the country-house whodunit: a sort of Agamemnon. The noir-ish ambience is seductive and the chorus of aunts and uncles irresistible – Eliot is best when he's being facetious – but Lord Monchesey's crisis of conscience brings ominous signs of the high horse. **The Cocktail Party** is brittle and bright, but then comes the religious bit, capped by the saintly Celia Copplestone's death-by-anthill. Eliot was fast becoming a Grand Old Man, his theatrical model the West End at its stuffiest. Your eyelids will droop over **The Confidential Clerk** and **The Elder Statesman** will have you fighting for consciousness.

In the 1950s, far too much was made of the 'Poetic Revival', partly on the back of the splendid casting opportunities to be found in the plays of Christopher Fry (1907–). Gielgud starred in **The Lady's Not for Burning** in 1948, Olivier in **Venus Observed** in 1950 and Edith Evans in **The Dark is Light Enough** in 1954. When the bubble burst, Fry took his falling-out-of-favour with all the equilibrium you'd expect from the author of these mild and fanciful works. He certainly didn't deserve to have the title of his most successful play served up in one of Margaret Thatcher's more ferocious conference addresses. 'Burning/turning' seemed a witty play on words to the elderly playwright Ronald Millar who had ghosted the speech and he was upset when Thatcher cheerfully misquoted it: '*This* lady's not for turning!' It turned out afterwards she hadn't the faintest idea that she was making a joke – indeed, she hadn't known that any such play existed.

There is an unbroken tradition in the British theatre going back to the fifteenth century. Can we forget so easily that our dramatic tradition is founded on verse drama, that our national playwright was a poet?

The missing name, of course, is Tony Harrison (1936–), who is as prolific a writer for the theatre as his contemporary and fellow native of Leeds, Alan Bennett. You could make comparisons between the two writers, and they would not be invidious ones. Both write about sex, class and death, even if Bennett's mordant wit provides an opaque filter which makes these themes less conspicuous than Harrison's. They share a common contempt for the merely fashionable, and they are thoroughly demotic – both making idiosyncratic films for television. Popular without being populist, they are thoroughly accessible, and thoroughly and unapologetically elitist – if that means believing in the absolute values of good and bad art and refusing to talk down to people from the class you were born into.

Harrison, a baker's son from Leeds, is highly cosmopolitan, multi-lingual (Greek, ancient and modern, Latin, Italian, French, Czech and Hausa), much travelled – a citizen of the world, as they say, living, often rather precariously, between London, New York and Newcastle.

Most of his work for the theatre is adapted from the Greek or the French – **The Oresteia, The Trackers of Oxyrhynchus,** based on fragments of a lost play by Sophocles, **The Misanthrope, Phaedra Britannica** – or from the middle English, The Mysteries. They're translations, 'carried across' from another language, but he mediates in his own voice between a foreign language and English verse, between one culture and another, between the past and the present. There's no more accurate description of this position than the epigraph that Harrison uses for his first volume of plays. It's a poem by Lion Feuchtwanger, who collaborated with Brecht on a version of Marlowe's **Edward II:**

Verse drama:
The Trackers of
***Oxyrhynchus**.*

I, for instance, sometimes write
Adaptations. Or some people prefer the phrase
'Based on', and this is how it is: I use
Old Material to make a new play, then
Put under the title
The name of the dead writer who is extremely
Famous and quite unknown, and before
The name of the dead writer I put the word 'After'
Then one group will write that I am
Very respectful and others that I am nothing of the sort
and all
The dead writer's failures
Will be ascribed
To me and all my successes
To the dead writer who is extremely
Famous and quite unknown, and of whom
Nobody knows whether he himself
Was the writer of maybe the
Adaptor.

If you look at the photographs of **Trackers**: twelve Yorkshiremen in clogs dressed as satyrs with long tails, the ears of pantomime horses, and magnificently gross erect phalluses, it's hard to think there was a bolder playwright working in this country in the 1990s.

One more playwright of the ambivalent years remains to be described; Rodney Ackland (1908–1991). Younger than Coward and a little older than Rattigan, he differed from both these steely professionals in the total disorganisation of his life and the impulsiveness of his work. They died rich and famous, though it didn't stop them grousing; he lived on into the 1990s, penniless and enraged. At least he hadn't gone out of fashion, since he'd never been in it. His talent had always been too warm and nervy for the commercial theatre.

He was born Norman Ackland Bernstein: his father was a ruined businessman, his mother a principal boy in pantomime. Aged eighteen, he was struck as though by a lightning-bolt by Komisarjevsky's production of **The Three Sisters**. His first play, **Improper People**, was thought 'nearly as boring as Chekhov'.

Characters in Ackland's plays are almost always louche and chaotic. People who knew him well were fond of pointing out, not only that Ackland shared these qualities himself (that much was obvious), but that people who had too much to do with him soon started behaving in a louche and chaotic way themselves: it seemed infectious.

He was gay except when not. As a young man, he insisted on walking down the street hand-in-hand with his boyfriend: this, he hoped, would shock the middle classes out of their respectable stupor. One day he got on the local bus by himself and an elderly lady looked at him kindly and asked, 'How is your poor dear blind friend?' At the age of forty-two, he went to a party and met one Mabbe Poole, the second daughter of the Edwardian playwright Frederick Lonsdale. They fell in love and married and that was that: for the next twenty-two years they spent not a single night apart. Married life was a saga of unpaid bills, moonlight flits and skin-of-their-teeth escapes from the Inland Revenue. This was his heterosexual phase: when Mabbe died, he was gay once more.

Strange Orchestra is a rumpled mosaic of Bohemian life in a London flat: dreams, blindnesses and visions. The autobiographical **After October** was Ackland's only commercial hit. An entire household depends on a young playwright's success: when his play is a flop, they kid themselves that it went just fine. And if it didn't – well, there's always *next* October … More fantasy in **The Dark River**: in an old house on the banks of the Thames, the pending Apocalypse goes unheard.

In 1952, Terence Rattigan told Frith Banbury, the director of **The Deep Blue Sea**, that he had a small financial problem. His earnings in the current year had been unexpectedly high and his accountant wanted him to offload some of his profits. Did Frith, by any chance, know of a good play certain to lose money? Absolutely, said Banbury: Ackland, whom he'd admired for many years, had sent him a splendid piece entitled **The Pink Room**.

The eponymous room is a Soho drinking-club, a dive like the one in the John Betjeman poem where the hostess wakes up to find kümmel on the handle of the door. Its members are brittle neurotics, soaks and has-beens: metaphor for a faded pre-war world which has just about made through to 1945.

Inside the club, bits are falling off the ceiling. (The bullet-holes don't help.) Across the street, people can be heard singing 'The Red Flag': Labour has won the election. A new world is dawning, one of purposefulness and common sense. Trivial people are on their way out, particularly when they're middle-aged and smell of drink and stale cigarette smoke.

This brilliantly alive and touching play was vilely received. It was harsh, repulsive, negative. In those days the single critic who could turn the tide was Harold Hobson. But Hobson was a Christian uplift-chaser for whom the realism of **The Pink Room** was a moral affront. 'The audience at Hammersmith,' he wrote, 'had the impression of being present, if not at the death of a talent, at least at its very serious illness.'

Four years later, metaphors of British collapse would be the staple diet of the Royal Court, and few of the plays presented there were as good as **The Pink Room**. But the Court could offer protection. Ackland was on his own, save only for the continued support of Banbury. Rattigan, who had a horror of failure, never spoke to him again. Binkie shunned him. Ackland's peripatetic years began. He lost confidence. Hobson's review became an obsession.

There is a sequel. In his obscurity, he rewrote **The Pink Room**, taking account of the abolition of the Lord Chamberlain. Hugh Marriner, failed writer and perpetual scrounger ('Bloodiest of fools, I've come out without a single cigarette on me') became a naked self-portrait. Out went Marriner's wife, in came Marriner's boyfriend Nigel. 'Cut it out,' he yelps when Hugh tries to give him a hug. 'I'm not a girl.' Hugh's tipsy, all-too-successful pass at a drunk GI is deathlessly done:

BUTCH:	… So c'me on, where do I get it?
HUGH:	… anywhere round Piccadilly … there's always plenty of –
BUTCH:	Now let's get this straight, Mac: any form of sex'l intercourse comes natchral to me bar one. I never done it an' I don' intend to – an' that's pay for it.
HUGH:	(*after a pause, his voice low*) Butch …
BUTCH:	Yeah … ? C'me on, let's hear –
HUGH:	(*his mouth dry, his words barely audible*) I was going to say … Does it have to be a –
BUTCH:	I get ya … I get ya, Buster … An' I go for it. I go for it … OK? (*A pause. Hugh shoots a furtive look at the door.*)
HUGH:	Have you got anywhere, Butch? I can't take you to my place.
BUTCH:	Listen, kid, you know the Regent's Palace Hotel?

The 'furtive look at the door' anticipates the return of club-owner Christine: by now, of course, she's drunk as a skunk. Hugh's collapse into her arms comes later on, via a delirious course of logic:

HUGH:	Well, I've always, ever since I was a child, felt it was so 'rude', so absolutely unbelievable and sort of surrealist, for two people *not* of the same sex to have sex together that I must say it does give me a really rather terrific and most horribly, I'm afraid, perverted – kind of thrill.

In his despair and obscurity, Ackland had given the modern age a long-lost play of the 1950s, stripped at last of its evasions. **Absolute Hell**, as it was now re-titled, was produced in 1988 at the tiny Orange Tree Theatre in Richmond, London: Ackland lived in a council flat nearby. Not long after, it was seen on BBC television. It was produced, in 1995, four years after Ackland's death, at the National Theatre.

Each time that **Absolute Hell** is revived, it seems more surely one of the masterworks of its century, as great in its boldness as **The Deep Blue Sea** is in its tact. It gives us a glimpse of what the theatre might have been if all those long-forgotten battles had been won the first time round; if Oscar Wilde had turned his double life into a single one; if censorship had been abolished when Shaw denounced it; if Granville-Barker's theatre had been founded when he first conceived it; if it hadn't taken two world wars and all those prissy and inhibited decades to get where we are today.

Judi Dench in
Absolute Hell,
RNT revival.

America Dreaming

'In the United States there is more space where nobody is than where anybody is. That is what makes America what it is.'
GERTRUDE STEIN

1

There's a *Picture Post* photograph taken in 1945: two sailors and two girls are standing in the fountains of Trafalgar Square, trousers rolled up to their thighs, water above their knees. One girl has her arms wrapped round the two men, a half-knotted tie lying between her breasts on her Lana Turner jumper, and a sailor's hat cocked at a rakish angle on her dark hair; she looks straight at the camera, mocking the photographer. The other, blonde and demure, floats her hands away from her body like a dancer, neither encouraging nor rejecting the sailor's hand spread over the side of her stomach. They are tired, drunk, young, and guileless.

It is dawn, VE-Day, after a night when plump women in aprons made of Union Jacks danced with pinstriped civil servants, strangers kissed, the young princesses Elizabeth and Margaret mingled with the crowd outside Buckingham Palace, searchlights danced on the night sky, bonfires blazed in the streets, and for a moment the nation held its breath before putting its weary back into rebuilding a nearly bankrupt country, crippled by war.

Britain at the time was profoundly insular, undemocratic and riven by class division. The country was divided between those who were content to let it continue, and those who were keen for change. A poll of all voters was asked if people wanted Labour to govern 'along existing lines, only more efficiently, or to introduce sweeping changes'. 56 per cent made the second assumption. A Labour government was voted in with the hope of a new Jerusalem. The wonder is that it changed so little for so long.

In the six years of war, millions of British men left home for the first time in their lives, and had their eyes opened by experience and education, millions of women went to work, millions of both sexes occupied the magic heartland of the movies, and were seduced by the vision of the Promised Land. Hundreds of thousands of American soldiers grafted their world on to Britain – their own newspapers, magazines, films, music, even their radio station: 'They so often seemed to treat Britain as an occupied country rather than as an ally,' said a contemporary US journalist. They were better paid than the British, better fed, better dressed, and however vainly the old guard may have hoped to export cricket and soccer to the US, the traffic was all one-way – the waltz gave way to the foxtrot, Pinewood to Hollywood, and the received pronunciation of the BBC graduated to the Mid-Atlantic.

The American presence – and the 'special relationship' – started to saturate British life politically, economically and culturally, invoking unease about our lack of democracy, unsatisfied desire for consumer goods, and restlessness and insecurity about our own culture. We became willingly, enthusiastically, and comprehensively colonised. 'The immense popularity of American movies abroad demonstrates that Europe is the unfinished negative of which America is the proof,' said the novelist Mary McCarthy. Generation after generation has lost its soul to American films, novels, comics, rock and roll, or TV, from **I Love Lucy** and **Bilko**, to **Friends** and **ER**.

Now when you walk down a street, you pass a McDonald's, a Burger King, a Nachos, a Baskin-Robbins, a Kentucky Fried Chicken, a Planet Hollywood, Tower Records, Warner Cinemas, jeans, T-shirts, baseball caps, loafers, hightop sneakers that proclaim Gap, Nike, Coke, Levi's, Calvin Klein, Ralph Lauren, Donna Karan, Tommy Hilfiger. You choose between a Bud and a Beck's in a pub called the Sunset Strip where you watch a Superbowl game on the TV, agree a ballpark figure for your deal, take a rain check on a movie, slap high-fives, and find yourself in the centre of any large city in Britain – the unofficial 51st state of the Union.

What's a 'ballpark' or 'first base' or a 'rain check' to you? They're terms taken from baseball – a game not even played by amateurs in this country. When did we start to say 'No way' and 'at this time' and 'business-wise', or speak of 'hackers' or 'hookers' or 'dissing' or 'date rape'? We assimilate words without any consciousness of their derivation as we did in the days of Imperial India, when we absorbed 'juggernaut', 'chicanery', 'curry', 'ginger', 'sugar', 'toddy', 'pyjamas', 'pundit', 'nirvana' into our language. This hybrid English (known as Hobson-Jobson) was a lingua franca between the colonised and colonisers; this time, with Coca-Colanisation, the polarity has been reversed.

We can draw a map of Manhattan easier than a map of Manchester. We know more about bars in Boston, police procedure in Los Angeles, medical practice in Chicago, cattle ranching in Texas, than about trawling in Grimsby. We feel inadequate or embarrassed about the greenness of our countryside, the shape of our policemen's helmets, the modesty of our sandwiches, the size of our cars and our buildings. 'We were Britain's colony once, she will be our colony before she is done,' said a prescient US newspaper in 1921.

For the British cinema – more than half in love with American money and American movies – the 'special relationship' became an uncomfortable bear-hug, a struggle in a mortal embrace to find an authentic British identity. In the British theatre, however – and for British pop music – the 'special relationship' has been a benign and fruitful one: both parties have prospered opportunistically, more a commerce of cultures than a conquest.

The British theatre of the 1930s, '40 and early '50s – whatever the charms, skills and sunbursts of dissent – was drained of vigour, etiolated, bound up by class, public puritanism, hypocrisy, self-censorship and state censorship. The injection of the plays of Arthur Miller and Tennessee Williams and of American musicals into the repertoire of the British theatre emancipated it: the ailing patient sat up and walked.

In 1950, at a time when British theatre was toying with a poetic drama, there was real poetry on the American stage or, to be exact, the poetry of reality: plays about life lived on the streets of Brooklyn and New Orleans by working-class people floundering on the edges of gentility, and resonating with metaphors of the American Dream and the American Nightmare – aspiration and desperation.

Death of a Salesman in 1949 and **A Streetcar Named Desire** in 1947 were not freak products engineered by gifted writers out of nowhere. They emerged from soil that had been tilled for two generations by commercial producers and by philanthropists and – for a short time – state subsidy, from organisations like the Provincetown Playhouse, the Mercury Theatre and the Group Theatre, and from a succession of writers, directors and actors who not only believed in the power and importance of the theatre but that, above all, it should engage with real life.

And Broadway, far from being oppressively risky for producers of plays and prohibitively expensive for their audiences, was – in Arthur Miller's eyes – a benign and supportive world:

> The only theatre available to a playwright in the later '40s was Broadway. That theatre had one single audience – catering to very different levels of age, culture, education and intellectual sophistication. One result of this mix was the ideal, if not frequent fulfilment, of a kind of play that would be complete rather than fragmentary, an emotional rather than an intellectual experience. A play basically of heart with its ulterior moral gesture integrated with action rather than rhetoric. In fact it was a Shakespearian ideal, a theatre for anyone with an understanding of English and perhaps some common sense.

The same criteria underwrote the musicals of the time, musicals of real intelligence, wit, allure and imagination – **West Side Story, Gypsy, Guys and Dolls**, and **Carousel** – which entertained without patronising the audience – giving the best *to* them, believing the best *of* them.

This was indeed a golden age, but sadly within fifteen years – by the mid-1960s – it had dissolved in the face of rising costs and box-office tyranny, while the British theatre, inspired by American example and fuelled by state subsidy, grew from strength to strength.

2

Broadway became 'The Great White Way' when it was illuminated by electric light in the last decade of the nineteenth century. It stretched over nearly twenty blocks and included a rash of new hotels and a string of fifty-odd theatres. In the 1900–1901 season there were seventy plays or musicals being produced on Broadway. In the decades that followed that number quadrupled. In addition, there were seven vaudeville houses and six burlesque theatres presenting their shows to a population of just over three-and-a-half million inhabitants. The American theatre of the first twenty years of the century was not entirely devoid of any play of any content but you had to hunt hard to find a play that was more than anodyne family entertainment. *Plus ça change …*

In those New York theatres you could have seen several of George M. Cohan's well-machined mixtures of cockiness, aggressive optimism, patriotism and sentimentality, like **Little Johnny Jones** (which featured the song 'I'm a Yankee Doodle Dandy') or **George Washington Jr.** (hit song: 'You're a Grand Old Flag'). Or musical comedies with books by P.G. Wodehouse and music by Jerome Kern. You could have seen vaudeville – the altogether more robust American translation of British music-hall; or burlesque, which offered a display of brilliant costumes, or rather an absence of them, and 'a parade of indecency artistically placed upon the stage, with garish lights to quicken the senses and inflame the passions' as one incandescent observer noted; or you could have watched the sumptuous – and exquisitely designed – shows produced by Florenz Ziegfeld, who discovered the showbusiness Theory of Relativity: sex + money + elegance = success. The erotic chic of the Ziegfeld girls set a precedent and a benchmark for a century of sexual display.

The plays you could have seen differed little from what you could have seen at the same time in the West End of London: social comedies, trite melodramas, the premières (*before* their London openings) of Somerset Maugham's **Our Betters**, and of J.M. Barrie's **The Little Minister** – not to mention his **Peter Pan**, and **What Every Woman Knows**.

At the same time the prolific American playwright David Belasco (1853–1931) offered a beguiling combination of theatricality and realism. Known as the 'Bishop of Broadway' for his clerical clothes and episcopal dictates, and possibly also his celebrated lecherousness, he lived in offices over his theatre, furnished with a canopied Gothic bed. For many years he dominated the Broadway stage as playwright, actor, director and theatre owner. His plays (mostly written in collaboration) were commonplace, melodramatic and maudlin, and if Puccini hadn't put music to two of the best of them – the spirited **The Girl of the Golden West** and the less spirited **Madame Butterfly**, his name would still be celebrated only on the marquee of his theatre on 44th Street, even if his Civil War play, **The Heart of Maryland**, complete with smoke-blown battlefield and romance, was revived every year for twenty years after its première in 1895.

The son of Londoners who had come to California in the Gold Rush, Belasco grew up in San Francisco and graduated from a call boy to a child actor. He became what he described as a 'theatrical vagabond', performing poetry, singing, dancing, and acting in the mining camps and frontier towns of the Far West. He started writing plays in New York with his friend Henry de Mille, whose son Cecil later became a byword for

Hollywood extravagance, sententiousness and vulgarity, while his granddaughter, Agnes, brought spirited good taste to the choreography of musicals.

Belasco was a combination of the opportunistic showman and the artistic adventurer. He brought to the theatre a passionate literalism and love of spectacle that in some way prefigured the films that his friend's son was to make. Here is Belasco in **The Girl of the Golden West**, whipping up a storm for a love scene, like the director of **Titanic**:

> FANS r. and l. SNOW effect over door, canvas and silk machines r. and l. A loud SHRIEK on the air tank … windows open and close; now appliances over windows work; inside and outside doors open and close as though blown by the wind; curtains on canopy over bed are first blown in by attachment through trick stand and then blown out by fan in rear; small basket on wardrobe is knocked off; pot with flower is knocked from stand, blankets in loft shake but not too violently …

And the heroine gets to receive her first kiss.

Belasco believed in the *theatrical*, exploiting the power of the medium to its full, creating sunsets that supposedly rivalled nature's or providing real settings for naturalistic

*Belasco's **Girl of the Golden West**.*

plays – even going so far on one occasion as to buy a room and its contents and transfer it to the stage, complete with rundown furniture and peeling wallpaper, anticipating the hyper-realism of contemporary gallery installations. He was the father of modern theatre lighting and obsessed with technological innovation, but paradoxically he paid an unfashionable degree of attention to realism and detail in acting, a 'Method' devotee before his time. For this *hommage* to Stanislavsy, he was made an honorary member of the Moscow Art Theatre in 1923.

Belasco had long fallen out of fashion by the time he was lauded in Moscow, but he left two enduring legacies: he was the prototype for the American producer/director tyro celebrated in countless plays and films from **20th Century** and **42nd Street** to **The Producers**, and his commitment to the appearance if not the substance of reality paved the way for the coming of a generation of writers and directors who regarded the theatre as a legitimate way of examining the exterior and interior reality of the world about them.

Walt Whitman wrote this in 1871:

> Of what is called the drama or dramatic presentation in the United States, as now put forth in the theatres, I should say it deserves to be treated with the same gravity, and on a par with the questions of ornamental confectionery at public dinners, or the arrangement of curtains and hangings in a ballroom – not more, nor less.

The first person to agree with Whitman would have been Shaw, but it was far from being the whole truth – given that Shaw's first popular success **The Devil's Disciple** opened in New York two years before London, and Ibsen's **Ghosts** had been hailed as a 'great theatrical event' by the American novelist William Dean Howells in New York in 1894.

In any case precisely the same indictment of triviality could have been made of the London theatre, and would have stood unchallenged for many years. It was only the influence of Europe in America (as in Britain) that started to expose Whitman's picture as caricature.

At the turn of the century the Statue of Liberty was only fourteen years old, there were few skyscrapers and no subway. The city of New York was a new city, a city in ferment: new buildings, new immigrants, new cultures.

Nearly 20 million immigrants arrived in the United States from 1900 to 1920. Those who travelled first or second class – only in America? – were given permission to land after a medical inspection on board the ships in which they had arrived. The poor – the steerage class – were ferried to Ellis Island, where they waited in long lines, weighed down with their baggage, before their medical and intelligence tests. 'How much is two and one? How much is two and two? How do you wash stairs: from the top or from the bottom?' 'I don't go to America to wash stairs,' said a Polish immigrant girl who spoke for millions.

In 1900 the culture was essentially Anglo-Saxon but it was beginning to acquire a different complexion: a little bit Irish, Jewish, German, Greek, Russian, Estonian, Hungarian, Romanian, Italian – and a lot American. They all started to mark out their cultural territory and exert their influence, but few of these immigrants arrived with a developed sense of what theatre was and of those that did by far the most significant were the Jewish ones.

There's a theory that argues that immigrants will settle within walking distance with two suitcases from their point of arrival – hence the demography of London: Irish in the Paddington area (trains from Fishguard and Holyhead), Afro-Caribbeans in South London (ship to Southampton, train to Waterloo), Scots in the King's Cross area, Indians in West London (Heathrow Airport). Between 1881 and 1903, in response to pogroms in East Europe, over a million Yiddish-speaking Jews arrived in the United States, and most of them settled where they landed – New York – within walking distance of the docks. The Lower East Side became the centre for the Jewish community, and the Yiddish theatre blazed there as a beacon of shared language and common identity.

Yiddish theatre had begun to develop in the 1830s beyond the folk drama that had existed since the seventeenth century. The traditional 'Purim' play had strong similarities with the medieval Christian morality plays: tales from the Old Testament interspersed with occasional secular stories, performed by amateur actors, clowns and acrobats. These plays were written in brisk jingling verse with rough rhymes, spoken scenes interrupted by songs. With time the songs and the music became fully integrated with the speech, and the shows invariably ended with a climactic song-and-dance number – becoming a sort of *ur*-musical. Even if moral instruction lurked beneath the surface, above all these were *shows*.

A Yiddish theatre production.

139

The popularity of the Yiddish theatre in New York became proverbial; it was said that they ate their '*brogt mit theater*' – their bread buttered with theatre. Actors became celebrities and the theatres became rowdy meeting-places. The theatres competed with each other for stars, spectacular scenery and costumes, in escapist fantasies blended with practical instruction for the new settlers. A voracious appetite for new material developed and shows were cobbled together by giving a Yiddish gloss to a collation of Jewish and non-Jewish texts – a process, recognisable to many who have worked in the musical theatre, known in the Yiddish theatre as 'baking'.

This popular entertainment was known as '*shund*', which became a term of abuse when a more ambitious form of Yiddish theatre developed. *Shund* – that uniquely Jewish concoction of song, dance and spectacle, became assimilated into the mainstream of the American musical theatre and, in many respects, became its principal model. In the non-musical theatre a new generation of Jewish playwrights – those perhaps who spoke disparagingly of *shund* for its relentless escapism – began to deal with subjects like loss of faith, assimilation and the pogroms, developing stories out of intrinsically Jewish situations, and, in parallel with the theatre in Europe, experimenting with a wide range of styles. A Jewish theatre developed which moved away from the popular musical style of the *shund* toward serious drama with high moral purpose, reaching its apotheosis in the work of Arthur Miller.

Little of what we now think of as *American* culture would exist without Jewish immigration from Europe, but the other mass immigration, or deportation, from Africa had an equal if not greater impact. Without the transfusion of African music into Scottish and Irish folk music, popular music and the Broadway musical would have taken a different rhythmic and harmonic course, and jazz – that uniquely American music – would not have been invented.

The black population of the US was enslaved until the Civil War in 1861. As if the indignity of slavery was not enough, the newly emancipated blacks endured parody and pillory for the entertainment of the white population – North and South – in Minstrel Shows which played the length and breadth of America for about fifty years after Abolition. The shows were performed by whites in black make-up: a combination of singing, dancing, bright costumes, comedy sketches and instrumental numbers featuring the banjo, all based on the premise that the black people were energetic, tuneful, vigorous, happy, rhythmic, innocent fools.

Minstrel shows were divided into three 'acts' or 'sets' (from which the jazz expression comes). In the first set – the 'line' – the minstrels sat in a line across the stage, a straight man in the centre with the comics at either end; the second – the 'olio' – was straight variety – performing dogs, solo songs, acrobats, conjurors and dancers, and in the third – the 'after-piece' – comic sketches which might feature stereotypes like Jim Crow, the lazy plantation worker, and Zip Coon, the dandy from the city, who would shuffle and croon in their dialect, using black work songs and spirituals and, when those were exhausted, songs from cattlemen, loggers and wagon drivers.

Gradually black performers – and composers – started to be absorbed within the white ascendancy. It became possible to see black people in what were known as 'ethnic' theatres perform in 'blackface' for their white audiences, who were willing to accept black performers as long as they conspired in their own self-abasement.

However, promoters started to see there was a market for black performers in black shows and by the turn of the century two black dancers – William Walker and Bert Williams – were heading the bill in **Clorindy, or the Origin of the Cakewalk**. The Cakewalk was a dance invented by the pair, and it became a nationwide sensation and was then introduced to Europe, translated by the white couple Vernon and Irene Castle. The syncopated music laid the trail for the conquest of popular music by ragtime and blues and for the birth of jazz.

By 1914 Irving Berlin had incorporated these rhythms into a popular Broadway musical **Watch Your Step**, and the Minstrel Shows had mutated into vaudeville. Black music, dance, and song started to percolate through American music-making, but the tradition of the Minstrel Shows took a long time dying. The first film with sound, made in 1927, was **The Jazz Singer**: it featured a blacked-up white man – a Jewish Lithuanian called Al Jolson – singing about his mother. As Jolson used to say, 'You ain't seen nothin' yet!' and indeed it was many, many years before 'blackface' Minstrel Shows died out entirely. In Britain a primetime television show – **The Black and White Minstrel Show** – continued to be broadcast by BBC TV until 1964.

The dramatic representation of the black world took a much longer time to be included within the theatre repertoire – at least on Broadway. The sensation of the 1850s, however, was a powerful, if melodramatic tale of the sufferings caused by slavery: **Uncle Tom's Cabin**. The novel was published in 1852 and sold 300,000 copies. Later that year, the first stage adaptation appeared – with a new happy ending. In the South it was taken as an insult that would 'poison the minds of our youth with the pestilential principles of abolition', but by 1879 at least fifty productions were on the road – many in the South – playing in tents, riverboats, town halls, churches, opera houses or wherever a platform would hold them, and by 1890 there were at least 500 'Tom Shows'. Some of the companies were beneath the tolerance even of small towns: 'The cast gave the bloodhounds poor support,' said a paper in the Far West.

The stage version of the novel helped solidify Northern sentiment against slavery. It was, as the critic John Mason Brown, said, 'the greatest grease-paint curiosity of all time'. It was a peculiarly American phenomenon – a popular moral fable about the most significant fault line in American society: racism.

In 1915 D.W. Griffith's film **The Birth of a Nation** opened and demonstrated two things: that racism was deeply embedded in the American consciousness, and that it was foolish for the theatre to compete with the realism of film. While the American theatre had not been entirely insulated from the change in Europe, realism was still the orthodox aesthetic.

A new view of theatre started to filter into American consciousness through news of the European 'art' theatre, as well as from immigration and visits from foreign companies. The Abbey Theatre from Dublin visited New York in 1911, Max Reinhardt brought his spectacular production of the wordless play **Sumurun** (derived from 'The Arabian Nights') to Broadway in 1912, in 1915 Granville-Barker produced a double bill of Shaw's **Androcles and the Lion** and Anatole Franc's **The Man Who Married a Dumb Wife ...**, and in 1917 the light-footed elegance of the staging of Jacques Copeau's Vieux Colombier company gave strength to the ideas of young American designers.

New York's Greenwich Village became an American Left Bank, a breeding and stamping ground for radicals in the arts and in politics. Two new theatre groups were associated with this brave new world: the Washington Square Players and the Provincetown Players. They produced plays by Maeterlinck, Ibsen, Shaw, Wedekind, Chekhov and Strindberg, as well as new American plays, in a style that became known as the 'New Stagecraft': simple, suggestive scenery, influenced by Gordon Craig, using lighting to enhance mood rather than to rival nature or the movies.

Universities began to offer courses in play-writing, of which the best known is George Pierce Baker's, begun at Harvard in 1913. He intended to make his students feel that it was possible to write plays of imagination, originality and integrity in America. He succeeded: his most successful student was the son of an Irish-American actor, Eugene O'Neill.

3

This is Arthur Miller on O'Neill, speaking for every theatre-goer who's ever watched an O'Neill play, and every actor or director who's staged one:

> The repetitions in his plays are enough to drive you out of your mind. And, then, gradually, that drumming begins to take over. And you are swept away ... Finally, what comes out of it is the image of a writer who simply will not be stopped – he's going to do it his way, and that's the way it's going to get done. Whereas the theatre as a whole is such a compromising place.

Before Laurence Olivier performed in **Long Day's Journey into Night**, he pronounced the play 'supremely boring', but the play defied his own preconceptions and the audience's expectations, and the production was one of the triumphs of his regime at the National Theatre. In recent years productions in London of **The Iceman Cometh** (with Kevin Spacey), **A Touch of the Poet** (with Vanessa Redgrave), **Anna Christie** (with Natasha Richardson), **Desire Under the Elms**, and **The Hairy Ape** have confirmed O'Neill as an indelible part of the British theatre landscape – a craggy, daunting, often beautiful, but impermeable, rock formation, which always takes the traveller by surprise.

The theatre critic John Lahr – son, incidentally, of a famous vaudeville performer (and actor), Bert Lahr – wrote memorably about Eugene O'Neill:

> O'Neill bushwacked his way through the morass of old showbiz assumptions. He was the first to stage the life and the idiom of the American lower classes; the first to put a black man on-stage as a figure of complexity and substance; the first to adapt the innovations of European drama to America; the first to challenge the soullessness of the century's materialism; and the first American playwright to insist on working as an artist.

O'Neill (1888–1953) grew up as the country grew up. In 1915 the economy was strong, but the view of America as the cradle of opportunity – the Land of the Free and the Home of the Brave – was starting to look a little tarnished. Those who believed in the pastoral innocence of the small towns and wide-open spaces were having to admit the reality of big-city industrialisation and widespread disillusion. The creed of the American Dream and the triumph of the individual will was still broadcast with evangelical fervour, but it was impossible to ignore the polarities of rich and poor and black and white – or the war that was starting to engulf the whole of Europe. Restless self-doubt entered the American soul and Eugene O'Neill became the poet of that self-doubt.

Eugene O'Neill.

The story of O'Neill's beginnings as a playwright has the satisfying neatness of an American folk-tale – rags to riches, unperformed playwright to Nobel-prize winner. In the summer of 1915 a small group of writers and artists gathered on Cape Cod in Massachusetts to enjoy their summer holiday and to write plays. The group was led by George Cram Cook and his wife, Susan Glaspell, both of whom had been active in the Washington Square Players in New York. Cook was a revolutionary – he wanted to create modern American theatre by emancipating it from financial constraints.

They transformed a small old fish-shed on a pier into a theatre to present their plays.

143

The Wharf Theatre had a capacity of ninety, a little smaller than the theatre in Bergen in Norway where Ibsen had his first plays performed. Robert Edmond Jones – who had worked with Granville-Barker during his visit to New York the previous year – designed the productions.

The following year, Susan Glaspell asked a friend of hers called Terry Carlin if he had a play for the group to read. Carlin could not supply a play for the group, but had a friend who could – the twenty-eight-year-old Eugene O'Neill. The group read **Bound East for Cardiff** and much admired it. It was a one-act play about a dying sailor and his almost inarticulately grief-torn companions set in the thin light of the forecastle of a ship.

O'Neill had lived a life enough for two by that time, and the experience of that life less ordinary served as the raw material for his plays for the rest of his life.

He was the youngest of three: Jamie was ten years older, and Edmund died of measles as a child. O'Neill felt himself to be cursed from the womb: his mother was reluctant to have another child, was given morphine to alleviate the pain of the birth and she became an addict for life. With his guilt at his own existence, and his sense of rootlessness engendered by spending his childhood in hotel rooms and theatre dressing-rooms while his father toured, O'Neill was seasoned in self-destruction.

As an adolescent he scorned his parents' Catholicism, began to drink and visit brothels, went to Princeton University for a year, worked for a short time in a New York office, and started to write poetry. He got a girl pregnant and fled, joining a gold-mining expedition to Honduras – even if he did marry the girl shortly before his departure. He contracted malaria after a few months in Central America, returned to the US and, after checking tickets and stage-managing on tour for his father's company and avoiding his new wife and son (whom he only met when the boy was twelve years old), he boarded the *Charles Racine*, a Norwegian windjammer, as a working passenger on its two-month voyage to Buenos Aires.

After staying in Argentina for several months, he sailed back to New York, divorced his wife and stayed at a bar called Jimmy-the-Priest's: 'One couldn't go any lower. Gorky's Night Lodging was an ice-cream parlour by comparison.' It was to become the setting for **The Iceman Cometh**. He attempted suicide, worked as a reporter for the *Telegraph*, continued to write poetry, developed a mild case of tuberculosis, went to a sanatorium, where he stayed for six months and began to write one-act plays inspired by his life as a sailor.

When he joined George Pierce Baker's play-writing course at Harvard, he wrote to his teacher, 'With my present training, I might hope to become a mediocre journeyman playwright. It is just because I do not wish to be one, because I want to be an artist or nothing, that I am writing to you.' After a year at Harvard, he returned to New York, where he went from the salons of Greenwich Village to its saloons – straying from the debating of the intelligentsia to the drunken philosophising of the Golden Swan Saloon – better known as the 'Hell Hole'. He found himself with a pile of his manuscripts in

*O'Neill helps build the set for **Bound East for Cardiff**.*

Cape Cod in the spring of 1916. **Bound East for Cardiff** was performed in the fish-shed on a foggy night in late April, and in its cast was the author.

Once the summer was over, the group returned to New York, and the Cooks founded a theatre in a converted stable in Greenwich Village. They called themselves the Provincetown Players and the theatre became known as the Provincetown Playhouse. On 28 July 1916 the Provincetown Players produced **Bound East for Cardiff**.

Like all significant theatre companies the life of the Provincetown Players was a shortish one – about eight years. In O'Neill's years with the Provincetown Players the direction of American theatre changed utterly. Within four years O'Neill had a successful play – **Beyond the Horizon** – on Broadway. It became apparent to Broadway producers that plays with ambitions to be something more than merely entertaining were not necessarily anathema to the paying public: art and commerce could be combined. Modern American drama was created when a playwright of genius displayed a popular touch combined with an obdurate determination to speak in his own voice.

No great playwright can be imitated, and no great playwright ever achieved greatness by a study of the 'well-made' play. Indeed, throughout his life O'Neill defied the notion of neatness. He wrote, as he lived, incontinently, never using one word where six would do. His plays are often clumsily constructed and woodenly written; they are not witty; there are no quotable epigrams, there are no wise saws; melodrama often engulfs the action,

Kevin Spacey in the Almeida revival of **The Iceman Cometh**.

and gloom spreads over the stage like a sea mist; the audience is not tickled or teased or stroked. 'What are you trying to do,' said O'Neill's father after seeing **Beyond the Horizon**, 'send them home to commit suicide?'

And yet his plays invariably exert a hypnotic power. He opens his heart to the audience without reserve. 'I am interested only in the relation between man and God,' said O'Neill, and from his own life he excavated the pain and overwhelming loneliness of living in the first century of which it could be truthfully said that God is dead. You don't emerge from an O'Neill play feeling reassured or calmed, having your fears assuaged or your doubts smoothed. Life is a form of death, you feel, a lingering descent to the grave: 'a bad dream between two awakenings, and every day is a life in miniature', says a character in his historical play **Marco Millions**.

One ought to feel depressed by O'Neill's plays but in spite of the nihilism and the morbidity, you don't feel – even saturated with the alcoholic fumes and hopelessness of **The Iceman Cometh** – that humanity is despicable. You concede pity and even reluctant admiration for people that, as Tennessee Williams said, endure by enduring.

The country that proclaimed the paramount power of the individual and offered every individual the dream of self-betterment and self-fulfilment found in O'Neill a playwright who said in his plays: yes I am an individual and I stand alone, but life is *not* to be lived, there is no hope, and all your dreams are nightmares. It is hard to imagine a philosophy that is more alien to the ethos that underwrites the American way of life, but perhaps that is precisely the reason why O'Neill held – and continues to hold – such a grip on the imagination of American audiences.

In the 1930s and '40s they were being confronted in O'Neill's plays not by a system of beliefs or a social spectrum but by the bare-forked thing itself – the unembellished individual. In this respect O'Neill is quintessentially American – the man who stands alone. O'Neill confronts the audience with their worst fears, and like rabbits caught in the glare of headlights, they stare mesmerised: like the German soldier in the Wilfred Owen poem, O'Neill is the enemy they killed.

Couple to this O'Neill's lack of irony, unforgivable in an English playwright, his frequent portentousness, his demotic instincts, his respect for the 'common man', his unambiguous sincerity, his blazing idealism – about his art if not about humanity – and you go some way to understanding his hold on the American theatre of the 1920s and '30s.

He was not a moralist or a polemicist, but a maker of fables. You meet O'Neill's characters, you listen to their stories, you watch their destruction. You say they are frustrated and disillusioned, collapsing, cracking up, but you know that you are talking of the author, and you acknowledge his subject: himself. 'One goes expecting a playwright,' said Kenneth Tynan, 'and one meets a man.'

O'Neill colonised new continents of meaning and subject matter but as importantly explored novel ways of using the medium he'd chosen. There are few playwrights – outside Shakespeare and Brecht – who have been so relentlessly enquiring about form.

Eugene O'Neill was the son of a capable actor who squandered his talent on endless money-making tours of **The Count of Monte Cristo**, playing the protagonist Edmund Dantés at least 4,000 times. The son had the opportunity to spend a great deal of his childhood, adolescence and early adulthood observing the theatre at its most mechanical and least alluring. He saw and heard theatre from under the stage, from the wings, the flies, the prompt corner, the dressing-room, the green room, the box-office, the stalls, the gallery, the stage door and the bar next door to it.

He saw the power of theatre, but also its tired conventions, its cynical manipulation of the audience, and its craven desire to please at all costs. And he thought, it doesn't *have* to be like that, plays are only neatly constructed because of timidity, because their authors want to seduce the audience before wanting to make them feel and think. They are drawing on conventions of speech and characterisation that iron out or paper over the rough bluntness and corrugations of humanity.

Beyond the Horizon, his first full-length play, was about two brothers on a farm; one wants to go to sea 'beyond the horizon', the other wants to stay on the farm. They fall for the same girl and the brother who wanted to farm goes to sea, leaving the girl to marry his brother and together run the farm. He returns to find his parents dead, the child dead, the farm in ruin, the marriage gone stale, and his brother dying of TB, but still looking beyond the horizon to a dream that they'll all find happiness together.

The play – even by the standards of O'Neill – is overwritten and febrile, as if it was written in a state too turbulent to be curbed. To the audience of 1920 it was shocking and sensational, but 'as honest and sincere as it is artistic'. For the first time there was a successful play on Broadway of real power which dealt with the dreams and disappointments of real people, which made the inner pain of the characters transparent and sought above all to make the audience *feel*.

Like Lear, O'Neill was out there on the heath, unprotected, at war with the elements – 'the sulphurous and thought-executing fires' and 'oak-cleaving thunderbolts'. O'Neill wanted the audience to feel that all our lives are a struggle against forces that we can never control: our parents, the past, the land and the sea, and the wild commotion of our feelings for each other.

The subject of most Broadway shows – in some shape or form – was romantic love. This was treated in the conventions of the time as a game of bantering compliment and flattery, a coy tease. In **Anna Christie**, **Desire Under the Elms**, and the little-known study of Puritan conscience **Diff'rent**, O'Neill wrote about fate and free will, but the motor of the plays is sex: the cancerous power of lust.

Sex and swearing, prostitution, infanticide, incest, and drink 'distressed' the audience, as the *New York Herald-Tribune* said, but they found the power and blazing *sincerity* of the plays irresistible. O'Neill added to the 'distress' in **All God's Chillun Got Wings** by dealing with racial prejudice, and in **The Emperor Jones** by portraying the mental breakdown of a black man. Here was a play that for the first time presented a black actor at the centre of a play which confronted the audience with African-American history – the slave ships, the slave markets, the prison gangs, the demeaning jobs and constant humiliations – not as polemic or documentary but as psychological drama.

Like all O'Neill's plays it has visceral power, it is felt as a brutal attack on the nerves, an appeal to the senses beyond and below rational thought. And like almost all his plays there is a sense of let-down at the end. It is as if the playwright is doggedly determined not to allow the audience the grace of exaltation or redemption. He is determined to show that plays, like life, should end not with a bang but a whimper.

O'Neill wrote play after play with a feverish prodigality until he had a breakdown in 1934, each one of the plays offering a different approach to theatre: **Anna Christie** demanded naturalistic presentation, but a poetic distillation of reality, rather than the literalness of a Belasco; **The Emperor Jones** introduced expressionism to America, a kaleidoscopic profusion of theatrical devices – staging, lighting, sound, music – to suggest the protagonist's terror and hallucinations; and in **The Great God Brown** O'Neill tested the audience by mixing masks with realistic characterisation, contrasting the inner and the outer realities. Who can find himself beneath the mask?

In **Strange Interlude**, a novel-like portrait of America over twenty-five years, O'Neill attempted an 'exercise in unmaking' without the literal use of masks. The spoken dialogue was a mask for the characters' true feelings, which were spoken in asides. The audience was presented with what the actor was *saying* and what he was *thinking*. The staging of this device proved an intractable problem until the director decided to freeze the action while the thoughts were spoken.

The success of **Strange Interlude** is a salutary reminder of the fickleness of fashion in the theatre. The play won O'Neill his third Pulitzer Prize and enjoyed the longest run of any of his plays before the posthumous revival of **The Iceman Cometh** in 1956. It was the most celebrated play of the 1920s but when it was revived in 1963 in New York by the Actors' Studio it was reviled: 'probably the worst play ever written by a major dramatist,' said a critic.

If **Strange Interlude** intended to tear the mask from the social face of America, **The Hairy Ape** – in spite of O'Neill's perennial obsession with man's struggle with his own fate – intended to reveal the face under the grime of the exploited stoker, and the face under the make-up of the woman who thrives on his labour and is drawn to his plight, until she confronts 'the hairy ape'. A glance at the list of scenes of the play gives a sense of O'Neill's fearless theatrical ambition:

SCENE I:	*The fireman's forecastle of an ocean liner.*
SCENE II:	*Section of the promenade deck.*
SCENE III:	*The stokehole.*
SCENE IV:	*The fireman's forecastle.*
SCENE V:	*Fifth Avenue, New York.*
SCENE VI:	*An island near the city.*
SCENE VII:	*In the city.*
SCENE VIII:	*In the city.*

O'Neill taxed his collaborators as much as his audiences. The demands he made on his directors and designers and actors were unforgiving, and like all O'Neill's life and work, a legacy of the past. Of his father he said at the end of his life: 'He became a third-rate actor … he ended up in tragedy, embittered, with his life wasted and ruined. The pity of it was, he had a fine brain. I loved him …' O'Neill's contempt for his father's art shows in his mistrust of the actors in his plays, revealed in his oppressively prescriptive stage directions:

He is a short, squat, broad-shouldered man of about fifty, with a round weather-beaten red face from which light-blue eyes peer short-sightedly, twinkling with a simple good humour. His large mouth, overhung by a thick drooping yellow moustache is childishly self-willed and weak, of an obstinate kindliness. A thick neck is jammed like a post into the heavy trunk of his body. His arms with their big hairy freckled hands …'

And more, and more, instructions – or commands – for actors and directors. O'Neill had watched the lazy corner-cutting and lack of artistic ambition of his father and his fellows, and determined that no unthinking theatrical convention or tradition could go unchallenged, that no subject was too difficult to be treated, and that *nothing* was too ambitious to be staged. And if a subject deserved to be treated at length, then the actors must submit – five and a half hours for **Mourning Becomes Electra**, his modern gloss of Aeschylus's Oresteia, five hours for **Strange Interlude**, four hours and more for **The Iceman Cometh**.

No one can see **The Iceman Cometh** and pretend that the time passes entirely without boredom. As Kenneth Tynan said, 'He would be the king of snobs indeed who failed to admit to a *mauvais quart d'heure* about halfway through.' Dorothy Parker quipped after seeing it: 'It's longeth and it stinketh.' But the length of the play is part of the experience, its expanse is part of its architecture, a huge gloomy prison full of the fog of illusions. Real time passes: the audience and the characters are locked in the present tense in a bar – the end of the line, the last-chance saloon – in which all the characters are prisoners of the past, sustained by alcohol and dreams.

It's not hard to hear the voice of Beckett's tramps in the drunks' drollery of **The Iceman Cometh**. 'The iceman of the title is, of course, death,' said a friend of O'Neill's. 'Death cometh – that is, cometh to all living – and the old bawdy story … of the man who calls upstairs, "Has the iceman come yet?" and his wife calls back, "No, but he's breathin' hard."'

If O'Neill was unforgiving to his audiences and collaborators, he gave his family hell. By the end of his life, a sick old man, he railed against his sons – wastrels and reprobates, he said – and would support them no longer. One of his sons was arrested for heroin, the other slit his throat. It was if they were determined to prove his lifelong thesis: the terrible hold that the past has on the present.

The person to whom he forgave least was himself, and in **Long Day's Journey Into Night** he spared himself nothing. It was an excavation of his own life, his heart, his soul – call it what you like. It is the undiluted autobiographical truth. It may be a great play or it may be a rotten one: it honestly doesn't matter. Nor does it matter whether such-and-such a scene is well placed or well written: a playwright is stating the central agony of his life, and nothing intrudes between his vision and the way that it hits you.

He hoarded the play like a miser, clutching it to his chest for years. He forbade it to be published until twenty-five years after his death and it was never to be performed. His widow wisely disobeyed him.

Ronald Pickup and Laurence Olivier in the National Theatre revival of **Long Day's Journey Into Night**.

The play ends unforgettably. Three men – father and two sons – drunk, exhausted by the appalling truths that have passed between them, watch helplessly as the mother enters carrying her wedding dress. She's floating, remote. She remembers her days in the convent school, her hopes of becoming a nun:

> That was in the winter of the senior year. Then in the spring something happened to me. Yes, I remember. I fell in love with James Tyrone and was happy for a time.

It's the saddest play ever written.

4

It seems poetic justice that O'Neill – for whom dolefulness was a permanent condition – was the most celebrated American playwright of a period known as the Depression, which could be said, in economic terms, to bear out his dictum that the present is an inevitable consequence of the past.

After the First World War there was a huge expansion of prosperity. Wealth became more widely distributed to more people than had ever been possible before. Tens of millions of ordinary families became the owners of houses, cars, life insurance, even shares. The class barriers seemed to dissolve, anyone could become a millionaire. The American dream came of age.

Unrestrained growth also encouraged unrestrained speculation, and swollen by the bellows of an artificially inflated money supply and low interest rates, the New York stock market burst in October 1929. The value of thousands of stocks plummeted as panicked sellers dumped their stocks and by December shares had lost billions, and millions had lost their jobs, their homes, their savings and even their lives diving in despair from Wall Street skyscrapers. American business came to a virtual standstill.

It's easy to think of historical periods – the Dark Ages, the Thirty Years War – as if everyone was equally disabled by the oppressive climate of the time. However, neither the theatre – nor the movies – seemed to be debilitated by the the Depression. Indeed, the two best American comedies were produced within months of the Wall Street Crash – one before and one after, when, historians would say, the entire country was paralysed by the crisis.

The two plays exemplify the very best of American comic writing – a tradition that is still alive in the very best of American TV sitcoms – fast, sharp hard-bitten but not hard-hearted; in short, grown-up comedy. Both plays are satires: **The Front Page** by Ben Hecht (1894–1964) and Charles MacArthur (1895–1966) on the newspaper business; **Once in a Lifetime** by Moss Hart (1884–1961) and George Kaufman (1889–1961) on the Hollywood film industry in the early days of the talkies. Kaufman famously said that satire is what closes on Saturday night, and the 'satire' in these plays is more a matter of milieu than of indictment. It is essentially good-natured, always intended to stay this side of offence, to entertain rather than improve. Both plays had fast action, brilliantly crafted characters, and a cascade of wonderful one-liners, and both plays had the effect of flattering the objects of their derision. To this day journalists aspire to Hecht and MacArthur's models, and Kaufman and Hart's mockery of the movie world has been hugged to the heart of Hollywood.

For O'Neill the coming of economic catastrophe was predictably consistent with his determinism, which owed more to Freud than to Marx: the sins of the father – from the Founding Fathers to the present day – had been visited upon the soul of America. But however much O'Neill identified with the underdog and pitied the poor, he never embraced politics. Even when he anatomised the state of the soul of man under capitalism – as in

The Hairy Ape – he avoided polemic or political solutions. He was intensely private and his response to public events was to become more introspective and more concerned with myths of the past than with events of the present. He started to write a cycle of plays – which he never finished – dealing with the history from the revolutionary war to the Depression of an Irish-American family caught in an expanding vortex of materialism, possessiveness, social aspirations, racism and greed. Its title: **A Tale of Possessors Dispossessed.**

We are used to using the word 'Broadway' as a pejorative to describe a theatre entirely dominated by market forces and bland entertainment – a 'showshop' as O'Neill called it. It is bracing therefore to observe that, as well as the commercial success of O'Neill's plays (many of them played for over a year), which stubbornly failed to live down to the desire to please, there were other plays that reflected disquiet about the underside of the American Dream, even plays that reflected growing political radicalism. The most conspicuous and most successful of these was **Street Scene** by Elmer Rice (1892–1967). He struggled for over a year to find a producer who would present it or a director to stage it, then landed the young George Cukor, who walked out in the middle of casting leaving Rice to direct it himself. It opened early in 1929 and ran for two years.

Rice is a familiar phenomenon in the theatre; he was hugely celebrated in his day as bold, inventive, passionate, diverse and effective – many contemporary critics thought he knocked O'Neill into a cocked hat – now we peer down time's one-way telescope at a diminished figure, shrunk by fashion. His expressionistic play **The Adding Machine** blamed a rotten system for the dehumanisation of the 'white-collar slaves' – the office-workers – who had been stripped of their self-respect in the age of the machine. It presented people as robots, machines in the control of the faceless forces of industry and commerce.

His much more considerable **Street Scene** depicts twenty-four hours in the life of a New York street in front of a brownstone building at the height of a heatwave. The play has a vast cast, a cross-section of New York's melting-pot. It's a really muscular attempt to show the ruthlessness and dumb good-heartedness of life lived in the raw, infected by urban poverty. In 1947 Kurt Weill wrote music for the play: it became a kind of folk opera, a pre-echo of **West Side Story.**

To anyone who was connected with the British theatre in the 1970s the theatre of the 1930s off-Broadway and outside New York seems oddly familiar – politically active groups putting on plays with the intention of drawing in new audiences and exhorting them to overthrow the existing political system. In the underside of the rampant capitalism and individualism of America there has always been a seam of Utopian thinking, and in the shadow of the Depression left-wing theatre groups mushroomed across the country.

It was a short-lived phenomenon that largely dissolved in the face of Roosevelt's New Deal under which, in 1935, the Federal Theatre Project was set up by the Works Progress Administration to create jobs for unemployed theatre workers, and to provide 'free, adult, uncensored theatre' to audiences throughout the country. It was a glorious, noble idea and like all Utopian plans, something of a magnificent folly – like the vision of the eighteenth-century French social reformer, Charles Fournier, who imagined a Utopia in which the sea would lose its salt and taste like lemonade and the world would blossom with 37 million playwrights all as good as Molière.

10,000 people were employed at its peak in theatres in forty states, playing to millions of people – an estimated 12 million in New York alone. During its four years of existence, the project introduced audiences to a huge variety of theatre – classics, new plays, plays by black writers, plays based on the issues of the day written in teams (called Living Newspapers), children's plays, foreign-language productions, puppetry, religious plays, musicals and circus – all at low ticket prices; it nurtured a number of very talented actors, and it launched the careers of Orson Welles, John Huston and Arthur Miller.

Orson Welles (1915–1985) was twenty-two when he directed Marc Blitzstein's bosses v. workers opera **The Cradle Will Rock** for the Federal Theatre Project. After its short run ended he and his producer, a Romanian immigrant called John Housman, proclaimed their 'Plans for a New Theatre', to be called the Mercury Theatre: 'When it opens its doors ... the Mercury will expect to play to the same audiences that during the last two seasons stood to see **Doctor Faustus**, the Negro **Macbeth** and **Murder in the Cathedral** ... people on a voyage of discovery in the theatre ... who either had never been to the theatre at all or who, for one reason or another, had ignored it for many seasons.' There were to be cheap seats and productions rotating in repertoire.

The ambitious repertoire of 'great plays of the past produced in a modern way' – underwritten by private investment – was to include **Julius Ceasar, Heartbreak House, Danton's Death, The Duchess of Malfi**, William Gillette's nineteenth-century American farce **Too Much Johnson** and Ben Jonson's **The Silent Woman**.

Only the first three made it to the stage. Welles' modern-dress production of **Julius Caesar** presented a chillingly contemporary account of demagoguery, the mob and the assassination of a dictator, borrowing its look from the Nazi rallies at Nuremberg. It was a triumph and, much to the chagrin of the designers and actors, Welles claimed the success all for himself. Democracy was a fine principle but not where the Mercury Theatre was concerned. When the company made the radio broadcast of *The War of the Worlds* – a spoof news programme which reported the landing of alien forces from Mars and provoked widespread panic – the making of the legend of Orson Welles had begun.

Housman said later, 'The truth is ... the Mercury had fulfilled its purpose. It had brought us success and fame; it had put Welles on the cover of *Time* and our radio show on the front page of every newspaper in the country. Inevitably, any day now the offers

CAESAR RESEMBLES MUSSOLINI, GIVES THE FASCIST SALUTE

*Orson Welles'
production of
Julius Caesar.*

from Hollywood would start arriving. It was too late to turn back and we did not really want to.' Financial problems and Welles' growing lack of interest caused the Mercury Theatre to fold in 1938 and Welles and Housman decamped to Hollywood – taking some of their actors with them – to make the film which is invariably voted the 'number-one film of all time': *Citizen Kane*.

For the Federal Theatre Project 'uncensored' theatre proved to be a problem. It has never been easy for governments to license the jester as well as the judge and the Project's unbridled social criticism, viewed as politically dubious by Congressional conservatives, led to the disbanding of the Project in June 1939 and the death of the only serious attempt to try to introduce state-subsidised theatre into the USA. It was – as the director Harold Clurman said – 'the most truly experimental effort ever undertaken in the American theatre'. And in the Living Newspapers project it reminded the theatre that there is no more important experiment than to explore the events of the real world.

Harold Clurman was one of three directors – with Lee Strasberg and Cheryl Crawford – of the most important theatre company to be founded during the Depression: the Group Theatre. They were joined by twenty-eight actors who became a permanent company – a company that acted (and often lived) together for most of the decade.

A typical Group Theatre play was Sidney Kingsley's **Men in White**. Set in a big city hospital, it was a kaleidoscopic account – patients, nurses, doctors, boardroom, operating

155

theatre; it was atmospheric, warm-hearted, energetic, and in its busy mixture of hospital practice, love story and debate about medical ethics, it anticipated *ER* by about sixty years.

The Group was a romantic enterprise, based on two propositions: that art should reflect life, and that through art it is possible to make life better. Theatre had to provide for society what society failed to provide for itself. In his autobiography Arthur Miller said this of the Group:

> I had my brain branded by the beauty of the Group Theatre's productions. With my untamed tendency to idealise whatever challenged the system – including the conventions of the Broadway theatre – I can place each actor exactly where he was on the stage fifty years ago. This is less a feat of memory than a tribute to the capacity of these actors to concentrate, to *be* on the stage. When I recall them, time is stopped.

The Group set up projects to train their own members as community leaders and teachers, and in their programme for training actors lay the genesis of the Actors' Studio. With Stanislavsky's Moscow Art Theatre as the model, Lee Strasberg encouraged his actors to systematise their work, and the catechism of 'impro', 'emotional memory', 'private moments', and 'relaxation exercises' became built into the credo of generations of American actors, and generations of American actors became preoccupied with feeling rather than technique, more concerned with finding themselves than the character that the author had written. What could only have meaning as empirical practice became the 'Method'. To codify Stanislavsky's precepts as Strasberg did is to make the means the end. There are as many 'methods' of working as there are actors. As David Mamet has observed tartly: 'The "Method", and the schools derived from it, is nonsense. It is not a technique out of the practice of which he develops a skill – it is a cult.'

The Group never succeeded in obtaining sustained investment either in the shape of public subsidy or private endowment and eventually ground to a halt in 1941. 'The Group Theatre was a failure because, as no individual can exist alone, *no group can exist alone*,' said Harold Clurman.

During their ten-year span, the Group staged the premières of twenty-two new plays; they gave a first opportunity to many writers who subsequently had success on Broadway and in Hollywood; their play-writing competition unearthed the young Tennessee Williams; they created a recognisable acting style that was highly charged, introspective and real; they engendered a style of production in which the whole was greater than the sum of the parts; they enfranchised many gifted set and lighting designers; and in the plays written by one of their own actors – Clifford Odets – they gave a voice to the most celebrated and lavishly praised playwright of the decade.

Clifford Odets (1906–1963) was raised in the Bronx in New York, the son of European immigrants. His childhood was not as materially deprived as he later claimed, but he learned about poverty at first hand as a struggling actor and his three suicide attempts before he was twenty-five indicate a powerful deprivation of some sort. He found his solace working and living together with the Group – in the summers in the country, the rest of the time in the large communal apartment on West 57th Street in New York.

The Group was Odets' home and his university, where he learned about politics and theatre and developed the confidence to write. His first play – or his first produced play – was a one-act agit-prop 'poster play' in which a taxi union holds a meeting to decide whether to strike. It was called **Waiting for Lefty** – a title that alone would have earned him a place in front of the House Un-American Activities Committee twenty years later. It was first performed at a benefit performance of short plays for the League of Workers Theatres. Its scenery was borrowed chairs and tables; its budget was $10.

Waiting for Lefty didn't invite the audience to analyse, it asked them to feel. Don't wait for Lefty, Odets argued, act on your own: American self-help conscripted to the aid of radical political action. The audience merged with the actors planted among them, one of whom was the director, then an actor, Elia Kazan. 'Strike!' they yelled. 'Strike!' at one of those rare performances that merge fiction and reality, where art becomes politics – like the riotous first performance of Stravinsky's *The Rite of Spring* in Paris in 1913

Waiting for Lefty became the play of the day, and Odets the man of the moment. Within weeks theatre groups throughout the country wanted to perform it and censors tried to prevent its production on grounds of subversion, obscenity and blasphemy. Occasionally they succeeded, but three months after its opening the play moved to Broadway – once again defying the lazy British caricature of New York theatre as the temple of the bland.

Clifford Odets.

By 1935 Odets had four plays on Broadway produced by the Group Theatre – **Waiting for Lefty, Till the Day I Die, Awake and Sing!** and **Paradise Lost. Awake and Sing!** is an enduringly good play, for all the reasons that provoked the dedicated activists of the day to lament the dilution of Odets' radical vision. Odets wrote well and truthfully about the world, and you didn't need to be a Communist (although Odets briefly carried a Party card) or a socialist to deplore a system that had put 16 million people out of work and put breadlines in Times Square.

Awake and Sing! is underscored by the Depression and centres on an aspirant working-class Jewish family in the Bronx held together by the mother: 'Here without a dollar you don't look the world in the eye. Talk from now to next year – this is life in America.'

If Odets had a model – although he knew little of his work at the time – it was Chekhov. He shared Chekhov's realism about life's compromises, his cool draughtsman's eye, his forgiving heart, and his reluctance to let plot rather than character drive the action. He also shared Chekhov's politics: things should be better, and you must live your life better, my friend. But Odets was an American, and as such half in love with the dreams that he deplored.

Odets was acclaimed for his 'realism', as if he'd gone out with a notebook and copied the speech he heard on the street. All theatre dialogue is crafted (and crafty) distillation: the art is in the apparent artlessness, a truth beyond documentary reproduction. The language of **Awake and Sing!** crackles with wit, wisecracks, street slang, neologisms, speech as weaponry and defence. English is remade in Brooklyn with a rich inventiveness and poetry, like O'Casey's Dublin working class fusing Irish rhythms and vocabulary with the language of their colonisers: 'Eighty thousand dollars! You'll excuse my expression, you're bughouse!' Or 'Take your hand off! Come around when it's a flood again and they put you in the ark with the animals.' Or, 'Go out and fight so life shouldn't be printed on dollar bills.' Or 'Cut your throat, save time.' And more.

Awake and Sing!

In 1941, Odets moved to Hollywood. Like many (or most?) playwrights Odets was socialist in spirit, but he was a romantic at heart. Playwrights observe the idiosyncrasies, ambiguities and singularities of human behaviour; a playwright who conforms to an over-arching ideology, a unified field theory, is not an artist but a scientist or a propagandist. Systems are for politicians, art should be all the things that politics isn't: complex, mysterious, and thrilling. Odets was a romantic in the sense that he believed that people have the capacity to change each other, and that love is a force of redemption. Like most people who work in the theatre, it is less the *kind* of vision of unity that interested Odets than a longing for *any* vision of unity.

Voltaire was once asked why no woman had ever written a tolerable tragedy. He replied that 'the composition of a tragedy requires *testicles*'. He would have been confounded by two remarkable – and angry – American playwrights; one courted celebrity and controversy in equal measures all her life, the other became submerged in obscurity: Lillian Hellman and Sophie Treadwell.

Lillian Hellman (1906–1984) went through life like a flame-thrower, scorching her enemies with righteous anger, determined self-advertisement and self-regard. But she blazed with a pure – if melodramatic – talent in her two best plays, **The Children's Hour** and **The Little Foxes. The Children's Hour** was hugely successful on Broadway. The fact that it was banned in Britain – and produced privately at the Gate Theatre – indicates both the Neanderthal censorship that suffocated the British theatre and the mildly shocking nature of the play's story: the hounding of two schoolmistresses falsely suspected of lesbianism. Their lives are destroyed by gossip based upon a lie, the big lie always more convincing than the small one.

Lillian Hellman.

Hellman herself became the object of malicious accusation when she faced the House Un-American Activities Committee in 1952. 'I cannot and will not cut my conscience to fit this year's fashions,' she said magnificently to the Committee, adding characteristically, 'even though I long ago came to the conclusion that I was not a political person and could have no comfortable place in any political group.' In the face of this unimpeachable all-American rallying cry they didn't jail her but her partner, the thriller writer Dashiell Hammett, who was sentenced to six months' imprisonment for refusing to name ex-Communists; she was blacklisted by Hollywood until the 1960s.

Hellman's characters are etched in vitriol within a conventional frame. She takes her example from Ibsen, describing a society – often set in her native South – saturated with self-interest and bitterness. She writes as a moralist with a short temper.

Machinal by Sophie Treadwell (1885–1970) – which opened in 1928 and was revived at the Royal National Theatre in 1993 – too is a play written in anger. In the dead wasteland of male society – it seems to ask – isn't it *necessary*, for certain women at least, to resort to murder? This point was taken up by the *Observer* when the play was first produced in London: 'Really, young women cannot be allowed to dispatch their husbands because they happen to dislike them, and my sympathies were wholly with the victim of the crime and not at all with the heroine …'

It's a stark, desolate play based on a real-life murder. The beat is percussive, the characters balefully anonymous, the ensemble scenes hammered into half-hypnotised chorales. 'There is the attempt to catch the rhythm in our common city speech,' said Sophie Treadwell, 'its brassy sound, its trick of repetition, and the use of many different sounds chosen primarily for their inherent emotional effect.' But the dialogue is achingly true, throwing a lifeline to the real world: office life, seduction routines, journalese.

It starts in an office: cue for a throbbing paean to nine-to-five small talk emanating from all desks. The Young Woman is being wooed by the Boss. 'He fell in love with my hands,' she explains to her mother. But she flinches whenever he approaches her. Here they are on their wedding night:

HUSBAND:	Where are you going?
YOUNG WOMAN:	In here.
HUSBAND:	I though you'd want to wash up.
YOUNG WOMAN:	I just want to – get ready.
HUSBAND:	You don't have to go in there to take your clothes off.
YOUNG WOMAN:	I want to.
HUSBAND:	What for?
YOUNG WOMAN:	I always do.
HUSBAND:	What?
YOUNG WOMAN:	Undress by myself.
HUSBAND:	You've never been married till now – have you? (*laughs*) Or have you been putting something over on me?
YOUNG WOMAN:	No.
HUSBAND:	I understand – kind of modest – huh?
YOUNG WOMAN:	Yes.

A time, two lives and an infinity of sadness are evoked by the kind of exchange you might hear through a motel wall.

Kenneth Tynan wrote the epitaph on the American playwrights of the years of the Depression: 'They did their best work in the conviction that modern civilisation was committing repeated acts of criminal injustice against the individual.' And they demonstrated to the British theatre something that was buried from the time of Shaw and Granville-Barker to the '50s: that theatre, the medium that deals best with social relationships, might also bear the conscience of the society. It seems an odd paradox from today's perspective when American theatre – not entirely fairly – is characterised as being exclusively concerned with commercial success, that the British theatre in the '50s borrowed back something that seemed to have been lost. The New World gave life to the Old.

*Fiona Shaw in Stephen Daldry's production of **Machinal** at the RNT.*

Still Dreaming

'America is a vast conspiracy for making you happy.'
JOHN UPDIKE

1

The Broadway musical – that is, the 'book' (meaning 'play') musical – is a dramatic form that blends drama of character and narrative with song and dance. 'Words make you think thoughts, music makes you feel a feeling, a song makes you feel a thought,' said the songwriter Yip Harburg. In the best book musicals characters sing at the moment that their feelings become too charged for speech, and in the songs the emotional action – the relationships – moves forward. The best musicals have a thrilling seamlessness and a cumulative emotional charge; the worst are lumps of dialogue interleaved with musical interludes.

There's a version of the genesis of the musical that is comfortingly like biblical genealogy: X begat Y begat Z and so on. But theatrical history – like any other history – is never neat: the happy accident that occurred is that people with prodigious gifts decided to do things differently, or combined familiar elements in an unfamiliar way. It was a Darwinian evolution.

Such luck lay in the first book musical written by John Gay (1685–1732) in 1728. Lacking a genre, it was called a 'ballad opera' and like its distant Broadway descendant it brought together the words of high and low culture and popular entertainment. 'It has been productive,' an eighteenth-century critic wrote, 'of more mischief to this country than any would believe at the time.'

The mischief-making piece was called **The Beggar's Opera**. It was a wholly original concoction of scenes of low-life punctuated by songs of the day plucked from the street, the drawing-room and opera house – English, Scottish, Irish and Welsh folk songs, parodies of popular operas, and arias by the much-revered Purcell and Handel. Its characters were highwaymen, thieves, beggars, whores, and jailers. The hero is a hero – a highwayman fatally generous to women, who, in a mischievous Hollywood-like parody of a happy ending, is reprieved on the gallows by the author of the play within the play, the Beggar. 'It is difficult to determine,' says the Beggar, 'whether (in the fashionable vices) the fine gentlemen imitate the gentlemen of the road, or the gentlemen of the road the fine gentlemen.'

It was part satire, part social criticism, part romance, part 'pure' entertainment oppor-tunistically geared to the tastes of its intended audience, who enjoyed being voyeurs of low-life sex and violence. It's possible that Gay had seriously moralistic intentions; he certainly intended the piece to be presented more austerely than it ended up. He wanted all the sixty-nine songs to be unaccompanied so that the actors glided from speech to song to speech and back again, using the songs to express the characters' feelings when speech became inadequate. However, his patron (or 'producer'), the Duchess of Queensberry, insisted that there was a musical score to make the eclectic selection of songs cohere.

*Paul Jones, Belinda Sinclair and Imelda Staunton in the National Theatre production of **The Beggar's Opera**.*

A German musician was recruited – John Pepusch – who was an imitator of Handel and unfamiliar with many of the songs and with much of the English language. He 'mixed the sauce', concocting an overture and orchestrating the songs. Pepusch's score unquestionably helped the show become a huge success, but equally unquestionably softened its bite. In that sense the show could be said to be both the parent of the form of the Broadway musical and also of the spirit – ever eager to please whatever the subject matter.

The Beggar's Opera became a craze and there is little short of a live-cast recording that was not merchandised on the back of its success: songbooks, slang dictionaries, pamphlets, pictures, playing cards, fans, screens, clothes. It monopolised conversation, its actors became stars, and it made 'Gay rich and Rich (the theatre owner) gay'. It was revived every year for about sixty years after its opening.

Countless clones were bred from **The Beggar's Opera** and just as it had pillaged and borrowed from many sources, it was plagiarised, adapted and imitated for generations, as well as still being performed in its original form. The version that Brecht wrote in 1928 with music by Kurt Weill, **The Threepenny Opera**, is less powerful, less original, less politically acute and less witty. It comfortably plays on Broadway without any of its intended objects of scorn – the highwaymen of big business – being even slightly disturbed.

The ballad opera took root in America after the Revolution and was one of many ingredients that went into the barrel in which the Broadway musical was brewed.

The first home-grown musical was **The Black Crook**, which opened in 1866. In many respects it was an archetype: it had a plot of sorts – a derivative Faustian melodrama, characters of sorts, spectacle, dancing, an 'Amazon parade of legs', and was a triumph of marketing.

It had many rivals from European imports: operas from Paris such as Offenbach's **Belle Hélène**, comic operas from London such as Gilbert and Sullivan's **HMS Pinafore**, and operettas from Vienna, like Franz Lehar's **The Merry Widow**. Operetta bred its Broadway version, dripping in syrupy Ruritanian romanticism, such as **Rose-Marie** and **The Desert Song**.

Musical comedies – a British genre: genteel Cinderella stories – were Americanised by the composer Jerome Kern in collaboration with P.G. Wodehouse, paradoxically the quintessence of Englishness. With Guy Bolton, Wodehouse took the bold and original step of using recognisable American characters and real locations and of writing songs that evolved naturally from the plot.

The various musical genres – operetta, musical comedy, burlesque, revue, Minstrel Shows, and the Jewish *shund* – were like tributaries flowing into a wide, deep, and muddy river. On this river, appropriately enough, arrived **Showboat** in 1927, and with it the first example of what we now describe as the Broadway musical.

Showboat was written by Jerome Kern (1885–1945) and Oscar Hammerstein (1895–1960). Kern had written the music for a number of revues and musical comedies, and Hammerstein was a veteran of American operetta – he had written the book and lyrics for **Rose-Marie**. The two men – who had collaborated once previously – had become frustrated by the oppressive uniformity of tone and content of the current musical theatre, where artistic ambition meant mimicking the last success: you wrote your songs, wrapped your story round the best ones and hoped it would all make sense. As George Kaufman said, the shows had 'the kind of tunes you go *into* the theatre whistling'.

Kern and Hammerstein's show was derived from a doorstop of a novel of life on the Mississippi River by Edna Ferber. Kern and Hammerstein created almost fully formed characters who were revealed as much through song as through dialogue: music, character and plot were welded together to serve a story of the lives of a family of showboat performers from the 1880s to the 1920s – the period in which there was a huge migration from the country to the cities, and a maelstrom of expansion.

Instead of a line of chorus girls showing their legs in the opening number singing that they were happy, happy, happy, the curtain rose on black dock-hands lifting bales of cotton, and singing about the hardness of their lives. Here was a musical that showed poverty, suffering, bitterness, racial prejudice, a sexual relationship between black and white, a love story which ended unhappily – and of course show business. In 'Ol' Man River' the black race was given an anthem to honour its misery that had the authority of an authentic spiritual. And moreover, as a contemporary critic said, 'It never falls into the customary mawkish channels that mistake bathos for pathos.' Well, not often.

The music shadows the epic development of the story over thirty years, the move from a folk culture to urban commercialisation, from romantic ballads to clamorous jazz – or what passed for it. It was the first true Broadway score, the

Showboat arrived in 1927.

first to have a dramatic shape in which themes progressed through the show, in which scenes were underscored and songs emerged rather than just occurred. And Kern wrote *American* music, the kind that Irving Berlin was talking about in 1911 when he said, 'The reason American composers have done nothing significant is because they won't write American music … So they write imitation European music which doesn't mean anything.'

It's easy to exaggerate the importance of **Showboat**, to suggest that nothing like it had been seen before and nothing was ever the same again. It's not true: it was evolution rather than revolution, and it's worth remembering that the producer of the show was not a young rebel against the status quo, but the veteran of countless revues and the architect of much of Broadway's glamour: Flo Ziegfeld. The show opened out of town – directed by its two authors – and Ziegfeld's influence could be seen in the loss of at least an hour's running time during its pre-Broadway run, as well as in the spectacular sets and costumes.

What was special about **Showboat** was that it took existing forms – in particular operetta – and transformed them, integrating song and book more deftly and imaginatively than before, letting the content dictate the progression of the story rather than trying to second-guess the audience's response.

A succession of innovative imitations did not follow in the wake of **Showboat**. The tone of musical theatre was still one of jocular irrelevance, with the odd brilliant burst of reality in **Of Thee I Sing** – political satire; **Porgy and Bess** – black opera; **Pal Joey** – set in a sleazy night-club; and **Lady in the Dark** – set in the world of magazines and psychiatry. And neither Kern nor Hammerstein took advantage of their breakthrough; it was sixteen years – in 1943 – before Hammerstein collaborated with Richard Rodgers to produce the musical that signalled the second watershed in the evolution of the Broadway musical: **Oklahoma!**

Showboat's maturity and ambition at least encouraged competitors to attempt more sophisticated character, to look for more integration of songs into plot and to use dance as a means of story-telling – as in **On Your Toes** which had a jazz-accented score and George Balanchine's ballets – notably *Slaughter on 10th Avenue*.

The creators of **On Your Toes** were composers Richard Rodgers (1902–1979) and lyric writer Lorenz Hart (1895–1943). They started writing revue together, then a series of musical comedies which seemed to rain hit songs, culminating in **Babes in Arms** in 1937 – a let's-do-the-show-right-here-in-the-barn extravaganza which included 'My Funny Valentine', 'The Lady is a Tramp', and 'I Wish I were In Love Again'. In **Pal Joey**, adapted from John O'Hara's melancholy and mordant short stories, they introduced a new tone to the Broadway musical – stained with mordant wit, irony and cynicism. They dared to have a protagonist who was only half sympathetic and they showed an adult realism about sex. The show also introduced a remarkable performer as Joey, the opportunistic small-time heel: Gene Kelly.

If Rodgers and Hart gave a voice to a hard-boiled world of broken dreams and romantic delusion, Cole Porter (1891–1964) was the poet of the playboy: charming, louche, knowing. Just the titles of his shows give an indication of their escapist innocence in the years of the Depression leading up to the war: **Fifty Million Frenchmen**, **The New Yorkers**, **The Gay Divorce**, **Anything Goes**, **Red Hot and Blue!**, **Du Barry Was a Lady**, **Panama Hattie** and **Let's Face It**. The shows were essentially elegant necklaces – indelible melodies and brilliantly witty lyrics laced to a thing string of plot. Only in **Kiss Me, Kate**, in spite of a stammering book punctuated by one-liners, did Cole Porter write a score that was more than the sum of its considerable parts.

'It is always possible to create something original,' said George Gershwin (1898–1937), and in 1935 with **Porgy and Bess** – 'an American folk opera' about a black community on Catfish Row – he made good his promise. He had been writing jazz-influenced scores with intricate rhythms and sophisticated lyrics by his brother Ira and had had a series of successes with musical comedies, often featuring Fred Astaire and his sister, Adele, and incidentally introducing Ginger Rogers and Ethel Merman.

'When I'm in my normal mood,' said Gershwin, 'music drips from my fingers.' He was a musical prodigy, publishing his first song at the age of fourteen. He worked briefly for Irving Berlin until Berlin heard some of Gershwin's music: 'What the hell do you want to work for somebody else for?'

Porgy and Bess:
*'I try to put the pulse
of my times into my
music and do it in
an original way' –
George Gershwin.*

Porgy and Bess was not the first all-black show on Broadway. There'd been a number of revues and a few musicals which had popularised a form of jazz that replaced ragtime as the dominant musical comedy style, and introduced new dance steps such as the Charleston, to the musical stage. It's not so surprising that the first black – or first American opera – was written by the son of a Jewish immigrant from St Petersburg, able at least to transfer one race's suffering to another. It's more fortunate that the adaptation of Dorothy and DuBose Heyward's clumsy, sentimental and patronising play **Porgy and Bess** was undertaken by the Gershwins rather than Jerome Kern, who was originally asked to write it for Al Jolson. Even so, it's very much a white view of never-never-land natives, happy with 'plenty of nuttin'.

'True music must repeat the thought and aspirations of the people and the time. My people are Americans … I try to put the pulse of my times into my music and do it in an original way,' said Gershwin, and his way was neither through classical, jazz nor show music, but a fusion of European – and Jewish – rhythms, harmonies and melodies with black music; not a hybrid but an American original. Gershwin paid for his originality: the show was poorly received on its opening, cruelly indicted by the critics, and it wasn't until a revival seven years later – after his death – that it was acclaimed.

If you were looking for the common strain between all the significant contributors to the musical you'd have to say it was their Jewishness: Rodgers, Hammerstein, Kern, Hart, Berlin, Gershwin, Bernstein, Loesser, Styne, Freed, Laurents, Kauffman, Sondheim … and, of course, Offenbach.

Except – as Richard Rodgers pointed out – Cole Porter: 'It is surely one of the ironies of the musical theatre that, despite the abundance of Jewish composers, the one who has written the most enduring "Jewish" music should be an Episcopalian millionaire who was born on a farm in Peru, Indiana.' It was an irony not lost on Cole Porter who, as he said himself, wrote Jewish tunes.

What was it that drew the Jewish immigrants to the musical theatre? They had a tradition in their own imported theatre, they loved to play with their newly learned language – like the Irish with their hybrid English – and show business was a way of emerging from the ghetto. Irving Berlin (1888–1989) epitomised the Jewish immigrant song-writer. As an eight-year-old – then called Israel Baline – he teamed up with a singing beggar called Blind Sol in the streets; by the time he was twenty-three he was a national celebrity. Jerome Kern said of him, 'Irving Berlin has no *place* in American music. He *is* American music.'

If we take for granted now that a musical can fuse dialogue, song and dance in the service of dramatic narrative, it is because Rodgers and Hammerstein made it seem as inevitable and necessary as the invention of television. They changed the course of American musical theatre just as Chekhov and Ibsen changed the course of twentieth-century drama: in both cases transforming existing forms by embracing real issues, and examining real characters and situations.

In the case of the musical, an apparently endemically frivolous medium became a vehicle for serious situations and profound passions. The musical grew up. What had been fitfully attempted in **Showboat** became triumphantly achieved: a seamlessly unified depiction of narrative and character through dialogue, song and dance.

Rodgers and Hammerstein's first collaboration, **Oklahoma!**, emerged from a play that was performed unsuccessfully in 1931. It was by a writer who specialised in cowboy subjects; he was part Cherokee and grew up in Oklahoma. His name was Lynn Riggs and his play was **Green Grow the Lilacs**. Its dialogue was immured in dialect:

> If we ever had to leave this place, Aunt Eller, I'd shore miss it. I like it. I like the thicket down by the branch whur the possums live, don't you? And the way we set around in the evenings in thrashin' time, a-eatin' mushrooms and singin' …

Oklahoma!:
'No gags, no girls, no chance'.

Perhaps it was the promise of 'singin'' that drew Richard Rodgers to the play as a basis for a musical. His usual collaborator, Lorenz Hart, was not attracted to it, partly because he found the subject matter unappealing, and partly because he was deteriorating rapidly from alcoholism and becoming 'a source of permanent irritation' to Richard Rodgers. Rodgers approached Ira Gershwin; Gershwin declined, and Hammerstein, who'd been in a professional slump, accepted.

Like all musicals, **Oklahoma!** was 'baked' as in the Jewish theatre. It was a collaboration – music almost invariably following words – and from an early stage the collaboration included the choreographer Agnes de Mille who, along with the choreographer/director Jerome Robbins, changed the Broadway musical as comprehensively as Rodgers and Hammerstein. The characters and their situations dictated the way the music and the story-telling went. The play began with an old woman churning butter outside a farmhouse. In the musical the first stage direction read: '*Stage left, an old woman*

churning butter. Off-stage right, the voice of a lone cowboy singing "Oh What a Beautiful Morning".'

The show merged dialogue, lyrics, music – and, importantly, dance – into an unsensational love story set in the Midwest at a time when America was still defining itself and still busy creating its own legends about its past. It opened in wartime – and offered up a world in which the important feuds were between cowmen and farmers, rather than between fascism and democracy.

What made **Oklahoma!** remarkable was that it stubbornly refused to deal with Broadway in its own currency: 'No gags, no girls, no chance' was the word on the street before it opened. It wasn't about show-business or society people; it wasn't formulaic; it didn't relentlessly attempt to manipulate the audience's feelings; it was about very ordinary people and loneliness and unhappiness – and of course about falling in love. What it did, it did with huge conviction and energy, and where **Showboat** was elephantine in its epic narrative, **Oklahoma!** had a fleet-footedness in its story-telling, aided by the use of dance – a dream ballet – as a device for advancing the plot rather than diverting attention from it.

Oklahoma! opened out of town in 1943 under the title of **Away We Go!**. It moved from New Haven to Boston to New York, losing two scenes, a song, and acquiring a new title, **Oklahoma**, and then an exclamation mark. It ran for five years. Four years after its Broadway opening – in 1947 – it opened in London: 'The production brings home the jaded condition of the people of these islands after seven years of austerity and deprivation, when contrasted with the freshness of the Americans and their abounding vitality.'

With **Carousel**, based on the Hungarian play **Liliom** by Ferenc Molnár, Rodgers and Hammerstein excavated a similar seam of love, loneliness, sexual passion, violence and death. Once again character dictated the movement of the story, and once again a communal gathering, a clambake, like the picnic in **Oklahoma!**, provided an image of a community trying to live well and work together. And again the setting was a could-be-Arcadia: a fishing village in late nineteenth-century New England. **Carousel** used the same syntax as **Oklahoma!** – dream ballet, psychological melodrama, underscoring – bound together by music whose ravishing romanticism overwhelmed the incipient sententiousness of the story.

If the tone of **Carousel** threatened morbidity, **South Pacific** was shot through with an irresistible ebullience. Set on a Pacific island during the war, it was, naturally, a love story but in a plausible context without a threat of escapism or dream sequences or surreal fantasy. 'You've Got to Be Carefully Taught' confronted the audience with racial prejudice, and with 'Nothin' Like A Dame' there was no protective veil of stylisation: these were sailors fed up with war and rabid for sex. Real, indeed contemporary, life had occupied the Broadway musical stage.

The musicals of Rodgers and Hammerstein all deal with the great American themes: race, business, individualism and the community – insiders and outsiders. They have a

socially conscious dimension, and are politically progressive and didactic: 'You've got to be carefully taught' is their instruction. Yet for all their genius, it is hard to avoid a sense of frustration even with their very best work. It is as if we are invited to feel for the characters – even the unsympathetic ones – to see their unhappiness and grant our compassion, and just as we are holding out our hand to them, it's brushed aside: don't bother, we'll sing and dance and everything will be fine, Broadway will always have the last word. But musical theatre never thrives on subtlety: there will always be somebody to sing about things looking swell, and putting the first foot forward. Ambiguity, doubt and uncertainty will always be at war with the prevailing optimism – albeit an optimism held in good faith as much as from economic necessity.

Nicholas Hytner's RNT revival of **Carousel**.

With **Oklahoma!, Carousel** and **South Pacific** the danger is constantly present of tipping from real conflict into melodrama, or from sentiment to mawkishness. In Rodgers and Hammerstein's later shows – **The King and I, Flower Drum Song** and **The Sound of Music** – this tendency becomes a compulsion. It wasn't for nothing that Christopher Plummer, who starred in the film of **The Sound of Music**, referred to it as the sound of mucus. Oscar Wilde said that one must have a heart of stone to read about the death of Little Nell without laughing; curiously, it is hard to watch **The Sound of Music** without crying.

171

For over twenty years – from 1940 to 1966 – the Broadway musical sat in perfect equilibrium with the appetite of the audience, the talent of the performers, and the taste of the time. It was a form of theatre that, uniquely, could be said to have crossed class-barriers. Looking at the names of the best musicals of those years that weren't written by Rodgers and Hammerstein is like turning over the gold-embossed pages of an illuminated Book of Hours: **Pal Joey, Lady in the Dark, One Touch of Venus, Carmen Jones, On the Town, Annie Get Your Gun, Brigadoon, Kiss Me Kate, Call Me Madam, Guys and Dolls, Paint Your Wagon, The Most Happy Fella, Wonderful Town, Kismet, Can Can, Music Man, The Pyjama Game, Damn Yankees, My Fair Lady, Candide, West Side Story, The Music Man, Gypsy, Camelot, Bye Bye Birdie, Fiddler on the Roof, Funny Girl, Man of La Mancha** and **Cabaret.**

Hammerstein and Rodgers.

West Side Story and **My Fair Lady** are highly intelligent, beautifully crafted, heartfelt and touching, and Jerome Robbins' staging for **West Side Story** was as great as that of any director of this century – in a musical or otherwise. Impossible to patronise, these shows are supreme examples of dramatic art and with **Guys and Dolls** it's not hard to accept Kenneth Tynan's assessment of it as 'the second-best American play' – the best being **Death of a Salesman**.

Guys and Dolls is a 'fairy-tale of New York', peopled by many of Damon Runyon's characters but without the savage undertow of most of his stories – more Runyonesque than Runyonese. His world is a wholly successful fictional creation, as consistent and original as that of P.G. Wodehouse.

It's an irony that almost all the songs in **Guys and Dolls** were written by Frank Loesser before the dialogue, which merely serves to highlight Loesser's genius as a dramatic lyricist. Abe Burrows wrote the book after an abortive script by Joe Swerling had been abandoned. 'Make it funny,' said George Kaufman, the director. 'But not too funny,' added Loesser. Abe Burrows certainly made it funny, but the catalytic talent that made **Guys and Dolls** so successful was Kaufman – the 'Great Collaborator'. He insisted on regarding **Guys and Dolls** as a play interrupted by musical numbers. He felt this so strongly that he regarded most of the songs as 'lobby' numbers – every time a song started he sprinted to the lobby for a cigarette. Abe Burrows once overheard him, mid-sprint, mutter, 'Good God, do we have to do every number this son-of-a-bitch ever wrote?'

All musicals are love stories: **Guys and Dolls** is endowed with two, one of them between Nathan Detroit, promoter of the oldest established floating crap game in town, and Miss Adelaide, a night-club signer. Adelaide is constantly disappointed by the failure of her fiancé of fourteen years to marry her and in her 'Lament' she mourns her loss:

> ADELAIDE (*reading*)
>> It says here
>
> (*singing*)
>> The average unmarried female, basically insecure
>> Due to some long frustration, may react
>> With psychosomatic symptoms, difficult to endure
>> Affecting the lower respiratory tract.
>
> (*looks up from book*)
>> In other words, just from waiting around
>> for that plain little band of gold
>> A person ... can develop a cold.
>
> (*reads again*)
>> It says here:
>
> (*sings*)
>> The female remaining single, just in the legal sense

> Shows a neurotic tendency, see note,
>
> (*spoken*)
>
> note note
>
> (*looks at note, sings*)
>
> Chronic organic syndromes, toxic and hypertense
> Involving the eye the ear and the nose
> and the throat
>
> (*puts book down and rises*)
>
> In other words just from worrying whether the Wedding
> is on or off,
> A person can develop a cough

And more. She reprises the song in the second half, ending with these lines:

> So much virus inside
> That her microscope slide
> Looks like a day at the zoo!
> Just from wanting her memories in writing
> And a story her folks can be told
> A person can develop a cold.

There is no better example in the canon of Broadway musicals of writing that describes character, advances plot, makes you laugh and touches your heart.

For over fifty years the pop songs of the day – the Tin Pan Alley songs – were the songs from the shows. The songs you could hear sung in the street or the bar or on the radio were the songs you would hear sung in a theatre.

And then it changed.

With the rise of the cheap(ish) portable record players, with amplified sound, with the proliferation of radio stations, with increased prosperity among blue-collar workers, recorded music became the music of the masses. White working-class men – Elvis and Jerry Lee Lewis – took over black working-class music, rhythm and blues, and they were then mimicked by white British working-class boys – the Beatles to name but four – and the umbilical chord between Broadway and the mass of the population was cut.

The new Tin Pan Alley songs – rock and roll – couldn't be assimilated in a dramatic structure. The form couldn't carry narrative and character. The songs couldn't progress the story and if songs just stand still in a musical then the musical dies.

And the musical died.

Of course there continued to be some remarkably talented composers and lyricists, but the Broadway musical – the 'musical play' – had lost its heartland. And in the face of

Dramatic art in a singular state of grace: **West Side Story** *and* **Guys and Dolls**.

growing awareness that the US was engaged in a major war in a faraway country in Asia, that was causing increasing numbers of American soldiers to be sent home in coffins, it became hard to retain the implacable optimism that underwrote the Broadway musicals.

'When popular music seemed to stop caring about theatre music, people who wrote for the theatre stopped writing for the market. The musical naturally became a lot more experimental,' said John Kander, the composer of **Cabaret** – a triumphant experiment in pushing the musical into serious moral, if not musical, territory. And there was no one more experimental than Stephen Sondheim.

Stephen Sondheim (1930–) had the perfect Broadway pedigree: he was taught by Oscar Hammerstein, and he wrote lyrics for **West Side Story** and for **Gypsy** before writing his own shows – **A Funny Thing Happened on the Way to the Forum, Company, Follies, A Little Night Music, Pacific Overtures, Sweeney Todd, Merrily We Roll Along, Sunday in the Park with George, Into the Woods, Assassins, Passion**. Each time he showed a restless curiosity about form and a determination to resist conventional subject matter. With **Sweeney Todd** he created an idiosyncratic masterpiece that lifts a scab of *grand guignol* horror and finds a psychological reality underneath.

Sondheim changed the palette of the musical, replacing optimism and sentiment with disenchantment and acerbity. The music and lyrics have a wry and astringent, melancholic consistency and are clever without being ostentatious; they are sometimes linked to books that lack dramatic muscle and creak under the weight of their intellectual ambition, but that is a flaw gloriously on the side of the angels. In the Microsoft dictionary that comes with the Microsoft 95 software, the synonym for Sondheim is 'song'. He's the conscience of the American musical.

'I am a modern romantic,' said George Gershwin. In truth, *all* musicals are inherently and irrevocably romantic, and almost all occupy a predominantly white, middlebrow part of the spectrum. Popular musicals have never colonised music outside a quite narrow range. Even though George Gershwin said, 'Jazz is the result of all that energy stored up in America,' it never really manifested itself in the musical theatre. And the nearest classical music came to being assimilated was in the music of Leonard Bernstein in **On the Town, Wonderful Town,** and **Candide,** none of which penetrated the popular imagination.

Only in **West Side Story** – derived from Shakespeare – did the world of classical music, ballet and straight theatre combine in a miraculous synthesis. 'It's an American musical,' said Jerome Robbins (choreographer). 'The aim of the mid-'50s was to see if all of us – Lenny [Bernstein] who wrote "long-hair" music, Arthur [Laurents] who wrote serious plays, Oliver Smith [designer] who was a serious painter – could bring our acts together and do a work on the popular stage ...' They did, a uniquely successful collaboration.

The great musicals of the '40s and '50s are examples of dramatic art in a singular state of grace. They address the emotional experience of an audience directly and without inhibition. In this they are peculiarly American – marked by energy, wit and optimism, devoid of irony, cynicism and pessimism. They were born out of a particular historical moment in which progress seemed benign: decent, staunch, humble (but not too humble and not too black) folk progressing – 'with hope in their hearts' – towards the fulfilment of the American Dream. No English writer could have ended the story that **Carousel** tells with the wilful determination to purge darkness with hope. It's an assertion of national faith – 'You'll never walk alone'.

2

How do you acquire a popular audience for ambitious drama that seeks to scourge rather than soothe? In New York – up to the 1960s – there was an audience sufficiently large and sufficiently wealthy to support enlightened straight drama; its allegiance was to intellectual values rather than social ones – the opposite in London.

'The trouble began in the nineteenth century and was connected with the rise of the middle classes – they wanted their theatre soothing,' said a playwright who went on to write the archetype for precisely the sort of amiable and reassuring play that he was indicating: **Our Town**.

Its author, Thornton Wilder (1897–1975), started writing as a novelist and adaptor of a play whose author would rather die than soothe – Ibsen's **Doll's House** – but in **Our Town**, which opened in 1938, he became the chronicler of Middle America. His view of America now seems as dated but as beguiling as the Norman Rockwell illustrations of lower-middle-class aspirations in the *Saturday Evening Post*. 'Well, people a thousand years from now, this is the way we were – in our growing up, in our marrying, in our doctoring, in our living and our dying,' says the Stage Manager in **Our Town**.

Wilder insisted on a mode of staging that was revolutionary in its minimalism and its belief in the power of theatrical imagination. He defied the received wisdom of contemporary theatre and the notions of time and place, insisting on a bare stage, minimal scenery and props – the new 'Elizabethanism' of Granville-Barker. Four chairs would represent a car, the same chairs and a table would represent a house, with a narrator – the Stage Manager – to guide the audience through the statistics and the 'smallest events of our daily lives'.

Thornton Wilder evoked the world of 'the cottage, the go-cart, the Sunday-afternoon drives in the Ford, the first rheumatism, the deathbed, the reading of the will'. Whether or not he spoke for the mind and spirit of the country, he spoke for the assumptions of an audience who shared a heartland and who wanted their theatre soothing. He was not – as he said himself – 'one of the new dramatists we are looking for'.

A pale ageing virgin watercolourist tells a story of a man masturbating into a pair of her underpants. 'And that experience … ' says the man she is talking to. 'You call that a … ' 'A love experience? Yes. I do call it one,' she says.

The play is Tennessee Williams' **The Night of the Iguana**. It dramatises two sides of the author's character – one wild and paranoid, the other prudent and resigned. Shannon, a defrocked priest, discovers that Hannah Jelkes, the wise virgin, has also had a nervous breakdown and asks her how she has dealt with it:

SHANNON: How'd you beat your blue devil?
HANNAH: I showed him that I could endure him and made him respect
            my endurance.
SHANNON: How?
HANNAH: Just by, just by … enduring.

Williams had recently emerged from a period in a mental hospital and during the writing of **Iguana** was still under assault from his blue devils, fighting them off with drugs – alcohol, barbiturates, uppers, downers – and with his indestructible brand of stoicism which survived until his death over twenty years later. His paranoia resulted in him accusing his lover, Frank Merlo, of conspiring to encourage his dog to bite him. They parted after fourteen years and Merlo died two years later of lung cancer – leaving Williams tormented by guilt.

Williams called the 1960s – the period after Merlo's departure – his 'Stoned Age' and there was a terrible falling off in his successive plays. He was convinced that **Iguana** would be his last, and, effectively, it was his last testament. Like many last works, **Iguana** is about the redemptive power of love – any human contact is better than none. 'Nothing human disgusts me,' says Hannah, 'unless it's unkind, violent.'

Williams makes us see that to be human is to love, and that to love your fellow, however difficult, is the only possible hope. The philosopher Simone Weil could have been talking about his work:

Love for our neighbour, being made of creative attention, is analogous to genius … The love of our neighbour in all fullness means being able to say to him: 'What are you going through?' It is a recognition that the sufferer exists, not only as … a specimen from a social category labelled 'unfortunate', but as a man exactly as we are … To forget oneself briefly, to identify with a stranger to the point of fully recognising him or her, is to defy necessity.

Or, in other words – to quote Blanche Du Bois   we must always rely on the kindness of strangers.

Tennessee Williams (1911–1983) was born in Mississippi, the son of a travelling shoe salesman who was an alcoholic and a bully, and of a minister's daughter – 'Miss Edwina' – a Southern belle who lived on the verge of hysteria and who later became a patient in a psychiatric hospital. Williams was devoted to his sister, Rose, who was diagnosed in her teens as a schizophrenic and was given a pre-frontal lobotomy, which Tennessee knew nothing about until it had been performed – emerging as fiction in **Suddenly Last Summer**. He said:

> At the age of fourteen, I discovered writing as an escape from a world of reality in which I felt acutely uncomfortable. It immediately became my place of retreat, my cave, my refuge. From what? From being called a sissy by neighbourhood kids, and 'Miss Nancy' by my father, because I would rather read books in my grandfather's large and classical library than play marbles and baseball and other normal kid games, a result of a severe childhood illness and of excessive attachment to the female members of my family, who had coaxed me back into life.

As Grahame Greene said, childhood is the writer's bank balance, and Williams drew on it like a spendthrift. **The Glass Menagerie** – his first performed play – was based on his pre-war family life. The mother and daughter in the play were based upon his own mother and sister, and Tom – as Tennessee was then called – worked in a warehouse like the one in which Tom works in the play. Rose and Tom even kept a menagerie of little glass animals in their room. 'And how do you like yourself on the stage?' said the actress who played Amanda Wingfield, the mother, to Miss Edwina after she'd seen the play.

'"Mr Williams, would you please give us your definition of happiness?" "Insensitivity, I guess." '

Williams' family was the nourishment for his writing all his life – the overbearing patriarchs, the fading belles, the beautiful but frail young men. The South was his garden, planted with over-heated romantic relationships, saturated with sex and death, blooming briefly and decaying rapidly. To describe this garden he drew his syntax from the religion he'd acquired in his grandfather's rectories while his father was on the road selling shoes: Paradise, Purgatory and Hell.

For someone with such an apparently frail hold on life, Williams was extraordinarily tenacious and productive. He wrote, as he lived, compulsively. During his lifetime at least sixty-three of his plays and playlets (thirty-two short plays, twenty-four full-length and seven mid-length) were published or given a major production or both. In a period of twelve years – between 1945 and 1957 – he wrote with a wild energy: **The Glass Menagerie, A Streetcar Named Desire, Summer and Smoke, The Rose Tattoo, Camino Real, Cat on a Hot Tin Roof** and **Orpheus Descending**.

The point of his plays, said Williams, was 'just somehow to capture the constantly evanescent quality of existence', and most of his plays look back with elegiac fervour to a past that has been improved in the memory, to a golden world kissed by wistful idealism.

Time destroys, never heals. Only art survives. Looking for lost perfection, Williams' characters find themselves redundant – the old, the bereft, the forgotten, the tormented. He's the mouthpiece for the dispossessed – women, gays, blacks, the mad, the wayward, the lonely. He offers up the irreconcilable versuses of life – masculine and feminine, desire for love and desire for freedom, animal lust and genteel courtship, flesh and spirit, rich and poor, present and past – but he never judges his characters or evangelises for an exotic life: between the polarity of Stanley Kowalski's lust and Blanche's cowed nymphomania, there's Stella's wholly unneurotic sexual fulfilment. 'Life,' says Maggie in **Cat on a Hot Tin Roof,** 'has got to be allowed to continue even after the *dream* of life is – all – over …'

Williams was defiantly out of the closet, although in his work homosexuality is usually associated with guilt and martyrdom, and all sex is tainted with death. He was not a 'gay' writer any more than Lillian Hellman was a 'women's' writer, and his plays are not coded allegories larded with covert gay references. Nor does he write women as surrogate men in drag – even if in the first draft of **Sweet Bird of Youth** the ageing Hollywood film-star Alexandra Del Lago *was* a man called Artemis Pazmezoglu. Countless actresses will testify that few playwrights have written such good parts for women. He grew up in the South of the Depression years, where to be gay and white was barely better than being black, and he observed the sober, heterosexual, clubbable, gullible subscribers to the American Dream with the eye of the outcast. When he chose to put homosexuality in his plays – in **Streetcar**, in **Cat on a Hot Tin Roof** and in **Suddenly Last Summer** – it was as explicit as the times would allow.

The power of sex to redeem or destroy is at the heart of **A Streetcar Named Desire** and it's not a coincidence that the play is now an indelible part of American folklore. The first New York production was Marlon Brando's introduction to Broadway, and the film added a new idol to the pantheon of twentieth-century eroticism. Brando in Levi's and T-shirt – semi-articulate, sweating, dangerous, and beautiful, baying 'Stella!!' into the hot New Orleans night – became a frequent object of straight male envy and a universal object of gay and female lust.

The film, like the play, was directed by Elia Kazan, who was always a mixed blessing for Williams as a collaborator. Unarguably brilliant as an animator of actors, Kazan had a way of tipping the meaning of Williams' plays towards the conventional and sentimental: in the film of **Streetcar** he removed the homosexuality of Blanche's fiancé, whose suicide has brought her so much guilt, and he made Stella leave Stanley, never to return. But Williams himself was never too prescriptive; when told of a Moscow production which gave **Streetcar** a happy ending, he said, 'They're right, Blanche would have conned her way out of that mental home in a fortnight, and she'd have married Mitch.'

'I don't want realism, I want magic!' said Williams. He was well served by the designer Jo Mielziner, whose designs had a spare accessible elegance – or, as a contemporary put it – 'the balance and beauty and sanity of fine prose'. Williams challenged his directors and designers to rise to his extraordinarily expressive stage directions. He was a formal visionary, with a theatrical imagination that was barely understood in his times – much closer to Robert Lepage than to Granville-Barker. He wrote theatre poetry with theatre language – gauzes to spill the action seamlessly from interior to exterior, complex lighting, slashes of iridescent colour, projections, music, and sound effects – cries in the night, distant marimbas, the tinkling of a music box, the thrashing of an iguana's tail. He had the same ear for theatrical music that Chekhov showed in **The Cherry Orchard**:

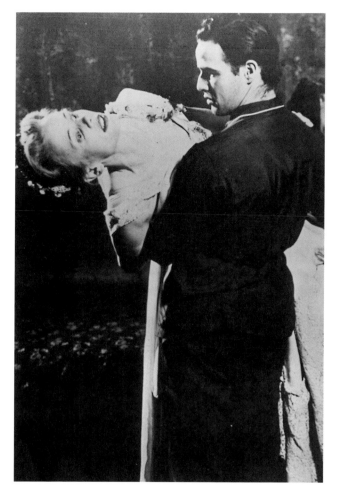

*Marlon Brando with Jessica Tandy in **A Streetcar Named Desire**: 'A frequent object of straight male envy and a universal object of gay and female lust'.*

> *Suddenly a distant sound is heard, coming as if out of the sky, like the sound of a string snapping, slowly and sadly dying away.*

This is the opening of **The Rose Tattoo**:

> *It is the hour that the Italians call 'prima sera', the beginning of dusk. Between the house and the palm tree burns the female star with an almost emerald lustre.*
>
> *The mothers of the neighbourhood are beginning to call their children home to supper, in voices near and distant, urgent and tender, like the variable notes of wind and water.*

Directors of Tennessee Williams plays frequently misread 'intense' and 'Southern' for camp. In performance his plays can seem too full of capital letters – over-heated, dipped in purple rhetoric, exuding over-sweet over-scented vapours – but often that is a consequence of the actors being lured into the siren-music of the language and ignoring the sharp and specific thoughts that animate it and the mordant wit that underscores it.

Williams was ferociously hard-headed about the meaning of language and the music of it. Ignore the punctuation, you change the rhythm, the sound and the sense. A sentence like this – 'We drank together that night all night in the bar of the Blackstone and when cold day was comin' up over the Lake an' we were comin' out drunk to take a dizzy look at it, I said, "SKIPPER! STOP LOVIN' MY HUSBAND OR TELL HIM HE'S GOT TO LET YOU ADMIT IT TO HIM!" – one way or another!' – has to be played on a single breath at least up to the comma. Williams needs actors with formidable skills and big lungs.

And, one should add, a sense of humour: his drollery runs under all his work like a fast-flowing stream. His first published work was a short story entitled: 'Can a Wife be a Good Sport?'. And he was once asked by a journalist, 'Mr Williams, would you please give us your definition of happiness?' He leant back, rolled his eyes, and said, 'Insensitivity, I guess.'

Tennessee Williams and Arthur Miller are the Romulus and Remus of post-war American drama: if they hadn't existed you'd have had to invent them. It's as invidious to make comparisons between Williams and Miller as it is between Chekhov and Ibsen – even if it was Chekhov who encouraged it, muttering to Stanislavsky, 'But listen, Ibsen is no playwright! Ibsen just doesn't know life. In life it simply isn't like that.'

And of course you can say that Tennessee Williams traced his lineage from Chekhov as Arthur Miller did from Ibsen – the one colonising the territory of the personal, the other the political, the rackety, forgiving poet of the heart and the assured and assertive poet of the conscience.

It is possible to admire them both. They grew in the same historical soil, were cultivated in the same theatrical climate, and their similarities are more conspicuous than their differences. Try attributing these quotes:

> The plays are my autobiography. I can't write plays that don't sum up where I am. I'm in all of them. I don't know how else to go about writing.

> It is about: the betrayal of people's hearts by the subtle progress of a corruption that is both personal and social ... the native power-drive of the individual and the false values with their accent on being 'top dogs', on fierce competition for a superior position, that defeat the possible true and pure and compassionately loving relations between people.

The first – intimate and confessional – is Arthur Miller, the second – that blend of territorial imperative with a whiff of Marxism – is Tennessee Williams from a letter he wrote when he was writing **Sweet Bird of Youth**. It was to his agent Audrey Wood, typed in capital letters on his Olivetti portable and sent from the Hotel Colon in Barcelona.

Williams was the son of a salesman; Miller wrote a great play about one. Both writers denied that they were realistic writers; both wrote 'memory' plays. Both were children of the Depression; both wrote about failed dreams. Both had a powerful public sexual persona – Williams through his unconcealed homosexual promiscuity, Miller through his all-too conspicuous marriage to Marilyn Monroe. And both denied an explicit political dimension to their work – as Miller said (and Williams would have agreed): 'There are no public issues; they are all private issues.'

It's characteristic of Arthur Miller to express his 'subjects' as 'issues' – a leaning towards advocacy of moral conceits. That's his legacy of Ibsenism along with his accumulation of an Ibsenesque technical arsenal and a leaning towards construction that, like Ibsen's, is often almost too neat – in sharp contrast to Williams' unpruned and often unweeded garden. The 'issue' that most concerns Arthur Miller is America's lack of a sense of its own history, and of the connective tissue between the past, the present and the future. But he's a playwright – he knows that the shortest route to bad plays is to write plays ballasted with the baggage of big themes.

His first successful play was **All My Sons** – the story of Joe Keller, a manufacturer of aircraft engines, who allows defective parts to be fitted to planes. Fatal crashes result, and he lets his business partner take the blame for them. His corruption is the original sin that corrodes everyone he's connected to – leading to the suicide of one son, the shame of his family, and eventually his own suicide.

All My Sons appears to be a linear moral equation, an Ibsenesque fable, but that's a superficial resemblance, even if it is concerned with the impact of private morals on public and vice versa. Miller is not a political writer, nor is he a moralist; and he is only a realist in the sense that he is concerned with the forces that affect people's lives rather than the superficial appearance of reality.

The real subject matter of **All My Sons** is not a moral conundrum but a question of whether we take responsibility for each other – are we social animals? 'Joe Keller's trouble,' said Miller, 'is not that he cannot tell right from wrong but that his cast of mind cannot admit that he, personally, has any viable connection with his world, his universe, or his society. He is not a partner in society, but an incorporated member, so to speak …' Arthur Miller is concerned with how you reconcile the individual with society and, if there is a touch of the evangelist in Miller, his message is that he refutes Margaret Thatcher's noxious axiom – he asserts that there *is* such a thing as society.

Arthur Miller (1915–) was born in New York – his father a first-generation Austrian-Jewish manufacturer of women's coats, his mother, born in New York, a schoolteacher.

Although not orthodox, the Millers could speak Yiddish, observed Jewish customs, and taught their children Judaism. The 1929 crash and the Depression provided Miller's sentimental education: the family business was destroyed, and the family was reduced to relative poverty. 'America … was promises, and for some the Crash was in the deepest sense a broken promise … I knew that the Depression was only incidentally a matter of money. Rather, it was a moral catastrophe, a violent revelation of the hypocrisies behind the façade of American society.'

Miller worked with the Federal Theatre Project until it was closed down in 1939, went to work in the Brooklyn Navy Yard and started to write for radio. His first stage play (and his first collaboration with Elia Kazan) – **The Man Who Had All the Luck** – was a failure but it did nothing to weaken his conviction 'that art ought to be of use in changing society'. It's hard to argue that art saves lives, feeds the hungry, or sways votes, but **Death of a Salesman** comes as close as any playwright can get to art as a balm for social concern.

Miller's original title for **Death of a Salesman** was **The Inside of His Head** – twenty-four hours in Willy Loman's life ending in his death, compressed into subjective action which jumps fluidly from the present to the real and the imagined past. It was a uniquely theatrical notion that exploited the theatre's poetic capacity to move between place and time, to make the present and the past co-exist in a compound metaphor. The designer and director of **Salesman** – Jo Mielziner and Elia Kazan – used a single setting for Willy's house and played all other scenes on various areas of the forestage, combining expressionism with detailed minimalist realism. The theatricality of Miller's conceit was illuminated by the failure of the film version, which inevitably reduced the theatre's fluency to film's linear literalism, flashbacks becoming cuts from one time and place to another.

When he was writing **Salesman**, Miller saw **Streetcar** and it opened:

> … one specific door, one that didn't deal so much with the story or characters or direction, but with words and their liberation, with the joy of the writer in writing them, the radiant eloquence of its composition, that moved me more than all its pathos. It formed a bridge … to the whole tradition of unashamed word-joy that … we had turned our backs on.

Inspired by Williams, in **Death of a Salesman** Miller created a new verbal language and a new theatrical one – even if the emblematic American profession of salesman was familiar to theatre-goers from Hickey in **The Iceman Cometh**. Miller provided Willy with a vocabulary and syntax that blended the clichés of everyday life with self-deluding aphorisms – 'America is full of beautiful towns and fine upstanding people,' with immigrant parables – 'Why, boys, when I was seventeen I walked into the jungle, and when I was twenty-one I walked out,' and with slogans for success – 'Be liked and you will never want.' These are repeated by Willy like a catechism for success, and are bound together by Miller's own vivid poetry – 'The woods are burning, boys' – and his sinewy rhetoric:

WILLY: I want you to know, on the train, in the mountains, in the valleys, wherever you go, that you cut down your life for spite!

BIFF: No. No.

WILLY: Spite, spite, is the word of your undoing! And when you're down and out, remember what did it. When you're rotting somewhere beside the railway tracks, remember, and don't you dare blame it on me!

*Elia Kazan and Arthur Miller in rehearsals for **Death of a Salesman**.*

The play is unarguably an indictment of a society that repressively puts financial success at the heart of the American Dream and presumes that there is nothing of value that can't be quantified. The salesman Dave Singleman is Willy's exemplar – 'And by the way he died the death of a salesman, in his green velvet slippers in the smoker of the New York, New Haven and Hartford, going into Boston – when he died, hundreds of salesman and buyers were at his funeral.' It is Willy's sentimental dream that it is possible to reconcile unbridled free enterprise with benign humanity and it is his tragedy that he never realises that his dream is a fantasy. Willy's defeat – and it is an utter one which leads to his suicide – is that he ends up believing, 'After all the highways, and the trains, and the appointments, and the years, you end up worth more dead than alive.'

Lee J. Cobb in **Death of a Salesman**.

Death of a Salesman is not a play that reveals an infinity of meanings but it is a remarkable play about the death of a salesman – less about the corrosive effect of capitalism than about the destructive nature of dreams. It is hard to watch this play now and accept the neatness of the plot mechanism that has the older son, Biff, becoming a drop-out when he discovers his father with another woman, or to disregard the sentimentality of the funeral scene. And it's hard to ignore the occasional rabbinical sententiousness – 'Attention must be paid to a man like this,' or 'A man is not a piece of fruit, Howard, you can't eat the orange and throw the peel away.'

Nevertheless each scene of **Death of a Salesman** is charged with feeling and theatrical energy, and it *is* the parable of twentieth-century America. It seems as unreasonable to blame the play now for its shortcomings as it is to blame the country whose icon is the Statue of Liberty for not always welcoming the concept it is honouring. As an audience member observed after the recent New York revival: 'It was like looking at the Grand Canyon' – an indelible part of the American landscape.

The struggle in Miller's plays is about the difficulty and the possibility of a man – and until **Broken Glass** it is invariably a man – taking control of his own life, 'that moment when, in my eyes,' said Miller, 'a man differentiates himself from every other man, that moment when out of a sky full of stars he fixes on one star'. It's a search for meaning in life that is resolved only in death. In **The Price** this debate becomes an explicit one between two brothers, between self-sacrifice on one side, and self-interest on the other: 'It's as though,' says the selfish brother, 'we're like two halves of the same guy. As though we can't quite move ahead – alone.'

His heroes – salesmen, dockers, policemen, farmers – all seek a sort of salvation in asserting their singularity – their 'name' – and redeeming their dignity, even by suicide. Willy Loman cries out, 'I am not a dime a dozen, I am Willy Loman ...!'. Eddie Carbone in **A View from the Bridge**, broken and destroyed by sexual guilt and public shame, bellows: 'I want my name,' and John Proctor in **The Crucible**, in refusing the calumny of condemning his fellow-citizens, declaims, 'How may I live without my name? I have given you my soul; leave me my name!' In nothing does Miller show his Americanism more than in the assertion of the right and necessity of the individual to own his own life.

Miller set **The Crucible** in the town of Salem in Massachusetts, where in 1692 nineteen adults and two dogs were hanged for witchcraft, and one man was pressed to death for refusing to plead, but the play was inspired by the events of the McCarthy era, by the actions of the witch-hunting House Un-American Activities Committee of the 1950s, in front of which Miller was invited to give evidence, in effect to betray his friends:

> It was as though the whole country had been born anew, without a memory even of certain elemental decencies which a year or two earlier no one would have imagined could be altered, let alone forgotten ... that the terror in these people was being knowingly planned and consciously engineered, and yet all they knew was terror. That so interior and subjective an emotion could have been so manifestly created from without was a marvel to me. It underlies every word in **The Crucible**.

Oddly, for all that it was engendered by specific events, **The Crucible** seems less of its time, and more enduring, than any of his other plays. For it he invented an entirely successful language – a coinage of seventeenth-century biblical cadences, pastoral poetry and regional English dialect, fused with potent theatrical rhetoric, and the play is a gloriously inspiring assertion of the individual dissenter against the latent tyranny of a repressive society. It's a deeply romantic – and deeply attractive – account of the nobility that we all aspire to and would wish we were capable of achieving in the face of having to make an absolute moral choice: as it were between betraying one's friends or one's country.

The Crucible. To a society intoxicated by sexual liberation, whirled in the vortex of the Vietnam War and the implicit civil – racial – war, Miller came to be seen as a ponderous moralist, and Williams as a pedlar of nostalgia – his preoccupation with female dependency and homosexual guilt being insufficiently liberated for the age. Miller's response was not to become more public and political but to write more about the past, as if to remind the country that history – like sex – had not been invented in the 1960s. He reclaimed the past as a means of understanding the future and his recurrent subjects were the Holocaust and the Depression, betrayal in private and public life, guilt, and loss of innocence: Cain wandering in a spiritual wilderness.

Miller asks the question: 'How are we to live our lives?' and Williams asks: 'How do we get through the night?' Both write about human fallibility – Miller trusting in its potential for improvement, Williams believing in its essential and irrevocable weakness.

Together they chronicle the curable and the incurable aspects of the world; paradoxically it is Miller who is the romantic, Williams the realist.

As Miller's and Williams' reputations began to decline in America, their international stature rose, and they have both enjoyed more honour and success in recent years in Britain. This is partly because the British theatre, sustained as it is by subsidy, generally feels confident (or complacent) about its present, hopeful of its future, and conscious of its past, whereas American theatre has been robbed of continuity. It's partly, too, that the British theatre has the virtuous habit of treating yesterday's classics as if they were contemporaneous. And it's partly that the British – fed on Shakespeare – have an appetite for theatre that uses such sinewy and passionate language with such unembarrassed enthusiasm.

That the prophet is not honoured in his own country is clear from a recent dilatory discussion in *The New York Times* with three theatre critics about the differences between British and American theatre:

CRITIC ONE: Arthur Miller is celebrated there.

CRITIC TWO: It's **Death of a Salesman**, for crying out loud. He's so cynical about American culture and American politics. The English love that.

CRITIC ONE: Though **Death of a Salesman** was not a smash when it first opened in London.

CRITIC THREE: It's also his earnestness.

Miller and Williams wrote with heat and heart, and from the perspective of the cool etiolated British theatre of the 1940s and '50s their work was felt like a distant and disturbing forest fire.

3

There was a period of about thirty years from around 1930 when that 'marvellous invalid', the Broadway theatre, seemed to be in a state of constant ecstasy: writers who became adjectival – O'Neill, Odets, Hellman, Hart and Kaufman, Hecht and McCarthur, Williams, Miller; actors like Katherine Cornell, Ethel Barrymore, Paul Muni, Fredric March, Katharine Hepburn, Uta Hagen, Irene Worth, Jessica Tandy, Arthur Marshall, Lee J. Cobb, Geraldine Page, Jason Robards, Marlon Brando, Julie Harris – who didn't *all* desert the theatre for the movies; directors like Elia Kazan, Jose Quintero, designers like Boris Aronson and Jo Mielziner. There was a place for serious theatre and there was a reasonable price to pay for it. But as Lillian Hellman said, 'I don't believe in the marvellous invalid theory. We forget that invalids can stay invalids. They don't always die and they don't always recover.' By the early 1960s it was clear that within the decade the tyranny of the box-office and the multiplication of production costs would create a Broadway dust-bowl.

It was at just this time that the British theatre, after decades of quiescence, was springing back to life at the Royal Court, the Royal Shakespeare Company, and the National Theatre; new playwrights, actors, and directors were emerging, with a cocky self-confidence. But the American theatre continued to provide the body of British theatre – if not with the life-giving jolt – then at least with a stimulating transfusion. The American experimental theatre which had grown up as a revolt against the commercial became an inspiring example to the British of how theatre could give minorities a voice to express themselves – about politics or race or drugs or gender – or, simply, sex.

If sexual intercourse was invented in 1963, so was a liturgy of liberation: 'DO IT!', 'SEIZE THE DAY!', 'FIND YOURSELF!', 'MAKE LOVE NOT WAR!', 'TURN ON!', 'DROP OUT!', 'OPEN THE DOORS OF PERCEPTION!'. A new American Dream was born – no less Utopian than the old one – whose component parts were a resistance to the suffocating conformity of the 'American Way of Life' and a defiance to an increasingly homogenised culture created by TV and advertising. All this was underwritten by a booming economy, relaxation of censorship, improved birth control, and an unpopular war. As the orthodoxies of the 1950s started to dissolve, the theatre – the art of the present tense – became transformed, and its transformation became a paradigm for what was happening in the rest of the country.

The new American theatre didn't look to Europe to embrace either the political or dramaturgical lessons of Brecht's Epic Theatre or the desolation – born out of an exhausted Europe – of Beckett's vision. If there was a dominant European influence in the theatre, it was the influence of Artaud, whose notion of deliverance from the tyranny of text chimed perfectly with the American goal of individual freedom. To this ideological mix was added existentialism (without socialism), stirred in with Freud, Zen Buddhism and a good dose of R.D. Laing's advocacy of the emancipation of the senses from the prison of reason. Peter Brook and Jerzy Grotowski became the spiritual godfathers of the new American theatre, encouraging the stripping away of accumulated conventions to reach what Brook and Grotowski called the 'holy' core.

The constituency of the theatre – performers and audiences – expanded to include previously ignored subjects: sexual issues, social issues, gender issues, the Vietnam War, and the concerns of special-interest groups like former prison inmates, the deaf, and old people. The conventional divisions dissolved: dance, gallery art, documentary, and political action became merged with theatre, and proscenium theatres were abandoned for studio theatres, thrust stages, in-the-round and 'site specific' environments – lofts, church basements, coffee-houses, parks and garages.

The playwright Sam Shepard described this world:

> There *was* a special sort of culture developing. You were close to the people who were going to the plays, there was really no difference between you and them – your own experience was their experience, so that you began to develop that

consciousness of what was happening ... I mean nobody knew what *was* happening, but there was a sense that something was going on. People were arriving from Texas and Arkansas in the middle of New York City, and a community was being established. It was a very exciting time.

Like the Group Theatre of the 1930s, many of the companies worked communally – writing plays as collectives and acting in ensembles. The ensemble was intended to be a paradigm of a perfect society, free of the authority of the playwright and the supremacy of text. It was a return to the communitarian spirit of the Federal Theatre Project and the Provincetown Players – and, indeed, of the Founding Fathers.

Companies like the Living Theatre, the Open Theatre, the Bread and Puppet Theatre, the Manhattan Project, and the Performance Group (later mutating into the Wooster Group) looked longingly to an American Eden uncorrupted by the competitive and hierarchical materialism of their parents, and to an aesthetic untainted by the commercial imperatives of Broadway or the boundaries of conventional play-making. Their binding belief was in iconoclasm.

The Living Theatre looking for **Paradise Now**.

No less Utopian, but far more irreverent, were companies like the gloriously camp and inventive Ridiculous Theatre Company and Off-Off-Broadway theatres like Café Cino and Café La Mama. Joseph Cino turned his one-room coffee-house into a theatre space which gave writers such as Lanford Wilson and Terrence McNally a platform – one memorably described by the playwright Robert Patrick as 'a cross between Lourdes and Sodom' – and Café La Mama, founded in 1962 by Ellen Stewart, gave opportunities to new directors, writers and producers and shows like the musical **Hair** – which now seems deeply conservative and sentimental: a hippie **Oklahoma!**.

It was an era that also gave birth to companies that continue to act as the *de facto* National Theatre of the USA: the Goodman Theatre in Chicago, the American Conservatory Theatre in San Francisco, the Guthrie Theatre in Minneapolis, the Alley Theatre in Houston, the Arena in Washington, the Mark Taper Theatre in Los Angeles, the Yale Repertory Theatre, and in New York – the Roundabout Theatre Company, the Manhattan Theatre Club, the Brooklyn Academy of Music, the Lincoln Center Theatre, and the Public Theatre, the child of Joe Papp and his New York Shakespeare Festival which presented Shakespeare for free in Central Park – the most important producing organisation of the post-war era.

Out of every corner emerged a theatre group speaking for disenfranchised or oppressed people – blacks, women, gays, Native Americans, Chicanos, Filipinos, Puerto Ricans, Asians. By the early 1980s there were twenty-eight gay and lesbian theatre groups across the country, and 110 women's groups giving a voice to many playwrights whose work rose above any diminishing adjectives – not so much 'women' playwrights, as good ones: Beth Henley, Marsha Norman and Wendy Wasserstein, for instance.

For the first time since the Federal Theatre Project of the 1930s, with the foundation of the National Endowment for the Arts, the US government flirted with subsidy for theatre.

However, the deep instinctive ideological wariness of state support for the arts ensured that the sums were small. The significant funding for the arts came through tax legislation – a covert form of subsidy in which the funding decisions are made by individuals rather than state bodies. If tax concessions on sums donated to the arts are regarded as a foregone tax – i.e. a subsidy – the theatre in America can be seen to be subsidised on a per capita basis at a much higher rate than in Britain. The difference is, of course, one of principle: the US government washes its hands of the responsibility for providing continuity to artistic enterprise, which means that for theatre producers in the US it is always year zero. They will always be in the position of Willy Loman, determined at all costs to be 'well liked'.

It's easy to parody the 1960s – in Britain as much as the US – as a rich kid's revolution about the right freely to enjoy sex, drugs, rock and roll and to write 'fuck' on walls and in plays, and it's easy to deplore a movement that, as much as the lowest common denominator in the tackiest Broadway musical, sought entirely to bypass the intellect to reach the heart or the groin. Auden's invocation to 'love one another or die' was taken literally: love, or more usually sex, was intended to salve the open wounds of racism, warmongering, and over-indulgence, and this simple expectation of redemption sat comfortably with the apparently irreducible American faith in individual and national progress.

But it wasn't all so disarmingly simplistic: many people started to become politicised in the 1960s and '70s – as they hadn't been since the Depression – by the Vietnam War and by the recognition of the long-established practice of apartheid within the Land of the Free. The campaign for civil rights for blacks was long and painful and is still unresolved. It ran parallel to the more successful – in terms of legislation and change of heart – campaigns of the women's movement and for gay liberation.

Much of the theatre provoked by issues was agit-prop but it's a virtue in an art form that only exists in performance that it *does* often deal with events happening on the streets outside the theatre, and that it speaks for and to a minority who can't find public expression in any other form. It was no less important to dissent in the USA than it was in East Europe, and while the passage of history may have rendered the works of that period redundant, that is not to discredit or dilute their power at the time. To have staged in 1967 Barbara Gerson's political parody of the feud between Kennedy and Johnson, **MacBird** (based on **Macbeth**), was no less an act of political dissent than staging **Hamlet** under Ceauşescu in 1980s Romania.

And few plays have as much power as those which, fuelled by polemical purpose and incandescent with indignation, illuminate the present from the perspective of the committed participant – like Larry Kramer's campaigning play about AIDS in the 1980s, **The Normal Heart** – even if it hasn't endured beyond the period when the public showed a wilful ignorance of the existence of AIDS.

Those adjectives applied to playwrights – 'polemical', 'gay', 'black', 'woman' – are part of a critics' arsenal, deployed as weapons of repression, which seek to belittle plays that are often about so much more than the issues, attitudes or events that have engendered them. And none more so than a play written by a black woman who died of cancer in 1965 at the age of thirty-four: Lorraine Hansberry (1930–1965).

Her first play, **A Raisin in the Sun**, resembles an Odets play in its use of a realistic mode to describe a world of which most of its audience were ignorant. 'The realistic playwright,' said Hansberry, 'states not only what is, but what can and should be.' The title came from a poem by Langston Hughes:

> What happens to a dream deferred,
> Does it dry up,
> Like a raisin in the sun?

Walter Lee Younger, a thirty-five-year-old chauffeur, lives in a one-window, three-room, cockroach-ridden Chicago tenement – 'a rat trap' – with his wife, mother, young sister and only child, and dreams the American Dream. The mother receives her late husband's life insurance and their lives are transformed: Walter wants to build a small business – a liquor store, his daughter wants to become a doctor, but the mother – a figure of indomitable stoicism and determination out of Gorky or O'Casey – uses the money to buy a house for the family in an all-white suburb. A man from the local 'Improvement Association' urbanely argues for racial segregation, his case underwritten by a discreet threat of violence. He offers to buy the house in order to 'spare them any embarrassment'. Walter insists on staying and announces that he will kneel before any white man who will buy the house for more than its face value. He's saved from the final degradation, but they move out and move on.

The play is an archetype of humane, liberal, politically informed art, impelled by a desire to show the individual foibles of socially aspirant individuals trapped in roles defined for them by other people, rather than to generalise about endemic racism. Said Lorraine Hansberry:

> It will be discovered that while an excessively poignant Porgy was being instilled in generations of Americans, his truer-life counterpart was being ravaged by longings that were and are in no way alien to the rest of mankind, and that bear within them the stuff of really great art ... each hour that flies teaches us that Porgy is as much inclined to hymns of sedition as to lullabies and love songs; he is profoundly complicated and interesting; everywhere he is making his own sounds in the night.

And the sounds they were making in her play were less about the failure of systems and the shortcomings of society, than about the capacity of people for self-deception, and their fallibility, regardless of race. All the same, the play never lets you forget that not to be aware of race in America is a privilege that belongs exclusively to whites.

*Sidney Poitier in **A Raisin in the Sun**: 'The realistic playwright states not only what is, but what can and should be.'*

A Raisin in the Sun gave a triumphant opportunity to its star, Sidney Poitier, and to its director, Lloyd Richards, who later directed all the plays of August Wilson (1945–), who made a halting start to writing plays in the late 1970s. By the late 1980s, Wilson had written three plays – **Joe Turner's Come and Gone, Fences,** and **Ma Rainey's Black Bottom** – which had played on Broadway and to audiences all over the country. The plays – all set in the past – are about the experience of a 'black community' that is all too aware that, although being black is a defining factor, it doesn't create a 'community'. Wilson is not a polemicist or an advocate of political transformation, but his indictment of social conditions is no less strong for being implicit. Said Wilson:

> What I've tried to do is to reveal the richness of the lives of the people, who show that the largest ideas are contained by their lives, and that there is a nobility in their lives. Blacks in America have so little to make life compared to whites, yet do so with a certain zest ... which is charged and luminous and has all the qualities of anyone else's life. I think a lot of this is hidden by the glancing manner in which white America looks at blacks and the way blacks look at themselves.

Wilson's plays assert the importance of constructing a history for yourself, when somebody else has been constructing a history for you and your ancestral voices are silent. 'The theme I keep coming back to is the need to re-connect yourself ... the sense of standing in your grandfather's shoes. Because I think it's vital. Having shared a common past we have a common past and a common future.' Apart from talking about re-connecting with Africa, slavery and the South, it could be the voice of Arthur Miller.

Joe Turner's Come and Gone.

195

Wilson's best play, **Joe Turner's Come and Gone**, is set in a Pittsburgh boarding-house in 1911, peopled by a group of wanderers who still bear the marks of slavery. His most accessible is **Ma Rainey's Black Bottom**, set in a white-owned recording studio where the black musicians are 'controlled' by the white technicians and owners. The blues was a wholly black music – the oral history of the black people, and in the play we see it appropriated, to be marketed as entertainment for whites. It's not schematic: it's as much about the differences between black and black and white and white as between black and white. As in the best theatre, Wilson creates a universe on stage – the world of the blues and the world of commerce are a metaphor for the world outside.

The tumour of racism in the body of American society was examined in Edward Albee's play **The Death of Bessie Smith** in 1959. The great blues singer was refused treatment after a car accident in Memphis and bled to death in the hospital, which in the play acts as a microcosm for a society that is poisoned by individual and institutional racism. In its unambiguous social commitment and its realistic style, it is almost wholly uncharacteristic of the later work of Edward Albee.

Albee (1928–) emerged in one of the small, off-Broadway theatres with a prodigiously successful one-act play **The Zoo Story** – an encounter between two lonely men on a bench in Central Park. It's a marvellously deft conversation piece between characters who inhabit two separate social and linguistic universes, and an engaged critique of detachment and

Early Albee.

materialism. 'The audience is so dead I have to shake life into it,' said Albee, and in a later play – the hugely popular **Who's Afraid of Virginia Woolf?** – he unquestionably succeeded in this ambition.

Virginia Woolf seemed on one level to be the *ur*-play of American middle-class marriage – a battleground littered with the corpses of failed idealism and disappointment – and that component was a large part of the allure of the play for its very substantial audience. George, the history professor, has been long married to the college president's daughter, Martha; Nick, the new faculty member, is newly married to Honey. George and Martha are childless and have created a child, a fantasy which dissolves during the course of an evening of epic drinking and argument. Nick and Honey are drawn into the vortex and obliged to surrender their own protective professional and sexual illusions.

Albee took on the attritional marriage play – Osborne's **Look Back in Anger**, or Coward's **Private Lives**, with fangs, claws, head and heart – and established an American template. He used language violently, waspishly, banteringly, caressingly, as a weapon, a defence, a vehicle for lying, for fantasy, for fiction, for evading the truth – and as a substitute for experience itself. The two couples engage in an exhaustive quartet, hectic, driving; obsessive variations of disharmonies resolving in an exhausted finale of sparse monosyllables.

Since **Virginia Woolf**, film and television drama have appropriated and diluted Albee's magnificently well-muscled and well-orchestrated marital rows without achieving the intensity of a play which, in its original production with Uta Hagen and Arthur Hill, had a huge theatrical potency – and isn't that, after all, the point of theatre? Kenneth Tynan said of Rattigan's **The Deep Blue Sea**:

> It has already been acclaimed as 'brilliant theatre', but there is a patronising ring to that phrase which I must set about demolishing. It implies that for a play to suit the theatre is not quite enough; that it is somehow improper to write deliberately for the medium you have selected – not print, not pure sound, but for the upturned host of credulous faces in a darkened hall.

But Albee would (rightly) scorn a description of **Virginia Woolf** as merely 'brilliant theatre'. The play conspicuously carries its ambitions to be more than a domestic drama, laden as it is (over-laden?) with rage and despair about the determination of American society to cling on to illusions and its reluctance to face realities; with time the comparisons with **Look Back in Anger** seem all the more evident. But it is the personal note that resonates most strongly in the play and one can't but think that, as the only adopted child of rich and unloving parents, Albee meant the 'invented child' to be something more than a metaphor. In one form or another the lack or loss of children – and of parents – underwrites Albee's plays as an emblem of emotional and spiritual sterility. His adoptive parents – a tall, powerful, frustrated woman married to a small, weak man – seem to have engendered a fictional world populated by self-created victims like George and Martha who, at the end of **Virginia Woolf**, arrive at some form of release like two exhausted beached swimmers:

GEORGE: (*Puts his hand gently on her shoulder; she puts her head back and he sings to her, very softly*):
Who's afraid of Virginia Woolf
Virginia Woolf,
Virginia Woolf,

MARTHA: I ... am ... George ...

GEORGE: Who's afraid of Virginia Woolf ...

MARTHA: I ... am ... George ... I ... am ...
(GEORGE *nods, slowly.*)

Virginia Woolf was born out of the Kennedy years and, after Kennedy's death and the growing corrosion of the Vietnam War, Albee and America changed. Whatever glimmer of optimism Albee possessed became extinguished. Perhaps it was a purely personal response to public events, or perhaps a philosophical one. Easy analyses and answers, easy indictments were no longer possible; doubt became the only plausible and principled response.

Albee refused to try to repeat the successful form – or formula – of **Virginia Woolf**, but it was also a defensive response to the bulimic praise that success brings in America. Clearly for Albee the form of his earlier plays was unable to portray the dementia in the dissolution of American society: he had never been a naturalistic writer and in his subsequent plays he rejected the realism of observed behaviour. He made an ironic exception in **Seascape** in which he insisted that two of the protagonists – lizards who spoke English – should be 'absolutely naturalistic'. 'It is just that the characters are lizards,' he said.

Albee has always regarded the text as the inviolable foundation of theatre, but that principle developed into a kind of absolutism: 'As opposed to many other people who feel that plays are complete only when they are performed, I am convinced that they are complete as a literary art which one can understand merely by reading.' To which one might respond, in Tennessee Williams' words: 'A play in a book is only a shadow of a play and not even a clear shadow.'

Albee is at his best when his plays are charged with passion; in latter years only **Three Tall Women**, which aches with a desire for love and reconciliation, seems as if the will isn't doing the work of the imagination. In **Tiny Alice**, **A Delicate Balance**, **All Over**, **Seascape**, **Counting the Ways** – oblique, detached, evasive, and abstracted, dressed in elegiac despair about the changes of age and the coming of death and lined with etiolated language – Albee seems like the Miss Havisham of American theatre.

By the mid-1960s Broadway had come to resemble the place it is now – a lavishly marketed department store filled with designer-label 'products', all conceived, manufactured, and exhaustively tested at an infinity of other venues – which might include the National Theatre of Great Britain, the Royal Shakespeare Company, the West End of London, Off-Broadway, Off-Off-Broadway and a variety of American not-for-profit regional theatres often linked with universities and colleges and funded by government, foundations, and corporate and individual patrons.

Meanwhile the British and European theatre has demonstrated that, if you want a theatre that takes artistic risks, sustains the best of tradition, develops new talent, feeds the commercial theatre, and does all this at seat prices which do not exclude all but the very rich, there is no alternative but to seek state support. In spite of that, however, out of the American theatre in the 1980s and '90s emerged the two most impressive playwrights of their time in the English language: David Mamet and Tony Kushner, proving that if God plays dice with the universe, nowhere is it more apparent than in the distribution of talent.

While America is everywhere in London, the only presence of Britain in New York, apart from Marmite and Oxford marmalade in chi-chi shops in Greenwich Village, two or three conspicuously successful magazine editors, Mobil Masterpiece Theatre on public TV, and a film or two a year, is a proliferation of British theatre on Broadway. *The New York Times* complained in 1998 that the British theatre was 'succeeding as lavishly as orchids in a hothouse'. This creaking metaphor bears witness to the fruit that the American theatre fertilised in the 1950s. It may be hard to bear as they welcome – and they do – yet another imported British production on Broadway, but this 'invasion' is an acknowledgement that British theatre has gained as much from American theatre as we have ever given to it.

Uta Hagen and Arthur Hill in **Who's Afraid of Virginia Woolf**: 'I … am … George … I … am.'

B.B.

'The proof of the pudding is in the eating.'
BERTOLT BRECHT

Bertolt Brecht (1898–1956) is such a complex and pervasive force that the simple things about him get obscured. He was a great poet: think Yeats or Pound. He was a brilliant man of the theatre, highly receptive to the avant-garde of his day, quick to improve it and somewhat too precipitate to turn it into theory. He was a Communist: not a left-winger, not a liberal, nor a humanitarian. From his twenties onwards, he thought and worked in terms of Marxist dialectic and he really wasn't kidding. His loyalty to Soviet home and foreign policy is part of the package: he had qualms but they were tactical rather than ethical and he kept them to himself. He was capable of emotional cruelty and shady dealing, both much exacerbated by the moral leeway inherent in Stalinist Communism. In the last few years of his life, a combination of history and his own long-practised wiliness gave him a theatre of his own: thus was born the Brecht we know.

He was a child of a middle-class business family in Augsburg, Bavaria. 'In future I shall produce nothing but flaming mud pies made of shit,' he wrote in the marvellous diaries of his youth. He'd already written **Baal** (first version 1918) an early version of **In the Jungle of Cities** (ditto) and **Drums in the Night** (first drafted 1919). (Dates with Brecht are always approximate: most plays were rewritten, some over decades.)

These three early plays are quintessentially the work of a young poet who wants to throw flaming mud pies at the world. They're sensual, pushy and anarchic. Violent confrontation is the basic form; obsessions are the only authentic kind of feeling; explanations are redundant; shocks illuminate. It's a romantic world, filled with echoes of Rimbaud, cheap movies and pulp fiction.

If Rimbaud was an influence, so were Gauguin, Rudyard Kipling and the early nineteenth-century expressionist Georg Büchner. There was an enticing role-model close to hand in Munich in the shape of Frank Wedekind (1864–1918), the author of the sexual ground-breaker **Spring Awakening** and that fabulous mantrap, **Earth Spirit**, better known as **Lulu**. Wedekind was also an actor, journalist, wit and cabaret-performer. Brecht played a mean guitar and often performed in cabaret: there's a delicious photo of him accompanying the clown Karl Valentin in a place evocatively called the Munich Lachkeller. Brecht is tootling on the piccolo between a tuba-player disguised as Toulouse-Lautrec and a gorgeous but very cross-looking brunette. At twenty, he attended Wedekind's funeral. 'Like Tolstoy and Strindberg he was one of the great educators of modern Europe,' he wrote of Wedekind, before adding a phrase which might have been written by Oscar Wilde: 'His greatest work was his personality.'

Drums in the Night was produced at the Munich Kammerspiel in 1922 and won him the Kleist Prize: 'The twenty-four-year-old Bert Brecht has altered the literary face of Germany overnight.' Brecht's lifelong collaboration with the designer Caspar Neher, a friend from schooldays, began here with work on Marlowe's **Edward II**. Brecht had asked the clown Karl Valentin to sit in on rehearsals; it was he who said that, since the soldiers in the battle scene would no doubt be frightened, their faces ought to be painted chalky white. Brecht would later quote this as the crucial moment in the birth of epic theatre. One other milestone in the shape of a piece of advice from the resident dramaturg: 'Invent a theory, my dear Brecht! When one presents Germans with a theory, they are willing to swallow anything.'

In Berlin he met Piscator: Marxist, propagandist and founder of the 'wreck-the-theatre' school of direction. Film, projections, puppets and assembly-lines all figured in his machine-age aesthetic: a lasting influence. Brecht also met Elisabeth Hauptmann, the first of his three major writing collaborators. Their role is controversial.

Production design for a Piscator production of an Ernst Toller play in 1927.

For Brecht, writing plays was making plays, and the first requirement was a fully staffed factory, bustling with talk, suggestions, readings-aloud, dictation, questions, rows and donkey-work. Both Robert Lepage and Baz Luhrmann have similar set-ups today, one hopes without the misery that Brecht's produced.

All three of his co-factory-workers – Hauptmann, Ruth Berlau and Margarete Steffin – were his lovers, sometimes concurrently, and all worked long and arduous hours. But what were they working *at*? How much did they write

themselves? Or did they just research? Or edit? Or transcribe? A recent book, *The Life and Lies of Bertolt Brecht* by John Fuegi, paints Brecht as a heartless predator, passing off his girlfriends' writings as his own. The book (which caused a scandal in scholastic circles) had at least one useful effect: it opened our eyes to the fact that much of the Brecht canon has till now been meanly credited: that others deserve much better billing. But to claim, as

Lotte Lenya in **The Threepenny Opera**.

Fuegi does, that (for example) Margarete Steffin was the prime creator of **Mother Courage** is surely stretching it: Steffin never wrote a work of stature on her own, any more than Hauptmann or Berlau ever did.

Mainstream Brechtians point out that 'collective' work was sound Communist practice, which would be more convincing if Brecht had spread the proceeds in a collective way. By the 1960s, both Berlau and Hauptmann felt that they'd been thoroughly taken to the cleaner's, and they said so. 'We are not two playwrights who have collaborated in writing plays,' Brecht replied angrily to Berlau. (But he didn't send the letter.) Margarete Steffin died without telling her story.

Hauptmann's contribution is the easiest to sort out, though it's still murky. She translated **The Beggar's Opera** from English and it seems that she had an equal hand in turning it into **The Threepenny Opera** in 1928. She wrote some of **The Rise and Fall of the City of Mahagonny**, including the 'whisky-bar' song and the Benares song ('Is here no telephone?'). Her uncovering of ancient Chinese and Japanese drama would inspire the Brechtian *Lehrstücke*, or didactic plays. One example, **He Who Says Yes**, is practically a straight crib; students of plagiarism have a stranger event to ponder in the case of **Happy End**, with its eerie resemblance to the Damon Runyon story, *The Idyll of Miss Sarah Brown*, which would later provide the basis of Frank Loesser's **Guys and Dolls**. The fact that the Runyon tale didn't appear in book form until three years after **Happy End** was produced seems on the face of it to settle the matter; but why did Hauptmann, who had written the outline, insist to the end of her days that she'd based it on an American magazine-story by the entirely non-existent Dorothy Lane?

Hauptmann may well have been a victim of Brecht's sharp practice – if so, she wasn't the only one – but a remark of Lotte Lenya's suggests another side to her. 'Last night I had a date with La Hauptmann,' she wrote to Kurt Weill in 1930. 'We kidded her terribly. I said that all anyone called her in Berlin was "Royalties Sadie", and that whenever she entered a theatre, the dramaturgs would yell, 'Hurry, put your plays away, La Hauptmann is coming to adapt them.'

The most gifted woman writer to move into Brecht's orbit was the one who got away. Marieluise Fleisser's **Purgatory in Ingolstadt** was set in her home town; when she arrived in Berlin for rehearsals, the intendant of the Berlin theatre took one look at her provincial clothes and asked her where she had left her hat. (She didn't own one.) Brecht had recommended the play: he sat in on rehearsals, exerted his *droit de seigneur* over the production, play and playwright and, finding himself ignored in a lunch-discussion between Fleisser and the intendant, unscrewed the top off his salt-shaker and threw the contents in the other man's face. The play was successful, so much so that (upsettingly for the author) it was widely assumed that Brecht had written it.

Her second play, **Pioneers in Ingolstadt**, is a fierce, feminist account of small-town life disrupted by a brigade of young sappers. One girl becomes a prostitute; another, after much persuasion, yields to her boyfriend in the belief that it will make him love her: she ends up, of course, as an object of derision and scorn. Once more, Brecht took over. More than thirty years later, she wrote a bitter description: 'The man obliterated me and no guardian angel came to my aid, only my hand was still my own and I was forced to drink myself into a stupor.'

The play caused a scandal, not least back home in Ingolstadt. Fleisser was shattered and the fact that Brecht chose this particular moment to marry Helene Weigel can scarcely have cheered her up. (When Hauptmann heard the news, she tried to kill herself.) Fleisser returned to Ingolstadt, married a swimming-champion and vanished into obscurity.

The Threepenny Opera was a commercial hit: to this day, every Berliner old enough to have seen it not only thinks it was the best thing ever, but swears that he or she was there on the opening night. **Happy End**, the Brecht/Weill follow-up, was a flop and for the first and last time Elisabeth Hauptmann found herself lavishly credited. Brecht and Weill had been working for years on **The Rise and Fall of the City of Mahagonny**: by the time it opened in Berlin in 1931, Brecht was a committed Communist. Neon-lit jungles, anarchy and catchy tunes were things of the past; he rowed with Weill, denounced the show ('culinary theatre') and walked out.

There's a memorable photo of Brecht, taken in the late 1920s. He's wearing an enormous leather trenchcoat, he's skinny, his hair is cropped, there's a huge cigar between his fingers and he's smirking lazily at the camera. He looks vibrant, chic, successful. Looking at the photo, you realise how attractive Communism was. It was the only interesting alternative to Hitler. It allowed pugnacity and affront. It affirmed a leanness and a ruthlessness in human relations. It was smart and sexy.

In **Man is Man**, Brecht made the sound Communist point that the human personality isn't fixed: that it changes according to circumstances. The same applies to Brecht the playwright: the flaming-cowpat poet of **In the Jungle of Cities**, all colour and chaos, has a different aim in every way from the cool didacticist who wrote the *Lehrstücke*. These works are short, severe, instructive.

Young Brecht: vibrant, chic, successful.

They were performed to audiences of workers, students and children. **The Lindbergh Flight** is a choral work (music by Weill and Hindemith) which celebrates man's conquest of the air. In **He Who Says Yes**, a little boy gives up his life in accord with ancient custom; in **He Who Says No**, he doesn't have to. The theme of individual death for the sake of collective good was a central prop of Communist thinking: Brecht returned to it in an important *Lehrstück*, **The Measures Taken**.

In it, a cadre of revolutionaries describe the life and death of their Young Comrade. A typical bleeding heart, he'd tried to alleviate the sufferings of the wretched in various ways, thus arguably delaying the day of revolution and certainly exceeding orders. So the other members of the cadre killed him. OK? This very accurate account of Soviet Terror caused a storm within the Party. Brecht had casually blown a well-kept secret: it was carelessness like this that got the Young Comrade bumped off.

The Mother, produced in 1932, was based on the novel by Gorky but continued the *Lehrstück* form:

> ANTON: When you joined our movement two weeks ago, Pavel, you said we could come to your place if we had any special job to do. Your place is safest because we've never worked here before.
>
> PAVEL: What do you want to do?
>
> ANDREI: We've got to print today's leaflets. The latest wage cuts have really stirred the men up.

Brecht was collaborating with a group of young left-wing actors who insisted on lucid narrative, sound politics and no artistic frills. The text is austere, uncluttered: so was the playing. The setting conveyed the beauty of unadorned and useful objects. (A much harder effect to achieve than old-style razzmatazz.) Seeing the play now, you realise just how much art went into it. The choruses, the placards, Eisler's difficult score, mark it out not as a popular work, nor as a useful guide to revolutionary tactics – was it ever? – but as a mannered, beautiful piece of experimental theatre.

Margarete Steffin was in the cast. She was twenty-four, working class, a committed Communist, already riddled with the tuberculosis that would kill her eight years later. In photographs, she has a sparrow-like beauty. Brecht swept her up; in 1933, when the Reichstag was burned down, he fled the country and within a few months, he, Helene Weigel and Margarete Steffin were settled in Denmark.

Brecht and the Brechtian crew had lost almost all they had: their homes, their incomes, worst of all their ability to put on plays. The Nazi State seemed firmly dug in for as long as the eye could stretch. From the Soviet Union came a threat of a different kind.

At the Soviet Writers' Congress of 1934, 'socialist realism' – a form which had never attracted Brecht in the slightest – was proclaimed the art form of the future. Artistic experiment was denounced. By 1936, *Pravda* was attacking 'formalists' such as Shostakovich and Eisenstein. Brecht's friend, the playwright Tretyakov, disappeared under suspicion of being a Japanese spy. Another friend, the German actress Carola Neher, vanished into the labour camps. These were Brecht's 'dark times':

> My teacher
> Tall and kindly
> Has been shot, condemned by a people's court
> As a spy. His name is damned.
> His books are destroyed. Talk about him
> Is suspect and suppressed.
> Suppose he is innocent.

Brecht wrote no more *Lehrstücke*: instead, he aimed at the novel-like richness which – in civilised Party quarters – was approved of. From now on, the plays became more ambiguous and more richly coloured, the characters more doubting and more three-dimensional. It's one of the paradoxes of Brecht's life that, by doing what he was told – but by doing it in a highly original, barely obedient way – he created his masterpieces.

His great epic, **Life of Galileo**, shows its hero paying the internal price of compromise. Brecht wrote it while following the show-trial of Nikolai Bukharin: colleague of Stalin throughout the revolutionary years. The connection was hit home by Isaac Deutscher in his Trotsky biography, *The Prophet Outcast*:

[Brecht] could not bring himself to break with Stalinism. He surrendered to it with a load of doubt on his mind, as the capitulators in Russia had done … The Galileo of his drama is Zinoviev or Bukharin or Rakovsky dressed up in historical costume. He is haunted by the 'fruitless' martyrdom of Giordano Bruno; that terrible example causes him to surrender to the Inquisition, just as Trotsky's fate caused so many Communists to surrender to Stalin.

Galileo is a moral adventurer of Shakespearian size: he's flawed, articulate, rank with the smell of his own mortality. His journey of self-discovery leads not to his death – the play is too subtle for that – but to resigned old age, lit by a flicker of hope. The form of the play – its grand solidity – now seems one of the best things about it. But Brecht resisted this, or felt it had been imposed on him. 'A great step backwards,' he wrote in his journal.

Mother Courage and her Children was written back to back with **Galileo**: once again, a sixteenth-century setting gives a robustness to the language and an Elizabethan sweep to the action. The difference is that Galileo has insight, both into himself and into the cause of his disasters: this is what makes the play a tragedy. Mother Courage learns nothing at all.

Her play supports a new and highly embarrassing Party line. In August 1939, Stalin signed a non-aggression pact with Hitler. Communists and fellow-travellers throughout the world were faced with a hideous test of loyalty. Brecht was as dismayed as anyone else: the USSR had 'saved itself, at the cost of leaving the workers of the world without guidance, hopes or help', he wrote gloomily in his journals.

Mother Courage drags her wagon towards yet another futile battle.

But publicly he was as loyal as ever. **Mother Courage** puts forward the Party argument for appeasement. Courage, the small-time profiteer, lives on the pickings of a war, the only point of which is to make a profit for the ruling classes. At the end of the play we see her dragging her wagon towards yet another futile battle. The lesson is clear. War is a capitalistic con-trick: stay out.

The play is perhaps not quite as unassailable as **Galileo**, but there are no better scenes in the canon of twentieth-century drama than Courage bargaining, or Katrin drumming on the roof. There are no better images – not even in Chekhov – than the cart with its dwindling team; no greater tests of acting than Courage, spitting on her hands, testing the weight of her wagon and deciding that she can, after all, despite her age and exhaustion, pull it along.

Nothing that followed matched these two masterpieces. **Mr Puntila and His Servant Matti** is a warning to anyone thinking of offering hospitality to a playwright. Fleeing from Denmark to Finland, Brecht and Co. found refuge on the country estate of a well-off Finnish landowner, one Hella Wuolijoki. She made the great mistake of showing Steffin a play she was writing about a drunken squire named Puntila: the rest is history. Fifteen years later, when Wuolijoki was no longer rich, her pleas for a share of the royalties went unheard.

The Good Person of Setzuan is an awkward throwback to ten-year-old Chinoiserie. In a greedy world, the sweet and gentle Shen Te (female) can only survive by posing as the harsh and exploitative male Shui Ta. When problems ensue, the visiting gods (who started all the trouble in the first place) escape into the heavens, leaving us to reflect that painful personality-splits are unavoidable under capitalism.

The Resistible Rise of Arturo Ui was written in a rush with an eye to America: it's a bouncy account of the rise of Hitler, quite baffling in its priorities. Hitler is an unruly puppet of the ruling classes, exactly as in some Communist schoolkids' primer of the early 1930s. But there's an excellent actor's *tour de force* when the Hitler character learns his gestures from a clapped-out actor.

On 12 May 1941, the travel documents arrived enabling the Factory to escape to America. They travelled via Russia. Steffin was moved *en route* into a Moscow hospital and there she died. Brecht got the telegram in the United States and it's clear from the private poems he wrote that he was devastated. The relationship between the secretary of dark times, and the woman who had nothing to give but dedication, is one of the great untold love stories of the century.

The only time that Samuel Beckett visited the United States, he observed, 'This is somehow not the right country for me. The people are too strange.' This might have been expected. Brecht, on the other hand, had written in his journal at the age of twenty-two, 'The answer: America …' and he'd fantasised about it ever since. Once he found himself actually living there, he floundered.

He settled in California, now a richly talented harbour of European expatriates. Billy Wilder, Fritz Lang and many others had found their feet with oiled rapidity. Brecht, so clever and quick in Europe, trotted along at the back of the class. He did his best to exploit the star-system, but somehow couldn't get the hang of it. He chased unsuitable marquee-names for abortive projects: Elisabeth Bergner in an adaptation of **The Duchess of Malfi**, Anna May Wong in **The Good Person of Setzuan**. Luise Rainer commissioned **The Caucasian Chalk Circle**, but didn't pursue it. ('I am *Brecht*!' he screamed at the three-time Oscar-winner. 'And you are *nothing*!')

The Caucasian Chalk Circle stands with **Galileo**, **Mother Courage** and **The Good Person of Setzuan** as Brecht's core of 'popular' classics. Its prologue and cracker-motto ending (a defence of land-collectivisation) are sanctimonious, but the rest is delightful. It's a superb director's piece and there's a neat self-portrait in the shape of the wise but rascally Azdak. This was the last of his major works. He hustled for jobs in film, but he hadn't the camaraderie or suavity to get them and the only screen credit he was given was for Fritz Lang's *Hangmen Also Die*, a mendacious account of Czech resistance. Life was quiet.

odd, i can't breath in this climate [he wrote in his diary]. the air is totally odourless, morning and evening, in both house and garden. there are no seasons here. it has been part of my morning routine to lean out of the window and breathe in fresh air; i have cut this out of my routine here. there is neither smoke nor the smell of grass to be had. the plants seem to me like the twigs we used to plant in the sand as children. after ten minutes their leaves were dangling limply. you keep wondering if they might cut off the water, even here, and what then? occasionally, especially in the car going to beverley hills, i get something like a whiff of landscape, which 'really' seems attractive; gentle lines of hills, lemon thickets, a californian oak, even one or other of the filling-stations can actually be rather amusing; but all this lies behind plate glass, and i involuntarily look at each hill or lemon tree for a little price tag you look for these price tags on people too.

One important event took place: he worked on **Galileo** with the great English actor Charles Laughton. Laughton was an unhappy Hollywood star, ashamed not only of his homosexuality but of his heaving, crumpled-marshmallow ugliness.

Simon Callow, in his Laughton biography, notes the similarities between the two men: their bluntness, their workaholism, their sloppy dress, their constant need for the 'bounce' and challenge of others, their lack of friends. (Each also had a masterful wife and a shadowy entourage of lovers.) Brecht loved Laughton's acting: it was sensuous, forceful, unsentimental. Asked why he acted, Laughton replied, 'Because I like to imitate great men.' Brecht was delighted: not to 'be' them, or to show off in their borrowed robes, but to *depict* them: at once critique, analysis and comment enter the acting frame. Laughton, in turn, thought Brecht was second only to Shakespeare.

Laughton in **Galileo**.

They started work in late 1944: trying out scenes, rewriting them, adjusting the translation, comparing scenes from Elizabethan plays, tramping around museums and art galleries. The première took place in June 1947 in a 260-seat theatre in Hollywood. The young Joseph Losey was the director, and seems not to have minded his junior status. Helene Weigel was the wardrobe-mistress: disgusted by the way Laughton's Galileo scratched his balls while thinking, she sewed up his pockets. Ruth Berlau took the production photographs and the first-night audience included Charlie Chaplin, Ingrid Bergman and Gene Kelly.

Nearly seven years had passed since Brecht had arrived in the USA. The war was over, Europe had been divided and it was time to leave. One small hurdle remained: an order to testify before the House Un-American Activities Committee. Brecht treated the panel to an immortal display of Schweykian guile. Asked about **The Measures Taken**, he replied about **He Who Says Yes**. When a speech from **The Mother** was read aloud, he pointed out that the translation was inaccurate. (It was also 'not very beautiful, but I am not speaking about that'.) At the end of the interview, the Chairman thanked him: Mr Brecht, he said, had been a good example to the other witnesses. The following day, Brecht scooted. Shortly after, **Galileo** opened in New York, giving him exactly what he needed to boost his status back home in Germany: a Broadway production with a great international star.

He arrived in the Soviet-occupied sector in October 1948. In theory he was there to direct a production of **Mother Courage**, but he at once set about planning a theatre company. His strength was a superb portfolio of plays, many unknown and unperformed in Germany. His weakness was that he wasn't especially close to the Communist leadership and his work wasn't much liked: just as in the 1930s, the Party elite preferred 'socialist realism' to anything Brecht was likely to offer.

So when, at the end of the year, the Berliner Ensemble was formed and given a state subsidy, it had no theatre: it was merely a company that gave guest performances here and there. The work was often carped at on ideological grounds and the Ensemble's production of Goethe's **Urfaust** caused an unholy row. 'One of the most important works of our great German poet,' complained the ruler of the GDR, Walter Ulbricht, had been 'formalistically defaced'. Things looked glum. In March 1953, Brecht wrote:

> our productions in Berlin are now getting almost no response press notices appear months after the opening night and contain nothing but a few feeble sociological analyses. the audience is the petty-bourgeois audience of the volksbuhne, workers constitute a bare 7 per cent.

The change came three months later. On 16 June, demonstrations broke out against wage-cuts: they soon spread into demands for political freedom. The streets were packed with protesting workers; the CIA cabled Washington for permission to arm them, the head of Russian Intelligence, Lavrenty Beria, arrived and the rising was put down with tanks. Its defeat triggered Brecht's celebrated squib:

> After the uprising of June 17
> The secretary of the Writers' Union
> Had leaflets distributed in the Stalinallee
> In which it was said that the people
> Had lost the government's confidence
> Which it would only be able to regain
> By redoubling its efforts. In that case, would it
> Not be simpler if the government dissolved the people
> And elected another?

The poem is often quoted as an example of witty defiance: in fact, Brecht made no attempt to publish it and it appeared in print only after his death. The course he took in public was very different. 'Please know that I stand with the forces of socialist progress at this moment,' he asserted in a letter to the Commander of the Soviet garrison. He also wrote to Ulbricht; this letter was in fact a touch equivocal, but one crucial sentence was enough: 'I need to express to you at this moment my allegiance with the Socialist Unity Party of Germany.'

From this point on, Brecht was a favoured artist. For years he had argued that his Berliner Ensemble should have a theatre of its own. Now all obstacles were swept away. The following year the Ensemble was installed at the Theater am Schiffbauerdamm, where **The Threepenny Opera** had opened twenty-six years before. From his protected nest, Brecht was free to swipe at censors, thought-police and art apparatchiks and he sometimes did so.

The Ensemble's 1954 visit to Paris made it a star of the international stage. In 1955 came the enormous honour of a Stalin Peace Prize: Brecht accepted it in Moscow in a speech translated for him by Boris Pasternak.

His influence in British circles dates from 1955, when John Gielgud's **King Lear** toured Europe. Brecht and Weigel came to a matinée at the Hebbel Theatre in West Berlin and met the company. A meeting took place over beer and sausages; later, George Devine, Peggy Ashcroft and others of the group crossed over to the East to look at the Theatre am Schiffbauerdamm. **The Caucasian Chalk Circle** struck Devine with its naked honesty; Jocelyn Herbert, later the core designer at the Court, noticed the use of real materials in the design, the exposed lighting bars and the permanent surround. Apparent to all was an eloquent piece of Brechtian dialectic: the stagings were simple and austere, but their context was a highly traditional auditorium dripping with gilt.

Brecht gave permission for the Court to stage **The Good Person**, with Ashcroft in the title role; the following year, it played in its opening season, the next-but-one production after **Look Back in Anger**. By now, the Ensemble had made its first, triumphant appearance in London. Brecht wasn't there: he had died, aged fifty-eight, on the eve of the Ensemble's departure.

Final act: Reputation. Throughout the 1960s and '70s, Brecht was revered by left-leaning theatricals as a sage whose slightest jottings could be relied on as a guide to morality, politics and life itself. In the 1990s the collapse of faith in Marxism put a stop to that. But although his Mao-like status hasn't lasted, his plays (or some of them) have quietly entered the theatrical mainstream. Whether they've entered as what they are, or in disguise, is harder to say. Some productions get praised for following his thinking to the hilt, others get praised for throwing his boring theories out of the window. Sometimes both are said of the *same* production.

His influence on the direction of plays – what they look like, how they're acted – is deep and lasting. Acres of print have been expended on his vision of the epic theatre – mostly not by him, although he's far from guiltless. Around the time of **Mahagonny**, he contrasted 'dramatic' (i.e. bad and bourgeois) theatre with 'epic' theatre. One provides the spectator with sensations, one forces him to take decisions; one shows man as fixed, one as capable of change; one is a matter of feeling, one of reason – and so on.

Brecht's favourite maxim was 'The proof of the pudding is in the eating,' so one's perhaps allowed to jump a couple of stages here. Boring, old-fashioned theatre aims at working up the audience into an intense but phoney emotional state. It relies on obvious effects and conventional ways of achieving them. It takes a cardboard-cut-out view of personality: dignified characters are dignified all the time, silly ones always silly. It links this view with a reactionary view of society: the most dignified character is likely to be an aristocrat, the silly one a chambermaid. This leads to its chief distinguishing factor: it's devoid of social analysis.

Trumpets and Drums, Brecht's version of *The Recruiting Officer* at the Berliner Ensemble.

'Epic' theatre makes use of what Brecht called the '*Verfremdungseffekt*', misleadingly translated as 'alienation'. It means a making-strange, a making-unfamiliar, a showing of something in a fresh and stimulating way. (When painters feel they can't any longer 'see' a painting they're working on, they sometimes look at it in a mirror: a classic *Verfremdungseffekt*.) The aim is always to reveal the social realities of a character, story or situation. Lucidity reigns: nothing is worse than a jumble of confused impressions. Brecht sometimes stressed the need for a certain detachment in the playing, but it's probably safe to assume that this was aimed at the inclination of some of his actors to ham it up. Thought and analysis, yes – but there's plenty of room for fire.

Later, at the Royal Court Theatre, under the leadership of George Devine, Brecht provided both a philosophical basis and a cue for a visual style: white light, a simple stage, real objects. Devine's policy of doing 'new plays as though they were classics and classics as though they were new plays' was in itself a Brechtian tactic: it meant giving working-class characters the fully dimensional quality that the West End theatre had denied them while, at the same time, restoring a long-forgotten realism to Shakespeare, Middleton and Otway.

The influence spread to the National Theatre via the agency of two young Royal Court directors, William Gaskill and John Dexter. Brecht reached the Royal Shakespeare Company (looking rather different) through the work of the designer John Bury, a Theatre Workshop veteran. The Brechtian influence is now so deeply rooted that to see a production that ignores it altogether (not just in part, for this is common) is to be as startled as waking up in a strange bed with no idea of how you got there. Has any production of Farquhar since Gaskill's **Recruiting Officer** featured snuff-boxes, sneezings and ladies waving their

*Maggie Smith and Colin Blakely in William Gaskill's **The Recruiting Officer** at the National Theatre.*

fans about? A few, but nobody liked them. Has any Shakespearian battle since Peter Hall's **The Wars of the Roses** failed to stress the realities of conscription, fear and death?

There's a polarity between which most of the modern theatre finds its place. Brecht stands at the one pole: Samuel Beckett at the other. Brecht was a public playwright, Beckett a private one. Brecht's energies were directed outwards, towards the Party, towards the struggle, towards the demands of his own career. Beckett explored the inner worlds of memory and existence. Brecht revived the 'epic': the theatrical string-of-beads, leaping from place to place and time to time. Beckett took the one-place, time-unbroken drama of Sophocles or Racine and distilled it to the point where its off-stage life is reduced to nothing.

Finally: Brecht's work has a political aim. Clarity is essential: how can the play be an effective arm of the struggle if it's incomprehensible? In his study stood a writing-aid in the shape of a toy donkey with a sign around its neck: it read: 'Even I must understand it.' Beckett's work has no 'effective' purpose, so it's free to be opaque – and it often is.

Fathers and Sons

'I know creatures are supposed to have no secrets from their authors, but I'm afraid mine for me have little else.'
SAMUEL BECKETT

1

To move from Brecht to Beckett is like walking around a crowded gallery, crammed with pictures, drafts and sketches – some good, some bad, none boring – only to find oneself pulled up by the sight of a large black box with an eyehole on one side. Within is a different world: clamp your eyeball to the hole and you'll discover a universe, drawn from a single, stern perspective.

Samuel Barclay Beckett (1906–1989) was born on Good Friday in Foxrock, Dublin, into a well-off Protestant business family. Photographs show a large Edwardian house in well-kept grounds. Photographs of his parents show a handsome, anxious woman and a round-faced, rubicund chap in a bowler hat. In 1916, he was taken by his father to a hill near the family home to see the flames of the Easter Rising. Later that year, he entered Portora Royal School in Enniskillen: Oscar Wilde's old school. He was good at sports, and would keep the rangy stance of the schoolboy athlete (and his passion for cricket) till he died. In 1923, he entered Trinity College: here began the omnivorous stocking-up of his awesome brain. He developed a love of Dante (a lifelong influence), Milton and Racine. He went often to the Abbey, where he saw the first night of **Juno and the Paycock** and the tempestuous première of **The Plough and the Stars**. Also **Playboy**, **The Wall of the Saints** and **The Tinker's Wedding**: the impact of Synge was tremendous.

Dublin was rich in music-halls; Beckett went to them all. Cinema was another influence: he saw all of Chaplin, but the comedian he preferred was the austere, impassive Buster Keaton. Keaton, in old age, would play in **Film**, claiming at first that he didn't understand a thing about it. After a few days, he warmed up. 'I'm beginning to catch on to this Shakespeare stuff,' he said.

In the 1870s, the young Shaw had prowled for hours on end through Dublin's National Gallery: it was one of the colleges of his self-made university, he said later, though its influence on Shaw is hard to spot. Beckett, as a Trinity undergraduate, was a regular visitor to the same collection and the results were vast: only his first play lacks a single, striking visual image – and he suppressed it.

Late Beckett.   Put like this, it sounds as though comedy, Keaton and painting were being lined up in Beckett's notebook under the heading 'Ideas for Plays'. In fact, at this stage of his life he had no intention of being a writer of any kind: he was under the firm impression that he'd be an academic, and so was everyone else. But when he was turning twenty, something happened. Looking back on it, it seems a contrary, warning sign. It recurred in various forms throughout his life, it's firmly embedded in his writing and it was in a roundabout way to open the door to his greatest achievements.

He fell ill. The symptom this time was a racing heart. Later he would describe it on page two of the first of his published novels, *Murphy*:

> Such an irrational heart that no physician could get to the root of it. Inspected, palpated, auscultated, percussed, radiographed and cardiographed, it was all that a heart should be. Buttoned up and left to perform, it was like Petrushka in his box. One moment in such labour that it seemed on the point of seizing, the next in such ebullition that it seemed on the point of bursting.

The dicey heart would be a fixture. Other illnesses pursued him all his life. There were tooth-infections, an abscess in a lung, cysts, an especially nasty cyst ('intra-osseous') in his palate, cataracts. They shared the putrid quality of something inside needing to be expelled, as indeed there was.

To say that Beckett was a clinical depressive is at once to add that depression is nothing to do with gloom or sadness. To be sad from time to time is universal. Gloom is an indulgence of the healthy. Depression is an insight into a world without ulterior meaning. It's a knowing-better. It expresses itself, in art, in crisp and practical terms. Properly used, it's dazzlingly creative. Its only drawback is the torture – mental and physical – that it inflicts on those who host it.

Aged twenty-one, Beckett travelled to Paris as Trinity College's exchange lecturer at the École Normale Supérieure. The following year, he met James Joyce: this encounter would change his life.

Joyce (1882–1940) had left Dublin for Paris in 1902. Shortly before his departure, Yeats – who had spotted the younger man as a coming talent – had engineered a meeting in a café in O'Connell Street. It was a momentous occasion, the clash of the *fin-de-siècle* avant-garde with the modern movement. Yeats, all set to offer advice, soon found himself decidedly at the receiving end. 'Why,' asked Joyce of the master, 'do you make speeches? Why do you concern yourself with politics? Why have you given some of your stories and poems a historical setting?' All these, he explained, were signs that 'the iron was getting cold'. Yeats, much shaken, argued for the general truths of folklore: Great Memory against the quibblings of the individual. 'Generalisations aren't made by poets,' Joyce replied. 'They are made by men of letters. They are no use.' Getting up to leave, he added: 'I am twenty. How old are you?' Yeats told him, but to his eternal irritation knocked a year off his age. Joyce was unimpressed. 'I thought as much,' he sighed. 'I have met you too late. You are too old.'

It's surely coincidence that Joyce's only play **Exiles** was turned down by the Abbey. If you open any page you'll be excited by some terse, allusive exchange. Read from start to finish, it's inert: 'bloodless', Beckett called it. Joyce was writing *Finnegan's Wake* when he and Beckett met in Paris. Beckett helped him by reading aloud (Joyce's eyesight was failing), did research and sometimes took dictation. That was the practical side of things. Emotionally, he was exposed to genius. He had either to take his place in Joyce's circle of acolytes, or meet the challenge. He started to write.

He returned to Dublin where a hideous row with his mother broke out: she'd been nosing through his papers and was shocked by what she'd found. A novel written around this time, *Dreams of Fair to Middling Women*, was only published once he was famous. Beneath its verbal bravura lies the authorial figure of Belacqua, named after the friend of Dante whom the poet passes on the Purgatorial outskirts. ('Belacqua' is also, of course, a rearrangement of Beckett's middle name: he liked these plays on proper nouns.) All his life this Florentine maker of musical instruments has enjoyed being idle. Now he endures the state of idleness for an equal period: cue for **Waiting for Godot, Endgame** and the rest of the Beckett output.

His racing heart continued racing and his depression failed to lift. 1934 saw him in London starting a two-year stretch of analysis under the young Kleinian Wilfred Bion. The teachings of Melanie Klein are based on the primeval conflict between the infant and the mother; as is often the case with psychoanalysis, hard-won insights are greeted with yawns by people who know the patient. '*Of course* Sam's mother was the problem.'

In 1936, he travelled through Germany to look at paintings and the following year he settled in Paris, where on Twelfth Night, at one in the morning, he was accosted in the street by a pimp who took out a knife and stabbed him, only just missing his heart. Beckett was rushed to hospital and put on the danger list. Of his three current mistresses – one Irish, one American and one French – it was the French one, Suzanne Deschevaux-Dumesnil, who turned out to be the stayer: she remained his stern and loyal partner till she died.

When war broke out, he was visiting Dublin. Anyone thinking of Beckett as a self-absorbed navel-watcher should remember that, though he could with ease have stayed in neutral Ireland, he chose for reasons of sheer principle to return to France. In Paris, he joined a Resistance cell. When it was betrayed, he and Suzanne made a hair's-breadth escape; for the rest of the war they lived in hiding in Roussillon, a village in Provence remarkable for its highly coloured earth. ('But down there everything is red!' says Vladimir in **Waiting for Godot**.) She kept house and gave occasional music lessons, he worked in the fields for a local farmer and wrote **Watt**. Four years passed.

By the end of the war, he was nearly forty, he'd been writing for fifteen years, he'd made no mark in the world and most of his work hadn't even been published. He'd been nearly killed, he'd fled the Gestapo and he'd lived for years in exile. Travelling to Ireland, he found his mother old and frail, shaking with Parkinson's. It was in her bungalow in Foxrock – just across the road from the house he was born in – that the tensions, drama and endless waiting fused into a revelatory moment. Writing about it later, in **Krapp's Last Tape**, he changed the locale but kept the insight:

> Spiritually a year of profound gloom and indigence until that memorable night in March, at the end of the jetty, in the howling wind, never to be forgotten, when suddenly I saw the whole thing. The vision at last. This I fancy is what I have chiefly to record this evening … What I suddenly saw then was this, that the belief I had been going on all my life, namely (*Krapp switches off impatiently, winds tape forward, switches on again*) great granite rocks like foam flying up in the light of the lighthouse and the wind-gauge spinning like a propeller; clear to me at last that the dark I have always struggled to keep under is in reality my most (*Krapp curses, switches off, winds tape forward, switches on again*) –

He would find his voice, he realised, not by fighting his depression but by expressing it:

by diving into the heart of the dark. Ten years after his psychoanalysis, he finally had what analysts call 'the breakthrough'.

There followed what he called 'a frenzy of writing': four novels, four short stories and two plays between now and 1950. In his first full-length play, **Eleutheria**, parody abounds – boulevard comedy, Strindberg, Yeats – and a Spectator climbs on to the stage from his box in order to pronounce on the action. There's a certain resemblance in all this to **The Old Lady Says No**: Beckett knew Denis Johnston from Dublin. But in **Eleutheria** the tricks seem tired and overstretched. Apart from this aborted play, he wrote in French: 'without style' as he described it. **En attendant Godot** (**Waiting for Godot** as it would be) came less than two years later.

Beckett named as his inspiration two paintings by Caspar David Friedrich, *Man and Woman Observing the Moon* and *Two Men Contemplating the Moon*: he'd seen them both in Germany. Other influences date back to his teens: the gags, cross-talk and comic business from the Dublin music-halls, the life-on-the-road of the tramp, as evoked by Synge. He and Suzanne, on the road to Roussillon, or living in suspense once they arrived there, have been cited as the originals of Vladimir and Estragon. But tense and idle waiting had been a theme of Beckett's since Belacqua.

Waiting for Godot *in London.*

219

If **Godot** had been a novel it could have made 'waiting' its action. Beckett's great theatrical insight was that, being a play, its action had to be waiting's opposite: 'filling the time'. Hence the endless questions: nervous, ferrety, persistent. Never has there been a play with so many questions in it. Everyone asks them, except for Lucky, whose speech is an answer. But answers in **Godot** are always useless, as Didi points out:

Caspar David Friedrich's Two Men Contemplating the Moon.

VLADIMIR:	What you seek you hear.
ESTRAGON:	You do.
VLADIMIR:	That prevents you from finding.
ESTRAGON:	It does.
VLADIMIR:	That prevents you from thinking.
ESTRAGON:	You think all the same.

After **Godot**, staying out of the public eye became a major preoccupation. By the time it opened in London, Tynan could boldly declare that he cared 'little for its enormous success in Europe over the past three years', before adding his seal of approval. 'It forced me to re-examine the rules which have hitherto governed the drama; and, having done so, to pronounce them not elastic enough.' Beckett came over for the hundredth-performance party. There were, he wrote, 'buckets of champagne and a powerful crowd. They were all very nice to me in London, critics and journalists included, they left me alone'.

America was a harder nut to crack: at the tryout in Miami the posters announced 'The Laugh Sensation of Two Continents'. By the interval, one-third of the house had left, and another third never came back. Estragon was played by a great and much-loved comic. 'How can you, Bert Lahr,' wrote a fan, 'who has charmed the youth of America as the Cowardly Lion in *The Wizard of Oz*, appear in this Communistic, atheistic and existentialist play?' It was 'existentialist' that wounded: tears in his eyes, he begged the director to tell him what it meant. Beckett wasn't put out by the fiasco. 'There is something queer about this play,' he wrote, 'I don't exactly know what, that worms its way into people whether they like it or not.' Lahr triumphed at last on Broadway, in a new production. Beckett was sent the tape. He liked the Pozzo and, 'The boy I thought very good.' What was the problem? 'Some changes and interpolations annoyed me mildly … ' He hated alterations, be they to the text of the play, or the look of the play … or to the rhythm of a speech … to anything at all, in fact, that he'd imagined when he wrote it. Which was everything.

He wrote **Fin de Partie** in a state of depression after watching and waiting while his brother died of cancer. He started with jotted exchanges between two characters, A and B. One was helpless – dying? – the other a minder of some kind. Or a relation? As always between minder and charge, there existed an element of mutual sadism.

In **Endgame** (as **Fin de Partie** became in English), the stage is a stage (with a real audience out there), a room and the inside of a head. Two high small windows like eyes. Outside, an empty world. A view (zero), light (sunk) and the horizon. But 'What in God's name could there be on the horizon?' Hamm is a ham, barnstormingly theatrical. 'Accursed progenitor!' That's his ancient father, kept in a dustbin. Hamm's old mum is similarly accommodated. Their very existence is a torture for the dying tyrant: he greets the death of one and the silent weeping of the other with malignant stoicism.

Clov the minder has so many absences to report that they become a running gag: there are no more sugarplums, bicycle-wheels, rugs, painkillers nor even coffins. Another absence is smell. In **Godot**, people have stinking feet, garlicky breath and they fart. In **Endgame**, even a blind man smells nothing. This is a world without warmth, physicality or affect. Lytton Strachey, writing in 1907, described the strange, ceremonial hall in which the tragedies of Racine are normally set. He could have been writing about the setting of **Endgame**:

> It will show us no views, no spectacles, it will give us no sense of atmosphere or of imaginative romance; but it will allow us to be present at the climax of a tragedy, to follow the closing struggle of high destinies, and to witness the final agony of human hearts.

All That Fall was written in English for BBC Radio. The challenge of sound evoked a host of childhood memories: Beckett, at fifty, was hitting the age when they start to bite. The walk to Foxrock station, the cart piled high with dung, the flat-tired bike, the irascible station-master. Did Mr Rooney throw the little girl out of the railway-carriage or not? 'We don't know, at least I don't,' Beckett wrote. 'I know creatures are supposed to have no secrets from their authors, but I'm afraid mine for me have little else.' **Krapp's Last Tape** reeks of memories: childhood walks in the Wicklow Mountains with his father; his mother on her deathbed in a house overlooking Dublin's Grand Canal; the bench on the weir where Beckett would sit and look up at her window 'wishing she were gone'; not to mention the revelation in her house in Foxrock, switched to the harbour of

Dun Laoghaire. The side of Beckett that is most forgotten – either because of the fame of **Godot**, or because of his exile – is the sensuousness with which he evokes his birthplace.

Happy Days has Winnie buried up to her waist in sand: that's just Act One. Beckett adored women: here the sheer existence of a woman, 'blonde for preference, plump', makes the filling and passing of time a cause for joy. In Britain, it would be a *tour de force* for his classic interpreter, Billie Whitelaw. **Play** has, as a great departure, an English setting: Sussex, the site of his and Suzanne's marriage the year before. English law required the groom to stay *in situ* for a fortnight. Beckett, stuck with nothing to do, drove round the Southern counties: Ash and Snodland, both in Kent, would find a small immortality in **Play**, as do Lipton's tea and the sound of a lawnmower.

This pocket masterpiece (eleven minutes long) places an adulterous trio where they belong, in purgatory. Beckett's staging places them up to their necks in urns of incongruously small dimensions. A spotlight darts from one to the other. As it hits each face, the tale erupts: it's as tacky as these things are apt to be.

'I had anticipated something better. More restful,' woman 2 complains, rather as though her holiday booking had let her down. The man, a doggy and downbeat type, is glad of the rest: 'Down, all going down, into the park, peace is coming, I thought, after all, at last, I was right, after all, thank God, when first this change.' The other woman makes the best of it: 'Silence and darkness were all I craved. Well, I get a certain amount of both. They being one. Perhaps it is more wickedness to pray for more.' All three are racked with repetitive images from the past; none of them knows quite where it is that they've ended up; none of them knows the whereabouts of the others. Nor do they know quite who or what is questioning them: 'And now that you are … mere eye. Just looking. At my face. On and off.'

As Beckett grew old, his plays grew shorter and more graphic. In **Come and Go**, three women in broad-brimmed hats, their faces in shadow, are seated on a bench: this exquisite miniature about death harks back to an Edwardian childhood. In **Not I**, a mere mouth is all that is left to speak of runaway psychosis. The visual starting-point of **Footfalls** is a woman walking restlessly back and forth: the footfall-rhythm is an integral part of the text. 'May' – Beckett's mother's name – appears both in its natural form and anagrammatised as 'Amy'. In **That Time** the head (only) of an old man in bed – flat on his back – is presented to us vertically, as seen from the ceiling. His long white hair fans out on the pillow behind/beneath him. Three streams of memory, a Dublin youth inseparable from Beckett's own being one of them.

Quite late in life, he began to direct his plays – a natural step for a writer to whom director and cast had always deferred. His method of work was unique, a bit like those autistic savants who carry a complete picture in their heads and draw it in detail starting at the bottom left-hand corner.

He learned the play by heart. He then prepared a production-book, specifying in detail every move and the time it should take and testing this out footstep by footstep in his

*Peggy Ashcroft in **Happy Days**;*
*Billie Whitelaw's mouth in **Not I**;*
Billie Whitelaw, Robert Stephens, and
*Rosemary Harris in **Play**.*

apartment. His punctiliousness in matters of physical detail hadn't changed since the days of his early novel *Murphy*:

> He raised his left hand, where Celia's tears had not yet dried, and seated it pronate on the crown of his skull – that was the position. In vain. He raised his right hand and laid the forefinger along his nose. He then returned both hands to their point of departure with Celia's on the counterpane ...

Rehearsals consisted of coaching the cast in the exact reproduction of the master-plan, starting with the first line and then – when finally the actor got it right – proceeding to the second. The only times his patience wore thin were when actors insisted on knowing more. 'Why am I doing this? Where have I come from?' Beckett's reply was always the same: that if he'd known more, he'd have put it in the play. Professional theatre directors are mostly horrified by this method. Is it a method at all, they wonder? Didn't it all look drilled and dead? The quick answer is that it looked incomparably spontaneous. This is to miss the point.

Beckett couldn't answer questions about the characters' off-stage lives, because he didn't believe their off-stage lives existed. After **Eleutheria**, and somewhere in the course of writing **Godot**, he turned his back on the representational element in theatre: that element that implies a life outside the door, a row of houses down the street, a three-dimensional past, a future.

His on-stage figures simply are. The mouth is a mouth; it's what it is and so are Hamm, Clov, Didi, Gogo, Pozzo, Lucky and the boy. They haven't come from anywhere, they aren't going anywhere else and they don't 'mean' anything other than what you see. They have the immediate, 'now-it's happening' quality of clowns or cabaret-performers.

Beckett avoided party politics, but he was active on a non-partisan level, adding his name to countless petitions for human rights, supporting prisoners (both political and not) and fighting censorship. He gave away great quantities of money and spent nothing on any of those things that make the lives of rich people easier in old age: a secretary to take telephone calls and answer letters, for example. His solution to the problem of the telephone was to answer it for one hour of the day, confiding the time of access to a small circle of trusted friends. He continued to drive himself around, although his steering was erratic at the best of times and it got no better when his eyesight failed.

His fame was a genuine burden. 'What a catastrophe for Sam!' exclaimed Suzanne when he was awarded the Nobel Prize for Literature in 1969. She meant it. His face was reproduced on posters, theatre-programmes and book-jackets as a convenient logo for tragedy. It seemed impossible to photograph it badly.

In private he was as beautiful as the photographs suggested. But any sense of tragedy was dispelled by his warmth and kindness. He was a listener, not a talker, and to see him paying attention was like looking through a window into a lost world of eighteenth-century courtesy. With women, he was grave and gentle: only the occasional glance of physical appreciation revealed the serial flirt. In an English pub, he evoked a world – not of Irish pubs, since gentlemen of his class could not, when he was young, be seen in public houses – but of Dublin club-life and Parisian café society. London barmen, stooping over the table merely to clear the ashtrays, would soon find themselves staggering back from the bar with trays of drinks: they recognised class when they saw it.

His influence is two-fold. On the one hand, he gave authority to the notion of the play as a work of art: as neither a representation of the world of everyday, nor as a comment on it, nor as an entertainment, but as itself.

The effect of his prose was more far-reaching. Just as Beckett learned from Joyce, so Harold Pinter learned from both. And the tone of Pinter's dialogue is so pervasive and so widespread that it's virtually the lingua franca of the modern English-speaking theatre. It's not (of course) compulsory and it isn't universal. But it's the baseline. Playwrights who write any differently do so either because they have that rarest of gifts, a style of their own, or because they've made a conscious effort to avoid it or because they don't know any better.

It's characterised, in Pinter's hands, by taut musicality, a crystalline clarity of focus and what Martin Scorsese described, in a different context, as 'a series of small shocks'. Its vocabulary is drawn from the whole of the pot: the skimmings as well as the dregs. It includes rarities, chat, philosophical flights and ribaldry. It also includes as an eloquent partner, silence.

2

The first night of Pinter's **The Caretaker** was thrilling even before it started. To be there was to feel you were watching history in the making, as indeed you were. It was at the Arts: a tiny London theatre, scene of many a past genteel experiment, oddly placed on the wrong side of Soho and boasting a pathetically faded theatrical tea-room on the first floor. Every so often the Arts lived up to its name by delivering some brilliant jolt to the system, and on the evening of 27 April 1960 there was a confident buzz. The auditorium was packed, the audience glittered, Pinter of course was there: sexy, genial, loud.

The play progressed exactly as everyone hoped it would: sharp, elliptical, conceding nothing to anything other than itself: it seemed to be making up the modern style as it went along. The phrase 'in your face' hadn't been coined yet, but that was the message: 'This is it, sort it out for yourself.' When themes emerged – which they did more or less immediately in the form of status, 'space', as it's called today, and territory – it was delightful that they weren't spelled out, that they bubbled up in an unformed, shadowy way, just as they do in life. The dialogue took ordinary speech, the kind you'd hear at home or at a bus-stop, and focused it so hard and fast that it seemed wildly exotic: it was like those dreams where you hear a foreign language for the first time and find yourself magically able to understand every word. Donald Pleasance, as Davies the vagrant, was vehement, pitiless, sentiment-free, Alan Bates authentically hard and street-wise: when Pleasance, Bates and Peter Woodthorpe sent a bag ricocheting like mad between them, it was as though all three had a vast hidden repertoire of juggling tricks of which this unexpected outbreak was a mere tantalising sample. The only bit that felt all right in a conventional way, but something of a let-down otherwise, was Aston's Act Two monologue about his psychiatric treatment, especially when the lights began to dim around him. When so much was cryptic, it seemed a shame to start explaining things.

Two years before, Harold Pinter had had a famous flop. Its fame was immediate, and this was what was special about it: it wasn't the normal kind of flop which everyone in the theatre tries to pretend hasn't happened. (The image is always of those wildlife documentaries in which a lion chases a herd of antelope, grabs one and wrestles it to the ground while the rest of the herd runs on paying no attention at all.)

Harold Pinter.

The Birthday Party had opened on tour, at the Cambridge Arts, when according to the local paper it received a 'great ovation'. OK, that was Cambridge. The following week it played far from dreaming spires in Wolverhampton, where Sean Day-Lewis, the critic for the *Express* and *Star*, called it 'the most enthralling experience the Grand Theatre has given us in many months'. Business was great. On the third week of the pre-London tour, the *Oxford Times* described it as 'brilliant, baffling and bizarre – Kafka, almost, spiced with humour'.

So the opening night on 19 May 1958 at the Lyric, Hammersmith had everything going for it. Only one thing went wrong. In those pre-technological days, reviews didn't come dribbling out over the rest of the week: they appeared *en masse* the following morning, and the morning after **The Birthday Party** they went mad. 'Half-gibberish', 'random dottiness', 'Mr Pinter, you're just not funny enough', were some of the comments, and those were the nice ones. Harold Hobson, the tide-turner (c.f. Ackland) who had backed Pinter a year before in his review of a student production of **The Room**, hadn't yet seen the show. Would he ever turn up? And what would he say if he did? Typically, he arrived at the Thursday matinée, where he comprised one-sixth of the audience: the receipts for the performance were two pounds and six shillings. Pinter watched from the empty dress circle: 'Oh, you poor chap,' said the usherette, on hearing he'd written the play. The matinée was funereal. Afterwards, Hobson limped away in Delphic silence, as was his wont. The show came off on the Saturday night, after a run of a single week. The following morning, Hobson's review was one of the greatest raves that he ever wrote, a rave which, if the play had still been on, would have ensured packed houses and a West End transfer. As it was, that same Sunday saw a nice little thriller being set up at the Lyric and the set of **The Birthday Party** thrown in the skips outside.

If Hobson had come to the opening night, if just one of the common-or-garden dailies had stood up for it, if the play had been done at the Royal Court for a limited run … was it sent to the Court? Rejected by it? Royal Court records were systematically destroyed throughout the 1960s, so the question remains unanswered. Was the production wrong? Judging by the photographs, the set looks peculiarly grand. Was Richard Pearson, who played the brooding, hidden, fantasising Stan, too much the squeaky-voiced bank-manager? Could the marvellous Beatrix Lehmann, a diamond-sharp intellectual, really have captured the slatternly, dozy Meg? Was Goldberg Jewish enough, or expansive enough? Had he the killer instinct?

Nothing is more stupid than blaming the critics, and there are such things as first nights that go off the rails. What was unusual was that the flop of **The Birthday Party** was immediately seen, not as a failure of the play but as a failure of the system. The liberal

*Beatrix Lehmann and Richard Pearson in the first production of **The Birthday Party**.*

establishment in the shape of BBC Radio and commercial television (those were the days), rushed to put things right. An important patron was Barbara Bray, a long-time Beckett associate and script editor on the Third Programme, who commissioned **A Slight Ache**. Michael Codron bought several of his sketches – **The Black and White, Request Stop, Last to Go** – as revue-material: they played side by side with Peter Cook material, and the mix was electric. In March 1960, Joan Kemp-Welch's television production of **The Birthday Party** went out to an audience of – wait for it – *eleven million* viewers. A month later, **A Night Out** was shown in a slick, suave television production by Philip Saville for ABC's Armchair Theatre: it topped the ratings. When **The Caretaker** opened

Donald Pleasance and Alan Bates in **The Caretaker**.

228

the following week, it was clear to anyone with eyes to see that there wasn't just an appetite for Pinter's plays: there was a cavernous public need.

Everything about him met the mood of the time: the oddball wit, the pugnacity, the idea that nine-tenths of human communication was an unwilling process of evasion and silence.

Most timely of all was the fact that he legitimised uncertainty. Before Pinter, it was the play-wright's job to know not only what happened on-stage, but why and what it meant and what had happened before. Uncertainty was a fault, a sign of muddle: if there'd ever been any doubt about this, it was dispelled by Shaw and given the *coup de grâce* by Brecht. Pinter brought us a world like the one we lived in: a world devoid of reliable answers. His genius was to create this world, not in a cloudy, ambiguous way, but in prose of diamond-hard lucidity. What was said in a Pinter play, and what was done, was clear as day: it was the rest, the rationalising clutter, that was missing.

Pinter was born in 1930 in Hackney, North London: a grey, once-respectable working-class sprawl, now dotted with soft-toy sweatshops and young middle-class couples doing up their first-time purchases. Jack Pinter, Harold's father, was a tailor with his own small firm; the mood at home was bookish and convivial and the family tree included Marxists, connoisseurs of music and a vanishing boxer.

Pinter's school, Hackney Downs, would be closed down in the mid-1990s as an irredeemable sink of anarchy, but in the 1940s it was a serious-minded, challenging place. (Steven Berkoff passed through it not long after.) Pinter joined, or formed, a set: a gang of six superior, clever boys. One of the others, Henry Woolf, would later become a living icon of the theatrical avant-garde, an actor who throughout the 1960s would appear (for pitiful pay) in any play that broke new boundaries: **Afore Night Come** was one, **AC/DC** another. 'Don't talk to me about racial prejudice,' Woolf said at around this time. 'I know all about it. I was brought up to believe that Jewish boys like me were clever and Gentiles were thick.' In fact the Pinteresque elite – 'The Boys' as they called themselves – was only two-thirds Jewish: two exceptional Gentiles were admitted.

The tone of the gang was joking, in a threatening kind of way: think of the withering virtuosity of the great lost Pinter actor Peter Sellers, or the intellectual wordplay of Lennon/McCartney ten years later. In-jokes and derisive nicknames were the rule. Money was short, so walks were long: exhausting treks down Mare Street, or across the Hackney Marshes, filled with furious argument with your best friend or silent challenge from your foe of the day. If a girl swam into orbit, she became half-threat, half-trophy. Books were shared discoveries, doors to a world beyond the bounds of Hackney: Joyce was an idol, so were Kafka, Shakespeare and Dostoevsky. Music: Bach. Poetry: Yeats. Films: Vigo, Bunuel, early Bergman. Clothes: as sharp as the purse allowed. Politics: 'Don't let them tell you what to do.' (Pete in **The Birthday Party**.) Utopia took the form of West End London: sooty paradise of films noirs, late nights, last buses and snogs in doorways. Drink was essential but expensive, drugs were something Aldous Huxley wrote books about.

This was the crucible of Pinter's writing: it wasn't until **Betrayal** in 1978 that he wrote a play in which you could imagine the characters behaving in a modern way: spending the evening watching television, or using a credit card.

Meanwhile he became an actor, trained in a sporadic way and was more or less continuously employed for as long as he chose to be. Good looks, a big voice and massive confidence. Anew McMaster (MacLíammoír's patron) was a notable employer, followed by the great British barnstormer Donald Wolfit. (Pinter's fellow-actor, Ronald Harwood, would later memorialise the Wolfit days in **The Dresser**.)

Pinter was in Ireland, working for McMaster, when he stumbled across a fragment of *Watt* in a poetry magazine: it knocked him sideways. Back in London, he searched for anything else by Beckett, but nobody seemed to have heard of him. Finally a copy of *Murphy* was run to earth in Battersea Library: a lucky find, since only 718 copies had ever been sold. Pinter took it out and has it to this day.

> I suddenly felt that what his writing was doing was walking through a mirror into the other side of the world which was, in fact, the real world … The book was also very funny. I never forgot the laughs I got immediately from reading Beckett. But what impressed me was something about the quick of the world. It was Beckett's own world but had so many references to the world we actually share.

Pinter's only novel, *The Dwarfs*, was written in the early 1950s: it's an early Pinter kit, packed with images and phrases which would recur in the years that followed. His first play, **The Room**, was written in 1956 at Henry Woolf's suggestion; in **The Hothouse**, written in 1958, a mental home becomes a metaphor for a world of arbitrary authority, c.f. *Murphy*.

In **The Homecoming** we see a home made arid and ugly by the absence of women. The mother is dead, Max, the father, does the cooking, we're told very badly. Lenny, one of three brothers, returns from North America, bringing his wife Ruth.

Her sex is inflammatory. 'I've never had a whore under this roof before. Ever since your mother died,' roars Max: a great Freudian slip. Male fantasies soon engulf the play. Not only is Ruth assumed to be a whore: she is one. She can't open her mouth without calling attention to her legs, her underwear, her lips. It's not long before Lenny finds himself waiting complaisantly downstairs while she makes love with his brother Joey. Joey and she don't have sex, and much is made of this: whoredom/womanhood has a playful, healing dimension, as Joey is pleasantly surprised to discover.

This is an essential modern classic about men: Ruth, the only woman, is the men's projection. Is the family Jewish? The locale is clearly Hackney and the celebratory nip of kirsch provides a moment of sense-memory. But the Jewishness isn't spelled out and a kind of 'ghost-play' about a young man bringing home his shiksa wife hovers somewhere in the background.

Of **No Man's Land**, John Gielgud – who gave a celebrated performance in the first production opposite Ralph Richardson – said very acutely, 'I always think that Hirst, the character Ralph plays, is very much like Hamm, the hero of Beckett's **Endgame** – a sort of tyrant who's dominated by his domestic staff.' The similarity extends beyond that: there's a sense of finality, of the shadows closing in, of witnesses being called to the end of a tyrannical life.

In **Betrayal**, Emma and Robert are married, Emma and Jerry are/were lovers and Robert and Jerry are best friends. Robert finds out on holiday with Emma, in a Venice hotel room; in the following scene he lunches with Jerry back in London. (Most of the scenes in **Betrayal** go in reverse order, but there are three beautifully placed judders forward and this is one of them.) We know that Robert's thinking about the affair – how could he not be? – but he doesn't mention it, so the effect is of two scenes being played simultaneously: the scene we hear, and the scene we can only infer. One is amiable, the other vengeful: the contrast is terrifying.

Is Robert's silence a betrayal? That's what the play suggests. It ends with another betrayal the night the affair began. A party is in progress. Jerry tells Emma that he loves her. When Robert walks in, Jerry more or less confesses what's been happening, with the result that Robert is faced with one of those unexpected, rather Zen moments when, if you do the wrong thing, it will haunt you for the rest of your life.

Gielgud and Richardson in **No Man's Land**.

Should he punch Jerry? Or simply tell him to lay off? Or ask him nicely? He does none of these. Instead, he simply affirms his love for Jerry, thus betraying Jerry, Emma and himself.

Images are used with infinite resource, echoing and recurring through the years. So are resonant proper names: O'Casey, Torcello. The recurrence is the key: Robert, Jerry and Emma are trapped in a set of actions, each one endlessly repeated, endlessly examined for new or deeper meaning. There's no way out. As in **Play**, the sequel to adultery is purgatory.

3

No one has taken up the Pinter style with more adroitness, or extended it further, than David Mamet (1947–). His plays – like Pinter's – are notated like musical scores with pauses, capitals and italics for emphases, dashes and dots for overlapping and interruption – 'You can delineate the intention by correctly delineating the rhythm of the speech.' And like a composer Mamet demands that the actor study the score fastidiously and perform it without the intrusion of 'personality':

> There is nothing we feel nothing about – ice-cream, Yugoslavia, coffee, religion – and we do not have to add these feelings to a play. The author has already done that through the truth of the writing, and if he has not, it is too late.

His rhythms are fast, deft, percussive, and syncopated, and often on the page the dialogue resembles concrete poetry, studded with varying verse patterns. From **Edmond**:

EDMOND:	Say it with me. (*Pause.*)
GLENNA:	What?
EDMOND:	'I am a waitress.'
GLENNA:	I think that you better go.
EDMOND:	If you want me to go I'll go. Say it with me say that you are. And I'll say what I am.
GLENNA:	… what you are …
EDMOND:	I've made the discovery. Now: I want you to change your life with me. Right now, for whatever that we can be. I don't know what that is, you don't know. Speak with me. Right now. Say it.
GLENNA:	I don't know what you're talking about.
EDMOND:	Oh, by the Lord, yes, you do. Say it with me. (*She takes out a vial of pills.*) What are those?
GLENNA:	Pills.
EDMOND:	For what? Don't take them.
GLENNA:	I have this tendency to get anxious.
EDMOND:	(*knocks them from her hand*) Don't take them. Go through it. Go through with me.
GLENNA:	You're scaring me.
EDMOND:	I am not. I know when I'm scaring you. Believe me. (*Pause.*)
GLENNA:	Get out. (*Pause.*)
EDMOND:	Glenna. (*Pause.*)
GLENNA:	Get out! GET OUT GET OUT! LEAVE ME THE FUCK ALONE!!! WHAT DID I DO, PLEDGE MY LIFE TO YOU? I LET YOU FUCK ME. GO AWAY.

'I come from a Broken Home. The most important institution in America,' Mamet once said, which might suggest that his plays put the domestic arena at their heart. But they rarely do and in his best and most successful play, **Glengarry Glen Ross**, like O'Neill and Miller, he takes on the workplace of that most emblematic of American occupations: the salesman. Four real-estate salesmen compete with a desperate urgency in a sales contest – the winner gets a Cadillac, the second a set of steak knives, and the other two get fired.

The salesmen live out the absurdly contradictory frontier ethic, posturing both as rugged loners and as good buddies. It's a man's world, with rhetoric as the man's weapon, shield and tool: words, tones, silences are used to impress, persuade, cajole, seduce, and bully. These men have the gift to use talk to promote themselves at everyone else's expense, and to profess friendship while cheating each other into a state of mutual

David Mamet.

isolation. 'The frontier ethic,' said Mamet, 'was always something for nothing ... take the land from the Indians and give it to the railroad,' and what's more if you don't exploit every possible opportunity – with women as much as in business – you're not only being stupid, but indictably so.

Mamet approaches his characters like an anthropologist, examining their patterns of behaviour and inferring their social conditioning from those patterns. In our turn we can infer in him a moralist filled with dismay at the persistence with which people sustain themselves with deluded propaganda and myths:

> The proclamation and repetition of first principles is a constant feature of life in our democracy. Active adherence to these principles, however, has always been considered un-American.

Mamet's plays aren't concerned with diagnosing or prescribing political systems; whatever illnesses he perceives are endemic and immune to political change. Nor is he a social satirist – **Speed-the-Plow**, a tale of two scam merchants who run a film studio trading a commodity that happens to be a 'buddy film', is a lethally accurate comment on Hollywood, but the play asks the question: are we capable of change? A twenty-five-year-old secretary has sex with one of the men for her own ends, but acts as a catalyst, temporarily jolting his conscience. He returns to his buddy glowing with idealism and conviction, only to be disabused of his new faith when he discovers the girl's deviousness.

These are people – the men and the woman – who, as the actor Joe Mantegna says, '... are in that grey zone. Are they good people? Are they terrible people? I think what David says is that there are no great people, there are no terrible people, it's only grey people: it just depends which side of the grey scale you're looking at ... '

Oleanna is another exploration of the grey scale. A two-hander about a self-important university teacher and a student who accuses him of rape, it's ostensibly a play about the phenomenon of political correctness, but Mamet's concern is clearly not a journalistic one, to provide a balanced debate on the subject – the cards are stacked too heavily against the student, who is motivated by revenge. The very lack of journalistic equity highlights Mamet's preoccupation with the characters' dogged inability to understand one another. 'We can only interpret the behaviour of others through the screen we … through the screen we create,' says the teacher to the student.

Why don't people get along? Why can't men and women love each other? 'My plays are about people trying to become connected. People who are confused … trying to do good … But no one knows how.' Mamet's view of the world is not so much a pessimistic one as a realistic one. He's not a fatalist: men and women, he says, can still make choices about how to live their lives but they do it within a society that's spinning apart. There's no more pithy, terrifying and brilliant speculation about how we live than in **Edmond**, a seventy-five-minute moral fable, which wastes not a single word or gesture, about a rapid descent into hell of a middle-class Manhattan businessman.

Edmond visits a fortune-teller who convinces him that he is a special person living in the wrong place and that his world is falling apart. He promptly leaves his wife and plunges into the New York underbelly in an attempt to free himself from routine responsibility and the constriction of his life. He breathes a casual resentment of women, blacks and gays. He's mugged and robbed, buys a knife at a pawn shop, stabs a pimp, sleeps with a waitress/actress and in a fit of wild anger murders her. He's arrested, convicted and imprisoned. Once in prison he severs his relationship with his wife, refuses to see visitors, is sodomised by his black cellmate and gradually comes to terms with his fall from grace. 'Every fear hides a wish,' he says. The play closes with Edmond and his cellmate philosophising at the end of the day. Their conversation over, Edmond kisses him goodnight.

Everything in Edmond's life – his sexual, social, and racial identity – has been destroyed. He has to start again, this time unburdened with the baggage of his background or his past actions or his profession. He must discover what he can control, and what is – as it were – in the hands of God. The kiss at the end, in the context of this lightning bolt of a play, is a flare of optimism, a humane benediction. Says Mamet, 'I think it's a very, very hopeful play.'

If Sam Shepard can be called the Jackson Pollock of play-writing, Mamet is the Edward Hopper. He builds his plays with meticulous care: spare, heightened, highly stylised language is crafted into a combination of euphemisms, approximations, ellipses, the omission of linking words and phrases, the juxtaposition of the stilted and fluent, the profane and the poetic. It's a marvellous paradox: the expert conjuror of words who writes characters who are disenfranchised from them, who blurt and stammer towards some, generally unrequited, desire to make contact as a step towards redemption.

*Al Pacino in Mamet's **American Buffalo**, 1984.*

1956

'I believe we started out with hope, and hope deferred makes the heart sick, and many hearts are sick at what they see in England now.'
JOHN OSBORNE, 1959

1

Some photographs: Port Said pounded into ruins by British bombers; half-sunk oil tankers in the Suez Canal canted over like dead rhinos; the unattended dead body of a Hungarian amid the rubble of broken paving stones as a Russian tank rolls down a Budapest street. It's 1956, a date that joins a grim calendar of wars and revolutions that resonates down the century: 1914, 1917, 1939, 1968, 1989, 1999 … The British were sending in planes and troops to hold on to their artery to a vanishing empire and the Russians were trying to quell revolution in Hungary. In the same year a revolution occurred in the British theatre at the Royal Court with the performance of John Osborne's (1929–1994) play **Look Back in Anger**. It indisputably stands as the landmark between the old and new worlds. Whether you liked the play then or like it now, even if you feel its influence was negligible and its significance symbolic, to ignore it is like ignoring the Beatles. 'I want to make people feel, to give them lessons in feeling. They can think afterwards,' said John Osborne in 1956. 'In some countries this could be a dangerous approach, but there seems little danger of people feeling too much – at least not in England as I am writing.'

To the child of the 1990s or '80s, the England of 1956 would seem as remote as another climate and another continent. Much of the country was still groaning under the after-effects of the 1939–45 war, which had left the country depleted of resources, exhausted and bomb-scarred. Terraces with missing houses looked like mouthfuls of missing teeth, and weed-infested wastelands spread over every large city like alopecia. The post-war Labour government had been replaced in 1951 by a Tory administration under the ageing Churchill, and the Brave New World which had yet to materialise had been replaced by what Jimmy Porter – Osborne's alter ego – described as a 'Brave New-Nothing-Very-Much-Thank-You'.

The coronation in 1953 of the young, shy and personable Queen Elizabeth II acted as a huge stimulant to the monarchy, still popular after the war. The ceremony and procession were watched by 20 million people in curtained rooms on mostly newly purchased TV sets with small screens set in wooden cabinets. And 10 million less privileged listened to the radio. For eight hours the British people celebrated like supplicants in a ritual: monarchy,

Osborne in the '60s.

after all, is the English religion. The monarchy was reborn, and with it the New Elizabethan Age, which offered a philosophical surrogate for a lost Empire – to which were annexed the ascent of Everest and the recapture of The Ashes, under the first ever professional captain.

That professionalisation of cricket wasn't replicated in most other areas of British life. Civilian institutions tended to be run by ex-officers and gentlemen, reproducing the polarities of the forces – for which conscription still existed (until 1960). A world made safe for democracy had been made safe for hierarchy. The popularity of the monarchy reinforced the status and inviolability of the aristocracy, which in turn gave a blessing to the tiers of the British class system – sanctified by the Established Church of which the Queen was the head. The country, like a Calvinist state divided between those who will be saved and those who are damned, was divided between the 'them' and 'us' of the managers and the managed.

There was much political myth-making about the coming of universal dissolution of class difference with growing affluence. 'Let's be frank about it,' said Prime Minister Harold Macmillan in 1957, 'most of our people have never had it so good.' That was certainly true for an ever-widening middle class, but it made little impact on a working class still suffering substantial poverty in spite of the Welfare State, whose priorities the Tory government had asserted when re-elected – along with the desire to see women return from their wartime jobs to home, hearth, and husband.

There was little opposition to the government. The Tory Party had assimilated much of the policy of the previous government and the Labour Party were wearied by the compromise and barter of their years in office. The radical left had been fragmented by Khrushchev's denunciation of Stalin and by the Soviet suppression of the Hungarian revolution, and were united only in opposition to the Suez adventure.

The voluntary suppression of dissent in politics was echoed in the arts and in what was then never called 'the media'. There was little dissenting intelligentsia, and television, radio and newspapers, run by people who knew what was good for you, offered a homogenised orthodoxy of opinion: regressively bland, demure, deferential, genteel, puritanical, complacent and suffocating.

Of course there were little bubbles of dissent – the Goon Show on the radio, for instance, and a group of novelists and poets which included Philip Larkin, Kingsley Amis, and Thom Gunn, who wrote about intelligent, provincial, lower-middle-class, educated, disaffected young men.

American music started to penetrate the carapace of British homogeneity – Charlie Parker and Miles Davis in jazz, Elvis and Bill Haley in pop – just at the time that Britain made her last gesture of independence from America in foreign policy over Suez. James Dean appeared in *Rebel Without a Cause* and the word 'teenager' entered the English vocabulary, as did 'Teddy Boys' – kids who defied the clothing orthodoxy by wearing long, coloured drape jackets with velvet lapels and thin, leg-hugging 'drainpipe' trousers. There were (small) riots at the showings of *Rock Around the Clock* and cinema seats were slashed. 'Its appeal is its simplicity,' said Bill Haley. 'Everyone wants to get into the act. With rock 'n' roll they can join in.' The 'young' were a disenfranchised tribe, of interest only to far-sighted record producers.

It's hard now, as our streets are a collage of street signs and shop fronts as vividly coloured as boiled sweets, and advertising hoardings beckon us to better lives with sex or sun or money, to imagine the lack of choice, the lack of colour, the lack of public joy, the sheer monochromatic greyness of everything in the 1950s. 'Dickensian' is not an idle adjective to apply to a country in which only a third of the population had exclusive use of bath, lavatory and cooker, nearly half had no bath at all, central heating was an exotic luxury and the smoke from coal fires smothered large cities with dense fogs. If one thinks back to the 1950s now, it seems like one long wet Sunday afternoon.

Look Back in Anger is set at the epicentre of that '50s inertia – an early Sunday evening in a small rented room in a dull Midlands town, with the air thick with boredom and … is it sexual frustration? The protagonist, Jimmy Porter, runs a sweet-stall in the market and is engaged in an attritional war with his wife, Alison, trying to goad her into life: 'If only something – something would happen to you, and wake you out of your beauty sleep! If you could have a child and it would die.'

He is cruel, violent, and iconoclastic, and he hacks away at his pet aversions with a wild and always beautifully orchestrated rhetoric: the upper classes, the middle classes, the Sunday papers, his wife, his friend Cliff, women, Americans, apathy and absence of feeling. Not exactly misogynistic – he gives far too much credit to the power of women for that – but demanding a commitment from them that is absolute.

Posh papers and ironing board: the first production of **Look Back in Anger** *– Alan Bates, Kenneth Haigh and Mary Ure.*

Alison becomes pregnant, her father (a sympathetic but bewildered ex-Indian army colonel) appears, and a play about a marriage becomes a play about a society. Alison leaves, and is replaced by Helena, an actress. The third act rhymes with the beginning of the first – Helena ironing one of Jimmy's shirts and wearing one of them for camouflage. Cliff announces that he's leaving and Jimmy is stricken. He expects disloyalty from a woman – but from a *man*? As John Osborne's hero Max Miller would have said, 'Go on, lady, make something of that!'

Alison returns; Helena leaves and husband and wife are reconciled in what is, for a play underpinned by sexual desire and frustration, an oddly mawkish duet: 'Poor squirrels!' says Jimmy. 'Poor bears!' says Alison. In a recent National Theatre production, this sentimentality was cleverly subverted: after Alison has grovelled and crawled to him ('I'm in the mud at last!'), and he has responded with his 'bears' and 'squirrels' speech, Alison (played by Emma Fielding) launched herself at Jimmy (played by Michael Sheen) and with the last strength in her body beat him with a wild ferocity – like the fights between Jimmy and Cliff, but this time for real. Then, warily, very warily, came the ending. But Osborne's intentions are unambiguous:

JIMMY: (*pathetically*) Poor squirrels!
ALISON: (*with the same comic emphasis*) Poor bears! (*She laughs a little. Then looks at him very tenderly, and adds very, very softly*) Oh, poor, poor, bears!
(*Slides her arm round him.*)

Look Back in Anger was written by an actor whose experience of plays – and adult life – had been formed in the raffish, tatty, congenial world of 'Number Two Tours of West End Successes' and weekly or two-weekly rep in Kidderminster, Ilfracombe, and Derby. Its form is borrowed from what Osborne knew of the plays he acted in or observed as a stage manager. **Look Back** was, as he said himself, 'a formal, rather old-fashioned, play' – three acts, with melodramatic, often contrived climaxes, indistinguishable in form from, say, Rattigan or Noël Coward. Compare these act endings from Osborne and Coward, both arresting, both teetering on the edge of self-parody, both unmistakably inviting the curtain to descend for the interval·

From **Look Back in Anger**:

JIMMY: (*grabbing her shoulder*) Well, the performance is over. Now leave me alone, and *get out*, you evil-minded little virgin.
(*She slaps his face savagely. An expression of horror and disbelief floods his face. His hand goes up to his head, and a muffled cry of despair escapes him. Helena tears his hand*

away, and kisses him passionately, drawing him down beside her.)

CURTAIN

From **The Vortex**:

FLORENCE: *(hysterically)* Love! You don't know what it means. You've lied to me – all these months. It's contemptible – humiliating. Get out of my sight!

TOM: *(turning and going upstairs)* Very well.

FLORENCE: *(suddenly realising that he is gone)* Tom – Tom – come back – come back – !

(She runs upstairs after him. NICKY at last stops playing and lets his hand drop from the keys.)

CURTAIN

It wasn't the form that made the audiences at the Royal Court sit up in the May of 1956, or even the setting which, with its evocation of the world of provincial bed-sitting rooms with peeling wallpaper, brown lino, candlewick bedspreads, and gas meters, served as a sort of mocking parody of the Home Counties drawing-rooms of West End plays. What was striking was the voice – and the voice unmistakably was John Osborne's own and above all else the voice was shouting out: 'Hallelujah! Hallelujah! I'm alive!'

As he makes clear in his autobiographies, **Look Back in Anger** describes his own life as an actor in provincial rep – Jimmy Porter's 'sweet-stall' of the play is his writer's decoy, his friend Cliff is probably Osborne's (gay) friend Anthony Creighton. The life was hard – little money, six-day weeks, rehearsals all day, performances at night, matinées on Wednesdays and Saturdays, learning lines, evading landladies, and on Sundays sitting round reading the papers, with no television to watch, no restaurants to go to, and pubs opening barely long enough to quench your thirst, let alone get drunk. In the 1950s, when sex before marriage was severely frowned on and homosexuality was a criminal offence, a life in rep offered a sort of cracked, tacky, tolerant Arcadia where actors enjoyed the gypsy freemasonry of the theatre and wore their hearts on their sleeves. 'Feelings were open, often raw, and most frailty smiled on or laughed away,' said Osborne.

Jimmy Porter seems at this distance indistinguishable from his creator. John Osborne wasn't from Oxbridge or public school, he hadn't done National Service, he hated authority, he hated conformity, he hated his mother, he was a conservative in everything but sex and, if he was anything in politics, he was an anarchist. He was wholly English in his cultivated eccentricity, his love of landscape and of liturgy, and he had enough self-knowledge to know that his prejudices and his passions were incurable: he would always remain a sort of demonic Peter Pan. His life was in his anger, and the anger in his life: anger was an existential force.

To ask, 'Feeling for what?' or, 'Angry for what?' is to ask a question that always infuriated Jimmy's creator. He wasn't *un*angry about the British attempts to hold on to the declining Empire in Suez or in Cyprus or Kenya or Malaya, or the Russians stamping into Hungary, or the government's acquiescence to the Cold War in testing H-bombs and preparing bomb shelters, but he was angry about his feeling of impotence and confusion in the face of these things. Far from looking back in anger, the play looks back with a fierce, despairing nostalgia for a world that was secure in its certainties *and* in its doubts.

The play never pretends to be objective. It is defiantly subjective and self-centred. There is no more solipsistic cry from the post-war years, when the world had become better informed than ever about mass starvation, tyranny, injustice, plague and poverty, than Jimmy Porter's 'There aren't any good, brave causes left.' But that's not the point. The point is this: at a particular moment of history Osborne came along and shouted: You've only got one life, however painful, alone or together, LIVE IT! As Tony Richardson said, 'He is unique and alone in his ability to put on the stage the quick of himself, his pain, his squalor, his nobility – terrifyingly alone.'

As Osborne said of Noël Coward, 'Like Coriolanus he was the author of himself,' and this was equally true of Osborne. His anger is about: the disappointment of love, the yearning desire for things to mean something, the longing to assuage loneliness, and the need to reclaim the past – or a mother who'd love him. He dreams of a lost Eden, in which anger is original sin. From **Déjà Vu**, his sequel to **Look Back** written thirty-five years later:

> Anger … is mourning the unknown, the loss of what went before without you, it's the love another time but not this might have sprung on you.

The British theatre, as Arthur Miller said, had been 'hermetically sealed off from life' – and from the American theatre. **Death of a Salesman, The Crucible, A View From the Bridge, All My Sons, The Glass Menagerie, A Streetcar Named Desire, Camino Real** and **The Rose Tattoo** had all been huge successes in New York – and smaller successes in London – by the time **Look Back in Anger** was produced. The fatuous presence of the Lord Chamberlain had reinforced the notion, to a generation now used to drama on television, that the British theatre was an archaic, redundant and class-bound form of entertainment. It was as though a spell had been cast, and the Prince had hacked through the enchanted forest to wake Sleeping Beauty from her sleep.

'I doubt if I could love anyone who didn't love **Look Back in Anger**,' announced Kenneth Tynan, with the rapture of an explorer planting a flag in new territory. The Royal Court Press Officer, asked for a description of the play's author, described him as 'an angry young man', and the press, in consort with the BBC and the newly enfranchised

ITV, moved into capital letters, manufactured a 'Movement' of 'Angry Young Men' (so much more *English* than the continental 'intellectuals'), and declared that a revolution was in progress. It was the first sighting of a phenomenon that was to become a familiar smudge on the English cultural scene: a 'media event', a phrase which John Osborne would have hissed at with boundless distaste.

Ironically, the despised 'media' were responsible for making **Look Back in Anger** nationally conspicuous: only with the showing of a twenty-minute excerpt of the play on BBC TV was its success at the Royal Court established.

It's an extraordinary comment on the state of the theatre at the time – and of British society – that the play that effected this seismic breakthrough was a play which, for all its abrasive, excoriating, maudlin, self-pitying and sometimes surprisingly tender rhetoric, seems to look back to the past with regret rather than anger. Nevertheless, Osborne introduced a hectoring, indignant, and passionate voice that belonged to the present tense, in an accent that was not attempting to conform to the oppressive homogeneity of 'received pronunciation'. And, like Edward Bond in later years, he was never afraid of offending the audience.

The British theatre still sets its clock by the revolution of 1956, accepts the theology and the pieties associated with that historical moment, and talks about before and after **Look Back in Anger** as if it were before and after Darwin. But most revolutions are evolutions, and the 'breakthrough' of 1956 was no exception. As John Osborne said: 'The theatre simply went on dying, as it has done for centuries. Like everything else.'

'The Brechtian bulldozer may not be our answer': **Luther**.

Osborne's later plays show a curiosity for adventure in form, scratching around like an animal looking for a new home, but always tethered to a strong central male character. He travelled from the Ibsenism of **Look Back** to the Brechtianism of **The Entertainer**, **Luther**, and **A Patriot for Me**, to the deconstruction of **A Sense of Detachment** – characters planted in the audience, actors stepping off the stage – to the phantasmagoric expressionism of **Inadmissible Evidence**. 'The Brechtian bulldozer may not be *our* answer. We need to invent a machine of our own. What this may be we shall have to find out,' he said in 1957.

Osborne's great experiment lay in his trust in the theatrical power of words, which spilled from him like an artist who draws without taking his hand from the paper; words to be spoken aloud, often titanic monologues by actors with an appetite and an ability for rhetoric – like Laurence Olivier, Albert Finney, Nicol Williamson, Paul Scofield, Ralph Richardson.

No English playwright had put language on the line like this since Lawrence – to reveal the beat of the human heart without ornament or decoration. Those who invariably expect bare-fanged vituperation from Osborne should listen to this declaration of love in **Hotel in Amsterdam,** preferably spoken by Paul Scofield with a slow, tender care for each adjective:

'A site of helpless-ness, of oppression and polemic': **Inadmissible Evidence** *with Nicol Williamson.*

... to me ... you have always been the most ... the most dashing ... romantic ... friendly ... playful ... loving ... impetuous ... larky ... fearful ... detached ... constant ... woman I have ever met ... and I love you ... I don't know how else one says it ... I don't know how else one says it ... one shouldn't ... and I've always thought you felt ... perhaps ... the same about me.

Inadmissible Evidence is his best play. Ostensibly set in a solicitor's office – 'a site of helplessness, of oppression and polemic' – the action whirls in a kind of vortex with the solicitor, Bill Maitland, being sucked down to its centre by despair, panic, envy of youth, fear of death. His life is a nightmare of snubs and desertions: even taxis ignore him. He listens to litanies of distress from his clients, and rails at the apathy of his seventeen-year-old daughter. Even given the ineradicable memory of Nicol Williamson's performance, it is impossible to divorce it from the sound of Osborne's voice, snarling and atavistic:

> If you should one day start to shrink slowly into an unremarkable, gummy little hole, into a world outside the care or consciousness of anyone, you'll have no rattlings of shame or death, there'll be no little sweating, eruptions of blood, no fevers or clots or flesh splitting anywhere or haemorrhage. You'll have done everything well and sensibly and stylishly. You'll know it wasn't worth any candle that ever burned. You will have to be blown out, snuffed, decently, and not be watched spluttering and spilling and hardening.

There is no better epitaph for John Osborne's work than Osborne's on Max Miller: 'I loved him because he embodied a kind of theatre I admire most. His method was danger.'

2

Look Back in Anger was the first new play to be presented by the newly formed English Stage Company, whose Artistic Director was George Devine and his Associate Tony Richardson. It was serendipity that brought the two men together, just as it brought them eventually to rent the Royal Court Theatre. They met when Tony Richardson directed Devine in a television adaptation of a Chekhov short story for the BBC, an organisation for which Richardson, characteristically, had no respect: 'an out-front-and-proud-of-it bastion of mediocrity'. Devine was an actor/director who had run the Old Vic School with Michel Saint-Denis and Glen Byam Shaw. They trained actors along French and Russian models, serious above all about taking the theatre seriously. For a while they seemed, plausibly enough, to be the triumvirate who would run the National Theatre when it was founded. They were fired by the capricious Tyrone Guthrie; Glen Byam Shaw went to Stratford and George Devine returned to acting.

When they talked about forming a theatre company neither the young Tony Richardson, nor the much older Devine, knew what they wanted: 'A new theatre – he didn't know what. I wanted a new theatre too, and I didn't know how.' If the ambitious young Oxford graduate didn't know how to go about it, then the older actor did, and together, for a few years, they made a happy marriage – the young adventurer with the (not-so-old) visionary, the impatient entrepreneur with the fastidious craftsman. Devine, handsome, compact, old beyond his years, pipe-smoking, wholly unostentatious; Richardson, the opposite – tall, dandyish, flamboyant, conspicuous.

Devine and Richardson joined with a cousin of the Queen who worked at the Royal Opera House, George Harewood, and the poet Ronald Duncan, who had already conceived a plan for a company that would produce new and uncommercial plays. They variously planned Sunday-evening performances, tours, and appearances at regional arts festivals, but it became clear that to be of any value the company had to be a professional one and they approached Devine to be its Artistic Director. Devine argued that they needed a London theatre, and insisted that Tony Richardson be appointed his Associate. The owner of the Royal Court finally agreed to a lease of thirty-four years and the English Stage Company was officially born.

The Royal Court had enjoyed a luminous period from 1904 to 1907 when Granville-Barker was its Artistic Director, and if George Devine had a spiritual father it was, unquestionably, Granville-Barker; his determination to make the theatre not a respectable art, but an art that was respected, mirrored the evangelical purpose that drove George Devine.

Devine hated the merely modish, the merely entertaining and the 'star system' – even if the Court frequently depended on stars. He believed that along with universal education it was the theatre that would liberate people – 'the lower classes who had been silent under the former system'. He wanted a theatre that made sense of the world about him:

> Had we not seen six million Jews murdered? Were we not seeing McCarthyism in the United States, the emergence of the coloured races; were we not experiencing a scientific adjustment of all our values? ... There had been drastic political and social changes all around us; the new Prosperity State was more than suspect, both political parties looked the same. No man or woman of feeling who was not wearing blinkers could not but feel profoundly disturbed.

Devine went on the hunt for new scripts and, as producers have done many times before and since, envious of the novel's cultural status, approached a number of novelists with the suggestion that they turn their hand to the theatre. With the exceptions of Doris Lessing, Angus Wilson – whose play had already been produced at Bristol – and Nigel Dennis, who adapted his own novel, **Cards of Identity**, he was disappointed. He was also disappointed by the response to an advertisement in *The Stage* for new plays. There was only one play of interest among the 750 scripts that poured through the door – John Osborne's **Look Back in Anger**, which had already been rejected by a score of managers and agents.

George Harewood showed a playwright friend the script of the play: 'Well, it's very excitingly written,' said the friend, 'but you can't put that on in a theatre! People won't stand for being shouted at like that, it's not what they go to the theatre for.'

And it was true, they didn't. But Devine was determined that they should, and they did, and, as Lindsay Anderson said: 'There was no bowing and scraping to us, the audience; and there was no bullying either. In English culture, where "serious" is most often used as a mocking epithet, this made the experience a refreshing or even touching one.'

There was a determination not to appease or toady to the audience, an attitude that could sometimes tip over into contempt if the audience were passive and glee if they walked out. But that robustness, or perversity or obduracy or courage, is very rare now in the theatre and was even rarer then. 'I wanted to change the attitude of the public towards the theatre,' said Devine. 'All I did was to change the attitude of the theatre towards the public.' He taught that if audiences were small it didn't mean that the work was bad, you were not wrong to have done it. You had to support the people you believed in; it simply meant that, next time, as Beckett said, you had to fail better.

A secular saint: George Devine.

George Devine introduced two canonical sayings to the theatre: 'Policy is who you work with', and the 'right to fail' – the first is endearingly pragmatic, a sort of embodiment of English empiricism, the second is a kind of arrogant, absurd, self-righteous, and necessary principle that must underlie any artistic endeavour. The demand for a 'right to fail' is more often a plea for the right not to have to succeed, but as a slogan it reveals much of the heart of Devine's character and ethos: ascetic, patrician, stubborn, modest, cocky, and courageous.

He engendered a system of values that gave the theatre of his time a goal: to be 'about something', to be ambitious for the work before the career – in short, he taught self-respect.

Devine came to be known by succeeding generations as a 'secular saint', not a bad description for a man who said that 'the theatre is really a religion or a way of life', even if, as Richardson said, 'He always had the cement and truck dust on his hands – that's why the hod-carriers would follow him to the top of the scaffolding.'

His partnership with Richardson lasted for nearly eight years – as long as the active partnership of Stanislavsky and Nemirovich-Danchenko at the Moscow Art Theatre, and perhaps as long as any theatrical regime can fruitfully endure before exhaustion, or inertia, take over. By the time Devine resigned in 1965 – because of ill-health – the Court, as the critic Irving Wardle said, had outlived its heroic phase. It had lost its exclusive position, and other theatres and television were now hungry to present the sort of plays that the Court had pioneered. 'We are supposed to be the spearhead,' said Devine, 'but how do you keep sharpening the spear?'

During his time Devine presided over the first performances of Osborne's **Look Back in Anger**, **The Entertainer, Luther,** and **A Patriot for Me**; N.F. Simpson's surrealistic *tour de force* **A Resounding Tinkle**; Willis Hall's **The Long and the Short and the Tall**; Pinter's **The Room** and **The Dumb Waiter** (although he didn't recognise their originality); Edward Bond's first play **The Pope's Wedding** (even though he thought Bond was 'second-string'); the first English productions of Ionesco's **The Chairs**; Brecht's **The Good Person of Setzuan** and Beckett's **Endgame, Krapp's Last Tape,** and **Happy Days** – Brecht and Beckett, his two household gods. In 1960 he presented Arnold Wesker's Trilogy: **Roots, Chicken Soup With Barley** and **I'm Talking About Jerusalem;** and **The Kitchen**.

Wesker's plays seem at the heart of Devine's ethos – passionately humane, socialist, very much 'about something', but were not wholly to his taste – which is why, directed by John Dexter, they were sent to Coventry, to the newly built Belgrade Theatre, to open first.

Arnold Wesker (1932–) was born in the East End of London. His background, rare among British playwrights, is working class and Jewish. If he has a model among his predecessors, it is Clifford Odets: he writes with the same paradoxical vein of romantic realism, underpinned by the conviction that people deserve better than they get. He's often spoken of as a conventional naturalistic writer, but in his best work – **Roots, The Kitchen** (inspired by his time as a teenage pastry cook) and **Chips with Everything** (from his National Service in the RAF), he defies reductive categorisation.

Chips with Everything is stylistically bold with a flair, which he first showed in **The Kitchen**, for showing the lives of a group of people in sharp detail, but also for making theatrical capital out of the surprising beauty of the natural choreography of a group of people at work. **Chips** is a play about conscription, class and rites of passage. Set in the early 1950s, it follows a group of conscripts in the RAF during their basic training. A rebellious upper-class boy and a working-class one become friends, but are driven apart by the determination of their officers to ensure that the upper-class boy remains loyal to his class by becoming an officer. He eventually submits and, in trying to improve the lot of his fellow-squaddies, finds himself part of the Establishment's repressive tolerance. The play is hard-nosed in its assertion of the indelibility of the British class system, even if it's always underscored by Wesker's indelible romanticism.

Perhaps it was Wesker's earnestness that Devine objected to, but from today's perspective Wesker's early plays seem among the finest achievements of that era, along with the work of John Arden (1930–). Arden's **Live Like Pigs** – about travellers on a housing estate – and **Serjeant Musgrave's Dance** – about a soldier who turns against war – displayed a great unbiddable talent: poetic and profoundly political.

Joan Plowright as Beattie Bryant in **Roots**.

Charles Wood (1932–) was another such talent, shepherded into the Royal Court by John Osborne, who directed his short play **Meals on Wheels** in 1965. Wood's trio of short plays, **Cockade**, had been presented a year earlier by the producer, Michael Codron, who for about a decade from the late 1950s was at least as important a supporter of new writers (Pinter and Orton among them) as the English Stage Company. Wood's play, **Dingo** – a savage, brilliant, imagistic play about the Desert War – subtitled **A Camp Concert**, was presented at the Royal Court a year later under club conditions, on account of the Lord Chamberlain's demand for a comprehensive re-write.

Wood as a playwright is something of a poet and something of a painter: the playwright speaks for himself; the poet is revealed in the text through the repeated rhythms, the hint of rhyme, the stylised translation of conversation, and in the emergence of an idiosyncratic and obsessional voice; the painter is latent in the stage directions: indelible images of a sandhill and a tank in the desert in **Dingo**; a decorated Indian elephant in **H**; a small Eurasian girl holding the hand of a Malaysian rubber planter in a clearing in the jungle while a record of a British night-club singer plays on a wind-up gramophone in **Jingo**; a moonlit soldier stumbling through a perpetual night under the burden of his full kit, a rough beast slouching towards Bedlam in **Tumbledown**, his screenplay for the TV film.

His work is not easy to perform. It's hard for actors to find naturalness within dialogue that is so highly distilled and so insistently singular, and it takes time, imagination and confidence to allow his scenes to realise their full potential. There's a remarkable scene in **Jingo** at the end of the play: the Brigadier responsible for the failure of the British to defend Singapore demands that an English woman gives him a spanking as punishment – the dismal demise of the British Empire, embodied in the childlike demand of an upper-class Englishman to be smacked on his bare bottom with the back of a pearl-handled hair-brush, is eerily touching and uncomfortably resonant.

Wood's writing invariably describes closed societies – the army (**Cockade** and **Dingo**) the British Empire (**H**), the theatre (**Fill the Stage with Happy Hours**), the film world (**Veterans**) – all having their private languages, their peculiar customs, and all steeped in an irreducible Englishness. But the consuming preoccupation of this humane and gentle man is the activity that devours humanity and gentility: war. As with Wilfred Owen, it is the pity of war that he is concerned with, but it is also the glamour – the weapons, orders, insignia, regalia, shoulder flashes, scarlet tunics, cap badges, ranks, battle honours, regimental history, and the private syntax of men amongst men. And the horror – the mud, the blood, the brains, guts, limbs and lives that get shed in foreign fields far from home. And before the confusion, folly and fear of battle, the strutting neatness, cleanness, pomp, order, hierarchy and absurdity of the soldier's life in peacetime.

There is no contemporary writer who has chronicled the experience of modern war with so much authority, knowledge, compassion, wit and despair, and there is no contemporary writer who has received so little of his deserved public acclaim.

Arnold Wesker's **Chips with Everything** was turned down by George Devine, and only presented by the Royal Court when a commercial producer agreed to share the costs. Why? Devine simply didn't like the play. Like any theatre director, his taste was fallible and his enthusiasms were inconsistent, but he did create a climate in which, above all, it was possible for a young writer to be taken seriously. It's hard now, when every theatre proclaims a 'new-play policy', to recognise the novelty of the Writers' Group that he set up, of which Arnold Wesker, Edward Bond, John Arden, and Ann Jellicoe were members. Ann Jellicoe's brilliantly original **The Knack** was a perfect example of Devine's catholic enthusiasm – the polar opposite of Osborne's rhetoric – a quartet of young people jostling for power in a play where words took a minor place to action and images.

Devine respected the primacy of the writer, but the Royal Court was never a 'writer's theatre' or a 'socialist theatre'. It took writers seriously, but often rejected them callously, and socialism was important only in the sense of the theatre being implicitly part of a broad left consensus. Devine's principles were aesthetic: rigour, asceticism and minimalism – what you left off the stage was as important as what you put on it; being 'theatrical' could have as much to do with austerity as excess. The designs of Jocelyn Herbert embodied this aesthetic and she – who lived with Devine – more than anyone animated his aesthetic. 'A theatre stage should have the maximum of verbal presence and the maximum of corporal presence,' said Samuel Beckett to Bill Gaskill, who succeeded Devine as Artistic Director.

It was an approach that demanded that the text came first, and that the director and designer served it with clarity, lucidity, realism, and grace. At its best the work had a limpid beauty, at its worst asceticism looked like poverty of imagination and purity became sanctimoniousness. Lindsay Anderson cited the Periclean ideal as the model for the Royal Court aesthetic: 'We pursue beauty without extravagance and knowledge without effeminacy' – more Sparta than Sloane Square, perhaps.

Tony Richardson's production of **The Seagull** in 1964 marked the end of the era. With poetic appropriateness, it played not at the Royal Court but at the Queen's Theatre. Peggy Ashcroft, who was a founder council member of the English Stage Company, played Arkadina; George Devine played Dr Dorn, and Vanessa Redgrave – by then Richardson's wife – played Nina.

> When at the end of the play [said Richardson] George announced, 'Konstantin Gavrilovich has shot himself,' in retrospect he was perhaps anticipating the end of the Court … After our Queen's season the Court withdrew into what it has become ever since – a minor liberal institution with good intentions. That's why Konstantin shot himself.

It's an epitaph that is nothing if not subjective; the Royal Court continued to produce fine work, and continued to be imbued, consciously or not, by the values of Devine, who died in 1966 at the shockingly young age of fifty-five. His legacy of unmannered acting, devotion to the text, unostentatious direction, simple and expressive design endured for many years.

So also did the sectarian fervour with which the Royal Court has always separated itself from the rest of the theatre. There was a time when it was frowned on to attend productions at the RSC if you worked at the Court, professional suicide not to be seen leaving before the interval, and actual suicide to profess enjoyment of the production. Christopher Hampton became the first Resident Playwright in 1968: 'I joined marauding bands to visit theatres, subsidised or unsubsidised … and got used to the command: "Well I don't think we can stay here." '

Devine acted as an artistic conscience for countless people in the theatre for several generations – and in particular for the authors of this book. Jocelyn Herbert's epitaph sums up what Devine gave to the Court – and what's required of every theatre venture: 'For a brief period our work, and our lives, had a centre.'

3

When Bill Gaskill succeeded George Devine in 1965, he intended to mimic Granville-Barker by presenting a 'true' repertory of plays with a permanent company. His success in that respect was intermittent, derailed by the exigencies of the precise casting demands of new plays. His flair for talent-spotting would come into its own on the arrival of the New Wave in the late '60s and early '70s. Meanwhile, his most remarkable achievement was to establish the reputations of two major playwrights – D.H. Lawrence, whose trilogy was presented posthumously in 1968, and Edward Bond.

The question most often asked nowadays about Edward Bond is: what happened to him? Though Bond hasn't disappeared from view and he isn't likely to. He hasn't lost his powers, far from it. Nor has he been forgotten: he remains in print, he's widely studied and written about, and he's respected to the point of reverence, rightly so. But at the time of writing he's estranged from the working theatre: his new plays either don't get done, or they do but it all becomes a miserable experience or they appear in semi-amateur productions. It's a cause of anger and contempt on Bond's part, depression and denial on the other.

He was born in Holloway, North London in 1934 and was evacuated to East Anglia during the war to stay with his grandparents: East Anglian dialect would later suffuse three of his most personal plays. He left school at fifteen, took on the ordinary office and factory jobs a working-class boy could expect to do and was called up for the obligatory two years' National Service. ('I'm a trained killer,' he would remind people in later years:

Edward Bond.

it had the typical Bondian touch of being extreme but true.)

Playwrights of Bond's generation grew up without a 'fringe' to produce their early plays, or a network of subsidised studio theatres, or anything to compare with the quick-off-the-mark script editors, who now roam round the circuits pressing commissions for film and television on anyone new who shows a spark of promise. Until 1956 there were – for the young unknown – only two possibilities: having your play produced by a commercial management or not having it done at all, which is why every one of Bond's first fifteen plays ended up in his bottom drawer. This isn't a hard-luck story. Worse things can happen to a young writer: years of fruitless 'play-development', for example, or being over-praised for a scrappy first attempt.

So the Royal Court was vital. In December 1962, **The Pope's Wedding** was produced for a single performance in the Court's quaintly named series of 'Sunday Night Productions Without Decor'. Like the play that followed, **The Pope's Wedding** has at its heart an unwitting, irresistible entrancement. We're in Essex: Dunmow, Bishops Stortford, Saffron Walden are all near to hand. Flushed with his success in a local cricket match, young Scopey gets a girl. They marry. Then haltingly, inexplicably, he becomes obsessed with a local recluse. He loses his job, his marriage falls apart and he kills the hermit. We aren't told why, and Scopey himself (it seems) has no idea. We guess that something about the man is real for him: killing him is a way of reaching it.

The corollary is that the rest of Scopey's life is bleak and pointless. But the sense of countryside, the generous tempo, the lads' banter give the play an attractive pastoral feeling, and the cricket match is thrilling: nothing that followed would have such joyful physicality.

Plays change over time, usually for the worse. Ten-year-old plays have a way of seeming talky, while twenty-year-old plays often sound like schoolboys late for assembly, brimming with over-elaborate explanations. Over twenty, reputation is up for grabs: it's classic status or bust. This is what 'classic' means: that a play can change its meaning and survive.

When **Saved** was first produced in 1965, what sprang to the fore, and what so outraged its enemies, was its harshness, its lack of affect and its violence. Reading it now is to discover something entirely different: a play of awesome power and beauty about the struggle of goodness for survival.

Len has a one-night-stand with Pam. She has their baby, by which time she's bored with him and bored with the baby too. But Len, like Scopey, is obsessed. He moves in with Pam and her family, he puts up with the noise of her screwing her new, testosterone-packed boyfriend, he adopts a curious Oedipal role with her mother and, when the baby is stoned to death in its pram by the rest of the lads, he plays no part in the killing, though he yields to a certain morbid curiosity about it.

*The baby-stoning in **Saved**.*

The title is un-ironic: Len is saved. By the end of the play, he's mending a chair. Granted, it's only a chair, but he is at least improving it. And in doing so – moving, as the stage-directions insist, through a series of classical poses – he achieves a redemption which the others around him are denied. Like Scopey, his journey is semi-unconscious: he's fixed on a course he can't defend, explain or articulate. The germ of virtue seems inherent in him. It's amazing that when Bond – in the wake of the **Saved** furore – described the play as 'optimistic', no one believed him.

The dialogue is terse, unshowy, richly nuanced; the construction is masterly, though we're presumably not meant to notice. Bond's great trick is to jump the connecting scenes, so that we arrive at each new state fresh and unjaded. The spirit is fiery, the observation sad and acute. A masterpiece.

It's a measure of Bond's extreme pugnacity that, after his first three shows, he wrote anything else at all. **The Pope's Wedding** was shelved after that single club performance. **Saved** was savaged, **Early Morning** banned. Playwrights have killed themselves for less. Bond wrote on, but the fact that the injustice of the world would now be his central theme is not surprising.

He wrote two prefaces to **Saved**, eleven years apart, and the differences between them are significant. 'Clutching at straws is the only realistic thing to do,' he wrote in 1966: he was referring to Len's acceptance of 'people at their worst'. By 1977, Len's immanent goodness counts for less than the rights and wrongs of violent action. 'Right-wing violence cannot be justified because it always serves irrationality; but left-wing violence is justified when it helps to create a more rational society, and when that help cannot be given in a pacific form.'

To say that Bond became a *more* political playwright is to misjudge the role of politics in great writing. **Saved** is as political as **The Cherry Orchard** or **The Daughter-in-Law**, assuming always that the audience pays attention. (Which it will.) What happened was that his politics moved from an intuitive, class-based sense that things were badly wrong to a revolutionary stance in absolutist 1970s style. Society can't be fixed, according to this perspective: demolition and replacement are required. Which means (to advance the argument a little) that mending a chair is a waste of time, however much this might please its owners. As for individual goodness, it's a mug's game. 'You can't do much by deciding to be happier, saner or wiser,' he wrote in the preface to **Bingo**. 'That partly depends on society, and you can only change your life by changing society and the role you have to play in it.'

Throughout the 1970s, Bond's prefaces ran ahead of his plays. These stern, assertive sermons are the work of the ideologue; the plays are the work of the poet. The fact that his politics were hardening-up showed first in the form of the plays, rather than in their content. The Brechtian *Lehrstück* popped up fast in **Narrow Road to the Deep North**; ditto in some excellent short occasional pieces for CND and Gay Sweatshop.

Lear is a Brechtian fantasia on Shakespeare's original. Bond had drawn from Shakespeare once before: **Early Morning** features the **Hamlet**-quartet of Oedipal mother, impostor-father, anguished son and treacherous pseudo-virgin. Now he challenged a greater play. His Lear, like the original, breaks through the carapace of his own apparatus to arrive at wisdom. This is the play in which Bond first displayed his truly fabulous ability for what Joseph Conrad called 'doing the police in different voices': peasants, bureaucrats, aristocracy, weird Goya-esque wanderers through a war-torn landscape are caught with amazing skill. Is there anyone, you start to wonder, whom he cannot write?

Lear himself is a new figure for Bond: flawed, gigantic, rather Russian in the manner of Eisenstein's Ivan the Terrible. **The Sea** is a dark pastorale with notes of high comedy. Two plays about writers followed: **Bingo** and **The Fool**. Both settle themselves, as though

Harry Andrews
in **Lear**.

by some kind of elastic reaction, around figures as opposite to Lear as could be imagined. Like Len and Scopey, each is good at heart and each is motivated by some vital inner force. But each is found severely lacking in political terms.

Bingo is about the last days of Shakespeare, and the first thing to say is that the central character is perfectly credible: never banal, never bathetic, the convincing author of not one but thirty-seven works of genius. Shakespeare's betrayal – the deed that compromises him, appalls him and will in a roundabout fashion lead to his death – is to sign away the rights of the Stratford villagers in their traditional common land. (True and well researched.)

No other playwright in the 1970s (or since) could have created such a persuasive simulacrum of Jacobean market-town life. Language, mind-set, social detail: all feel right. **The Fool** applies the same ventriloquial brilliance to the world of John Clare, the nineteenth-century 'peasant poet', briefly taken up by polite society and then dropped, to his great emotional and financial cost. Clare, we find, was chasing his Mary ('Mary, or sweet spirit of thee … ') at the very moment that his fellows were robbing the houses of the gentry: this class-betrayal will cost him dear. Scene Six – in which Clare is taken to the asylum – is one of the very best old-fashioned narrative scenes of modern drama, and the last of the kind that Bond would write up to and including the time of writing.

*John Normington in **The Fool**.*

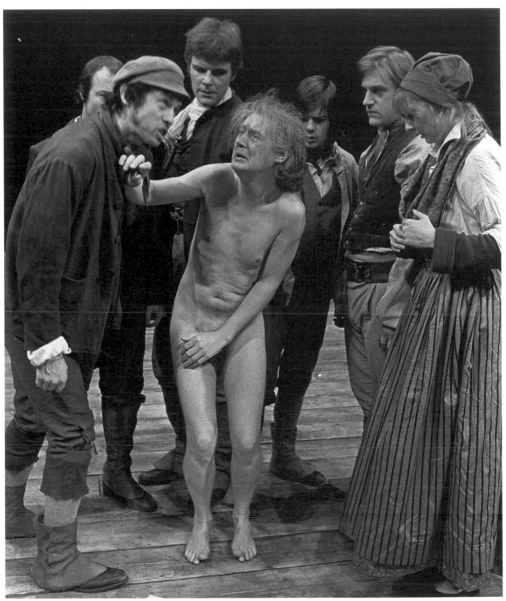

The role of political spearhead, in each of these two plays, is deputed to a secondary character: the 'Son' in **Bingo**, Darkie in **The Fool**: they seem direct successors to Scopey's potent sexual rival in **The Pope's Wedding** and Len's in **Saved**. Bond always has precise descriptions for these challenging figures: '*tall*', '*dark*', '*big-boned and muscular*', '*Fred holds a fishing-rod out over the stalls*'.

But in **The Bundle** the balance is changed: the central figure, Wang, is no longer a doubtful wobbler but a clear-sighted revolutionary. Finding a baby abandoned at the water's edge it takes him no more than half a page of inner debate before deciding on the sensible course. Why save *one* baby? When millions of babies are starving all over the place? And when saving this particular baby would distract him from his revolutionary purpose? Which will save who knows how many other babies? Having thought this through, he throws *this* baby, which happens to be the only one in sight, as far as he can into the river. *Splash!*

The Worlds continues swiftly in the same direction. This is the first Bond play in which we realise, with a louring frown, that we're being talked to, not by the character but by the writer.

ANNA: Listen. There are two worlds. Most people think they live in one but they live in two. First there's the daily world in which we live. The world of appearance. There's law and order, right and wrong, good manners. How else could we live together? But there's also the *real* world. The world of power, machines, buying, selling, working. The world depends on capital: money!

From **The Worlds** onwards, Bond would concentrate on the certainties of grand analysis – the 'real' world – as opposed to the cryptic, contradictory nature of 'the daily world in which we live'. To put it simply: he used to ask questions, now he gave answers. Scopey and Len invite interpretation and to a great extent reward it: this is their fascination. Anna and Wang tell us exactly what they're thinking and exactly why.

It's possible to see Bond's progress as his answer to the problem of uncertainty. In the modern world, and most decidedly in the modern movement, a play can be only a partial view of its subject. A playwright has somehow to acknowledge this without producing a lazy, scrappy effect. Pinter, Stoppard or Caryl Churchill (for example) all make uncertainty a virtue, in their different ways. Bond's answer to the problem was Utopian socialism: a system of belief within which uncertainties are dissolved. Looked at this way, once his horrible early years were over, nothing 'happened' to Bond at all: he chose a particular path and stuck to it.

4

Three months after the opening of **Look Back in Anger** the Berliner Ensemble made their first visit to London. Brecht wrote this for the backstage noticeboard of the Theater am Schiffbauerdamm in East Berlin:

> For our London season ... our playing needs to be quick, light, strong. This is not a question of hurry, but of speed, not simply of quick playing, but of quick thinking. We must keep the tempo of a run-through and infect it with quiet strength, with our own fun. In the dialogue the exchanges must not be offered reluctantly, as when offering somebody one's last pair of boots, but must be tossed like so many balls. The audience has to see that here are a number of artists working together as an ensemble in order to convey stories, ideas, virtuoso feats to the spectator by a common effort.

It was the last thing he wrote. He died on 14 August 1956, and the company opened in London on 27 August in **Mother Courage**, with Helene Weigel playing the title part. The reception was divided, the division exemplified by this debate which took place on television between Kenneth Tynan and Richard Burton:

TYNAN:	Is there any great playwright whose work has never tempted you at all?
BURTON:	Brecht.
TYNAN:	Why not Brecht?
BURTON:	Loathsome, vulgar, petty, little, nothing.
TYNAN:	Large, poetic, universal, everything.

Mother Courage had not been seen in London, even though it had been played in translation in every capital city in Europe, but it had been performed the previous year at a small arts festival in Devon. It had been directed by Joan Littlewood, who also played the name part. It wasn't a success, quite possibly because Littlewood's heart wasn't really in the venture. 'Brecht, like Sartre,' she said, 'never seemed to know exactly what he was saying.' She'd tried to back out of acting in it as well as directing it, but Brecht had insisted on her playing the role:

> I might have got away with it but for that fucking hen. I had to pluck it in the first scene and it was stinking ... Mother Courage had to stop herself vomiting for wellnigh half the play.'

Perhaps its lack of success – or Kenneth Tynan's anatomy of its failure – give an indication of what Littlewood was up to, and how far-sighted in her radicalism she was:

> As director she has sought to present, with fourteen players in a concert hall, a play which the author intended for a company of fifty in a fully equipped theatre

with a revolving stage. She has made a vice of economy by allowing actors to change the scenery in full view of the audience ... The result is a production in which discourtesy to a masterpiece borders on insult, as if Wagner were to be staged in a school gymnasium.

God forbid that we should let in the uninitiated.

It was exactly the elephantine expectations of Brecht's enterprise that she was trying to get away from. Nowadays theatre companies all over the country will recognise the virtue of her ambition.

The theatre, she said, should have:

An awareness of the social issues of the time, and in that sense, be a political theatre. A theatrical language that working people can understand, but is capable of reflecting, when necessary, ideas, either simple or involved, in a poetic form.
An expressive and flexible form of movement, and a high standard of skill and technique in acting.
A high level of technical expertise capable of integrating sound and light into the production.

These aims – set out in a manifesto for the company that she ran in her twenties with her husband – remained constant until, burned out by her success as much as wearied by battles to keep her company going, she retired from the theatre and – like Granville-Barker – moved to France.

There's been no figure like her in British theatre. If George Devine thought of his theatre as a church, hers was more like a pub. She wanted what her French contemporary, Jean Vilar – director and actor-manager – described as 'an auditorium where you can embrace your neighbour, eat and drink and piss on the floor'. She was wholly unclubbable – a self-educated working-class woman, who defied the middle-class monopoly of theatre and its domination by metropolitan hierarchy and English gentility. She was no respecter of fame or taste – 'Good taste – no vulgarity!' she said of a performance of **Hamlet**.

Her socialism lay less in believing in abstractions about redistribution of income than in realising the latent potential of every individual. She was in favour of 'that dull working-class quality, optimism', a necessary virtue in a life dedicated to demonstrating that political theatre wasn't always an oxymoron.

Jean Vilar said to her once, 'Why is it always the women who resurrect the theatre in England?' He was thinking of Miss Horniman, and of Motley (the designers Margaret and Sophie Harris, and Elizabeth Montgomery), and of course of Lilian Baylis at the Old Vic.

Joan Littlewood was born in 1914 two streets away from Lilian Baylis's house in South London, the illegitimate daughter of a teenage housemaid. She was awarded a scholarship to RADA – then a sort of finishing school for debutantes – and although she won prizes, was never lured to the West End or to any theatre seeking to mimic its values. She became an assistant stage manager/actress in Manchester, where at the age of twenty she met Jimmie Miller, a playwright, folk-singer and Marxist, who was a moving force in the Manchester Workers' Theatre Movement.

With Miller she joined a company called the Theatre of Action. They performed in schools, churches and town halls with a few lights and rudimentary scenery. Their first production was an anti-war (it was 1936) agit-prop show called **John Bullion.** You could see all the seeds of her later work – headlines projected on to the backdrop, a clergyman giving a sermon on the virtues of peace while his double talks of investing church money in arms, three bankers on high stools dressed like Michelin men, polemic, personal testimony, statistics, tableaux, songs, and dances.

The company were largely untrained working-class enthusiasts, who, if they were lucky enough, subsidised their acting by working. Most of the company resented the 'artiness', the 'ballet … all that jigging about'. They wanted the message and no messing and, like many – or most – left-wing theatre groups, the Theatre of Action split into fragments and Miller and Littlewood left to form their own company.

Joan Littlewood.

With Europe tilting closer to war, they concentrated on anti-war plays – Lope de Vega's **Fuenteovejuna** during the Spanish Civil War in 1936, Hayek's **The Good Soldier Schweik** during the Munich Crisis in 1938. There was no other theatre in Britain that was so ambitious with form, let alone engaging with politics, but as Jimmie Miller (who by now had metamorphosed into Ewan McColl) balefully said of the shows: 'Even when they were successful, they weren't successful in our terms – in changing the nature of the *audience*.'

During the war, Littlewood worked largely for the BBC and in 1945 she suggested that they revive the company. By this time she was living with Gerry Raffles, who she'd met when he was at school in Manchester. He became the company's manager and her lifelong companion. Together with Ewan McColl, they formed Theatre Workshop to create theatre for the working class under this banner: 'The great theatres of all time have been popular theatres which reflected the dramas and struggles of the people.'

For seven years they toured Britain – one-night-stands mostly in chilly village halls and community centres: cheap digs, travel, unload, rig, warm up, perform, de-rig, load, back to digs, travel … They tried persistently and without success to secure an Arts Council grant, and supplemented their income from tours to Scandinavia, Germany and Czechoslovakia.

In 1953 they gave up the life of one-night-stands, when Gerry Raffles arranged a lease on a dilapidated music-hall – the Theatre Royal, Palace of Varieties – in a working-class district in the East End of London, with a neat poetic irony called Stratford. It's hard, by any standards, to feel that Littlewood was betraying either the political or theatrical cause by settling in London after so many years on the road, and she knew better than anyone about the response of the working class to plays about the hardships of their lives: 'We'd sooner see how the other half lives.'

But Ewan McColl 'walked out, quit, buggered off – and, not to put too fine a point on it, resigned', leaving the company to join a folk group:

> There was a feeling that it was time we settled down in a place where we could get the attention of the national theatre critics. Before this, the level of discussion had been 'What are we doing wrong when we take a play about mining to the Welsh coal villages and the miners don't care?' … But the new questions were going to be, 'How are we going to get Harold Hobson? What is he going to think of us?'

So, without their company writer, Theatre Workshop began to produce classics, and the collective leadership declined to a triumvirate – Littlewood, Raffles and John Bury, who as actor, designer and factotum had worked with the company for several years.

The Theatre Royal was in shabby condition and most of the actors lived in the building, cleaning, repairing seats, mending curtains and carpets, putting up posters – as Littlewood said, with 'the enjoyment of making the impossible possible'. They were almost totally reliant on the box-office income, with only a very small subsidy from the local council. The Arts Council, with their unerring gift for backing the wrong horses in the wrong race, gave the company £100 in 1954 with ill-grace, £1,000 by 1957 and only in 1972 a significant grant. The Arts Council, ever anxious to protect their (in practice meaningless) 'arm's-length' principle, were wary of Littlewood's politics and of her transparent contempt for their bureaucracy.

In the first two years at Stratford East, they performed thirty-six plays, mostly classics such as **The Alchemist, Richard II, Edward II, Arden of Faversham, Celestina, An Enemy of the People.** Joan Littlewood sent a young actor to see **Richard II** at the Old Vic to 'cure him of a misplaced respect for the English Establishment'. No cut-glass accents, no posturing, and John of Gaunt's dying speech – 'This royal throne of kings, this sceptr'd isle' – played with bitter irony. No doubt much of the acting was merely serviceable and no doubt much of the poetry was dulled, but there was an undeniable freshness about the approach, which anticipated Peter Hall's **Wars of the Roses** several years later – designed by Littlewood's designer, John Bury.

As in the early years of Théâtre de Complicité, the company acquired more of a reputation abroad than in Britain. They appeared with great success as Britain's entry in the Paris International Theatre Festival in 1955, to the chagrin of the theatre establishment. Ewan McColl's fears for the company becoming obsessed with critics took some time to be tested – it was eighteen months after the opening of Theatre Workshop before any London critic took the tube to Stratford East.

1956 was as much an *annus mirabilis* for the Theatre Workshop as for the Royal Court. Everyone who has ever run a theatre dreams of this moment: 'A tattered bundle appeared on my desk. It was from Ireland … The typing frequently went careering off the page, there were beer stains and repetitions, but you'd hardly read five pages before you recognised a great entertainer.' The 'great entertainer' was Brendan Behan, and even though he was twice sent his train fare, he didn't answer the summons to the Theatre Royal until his play was well into rehearsal – detained by drink.

Behan (1923–1964) sprang from the Irish literary heritage, from the popular culture of song and anecdote and from the IRA. All three were combined in a fourth and fatal tradition: that of the drunk who's funniest just before he crashes unconscious on to the bar-room floor.

The title of the play that appeared on Littlewood's desk was **The Quare Fellow** – the nickname given to a prisoner about to be hanged. It had been produced in 1954 in Dublin by a pocket-sized, fifty-seat theatre, the Pike, the Abbey Theatre having lost two-thirds of the first script he submitted and rejected all of the second. The play was set in Dublin's Mountjoy Jail, which is where Behan had served a sentence for IRA activities, and covers the hours before the execution of an axe-murderer, a character who never appears. It's soaked with gallows humour – an overwhelming indictment of capital punishment without a hint of piety or sentimentality: a beautiful play, unjustly forgotten.

Littlewood's production transferred to the West End later in the year, and when publicity called, Behan served as a TV chat-show drunk providing boozer's jokes – what the press call 'outbursts' – or incomprehensible pauses or collapses. In interviews Behan liked to present himself as a child of the Dublin slums. In fact, he was born into a clever, artistic family: one of his uncles had written the Irish National Anthem, his mother liked nothing better than to take the children for walks round Dublin, pointing out the houses of Sheridan, Shaw, Swift and Wilde, while his father, a house-painter by trade, would sit them down at night to listen to extracts from Dickens, de Maupassant and Zola. The house was filled with music (echoes of the Shaw establishment): father was an excellent violinist, mother a walking compendium of popular songs and patriotic ballads; this was a fierce Republican household. Another lasting influence was his adored and wealthy grandmother who started him off on porter as soon as he was big enough to carry the jug from the pub, and moved him on to whisky at the age of eight. 'It'll cure the worms,' she explained.

He left school at fourteen and took part in various IRA missions, as a result of which he spent most of the ages of sixteen to twenty-two behind bars. His stretch in an English Borstal, under an enlightened regime, was a blessing: he took up his education, carried on reading and started writing. He spent several years in Paris (where Beckett, who had a soft spot for ex-prisoners, was predictably kind) and then returned to join the world of Dublin's literary bohemia.

Two years after the success of **The Quare Fellow** he wrote – partly under threat of execution by an exasperated Gerry Raffles – **The Hostage**, and once again demonstrated that without Irish writers the British theatre would be poorer, paler and in every sense more sober. **The Hostage** is an uncategorisable play – part music-hall, part farce, part satire, part tragedy. It's about Ireland and England; set in a Dublin lodging-house where a kidnapped cockney soldier is being held as hostage for an IRA prisoner sentenced to hang. The IRA, it should be remembered, was at the time an ineffectual sideshow: this is what gave the play its comic basis, admittedly hard to restore at the present time. It's also what made the fact that the Tommy gets shot at the end of the play neither atrocious nor heroic: just a dead-pan view of futile combat. Behan was bidding farewell to the political attitudinising he'd enjoyed so much as a boy.

The Hostage was funny and sad and real, but unquestionably softened for the London audience by Littlewood's utterly singular form of music-hall, camp antics and pub humour. The programme emphasised that Behan, the ex-IRA militant, felt 'only love and understanding' for the British people; Princess Margaret came and 'laughed herself to tears'. Nevertheless, Littlewood's production was one of those rare evenings in the theatre where the action seemed so spontaneous that it was as if the play was being invented in front of your eyes, which of course, in many cases, it was.

Behan never lamented the cavalier treatment of much of his dialogue; he was too busy glorying in his celebrity. Childlike and tragic, in conquering London, he'd made himself the equal of those Irish heroes: Sheridan, Wilde and Shaw. This was the pinnacle of his hopes, and he never got over it. He died at the age of forty-one leaving behind a single unfinished work, **Richard's Cork Leg**, which reads like a prototype for a Joan Littlewood production of a play by Brendan Behan. 'I was so angry with Brendan for dying that I felt like kicking his coffin,' said Littlewood.

Littlewood's success brought more bulky packets to her desk – a play from Henry Chapman set on a building site: **You Won't Always Be On Top**; another, about ponces, spielers, lags, tarts and layabouts, from a cockney writer called Frank Norman, who'd never ever seen a play: **Fings Ain't Wot They Used T'be**; and another from a nineteen-year-old Salford girl called Shelagh Delaney:

> Dear Miss Littlewood,
> Along with this letter comes a play, the first I have written. I wonder if you would read it through and send it back to me because no matter what sort of theatrical atrocity it might be, it isn't valueless as far as I'm concerned.

The play was fresh, naive and touching – a forty-year-old mother goes off with her boyfriend, leaving her daughter to spend Christmas alone. The daughter goes to bed with a Nigerian sailor, who leaves her. She's now pregnant; a gay art student moves in, sleeps on her couch and looks after her. It was called **A Taste of Honey**.

'We are both creatures of Joan's imagination,' said Brendan Behan to Shelagh Delaney. 'Perhaps they were,' commented Littlewood, but while the writers were grateful to her for their success, time and authorial pride made them equivocal about just how much of a real *auteur* of the theatrical event she had been. All her great successes were with plays that arrived in an incomplete and inchoate form and were moulded into shape like raw clay – she cut, moved scenes around, improvised with the actors, added music (often opportunistically and occasionally sentimentally) – a jazz band in **A Taste of Honey**, Republican ballads and music-hall songs in **The Hostage**, and a score by Lionel Bart to Frank Norman's play, turning it into a fully fledged musical.

She didn't disrespect writers, and she was very widely read with a considerable knowledge of European and classical drama, but she had a contempt for 'text' – she hated the notion of what was said and done on stage being inert or fixed. She believed in 'the chemistry in the actual event', which included encouraging the audience to interrupt the play and the actors to reply – an active form of the kind of alienation that Brecht argued for but never practised.

She always worked with a company of actors, many of whom stayed with her for years, and had a contempt for stars, or at least for the system that required them and the sycophancy that supported them – she described Olivier as 'the most stupid ham that ever conned people into taking him for an actor'. Her energy never lapsed; she was always in motion, like a genial but often aggressive pug dog, prodding and

The Hostage and
A Taste of Honey.

cajoling the actors, barking the play into life. Kenneth Tynan said she had a 'perky crumpled face looking always as if tears had dried on it'. She used the company to research the social realities of each play, and to find the physical ones she made them do acting exercises, often blindfolded or barefoot, to use their sense of hearing, smell and touch.

Much ahead of her time, she did movement training with the company – influenced by the Czech teacher Rudolf Laban – to develop the use of the body as an expressive instrument, and she regularly did vocal exercises, although elocution was always excluded.

Littlewood's productions were paradoxes: the acting could be coarse but it was not crude – although she loved vulgarity, Littlewood was far from a vulgarian. She was like the painter Stanley Spencer: both yoked a desire to celebrate unhymned lives with a desire to communicate with those disenfranchised from art. Like Spencer, Littlewood insisted on a truthful observation of life within a non-naturalistic context, and, like Spencer – another paradox – she was the most British of artists as well as being a passionate Francophile and an internationalist.

The Quare Fellow, **The Hostage**, **A Taste of Honey**, and **Fings Ain't Wot They Used T'be** transferred to West End theatres – the last three playing at the same time: 'We are forced to export our shows to the West End and are always losing our companies. We are hamstrung by the money-grabbing commercialism of the West End.' Forced to sell her goods in a 'shoddy market' by the snobbish parsimony of the Arts Council, having to put together an *ad hoc* company yet again, having to fight the Lord Chamberlain, seeing the actors that she had held together so long, despite derisory wages, begin to disperse, Littlewood became exhausted:

> I had to spend my time running from one to the other reviving tired performances, playing all sorts of tricks to combat the artist's deadly enemy – slowness, milking the part. Mounting a show is easier than keeping it alive. Success was going to kill us.

'We'd burned ourselves out,' said John Bury, and in 1961, after directing **The Hostage** in New York and an unsuccessful American play by James Goldman – financed by Hal Prince – Littlewood threw it up, just walked away from the Theatre Royal: 'It was because I could not face the prospect of passing the rest of my life in that crumbling old slum. Long ago I'd set my sights on a very different kind of place.'

Littlewood lost interest in the theatre for a while and went to Nigeria to work with Wole Soyinka on a film project, and directed a film of **Sparrers Can't Sing** – a story of East End life that she'd directed in the theatre. Gerry Raffles continue to run the theatre and nursed a long-held idea of doing a play about the First World War, which he finally lured Littlewood back to direct. Two writers had already failed to produce anything worth staging, a third – Charles Chilton of the BBC – was working on it, and came up with a cumbersome script and 800 songs from the period.

It was Littlewood's idea to tell the story through the songs. She added period dances and sketches, but what transformed it from social documentary to art was her idea of staging the war by means of a Pierrot troupe playing 'The War Game'. It was a brilliant theatrical metaphor, the chirpy idiom of the Edwardian age subverted by the reality of the war. 'After all,' said Littlewood, 'war is only for clowns.' She added a newspanel like one she'd seen in East Berlin to feature statistics – BATTLE OF SOMME ENDS … TOTAL LOSS … 1,332,000 MEN … GAIN NIL … and she added projections – recruiting posters, soldiers marching to the front, soldiers gassed, soldiers wounded, soldiers dead.

It was the story of men led by donkeys – the courage and stoicism of the working class set against the blind stupidity and self-interest of the ruling class. It was drenched in indignation, but for all its homespun Marxism, it was impossible not to feel sympathy – and horror – for Field Marshal Haig imprisoned in his vain illusions that one more big push would end the war: 'I am the predestined instrument of providence for the achievement of victory for the British Army. And I ask it oh Lord, before the Americans arrive … '

A.J.P. Taylor's *Illustrated History of the First World War* is dedicated to Joan Littlewood. His aim was indistinguishable from hers:

> In the narrative, the war is an academic exercise … The illustrations show men. This war was our war too. Maybe if we can understand it better, we can come nearer to being, what the men of that time were not, masters of our own destiny.

The show awakened race memory: the war was the event that had shaped the consciousness of the nation, and it worked for all generations – those who had endured the war, their children who had grown up in its shadow, and *their* children, ignorant and appalled by it. It reunited the audience with their past, half a century of mourning for a lost generation. It was nostalgia as the dictionary defines it: a form of melancholia induced by prolonged absence from one's own country or home – not a bad sensation to induce in a Britain still riven by class differences. The marvel is that it was so funny as well. It's the natural heir of **The Beggar's Opera**.

McColl, combative to the last, believed that **Oh, What a Lovely War!** was the final nail in Theatre Workshop's coffin:

> It is sometimes said that shows like **Fings** and **Lovely War** were the high point of Theatre Workshop's existence. I think they were the nadir, the low point. They symbolised the ultimate failure of Theatre Workshop. Here was a show, **Oh, What a Lovely War!**, which was ostensibly an anti-war show. Yet it was running in the West End, with all these colonels loving it … Theatre, when it is dealing with social issues, should hurt.

Victor Spinetti teaches recruits how to kill Germans.

It begs the question: is the theatre a medium in which you *can* castigate your customers? There's a puritanism about denying an audience entertainment whilst providing enlightenment; it's the same urge as the nineteenth-century social evangelist distributing pamphlets rather than bread to the deserving poor, seeking to exchange the actor's robe for the coat of the social engineer. Isn't it a form of elitism to prescribe the response of the audience and to disdain an audience for its incorrect class profile? Aren't colonels precisely the people whom an anti-war play should be reaching?

The orthodox history of British theatre hasn't been generous to Littlewood. It's elevated the ascetic air of the Royal Court, whose self-proclaimed legend of a 'writers' theatre' has been amply chronicled against the scant accounts of Littlewood's work. History favours those who write things down. Why are the theories of Brecht and Stanislavsky so remorselessly picked over? Answer: because their ideas are codified and can be studied and set for exams. Littlewood's productions defied study: their legend lay in their spontaneity.

Joan Littlewood had no time for the Royal Court – 'too soft-centred – very middle-class and proper, like their leader ... ' It was certainly true that at the Royal Court there was always a comic contrast between the meticulous observations of working-class life on stage and the patrician audience with their chauffeur-driven cars parked two-abreast outside the foyer when the theatre had a hit. But Littlewood herself never attracted the audience that she had set out to win. Said actor Harry Corbett – later Steptoe's son on TV, 'No way was there a local following, only in the sense of a few eccentrics – Johnny Speight was one – and they were leaving their working-class environment.'

Her achievements, however, have resonated throughout British theatre. She broke up the fabric, revolutionised the way that plays were presented, the way that they were written, and the way directors and actors and writers collaborated. Her revolution, her propagation of the notion of 'popular' theatre – meaning theatre for non-metropolitan, non-middle-class audiences – has been as enduring as the Royal Court 'revolution' of 1956.

After **Oh, What a Lovely War!**, which opened in 1963, she stopped, and, after the death of Gerry Raffles, turned away from the Theatre Royal. Joan Littlewood has not worked in Britain for over twenty-five years, and it's been our loss. Time hasn't diminished her resentment of the theatrical establishment in any form. She always felt cold-shouldered – be it by the Royal Court, the National Theatre, the Royal Shakespeare Company, or the apparatchiks of the Arts Council, and when universal recognition arrived it was too late for pleasure.

She managed, at least for a while, to run a company that combined high ideals, no pretensions, artistic integrity, political sincerity, and commercial success. Her troupe of actors brought together a chaotic patchwork of styles, making a seamless unity without diminishing their individual colours. Her work was witty, skilful, vulgar, populist but not patronising, and **Oh, What a Lovely War!** successfully brought together the traditions of popular entertainment – music-hall – with the aims of propaganda. This was political theatre that, unlike most of the genre, neither patronised its audience, nor tried to reprimand or reform them. It sought to inform and to entertain, and it broke your heart in the process.

Ireland a Republic

'Now Ireland has her madness and her weather still, for poetry makes nothing happen.'
W.H. AUDEN: In Memory of W.B. Yeats

1

For many British theatre-goers in the late 1950s, Brendan Behan confirmed an Irish theatrical revival. The real revival came in the 1960s, and it was the opposite of Yeats's. That was invention, this was fact. It took shape around two first-rate plays by emerging writers: Tom Murphy's **Whistle in the Dark** in 1961 and Brian Friel's **Philadelphia, Here I Come!** in 1964. But one other playwright slipped in first.

The plays of John B. Keane (1928–) share a lot with nineteenth-century melodrama: the racy plot, the well-timed entrances, the thrilling climax. But they're more complex than they look. They're a prescient record of the economic and social changes that would, in time, transform the country – and its theatre too.

In **Sive**, written in 1959, the heroine and her rapacious family have neither running water nor electric light. But when Uncle returns from selling his pigs he brings home the handsome sum of £16.10s. Shopkeepers fall over themselves to offer him credit; even penniless old Nanna can afford to sneer at people who were brought up to drink their tea out of jampots:

> There is money-making everywhere [explains an itinerant tinker]. The small man with the one cow and the pig and the bit of bog is coming into his own. He is pulling himself up out of the mud and the dirt of years. He is coming away from the dunghill and the smoky corner … The farmer will be the new lord of the land. What way will he rule? Which way will he hold up under the new riches?

As the city invades the countryside, even a patch of grass takes on a different meaning. In **The Field**, a stranger spots a piece of grazing land as an excellent source of building gravel; Bull McCabe, the village tyrant, is driven to murder. 'I'm a fair man and I want nothing but what's mine!' the old man bellows. 'A total stranger has come and he wants to bury my sweat and blood in concrete. It's agin' God and man … ' Keane is hot on hypocrisy but soft on the Church: Father Murphy is clearly a decent chap; but who promotes the cruel morality that ties Maimee to a husband who orders her about, hasn't bathed for a year and, by the end of the play, has got her pregnant for the tenth time?

Big Maggie revolves around a widow who treats her family like dirt. But she has her problems too: she's a small-time shopkeeper in an age when 'the supermarkets are sprouting up like daisies'. By the end of the play, two of her brood have emigrated to England; a third will follow.

Emigration was the starting-point for Friel and Murphy. They shared other things too, in these early years. Themes of male virginity, boredom, drink; the use of song to summon the past and cleanse the present; the power of fathers. Mothers are usually a background presence; neither parent, it seems, will share the spotlight with the other, and it's the fathers, with the harder pair of elbows, who get there first.

Brian Friel (1929–) was born into the Northern Irish Catholic community in Omagh, County Tyrone and brought up in Derry. In his teens he studied for the priesthood: a bleak experiment. He was a schoolteacher until his early thirties and he found his confidence as a playwright during a residency in Minneapolis, at the theatre run by the great Irish director Tyrone Guthrie. For six months he skulked about at the back of the stalls, wondering what he was meant to do, let alone what right he had to be there. One day a doorman tried to stop him coming in. One of the actors intervened. 'He's OK,' he said. 'He's an observer.' 'That fortuitous christening,' as Friel described it later, 'gave me not only an identity but a dignity.'

'Observer' was the happiest word the actor could have chosen. It convey's Friel's reticence, his coolness and the X-ray quality of his writing: there's no fact so solid but it will, if studied hard, dissolve to reveal a tissue of possible fact beneath. And that in turn …

Philadelphia, Here I Come! is set on the eve of young Gar O'Connell's departure for the United States. (Two actors play him: Friel's plays are rich in mirror-images and doubles.) His friends are louts, his father is brusque. His girlfriend is delightful, but Gar has missed his chance. No wonder he longs for 'a vast restless place that doesn't give a damn about the past'. But America now seems weird and uninviting. Why is he going? He doesn't know.

Freedom of the City derived from the 1972 Bloody Sunday shootings, but its theme is myth: the weaving of convenient fantasies around an inconvenient truth. Three Catholic demonstrators take refuge in the nearest place to hand which, to their great surprise, turns out to be the Mayor's parlour in the Guildhall, Derry. One is a housewife, one a respectable, trusting fellow, one an intelligent bigmouth. Emerging with their hands on their heads, they're shot dead by the army. Their transfiguration now ensues: the army labels them as terrorists, a balladeer sings of their martyrdom in the tradition of Pearse and Connolly, a priest laments their death but blames the influence of godless Communism.

These ambiguities evaded the London critics: 'It suffers fatally from this overzealous determination to discredit the means and the motives of the English in the present Ulster

Brian Friel.

crisis,' said the *Evening Standard*, while the *Daily Mail* disclosed that 'the play has angered senior army officers in Ulster'. The theme of myth returned in **Aristocrats** in 1979: here the myth is the very existence of a social class. Friel was on a roll: **Faith Healer**, one of his finest plays, followed that year: a sombre, coded meditation on the life of an Irish writer.

FRANK: Was it all chance? – or skill? – or illusion? – or delusion? Precisely what power did I possess? Could I summon it? When and how?

The healer has – at times – a gift he cannot explain. Or does he? What if it's all a fraud? We learn of his huckstering tours in England, Scotland, Wales. Grace, his wife (or mistress?) corroborates some of his story, but by no means all; Teddy the fit-up-man's account is equally elusive. Something happened in Scotland, in a place called Kinlochbervie: was this where Frank heard the news of his mother's death? Or where Grace's child was buried? Was it misty, as Grace describes it? Or do we believe in Teddy's 'fantastic little village sitting on the edge of the sea, all blue and white and golden, and all lit up and all sparkling and all just heavenly'? Or are all these truths subjective?

What's certain is that, when Frank went home to Ireland, he found himself in a rural backwater being challenged to cure a hopeless case. He failed and was lynched. 'It is dangerous to leave one's country,' said James Joyce, 'but still more dangerous to go back to it, for then your fellow-countrymen, if they can, will drive a knife into your heart.'

Translations was written for Field Day, the touring company formed in Derry in 1980 by Friel and Stephen Rea. It's about language as hegemony: as a way of imposing one reality on top of an old one. In nineteenth-century Donegal, the English military is busying itself regularising place-names, i.e. transforming Irish names into their civilised equivalent. The British are quickly out of their depth in a land where peasants shake hands with the ancient world:

And when I heard Jimmy Jack and your father swapping stories about Apollo and Cuchulainn and Paris and Ferdia – as if they lived down the road – it was then that I thought – I knew – perhaps I could live here … '

It's Yolland, a young English soldier speaking. When he falls for Maire, a hedge-school trainee, we find that language can be redundant. She knows only one sentence in English and it isn't a useful one: 'In Norfolk we besport ourselves around the maypole.' Yolland woos her in botched translation; later, when they declare their love, the language-barrier makes the scene all the more rapt and eloquent.

This is the play that established Friel in English eyes as a master playwright. **Dancing at Lughnasa** was a huge international crowd-pleaser, thanks to the title scene: who could resist the sight of five delightful women breaking into a joyous Bacchanalia? But the rest of the play is heartbreaking. The women's lives are painted sensuously: we smell their Woodbines, taste their soda bread, feel the cold of the kitchen floor.

KATE: You work hard at your job. You try to keep the home together. You perform your duties as best you can – because you believe

273

Stephen Rea in **Translations**.

in responsibilities and obligations and good order. And then suddenly, suddenly you realise that hair cracks are appearing everywhere; that control is slipping away; that the whole thing is so fragile it can't be held together much longer. It's all about to collapse, Maggie.

Agnes and Rose will lose their market for the gloves they knit, Kate, the teacher, will lose her job. A pair of appalling deaths spells out the destruction of the rural idyll.

Lughnasa couldn't have conquered the world in the way it did without Friel's masterly control over its opposing themes: past/present, discipline/freedom, language/dance. This is what helps a play to 'travel': to surmount cultural differences, translations, bad translations, bad productions, even expressionist German productions.

Prose doesn't travel as well as structure does, which perhaps is why the plays of Tom Murphy (1935–) aren't seen as often as they should be outside Ireland. His themes become apparent, not when you track the play in time over a two-hour traffic, but when you pay acute attention to any thirty seconds of it. He's the poet of modern conversational prose: subtle, unforced, robust, always worth a backward look to check what was really being said. The dialogue never seems 'polished' or nudged into place: it's like a mountain stream, full of rapids, lulls and invisible depths.

His short play, **On the Outside**, written in 1959, waited fifteen years for a stage production, thanks to the Abbey. Outside a country dance-hall, Frank and Joe, short of

Tom Murphy.

the entrance-money, hover between the heaven of sex and music and the hell of a traipse back home. 'I'm not sticking around here much longer,' fumes Frank. 'England. I'm bailing out of that lousy job. Lousy few bob a week. Twenty-two years old and where does it get me? Yes, sir – I'm a pig, sir – if you say so, sir!'

A Whistle in the Dark, premièred in 1961 at Joan Littlewood's Stratford East, takes up the threat of leaving. Michael, a young Irish emigrant, works in Coventry: his hopes of becoming a functional member of the working class are shattered by the arrival of his brood of brothers and his terrible father, fists a-swinging. Nothing could be more absurd, or more demeaning, than his Dada's trumped-up punch-up with a rival emigrant Irish clan:

DADA: No. No. I was nearly away myself. After the second fella I got this kick, right here (*feels his groin*). And lucky thing for me, the third guy wasn't too anxious 'cause I was hunched. Anyone'd be. And the pain, and winded, you know. And I started to get away quick as I could, and when I got to the main street, I had to throw myself on a seat there. Lord, I was bad, but I didn't care who was looking. Sick as a dog, hunched completely, not worth two-pence. And I couldn't stir, I'm telling you. Not for hours … I'm not as young as I was, boys.

Dada becomes a figure of tragedy. So does Michael, destroyed by a single act of atavistic violence. You can travel as far as you like – the play suggests – but you can't escape.

In **A Crucial Week in the Life of a Grocer's Assistant,** the hero neither bolts nor buckles. Instead, he stands in the road of his awful, unbearable home town, shouting its secrets for all to hear:

JOHN JOE: We have flour-bags sewn together for sheets … Oh, but we know Mrs Smith doesn't use a sheet at all. Did you know that, Mrs Smith? We know that from the day Peter Mullins climbed in your back-room window, because it was the only room in your house he hadn't seen. But he said it was clean, but he wouldn't give you two-pence for the sticks of furniture.

'Mother of God!' gasps his mother. 'Lord! We're disgraced!' From now on, Murphy would widen his field. **Famine** is a Brechtian epic. **The White House** exposes masculine malice, friendship and unease in the dusk of the Kennedy myth. Its form is based on the almost Kabuki-like artificiality of pub manners: whose round is when, when is it rude to stop, how drunk do you need to be to excuse your bad behaviour?

Murphy uses very little of the armoury that playwrights normally deploy to keep you watching: suspense, surprise, the artful teasing-out of telling detail. He shoots an arrow into the air on page one, and allows it to hit the target (or not) with Zen detachment. In **The Gigli Concert**, the arc is faultless: this is one of those rare plays in which, when the lights go down at the end, every element has been gathered up and dealt with.

It's also one of those unnaturally satisfying plays in which almost nothing happens. There's a proposition: an unhappy man consults a quack healer. He wants to sing like Gigli. In fact, he's just unhappy. Except there's no 'just' about unhappiness: it is (as we soon discover) complex, rich and slippery. The passage of the play is the transferring – to and fro, but finally, decisively, patient-to-healer – of a quality which itself becomes transformed: from vague, unplaceable longing, through deep melancholy to a final, grand apotheosis. When at the end of the play it's not the patient but the quack who sings like Gigli, his unhappiness is heroic. An all-time classic.

From Bloody Sunday onwards, playwrights from the North were drawn into the Troubles. David Rudkin (English-based, but born in Armagh in 1936) had knocked the London theatre sideways with **Afore Night Come** for the RSC in 1961: this mythic evocation of blood-sacrifice in a Midlands orchard took as its ritual victim an itinerant Irish worker. **Cries from Casement as His Bones Are Brought to Dublin**, first written for radio, tests the equation between colonial overlordship and passive sex. In **Ashes**, failure to conceive a child becomes a metaphor for sectarian death-of-life.

Stewart Parker (1941–1988) produced a pair of playful musings on sectarian violence in **Spokesong** and **Catchpenny Twist**, and a brilliant triptych, full of parody and pastiche in the Denis Johnston mould: **Northern Star**, **Heavenly Bodies** and **Pentecost**. Bill Morrison's (1940–) **Flying Blind** turned the horror into farce. Both Graham Reid (1945–) in **Remembrance** and Martin Lynch (1950–) in **The Interrogation of Amrose Fogarty** delved into the gritty roots of Loyalist violence; a theme taken up more recently by Gary Mitchell (1965) in **Trust**. In Ron Hutchinson's **Rat in the Skull**, violence across the divide is a subversive pleasure, indulged in under the nose of the common enemy.

Frank McGuinness (1953–) broke the surface in 1982 with a study of working women: **The Factory Girls. Behold the Sons of Ulster Marching Towards the Somme** showed off both the scale of his imagination and the subtlety of his sexual politics. **Carthaginians** took drama of the Troubles to a new and different level: sexual, mythic and reflective.

Young Irish playwrights have very different views of narrative. It's an unexpected replay, a century later, of the schism between the story-driven drama of Boucicault and his heirs, and Yeats's plays of atmosphere. Sebastian Barry (1955–) falls into the second category. His plays are 'states', not sweeps of action: they dwell on memory and their style is limpid. But his best-known plays deliver crisp, no-nonsense analysis of some tectonic slippage in Irish history. **The Steward of Christendom** delves into Barry's own family background to show us the Catholic Dublin copper – now indigent, old and mad – who, on a memorable day in 1922, turned over Dublin Castle to the insurgent general, Michael Collins. **Our Lady of Sligo** is a mirror-image of **The Steward**: Mai, a dying alcoholic, stands for a Catholic bourgeoisie left floundering by the advent of nationhood.

Barry's success in Ireland, Britain and the United States is a quiet and mostly unremarked revolution: before **The Steward**, non-narrative theatre had been strictly a cult form. Martin McDonagh (1970–) is in every way Barry's opposite. **The Beauty Queen of Leenane** is story-based entirely: this is a tragi-comedy of peasant life, part of not one but two Aran Island trilogies. The coincidence with Synge's old patch had English reviewers scrabbling for comparisons with **Playboy**, but it was hard to make them stick and when McDonagh, in his many media appearances, turned out to be a chic young guy, wearing the nicest Armani suit you've ever seen and sporting a marked South London accent, bemusement turned to fury. 'If this is an Irish playwright, I'm a banana,' cried the chorus.

McDonagh is Irish/British, born in London: this is what emigration is all about. If he's the most street-wise of young Irish writers, he's also the one who draws the most from Irish theatrical history. **Beauty Queen**, just like **The Cripple of Inishmaan**, produced in 1996 at the Royal National Theatre, puts the narrative thrills and spills of Boucicault and John B. Keane into ironic quotes.

Conor McPherson (1971–) began with stories unadorned: in **This Lime Tree Bower** the characters unfold their tales as raconteurs might do in a pub. But in **The Weir**, stories are the bricks and mortar of the play: it ends in memorable epiphany. No politics here: McPherson will not write about the 'struggle', nor the era of stagnation, nor the agonies of the North.

For Yeats, the notion of a national drama was a problem, one to be solved by smoke and mirrors and much invention. Now that battle is won, the Irish playwright can be simply a playwright. The single factor about the new generation is the lightness with which it bears the burdens of the past. Which makes it no less Irish. The idea of 'nation' is a self-replenishing vessel: the more is spent, the more wells up from below.

Last Orders on the Titanic

Last orders on the Titanic
Get up and paint your face
Deckhands in dungarees
And millionaires in lace
TONY BICAT'S lyrics from DAVID HARE's **Teeth 'n' Smiles**

1

There's a curious, uncalled-for thought that comes up once in a while: when you go for a new job, for example, or look at a flat you're considering moving into in a street that you've never visited before. Afterwards you do some ordinary, everyday thing: have a cup of coffee in a local sandwich bar, or buy an *Evening Standard* from the newsagent on the corner. And you realise that, if you get the job, that sandwich bar is where you'll buy your coffee every morning. If you take the flat, that newsagent will be part of your life: you'll know the opening hours and where the cat-food's kept, the man behind the counter will reach for your paper the moment you walk in the door and the pavement outside is where (from time to time) you'll stand at 6 a.m., hungover, cold and sockless, reading your reviews. Or else you'll never see it again as long as you live. One or the other, you just don't know.

There's an opposite thought that comes in familiar places: when you're visiting your old school, or at country funerals or when you're selling up your parents' house. For years, you've dreamt about those walls, those doors, that creak on the stairs: you know every patch of damp and every square of carpet. Now you realise that there's no real reason ever to return. You might, of course, but you probably won't. This is it, the end: it feels as though the place itself is disappearing.

Writing about the 1970s feels like both of these. If you've spent a part of your youth convinced that you were making history (which is how the '70s felt), and doing so (or not) in the way young people do, not in a thought-out way, but through intuition, luck and the support of friends, then that bit of your life becomes the bit you don't revisit when you're middle-aged. You put a mental fence around it: it's the wild garden of memory. You fear that, if you start digging it up, you'll never stop: that you'll end up spending your sleepless nights reliving that drunken row you had in the pub next-door with a playwright who never forgave you, or pining over that fierce political epic you should have staked your subsidy on, never mind the enormous cast. Or wallowing in those times you knew you'd made it. Or just drowning in nostalgia.

Jonathan Pryce
in **Comedians**.

And you fear the opposite will happen: that once you've faced the past, it will dissolve, to leave you standing alone.

The 1970s were in fact a decade, though many a revisionist mouse has nibbled bits off it one end or the other. It's a popular theory that the 1960s, era of sex, drugs, and rock and roll, began in around 1966, with the *Time* magazine cover story on 'Swinging London' and the release of *Revolver* – and trickled on until the mid-1970s, culminating (let's say) with Pink Floyd's *Wish You Were Here*. And it's a fact that Margaret Thatcher, spirit of the rampant 1980s, became Prime Minister as early as 1979. So by that particular calendar, the '70s hardly existed at all.

But theatrically speaking they form a distinct arc, one that runs from revolution to revision, from rage to wry acceptance, from heady independence to cautious crossover. You can also see the decade as part of a larger arc, as the final stage of the decline of a programme of liberal state patronage that had begun in the 1940s. No one, however, thought this at the time.

If you look at the plays that appeared in any one year, it's hard not to feel that things were livelier then. The list feels meaty and ambitious – and many of the most striking titles were first produced in theatres outside London. It wasn't only because of the younger writers, strong though they were: many of the '50s and '60s playwrights were still at work, and they shared much more with the younger generation than anyone thought: a daring in choice of subject, a muscularity of approach and an unashamed theatricality – whether it came from language, story, scandal, gladiatorial conflict or the primitive power of star performance.

Examples: 1972 saw John Osborne's **West of Suez** alongside the scattergun polemic of **England's Ireland**, co-written by Howard Brenton, David Hare, Tony Bicat, Brian Clark, David Edgar, Francis Fuchs and Snoo Wilson: Stoppard's **Jumpers** and Caryl Churchill's **Owners**; Charles Wood's take on acting genius and colonialism, **Veterans**; E.A. Whitehead's marital gut-wrencher **Alpha Beta**; Fugard/Kani/Ntshona's anti-apartheid heart-stopper **Sizwe Bansi is Dead**; and David Storey's marvellous **Home**; plus Hare's **The Great Exhibition** and Brenton's **Hitler Dances**. 1973 brought two vintage Bonds: **The Sea** and **Bingo**; Christopher Hampton on the complex truth of genocide in **Savages**; Alan Bennett on the ludicrous truth of sex in **Habeas Corpus**; John Osborne's two-fingers-up **A Sense of Detachment**; Trevor Griffiths' **The Party**; the Hare/Brenton **Brassneck**; Brenton alone on bombs and anarchy in **Magnificence**; Snoo Wilson on sex and anarchy in **The Pleasure Principle**; plus Arnold Wesker very much around with **The Old Ones**; and a beautiful early Mike Leigh, **Wholesome Glory**.

Mike Leigh (1943–) is odd-man-out in the list, partly because of his unique working-method: a long, meticulously guided process of improvisation, starting with the creation of solo characters, proceeding to the interplay between them and only finally coalescing in story and shape. (The title comes last.) But he was also one of the few new play-makers to explore the tragic potential of working-class life, and to do so with the delicate understatement which is usually reserved for people higher up the social scale. As in the plays of Robert Holman and Peter Gill, the politics aren't spelled out, and they don't need to be: they are inherent in the depth of attention given to unsung, unprivileged lives. A fine Leigh play came at the end of the decade: **Ecstasy**, in which a raucous Kilburn-Irish drinking party is somehow imbued with a sense of isolation. More isolation in the satirical **Abigail's Party**, where we see the results of pulling up your working-class roots: coldness, pretentiousness, fakery.

The hardest thing to convey to anyone who wasn't around in those days is how important the politics were. Capitalist Britain was driving over a cliff, and the only point of disagreement was whether this was a good thing or a bad one. *Les Événements* of 1968 were fresh in the memory; that same year had seen the proprietor of the *Daily Mirror* fending off the apocalypse by trying to rope in Lord Mountbatten as head of an unelected coalition government. Union power was vast and much resented by Middle England; in 1970, Harold Wilson lost to Edward Heath on this very issue. Heath did no better: his era was marked by further union torment, rampant inflation and the accumulation of huge fortunes by wily speculators. In Northern Ireland, internment was introduced and the Protestant Unionists scuppered the peace initiative.

After the miners' strike, the State of Emergency and the three-day week ('Who governs?') Wilson returned to power as head of a Labour Party well to the left of him. Tony Benn was now the terror of the shires and schoolchildren became notorious for refusing to learn anything at all. The Festival of Light was formed to fight 'permissiveness', the National Association of Freedom was formed to fight the Communist threat, one of its founders was blown up by the IRA and the nation was swept with yet another sign of crumbling order: 'mugging'.

Wilson resigned in 1976, convinced that he was under MI5 surveillance. Pickets at Grunwick's, crisis at Leyland and the Winter of Discontent were the run-up to Margaret Thatcher's victory in the election of May 1979. 'It wasn't at all difficult this morning to vote Tory,' Peter Hall wrote in his diary. 'In fact it positively felt good: wanting change … and we have to have change.'

Not every playwright of the '70s was politically on the left, but being left-wing was the mood of the time and the extent to which a writer did or didn't chime with it was the crucial definition. When playwrights formed the Theatre Writers' Group to campaign for better fees and rehearsal conditions, it seemed natural for it swiftly to transform itself into a union seeking affiliation with the TUC; natural for its members to regard themselves as 'employees' of whatever theatre was lucky enough to get their plays; natural, too, that almost every writer of the new wave was a member. Its support from previous waves was self-selecting: Edward Bond but not John Osborne, John Arden but not Tom Stoppard.

Revolution was in the air. Not just any revolution: '*The* Revolution'. What was it, exactly? Did anyone know? Did anyone want it? Yes, a few. But what about everyone else? It now seems strange that a violent social convulsion that wasn't going to happen, and which almost nobody would have liked if it had, became such a powerful working hypothesis. All kinds of arguments could be clinched by the charge that such-and-such a course of action would be non-revolutionary. Least revolutionary was the play that uttered not a hint of positive change ('showing society as static'), which is why so many plays of the period feature the arrival in some improbable setting of an argumentative worker.

A pair of bookends helps to define the decade. In 1970, **Occupations** appeared: the first major play by the socialist playwright Trevor Griffiths. In Griffiths' words, it's 'a sort of Jacobinical response to the failure of the '68 revolution in France'. It probes the moral and emotional cost of revolutionary leadership in a thoughtful, complex way. Here Gramsci, the Italian Marxist, confronts Kabak, the Man from Moscow:

GRAMSCI: But then I thought, how can a man love a collectivity, when he has not profoundly loved single human creatures. And it was then I began to see masses as people and it was only then that I began to love them, in their particular, detailed, individual character. You would be wrong to see this ... love ... as the product of petit-bourgeois idealism. It is the correct, the only true dialectical relationship between leaders and led, vanguard and masses, that can ensure the political health of the new order the revolution seeks to create. Treat masses as expendable, as fodder, during the revolution, you will always treat them thus. I tell you this, Comrade Kabak, if you see masses that way, there can be no revolution worth the blood it spills.

Gramsci isn't making a merely theoretical point and neither is the playwright: anyone hearing the speech at the time would very reasonably assume that it had some down-to-earth practical application. Griffiths' later plays brought the same intellectual vigour to other political themes. **The Party** is a *roman à clef*, based on the radical salons held at the time by the television producer Tony Garnett. We see, at one such gathering, the impotent first-generation middle class getting soundly trounced by a prophet of grassroots conviction. Two long elucidations of Marxist theory turn out to be as engrossing as Brecht would have predicted; one is delivered by an LSE lecturer (based on Robin Blackburn), the other by a veteran working-class activist: this transparent portrait of Gerry Healy, the leader of the Trotskyist Socialist Labour League, was surprisingly (and very successfully) played by the newly ennobled Lord Olivier.

Comedians takes on a profound and curious subject: the relationship between reaction and jokes. Do we laugh at what we despise? And what do we find despicable? And why? Putting the question the other way round: is comedy of class anger actually funny? Or is it simply weird? This play is a flawless piece of naturalism: time, space, and character are handled to perfection. The mystery at the heart of the play is never solved: how could it be? A brusque poetic patch-up encourages us to keep on thinking about it.

But the play is not simply an anatomy of laughter, it's about class and social Darwinism. Can we change the world? And if so do we achieve it by gradualism or by revolution? The final scene of the play is an argument on this subject between the old comedian, Walters (played in the first production by the old comedian, Jimmy Jewel), a humane man who believes that you change the world by persuasion, even by comedy, and Gethin Price (played by Jonathan Pryce), a near-psychotic poor working-class boy who believes in nothing short of a revolution, fuelled by hate. His comic performance consists of a virtuoso harangue of a caricatured couple of middle-class dummies. In his defence of it he quotes Robert Frost:

> I found this in another book. I brought it to show you. Some say the world will end in fire. Some say in ice. From what I've tasted of desire I hold with those who favour fire, but if it had to perish twice, I think I know enough of hate to say that for destruction ice is good and will suffice. It was all ice out there tonight. I loved it …

An opposite bookend to **Occupations** arrived in 1980. **Nicholas Nickleby**, adapted from Dickens' novel by another leading socialist playwright David Edgar, showed the cruelties of primitive capitalism being softened, modified, conquered by the power of love and humanity. Which raises a crucial question: if that can happen – and if, whatever Gramsci and Bertolt Brecht might think, it's desirable that it should – who needs a revolution? This show was a milestone: deploying the full panoply of 'alternative' '70s spectacle, it marked the end of an old myth and the start of a new one.

*Roger Rees and David Threlfall in **Nicholas Nickleby**: 'The end of an old myth and the start of a new one'.*

2

Throughout the 1970s, the feature of the past that seemed most ripe for rejection was the stale, pat, boring relationship between the proscenium-arch stage and a middle-class audience. Enormous efforts were made to take productions out of the ghetto. Enormous energy went into moving the stage about: putting it round the walls, in the middle, playing on ice-rinks (Howard Brenton's **Scott of the Antarctic**), lecture-theatres (Pip Simmons's **Woyzeck**), in swimming-pools (Ken Campbell's **The War of the Newts**), on the back of a motorbike (Marcel Steiner's Smallest Theatre in the World); often turning the stage and audience areas into a single, merged performing-and-acting space. The *mise-en-scène* became amazingly showy and often surprisingly cheap. Paint and canvas were as out of date as sticks of Leichner 5 and 9, when the alternatives were real brick walls, real neon, real grass growing on the floor, real waterfalls, a real 1950s Cadillac and real scaffolding poles and railway sleepers everywhere.

Public funding kept up with the new developments, more or less. Arts Council funding for alternative theatre in 1969/70 came to £15,000; ten years later, funding from the Drama Panel alone amounted to £1.5 million. The Arts Council was nevertheless regarded as an Orwellian arm of the state: 'the thought police'. It occupied ludicrously grand offices in Piccadilly, its officers had an annoying tendency to check figures and its function, as far as anyone in alternative theatre was concerned, was to be milked, bilked and complained about. Looking back from the 2000s one sees something very different: a haplessly well-meaning organisation, thickly infiltrated with liberal well-wishers, all of whom wanted nothing more than to shower money on interesting young people and take it away from clapped-out old ones.

Small theatres sprang up like mushrooms. The impetus came from two directions: from young people looking for somewhere to play and finding it, and from established theatres – the Royal Court and the RSC – who realised the value of the new movement, wanted to be part of it but didn't (frankly) want to risk it on their main stages. Outside London, the big repertory theatres – 'regional centres of excellence' as they were pompously called – soon followed: Birmingham, Sheffield, Bristol, Leicester, all had studio theatres. But the lack of a studio theatre could be a virtue: **Comedians**, **The Churchill Play**, **Brassneck**, and **Touched** were first commissioned and produced at Nottingham Playhouse (which seated 750), underwritten by a conviction that the hub of the theatrical universe was Nottingham or Glasgow or Manchester, not London. And sometimes it was. In Liverpool, the Everyman was major 'studio', home of Alan Bleasdale, Willy Russell and Bill Morrison.

In London, mushroom-theatres were the 'fringe': a word that meant a lot to anyone who was young and cared about the theatre. The newly formed *Time Out* put 'fringe' not trailing after its West End listings, but before them – an eloquent signal to its readers. Every outpost had a different personality. Oval House, previously a youth club, seemed still to be partly one, full of long queues for the food and Gestetner machines whirring somewhere in the background: here Peter Oliver hosted the cream of the touring circuit. The Bush was basic/utility, a sort of Trabant among theatres, but the plays were good: Snoo Wilson again, Robert Holman, Mike Bradwell's Hull Truck, two good Stephen Poliakoffs, **Hitting Town** and **City Sugar**, a debut work, **Happy Yellow**, much praised by Harold Hobson, by a recent Oxford graduate named Tina Brown. The King's Head was amiable and showbiz. The Royal Court's Theatre Upstairs was cutting-edge: it also fancied itself and threw good parties. Was the Hampstead Theatre Club 'fringe'? Not really, and it was never bloodied by scandal, so its qualities didn't show up on the Richter scale or any other. The Open Space, in Tottenham Court Road, was run by the argumentative Charles Marowitz and his associate Thelma Holt: it was housed in a large and anonymous cellar, quintessential Off-Off-Broadway and site of one of the most chilling performances ever seen: William Burroughs' impersonation of Judge Hoffman in a dramatisation of the trial of the Chicago Seven. Riverside Studios was crisp, cool and uncompromising: new plays, Kantor and the classics. The Warehouse – a satellite of the RSC – had all the atmosphere of a Tesco's loading-bay, but the standard of production, under Howard Davies and Bill Alexander, was excellent. Shakespeare and Chekhov (brought down from the Stratford season) and (London-grown) new Barker, Keeffe, mid-period Bond and Peter Whelan.

The Half Moon was situated in a disused synagogue down a foggy Hitchcockian alley in Whitechapel. First you had to get there ... when you did, you felt surrounded by a magical, stirring sense of history. It was here in Whitechapel that the decade's best productions of plays by Brecht were seen: Guy Sprung's **In the Jungle of Cities** in 1972, Jonathan Chadwick's **The Mother** in the following year: both were raw, alive and beautiful. Also much Steve Gooch, notably **Female Transport**.

In the competitive 1980s, lunchtime theatres would disappear along with long lunchtimes, but in the leisured '70s they started off many playwrights' careers. The nicest lunchtime theatre was the Soho Poly, initially just off the Charing Cross Road and later in a minute cellar behind BBC Broadcasting House. It was run by the novelist Verity Bargate: an elegant, anxious, Jean Shrimpton-like figure, always there to usher the audience in; then, once the play had started, waiting alert on the stairs outside. She had a classy eye for writers: early Snoo Wilson, Hanif Kureishi, Barrie Keeffe, Pam Gems, Olwyn Wymark, Mustapha Matura. The Green Banana was another significant lunchtime spot: first London sighting of Howard Brenton's **Gum and Goo** in 1969. 'Inter-Action', founded by the irascible Ed Berman, presented Bond, Tom Stoppard and early David Lan.

Small touring companies were another alternative to the conventional theatre set-up. Foco Novo was founded in 1972 by Roland Rees, David Aukin and Bernard Pomerance (author of **The Elephant Man**): it did politically committed plays, directed by Rees. Nancy Meckler's Freehold pushed physical expressiveness to a new level; the Pip Simmons Group specialised in visceral impact; the People Show created surrealistic events, sometimes baffling, always resonant; Cartoon Archetypical Slogan Theatre shows were brash and polemical. In 1975, two special-interest notable groups were founded: the feminist co-op Monstrous Regiment and Gay Sweatshop. David Hare and Tony Bicat formed another small-scale touring company, Portable Theatre: its early dates included that penniless hell-hole of commitment to the South, the Brighton Combination, and Jim Haynes' London Arts Lab, where you had to climb over the sleeping-bags to get to the stage. **Christie in Love** was one of Portable's early triumphs, **England's Ireland** finished it off.

Joint Stock, founded in 1974 by Hare, David Aukin and Max Stafford-Clark, brought something new to the touring circuit. When William Gaskill, now no longer running the Royal Court, came on board to co-direct Heathcote Williams' **The Speakers** with Stafford-Clark in 1974, it marked the start of a long and fruitful relationship between two contrasting innovators. Gaskill's concern was the text, the truth, the analysis; Stafford-Clark, eleven years younger, had run the Edinburgh Traverse Theatre before starting up its smaller offshoot, the Traverse Theatre Workshop, in order to experiment with ways of staging plays, the use of music in theatre and the dynamic within the group itself.

The Speakers is a masterly piece of reportage, written when Williams was in his early twenties, about the soap-box orators at Marble Arch. The production placed the scenes at different points around the theatre space, while the audience moved from one to the other, as in life: the original English promenade. David Hare's **Fanshen**, condensed from William Hinton's unreliable memoir of the Chinese Revolution, plunged the cast into an arduous programme of self-criticism on the Chinese model. Joint Stock was from now on a collective, though the fact that two of its members were directors, and strong-minded ones at that, would cause recurring hiccups in the collective process.

Joint Stock in action:
The Ragged-Trousered Philanthropists.

Yesterday's News was based on another real-life subject: the recent killing of a group of British mercenaries in Angola. The research – during which the actors interviewed many of those concerned – was brilliant. But no play emerged. So the research became the play: this was the original show in which the actors sat on a row of chairs and acted out the testimonies of the people they'd met. They did so with the care and subtlety that they'd have given to great writing, which is what it seemed to be. Howard Brenton's **Epsom Downs** was a brimming canvas of Derby Day; Barrie Keeffe's **Mad World My Masters** a rumbustious farce about con-tricks, distantly related to the Middleton original; **The Ragged-Trousered Philanthropists**, adapted by Stephen Lowe from Robert Tressell's novel, took its shape and atmosphere from a daily workshop routine of painting and decorating, plus games, role-swapping and song.

The actor and writer Ken Campbell (1941–) would later become renowned for his compelling one-man shows – they take as their jumping-off point the extraordinary nature of the universe – but in the '70s his touring company, the Ken Campbell Road Show, was a challenge both to the po-faced mainstream and the equally po-faced new politicos. Its basis was the stories people told you which they swore were true but which secretly nobody really believed (the phrase 'urban myth' hadn't yet been coined), but it soon branched out into quizzes, escapology and bar-room stunts: the ferret-down-the-trouser contest was one of the few things in modern theatre that made the audience laugh so much that people really did roll in the aisles. The acting style was a mix of panic, hectoring and genius: 'Oh, you mean *real* acting!' said a notorious Irish ham before proceeding to let rip as never before.

Ken Campbell capering.

287

Like many of Campbell's most successful projects (or 'capers' as he'd refer to them), he'd take someone else's idea, and turn it into something inimitably his own. Most of Campbell's capers looked as if they were going to be follies and turned out to be inspired gestures of showmanship. **The Road Show** eventually became a part of theatrical folklore; **Illuminatus**, a day-long play at the Liverpool Theatre of Science Fiction, ranks beside **The Wars of the Roses** and the Hare Trilogy as great days of theatre. It was as ambitious, as long, and certainly as entertaining, as **The Ring**. **The Warp**, an unforgettable cocktail of science fiction, sex, stories and adventure, played at the ICA in London in 1979, where it lasted twenty-two hours. A critic observed (correctly) that 'the world may soon divide into those who have been through **The Warp** and those who have not'. Those who did not were the poorer for it.

Campbell has been a lifetime opponent of 'brochure' theatre – the sort of theatre that gets done because something has to be programmed and announced in the brochure. For him theatre has to be an event, or nothing. If an actor fails to provide the necessary energy and invention to satisfy him he can be hurled against the wall with Campbell screaming in his all too imitable voice, like an exhaust pipe with a broken silencer: 'Act PROPER!'

His two shows for Nottingham Playhouse – **Bendigo: The Little Known Facts** and **Walking Like Geoffrey** – were unclassifiable, part musicals, part comic extravaganzas, part circus. In 1976 Ronald Bryden, then critic of the *Observer*, wrote of the latter show: 'If there's a future for British theatre it must lie here.'

3

A significant poke at the revolutionary myth came in 1978, in the form of an address delivered by David Hare to a conference on political theatre in Cambridge. Hare was by now a star among left-wing playwrights, one of a kind with Howard Brenton, David Edgar and Trevor Griffiths: that, at least, was the view from the mainstream. From the left, he was viewed with ambivalence. On the plus side was the zest with which he probed the darker side of capitalist corruption. On the minus side was his seeming lack of interest in the socialist alternative. (**Fanshen** apart – but that was in China.) Wasn't he, as one commentator put it, showing capitalism 'enduring, despite attempts to alter it'? How was that supposed to advance the revolution?

In his Cambridge address, Hare met the question head-on. 'Why is it,' he asked, 'that in advanced industrial societies the record of revolutionary activity is so very miserable, so very, very low?' The question was tactfully put: the workers' reluctance to man the barricades was seen as disappointing, rather than something to be greeted with the 'phew!'s of relief it would get today. And he wasn't claiming that the revolution had failed *across the globe*: in China, 'The Party answers to the people and is modified by it,' a view which was at the time widespread.

But his message was clear: the Revolution was a middle-class fantasy. Was it merely (he went on to ask) because of their artistic failure that dramatists had 'lately taken to brandishing their political credentials as frequently as possible throughout their work, and that political groups have indulged in such appalling overkill'? Was it this that caused the 'sinking of the heart when you go to a political play and find that the author really believes certain questions have been answered even before the play has begun'? Most theatre was hard work and nothing else, he added, before signing off with the paranoia-inducing observation: 'It is no coincidence that some of the British theatre's loudest theorists are notoriously incompetent inside a rehearsal room.'

'I was born on the pavement,' David Hare (1947–) said in an early interview, meaning that nothing felt quite so culture-starved as his respectable suburban South Coast background. Every other social stratum – working class, upper class, bohemian, you name it – had a richness missing from the streets of Bexhill-on-Sea.

So it's no surprise to find him, as a grown-up playwright, exploring worlds of glamour and excitement. The glamour of success is only part of the search, and it's not a large one. More important is the glamour of decay, the glamour of illicit sex, the glamour of corruption and crime. The glamour of place is a prime ingredient. No playwright creates more evocative rooms: whether they're in echoing country houses, cheap two-room conversions or arty basements glowing dimly in the London blackout, they share a density of atmosphere which makes you shiver. The tattiest seaside boarding-house, or the emptiest provincial night-club, has a desolate magic about it, just as it would in a novel by Graham Greene or Patrick Hamilton.

Pervading all these resonant places is a sense of something lost. Just *what's* been lost appears from time to time in the form of a woman. She may be a woman of startling goodness, or impossible integrity, or she may be simply kind and loving, but she's always a beacon of light. Much has been written about Hare the acerbic chronicler of his times: this is to mistake sharpness of tone for a flinty nature. He has the pen of a polemicist but the soul of a romantic.

David Hare.

He joined the Royal Court in the late 1960s when Christopher Hampton stepped down as literary manager. The job had been designed as a way of supporting a young playwright, but it effectively stopped anyone of normal constitution from writing anything at all and the pay was only seven pounds ten shillings a week. Challenged to find a replacement, Hampton came up at lightning speed with his old schoolfriend from Lancing. Hare was already a name on the alternative touring circuit as a directorial mover-and-shaker who also wrote plays. He looked very much as he does today: rangy, boyish and debonair except when some setback, real or imagined, drove him to white-faced, tight-lipped fury.

Setbacks at the Court were many, since his arrival prompted fierce resistance from most of the old guard. The ridiculous thing about this was that Hare and the principal anti-Hareite, the director Lindsay Anderson, had so much in common. Each was a romantic, and a romantic in particular about England; each nursed an Oedipal anger at England's failings; each was brilliant, combative and outspoken. Part of the problem was that the Court saw itself as a place where playwrights were discovered and Hare, it soon became clear, had no intention of being discovered by anyone other than himself. His confidence was seen as a presumptuous challenge, fictitious battle-lines were invented and the result, very unfortunately for the Court's main stage, was that an entire generation of radical playwrights was soundly put off.

Slag, Hare's spiky take on feminism, was premièred in 1970 at Hampstead, about as far from Sloane Square as you could get while still being in London. So was his first look at the profane underbelly of politics, **The Great Exhibition**. Over the next few years he made the occasional return trip to Sloane Square – a revival of **Slag** in 1972, **Teeth 'n' Smiles** in 1975 – but essentially he progressed from fringe to mainstream by means of a wide detour: the West End, Nottingham Playhouse, Joint Stock, television, the National Theatre.

Knuckle, produced commercially in 1974, was a turning-point. Curly, a cynical arms-dealer, searches for his vanished sister through a seedy world of shady land-deals, adulteries and celebrated South Coast murders. She, a political radical, is the first Hare beacon-heroine. The mood of disillusion is consistent and, in lightly pastiching the tone of the thriller, Hare discovered a voice of his own. It's crisp, suave, punchy: a metropolitan style without the middle-class twiddles.

1978 saw three big milestones. His television film, *Licking Hitler*, is set in the seductive world of wartime propaganda. An upper-class girl and a Red Clyde intellectual make love across the class divide; a coda showing her post-war politicisation serves as a template-in-miniature for the stage play that followed.

In **Plenty**, Susan Traherne is parachuted into occupied France, where she fights a gallant war. But her stubborn integrity is unwelcome in peacetime Britain, a place of shifty compromise. She drinks, makes embarrassing scenes, damages her lover and husband, has breakdowns. Her life is a downward spiral: a difficult graph for the playwright to handle while keeping us wondering what will happen next: Hare adjusts the graph by twisting the

*Kate Nelligan in **Plenty**.*

shape of the play, by letting us see her aged and bitter, going back in time, showing the troughs and high points, finally ending the play in a blaze of optimism. Susan, young once more, is glimpsed in a sun-drenched France. 'There will be days and days and days like this,' she declares. It's ironic, but also not: the hopes were real.

The third big event of 1978 was his Cambridge address: a provocation which 'left many members of the political theatre movement reeling as if from an unexpected, undeserved blow', as a historian of the period puts it. For some, it branded Hare a renegade; for others, it was proof that he'd never belonged in the first place, that his place in left-wing theatre was just one more symptom of his knack for being in the right place at the right time. The truth was simpler. For Hare to move on as a playwright, he had to release his imp.

Every first-rate playwright has an imp. It's the unofficial, unacceptable part of the writer's psyche. It's vain and attention-seeking: it will stay in the background for a promising play or two, sulkily pressing the buttons and turning the wheels but, after that, it demands its freedom. If it isn't let out, it goes on strike or pulls the switches: then the machine will stop, or the wheels will revolve uselessly. Once the imp is released, it becomes uncontrollable: it goes rampaging from play to play, changing its name, its sex and appearance but always holding fast to its perverse and contrary nature. Goldberg, Pinter's Jewish uncle-interrogator, is the prototype for a line of authoritarian brutes; Bennett's matriarch/aunt is unstoppable in all her guises. Edward Bond's imps are working-class young men: the political rigidity of his later plays can be seen as a form of National Service, redirecting their physical violence towards acceptable ends.

Hare's imp is an emotional tyrant and a right-wing charmer. He appears as the South African media-monster Lambert le Roux in Hare and Brenton's satirical crowd-pleaser **Pravda**, the Thatcherite Marion in **The Secret Rapture**, the brusque, bull-dozing Tom in **Skylight**. Each of these incarnations has life and vibrancy, but none has the enchanting quality of Victor Mehta in the play that followed the Cambridge speech, **A Map of the World**. He's a celebrated Indian author, self-professed reactionary, lady-killer and wit.

All old civilisations are superior to young ones. That is why I have been happiest in Shropshire. They are less subject to crazes. In younger countries there is no culture. The civilisation is shallow. Nothing takes root. Gangs of crazy youths sweep through the streets of Sydney and New York pretending they are homosexual. But do you think they are homosexual really? Of course not. It is the merest fashion.

How can we help the starving of the Third World? It's very simple. By example: 'By what one is. One is civilised. One is cultured. One is rational. That is how you help other people to live.'

Stephen, Mehta's opponent both in love and ideology, musters a number of excellent liberal arguments to prove that Mehta is talking nonsense. By any rational tally, Stephen would win hands down. Yet Mehta has more life, as how could he not? He's the playwright's secret double, free to be outrageous. Hare himself speaks deprecatingly now of **Map of the World**. But it's delightful: part Shavian debate, part masked ball of the id.

Hare's trilogy of state-of-the-nation plays was a crowning moment in the life of the National Theatre in 1994. The plays all ask the questions: How does a good person change people's lives for the better? Can an institution established for the common good avoid being devoured by its own internal struggles and contradictions? Is man a social animal interested in justice, in equality, in love? The second play, **Murmuring Judges**, is the grandest in architecture, the third, **The Absence of War**, the timeliest, being a study of a Labour Party hero at a time of transition. **Racing Demon**, the first of the plays, is a warm and intimate study of failed love. It's the play in which Hare drew on his own lower-middle-class roots to create something both prosaic and entrancing: a world of sooty streets, bicycle-clips, Hancock tapes and clarinet lessons.

*John Thaw as Labour leader in **The Absence of War**.*

It's also, of all Hare's plays, the one in which he most nearly allows for unconscious emotion. Young Tony, 'a combustible curate', can relate to God all right. What he cannot do is relate to other human beings. His parents were killed in a motorway crash, but he angrily refutes any suggestion that he's in grief. 'All that stuff, it's just a load of nonsense. All that matters is that I'm healed.' But he doesn't look it: he's so angry that he can hardly function. And you can't help noticing that he's found, in God, a substitute father who can be relied on not to die on him – and in Lionel Espy, faith-wracked priest, a father-figure he can rage at for his all-too-human inadequacies.

Tony has a beautiful speech about his own mundanity; it's pure Bexhill-on-Sea:

> Like everything else in England it turns out to be a matter of class. Educated clerics don't like evangelicals, because evangelicals drink sweet sherry and keep budgerigars and have ducks in formations on their walls. (*Nods, smiling.*) Yes, and they also have the distressing downmarket habit of trying to get people emotionally involved. (*Stares at them.*) You know I'm right. And – as it happens – I went to a grammar school, I was brought up – unlike you – among all those normal, decent people who shop at Allied Carpets and are into DIY. And I don't think they should always be looked down on. And tell me, please, what is wrong with ministering to them?

Amy's View is a touching and entertaining account of loving, mothers and daughters, dependency and how we never know how things will turn out. It was also, explicitly and implicitly, a passionate defence of the theatre – and one that gave a cracking part to Judi Dench. In **The Judas Kiss**, Hare wrote a study of *folie d'amour* in a play about the fatal attraction of Oscar Wilde for Lord Alfred Douglas.

There are jokes in David Hare's plays which, when read on the page, or in rehearsal, tend to baffle. They're often the jokes that get the biggest laugh on the night. He and his public share a private line: this is doubtless, in a coded way, what Tony the priest is talking about. Hare re-invents himself with tireless energy and he never gets bored. So his finest play is probably still to be written. As he puts it: 'You have to start at nine in the morning. If you do, you'll finish the play. If you don't, you won't. It's as simple as that.'

An oddness to the modern eye is that the revolutionary spirit of the 1970s seems to have been happening ten years too soon. It was the Thatcher era, surely, that was cruel and heartless? It brought monetarism, the wholesale dismantling of industrial Britain, unemployment nudging 3 million, let alone the Falklands, Clause 28, the Poll Tax, city yobs popping the champers.

All this is true; but what fuelled the political plays of the 1970s was not, except in the case of Northern Ireland, state repression: it was the belief that the post-war Labour victory had been squandered by twenty-five years of compromise and cave-in. This may seem surprising, since none of the writers concerned was exactly old enough to have been downing celebratory pints on VE Night. But a sense of history was a powerful force in the '70s coming-of-age: copies of Angus Calder's *The People's War* were passed around till they fell to pieces. Post-war betrayal provides the central theme of **Brassneck**, Stephen Lowe's **Touched** and **Plenty**. Caryl Churchill's **Light Shining in Buckinghamshire** finds a parallel in the forgotten radicalism of the English Civil War. 'AFTER' is the title of the closing scene: it's set in the wake of loss. One character thinks that Jesus came but nobody noticed. 'We missed it. I don't see how.' Another's a thief. Another, in hope of mending the world's inequalities, has cut down his diet from eggs to porridge to berries. Now he's found a way to rob no one of anything:

> BRIGGS: It was hard to get my body to take grass. It got very ill. It wouldn't give in to grass. But I forced it on. And now it will. There's many kinds; rye grass, meadow grass, fescue. These two years I've been able to eat grass. Very sweet. People come to watch. They can, I can't stop them. I'm living in a field that belongs to a gentleman that comes sometimes, and sometimes he brings a friend to show. He's not unkind but I don't like to see him. I stand where I am stock still and wait till he's gone.

Caryl Churchill's plays are a meeting-ground between a fiercely lucid intelligence and a sense of mystery. She's a political radical whose views on feminism, money and exploitation have been consistent over a long career. But life, in her plays, has a secret underside: magical, sexual, criminal. However much her characters seem to know what they're doing and where they're headed, one always feels a shifting of the ground beneath them. Cracks of uncertainty open up in the interstices of the dialogue; even the most transparent statements hint at more beneath. From **Top Girls**:

> MARLENE: Are you suggesting I give up my job to him, then?
> MRS KIDD: It had crossed my mind if you were unavailable after all for some reason, he would be the natural second choice I think, don't you? I'm not asking.

But of course she is. Marlene, the power-shouldered Thatcherite, has elbowed Mr Kidd aside and collared the job that his passive-aggressive wife regards as the man's prerogative. There is a rich irony in the appeal to female solidarity to let the man take over, not that they get very far in the face of the new-style, right-wing, entrepreneurse: note Marlene's aggressive tilt of the chin on 'then?'. If you read Mrs Kidd's reply aloud, you can see at once how troubled it is. There's a preposition missing and an absent comma, always meaningful in Churchill's dialogue: here a sign, perhaps, that things are

Caryl Churchill.

getting out of control. 'For some reason' sounds ominous: what does she have in mind? Disease? Death? Clichés keep swimming into view: 'Crossed my mind', 'the natural second choice': they seem designed to conceal what she really means.

Churchill was born in 1938 in London, grew up partly in Canada and studied at Oxford. Just after graduating, she wrote a manifesto about the theatre: it called for plays that revealed new worlds beyond and beneath the surface of ordinary life, very much the kind of play she would write herself – though none would be produced professionally until **Owners** in 1971. Meanwhile she got married, had three sons and wrote a number of plays which were either turned down or she suppressed. Encouragement came from Martin Esslin and John Tydeman at the BBC, who produced her short radio plays, and the literary agent Margaret Ramsay, who had spotted Churchill young and didn't at all object to her client's slow progress: she saw it, if anything, as a badge of honour.

Tributes to Peggy Ramsay should by rights be dotted throughout this book. From the moment she started her business in the early 1960s till her death in the 1990s at a great but mysterious age, she was of all agents the most inspired and idiosyncratic and the one who most decisively pushed the New Wave into the public eye. Nothing about her was predictable, not the seldom-admitted childhood on a South African ostrich farm, nor the fabled marriage which she allegedly escaped by climbing through a bathroom window, nor her rise from chorus girl to top agent. Her list of clients ranged from the new and maverick – Orton, Bond, Hare – to the plushly prosperous, and it was no secret that the mavericks were her favourites. She worshipped the individual voice and dreaded the possibility that success might rob it of its 'special' quality. 'Whatever you do,' she would warn her younger clients, '*don't* end up like Robert Bolt. He's sold out for money, dear! Sold out for money!' Bolt was a client of her own, one for whom she had struck some highly lucrative film deals: it was just one of the many contradictions about her that a commercial negotiator of such acumen should carry the torch for art with more impassioned fervour than almost anyone around her. Letters to her clients – typed in blue on what appeared to be an antique Remington – were never confined to the dull minutiae of contracts: they included advice on marriage, fierce exhortations and keen-eyed character-assessment. The message was always the same: to be an artist is an awesome responsibility, one to be deployed with total integrity or not at all.

By the time of **Owners**, Churchill had spent ten years honing her distinctive style: it's anxious, sharp, funny. The play is set in Islington, where Churchill lived; its perimeters are the local ones of a housebound mother, its settings the landmarks that you pass while wheeling the stroller: the estate agency, the butcher's shop. The undertow is a violent brew of blood, fire and mutilation. Selfish love is seen as a form of devouring capitalism, swallowing up the object of desire, be it the man you love or a baby. Marion deals in property: her driven energy stands in pitiless contrast to the Yoga-like detachment of her one-time lover:

ALEC:	It was all here before you were born and you don't resent that.
MARION:	But once you have things you don't want to give them up. It's quite different.
ALEC:	No, it's just the same.
MARION:	But I want to hold on. Everything I was taught – be clean, be quick, be top, be best, you may not succeed, Marion, but what matters is try your hardest. To push on. Onward Christian soldiers, marching as to war. That was my favourite song when I was seven. Fight the good fight. Where's your fight?

Underlying it all is a fear of madness. Marion speaks from the heart of a psychic storm; Alec, she claims, has had a breakdown. ('Or up. Or through,' he replies.) And what about Marion's rent-collector, Worsley, newly scarred each time we see him by another suicide-attempt?

Light Shining in Buckinghamshire evolved from a method unique to Joint Stock. A programme of research, involving cast, directors and actors, was followed by a break of around two months during which the playwright wrote the play. Rehearsals followed and then the show. The point to underline is that, during the writing-gap, the playwright worked alone. Joint Stock wasn't one of the many '70s companies where the script was created by all concerned, nor was it quite a 'writers' company' on the lines of the Royal Court: it was a mix of both. It suited Churchill perfectly, since it gave free play to both her intuitive self and the cooler analyst in her. No other playwright was to make such fruitful use of this duality.

Light Shining also released her passion for re-inventing forms. Here, she inverted the familiar fringe convention of doubling: instead of one actor playing a series of parts, the parts themselves were written to be rotated around the actors. This could happen to anyone, or be said or done by anyone, was the message: it's the circumstances that count.

Since then, every full-length Churchill play has been fuelled by a full-scale formal innovation, something which, by shaking up our notion of what a play is like, makes us apply the same astonishment to life. The other result is that the stock response to political drama – 'Oh, that's so *obvious*!' – can never be made. In **Moving Clocks Go Slow**, time runs backwards as well as forwards; **Traps** is an Escher-like display of impossible actions. **Cloud Nine**, Churchill's first big popular success, sprang out of a Joint Stock workshop based on sexuality: the participants included a married couple, a gay couple, one and a half lesbians, a single heterosexual man. Churchill pointed up the changes made, or perhaps required, by making the action span a century, during the course of which the characters age a mere twenty years.

*Adventures in the gender game: Jim Hooper and Antony Sher in **Cloud Nine**.*

The all-male **Softcops** was written in tandem with the all-woman **Top Girls**: it was the latter which became the classic, thus defying the rules of formal coherence. Each act of the play comes out of a different box. The first is a conversation-piece between great women of myth and history: they exchange views, news and highlights of their unusual careers around a table in an Italian restaurant without for a moment wondering how they got there. Act Two is city comedy: we see Marlene's unstoppable rise. Act Three, in social-realist style, brings her nemesis to the fore: the 'failed' sister who has clung to her ideals whatever the price. It's the most sustained emotional scene Churchill has ever written, and it's terrific. The oblique strokes are the cue for the next speech to start: they're Churchill's invention, now widely used:

MARLENE:	I had to get out.
JOYCE:	Jealous?
MARLENE:	I knew when I was thirteen, out of their house, out of them, never let that happen to me/never let him, make my own way, out.
JOYCE:	Jealous of what you've done, you're ashamed of me if I came to your office, your smart friends, wouldn't you, I'm ashamed of you, think of nothing but yourself, you've got on, nothing's changed for most people/has it?
MARLENE:	I hate the working class/which is why they're going
JOYCE:	Yes you do.
MARLENE:	to go on about now, it doesn't exist any more, it means lazy and stupid/I don't like the way they talk. I don't
JOYCE:	Come on, we're getting it.
MARLENE:	like beer guts and football vomit and saucy tits/and brothers and sisters –
JOYCE:	I spit when I see a Rolls-Royce, scratch it with my ring/ Mercedes it was.
MARLENE:	Oh very mature.

Gary Oldman in **Serious Money**.

Serious Money, written in the late 1980s, dealt with the noisy lads of the Thatcher money-market: they speak in verse, the heroes' medium. Even more unsettling was the fact that the play offered not one word of reproof of the lads' frightful activities. City traders came to the play and cheered. Didn't this mean that it had backfired? Well, no: it simply let the audience make its mind up. **The Skriker** brings Joycean wordplay to a Hieronymous Bosch world of bogies and goblins. But who, or what, is the Skriker, exactly? Is she, as she claims, an ancient sprite, capable of turning herself in a trice into a perfectly ordinary person of the kind you'd run into in a pub or at an adventure playground? Or is she, in reality, that perfectly ordinary person, bizarrely perceived by a girl whose reason has cracked? Once more, time plays tricks: underworld centuries shoot past in earthly seconds: the opposite happens too.

Blue Heart is an exercise in exasperation: in each, a play begins only to be angrily scrawled over. The first sets up the arrival of a relation from Australia, goes into spin and collapses. Crowds of small children erupt from the chaos and so does an enormous bird. (Peggy Ramsay appears in disguised form in many of her clients' plays: is this the South African ostrich?) The second, **Blue Kettle**, starts so well that you almost wish that Churchill had let it alone. A young man finds his mother. Then he finds another. Then a third one. What? The truth is that he's a fake: a painful inadequate, driven to find affection wherever he can. By now the play has been invaded by a virus that turns words to nonsense. This play is so mature that it feels like a brilliant first.

4

America was less of an influence in the 1970s than you'd imagine. Most of the really exciting American companies had been to London in the previous decade – the Bread and Puppets, the marvellous Joe Chaikin production of **America Hurrah!**, the Living Theater. Everyone knew about New York happenings, Off-Off-Broadway and one-off performances in East Village lofts, but first-hand accounts were rare: it's hard to convey quite how remote America seemed in those days. Interesting testaments to New York avant-garde activity came in the shape of the Evergreen editions of plays by writers like Lanford Wilson, Terrence McNally and (by far the best) Sam Shepard, and many were done on the alternative circuit. When Shepard himself showed up in London, he seemed surprised that these short plays of his had made such an impact. Most of them, he said, he'd knocked up because he hadn't anything else to do, they'd been thrown on at La Mama at impossible hours of the night and hardly anyone had seen them. But whether he was kidding or not was hard to say.

In November 1964 a twenty-three-year-old son of an air-force pilot, who had spent his childhood as an 'army brat' on army bases from South Dakota to Florida to Utah to Guam, barged into Edward Albee's apartment in Greenwich Village with a suitcase full of manuscripts. The young man was Sam Shepard, and Albee became a champion of his talents as he did of many other aspiring playwrights.

Of all American playwrights, Sam Shepard seems as indissolubly and unmistakably American as John Osborne is English and Lorca is Spanish. Few playwrights give you a sense of landscape – real landscape, that is, not the metaphoric landscape of the mind. Shepard draws the map of both.

He settled as a teenager on a working ranch in Duarte, a suburb on the outskirts of Los Angeles – the small-town America of the '60s that recurs in play after play of his: local high school, fighting with his father, stealing a car to drive to Mexico, drag-racing, drug-taking, making friends with the few blacks in town, jazz, drumming for a rockabilly band – Holy Modal Rounders – and looking up to the guys who 'didn't have any real rules' – cowboys, rock stars, sportsmen, druggies, rebels with and without a cause.

Shepard's themes are the myths of the American West – the loss or betrayal of the American Dream, the search for roots, the sanctity of the family – set in the southern landscape, on the meniscus of the excesses of late Californian consumerism and the myths of the last frontier:

Welfare State International and Bread and Puppet Theatre: Taking theatre to the people.

I just feel like the West is much more ancient than the East ... There are areas like Wyoming, Texas, Montana and places like that, where you really feel this ancient thing about the land. Ancient. That it's primordial ... It has to do with the relationship between the land and the people – between the human being and the ground. I think that's typically Western and much more attractive than this tight little forest civilisation that happened back East. It's much more physical and emotional to me. New England and the East Coast have always been an intellectual community ... I just feel like I'll never get over the fact of being from the West.

His early plays – **La Turista, Chicago, Red Cross, Icarus's Mother, Cowboys No 2, Angel City** – have an unaffected freedom about them, influenced by jazz, Jackson Pollock's action painting, and by Joseph Chaikin, from whom Shepard learned the cardinal value of spontaneity – or the appearance of spontaneity – in performance and writing. In those plays there's an artlessness and openness, a lack of sub-text or message – like a band playing for the sheer joy of the sound.

In the early '70s – in the wake of the failure of **Operation Sidewinder** at the Lincoln Center – Shepard moved to London, weaned himself from drugs to alcohol, and wrote **The Tooth of Crime, Blue Bitch, Geography of a Horse Dreamer, Little Ocean** and **Action**. He wrote with a guileless enthusiasm about purity and corruption in America, drawing his images from crime, magic and live music – words tumbling out with a prodigal profusion, sometimes pure sound and rhythm, long visionary speeches erupting like extended guitar solos. He made hip the 'theatricality' of theatre.

Julie Walters and Ian Charleson in **Fool for Love***.*

When he moved back to the US he wrote more thoughtfully, less spontaneously – mostly about the family as an institution, and his own family history. 'What doesn't have to do with the family?' he said. 'There isn't anything.' Families are the most potent totem at the heart of the American myth, and in Shepard's plays even if they begin in precarious stability the centre never holds: violence and disorder explode in **Curse of the Starving Class** (about his teenage years in Duarte), in **Buried Child**, and in **True West**. Mother is estranged from child, father from mother, brother from sister, lover from lover, and in **Fool for Love** and **A Lie of the Mind** couples can neither stay together nor live apart. 'We're just this incredible race of strangers,' said Shepard in an interview.

He might borrow an epigraph for his plays from Gloucester in **King Lear**:

> Love cools, friendship falls off, brothers divide; in cities mutinies, in countries discord, in palaces treason, and the bond cracked 'twixt son and father. We have seen the best of our time.

5

As the critic John Gross remarked, 'There are false sunsets as well as false dawns.' A false, or at best unreliable, sunset had been lengthening the shadows over English drama since the mid-1950s, ever since Colonel Redfern made his entry into Jimmy Porter's domestic hell:

COLONEL: Perhaps I am a – what was it? An old plant left over from the Edwardian Wilderness. And I can't understand why the sun isn't shining any more. You can see what he means, can't you? It was March, 1914, when I left England, and, apart from leaves every ten years or so, I didn't see much of my own country until we all came back in '47. Oh, I know things had changed, of course …

I think the last day the sun shone was when that dirty little train steamed out of that crowded, suffocating Indian station, and the battalion band played for all it was worth. I knew in my heart it was all over. Everything.

We get the point: something is breathing its last. But what? Decency? Upper-middle-class values? Yes, and rather admirable they seem to have been, if Colonel Redfern is anything to go by. Empire? Well, we heard the Indian bit and yes, we suppose that's partly what he's talking about. Sounds a bit Merchant-Ivory, though. And why should a left-wing playwright care so much about the Empire? Wasn't it *good* that we gave it away? Shouldn't we stop complaining?

Colonel Redfern's valedictory tone had echoes throughout the 1970s and in true Osbornian style the passing of the *ancien régime* was never complete without a sense of heartache and a romantic glow. Both are combined in a lyric of Tony Bicat's, written for David Hare's **Teeth 'n' Smiles**:

> Last orders on the Titanic
> Get up and paint your face
> Deckhands in dungarees
> And millionaires in lace

The 'Titanic' metaphor was as plain as 'Rule Britannia', though it conveyed the opposite message: H.M.S. Britain was holed beneath the waterline and sinking fast. The notion that the apocalypse, when it came, would be both stylish and nostalgic – that waiters would be circling the tables in an art-deco lounge while millionaires plummeted from the decks – was a complicated one: it needed careful spelling-out and duly got it. Darwin, the senior diplomat in **Plenty**, is Colonel Redfern's brainier descendant; Howard Barker's prison governor in **The Hang of the Gaol** is another and Brenton's effete politicians are closely related. Mrs Rafi in Bond's **The Sea**, cruel and wilful though she is, faces her extinction with nobility:

> MRS RAFI: I'm afraid of getting old. I've always been a forceful woman. I was brought up to be. People expect my class to shout at them. Bully them. They're disappointed if you don't. It gives them something to gossip about in their bars. When they turn you into an eccentric, it's their form of admiration. Sometimes I think I'm like a lighthouse in the world. I give them a sense of order and security. My glares mark out a channel to the safe harbour. I'm so tired of them.

One playwright would have nothing to do with any of this. For Tom Stoppard, traditional values weren't a dying system to be mourned in a half-affectionate, half-guilty way. He loved and defended them.

Stoppard was born in Zlin, Czechoslovakia in 1937, the second son of a physician, Eugene Straussler, who worked for Bata, the shoe manufacturers. In 1939, the family fled the Nazi invasion, taking refuge in Singapore. In 1942, mother and sons were forced to flee once more, this time to India. Dr Straussler stayed in Singapore and shortly died. His two sons gained their new surname from a major in the British Army, who married their mother in 1946 and brought them all to England.

'The whole Czech thing about me has got wildly out of hand,' Stoppard claimed in a 1988 interview. 'I wasn't two years old when I left the country and I was back one week in 1977. I went to an English school and was brought up English. So I don't feel Czech.' But Stoppard's interviews are works of art, as subtle and allusive as his plays and less reliable. No other living playwright has been interviewed half as often, for the simple reason that he's the lazy interviewer's dream. No need for the busy hack to cut or clarify: every sentence tells, every word has a dancer's poise, every punchline hits the spot like a well-aimed dart. Whole paragraphs re-appear in later interviews, each time better structured, sometimes embellished with an artful searching for the appropriate phrase. 'I'll say anything in an interview,' he once admitted. Was that intended to put us off the scent? Or put us on to it? The answer is both. Stoppard the playful wit is a public figure, script-written to perfection by the master. But there are other, hidden Soppards. Stoppard the celebrity-on-view is a modest man, responding with old-world courtesy to the stupidest questions. 'You can make a case for what you're saying but,

Early Tom Stoppard.

wielding Occam's razor upon it, the same thing can be said in a much simpler way.' Stoppard the political thinker is a lucid, forceful voice, most often heard when goaded; of Stoppard the intuitive artist we hear much less and Stoppard the romantic never speaks.

His disclaimer of 'the Czech thing' came in answer to the suggestion that it explained his sympathy for Václav Havel, who was at the time in prison – as though any decent person wouldn't feel the same. But if that was absurd, it would be equally ridiculous to dismiss the relevance of his extraordinary childhood: driven by war from the country of his birth, orphaned by war, exiled by the spread of the Soviet Empire. England was the floor on which he laid his sleeping-bag with all the determined masterfulness of the late arrival. He learned the rules and studied the small print. His attachment to British free speech was fierce and foreign, like an enlightened explorer seeing the value of a native tradition long after the actual natives had forgotten the point of it. In a culture ruled by Oxbridge graduates, he became an intellectual star without the help of either university. His command of the language was, and is, prodigious. So are his jokes.

There's a crucial speech in **The Real Thing**, which appeared in the early '80s. It's joke-free and that's the point: this is the playwright talking. Annie has asked her lover Henry, a writer, to polish another writer's play. She can't understand why he's so reluctant. Does it matter if the other chap is just a bungling amateur? 'What's so good about putting words together?' she asks. Henry gets out his cricket bat:

HENRY: Shut up and listen. This thing here, which looks like a wooden club, is actually several pieces of particular wood cunningly put together in a certain way so that the whole thing is sprung, like a dance floor. It's for hitting cricket balls with. If you get it right, the cricket ball will travel two hundred yards in four seconds, and all you've done is give it a knock like knocking the top off a bottle of stout, and it makes a noise like a trout taking a fly … (*He clucks his tongue to make the noise.*) What we're trying to do is to write cricket bats, so that when we throw up an idea and give it a little knock, it might … travel … (*He clucks his tongue again and picks up the script.*) Now, what we've got here is a lump of wood of roughly the same shape trying to be a cricket bat, and if you hit a ball with it, the ball will travel about ten feet and you will drop the bat and dance about shouting 'Ouch!' with your hands stuck into your armpits (*indicating the cricket bat*). This isn't better because someone says it's better, or because there's a conspiracy by the MCC to keep cudgels out of Lord's. It's better because it's better. You don't believe me, so I suggest you go out to bat with this and see how you get on …

The writer he despises is a working-class lad, possibly hard-done-by, certainly in trouble. For Stoppard, this is irrelevant. There are, in art, absolute standards of good and bad. To fudge them is a kind of blasphemy. Note the prop on which the speech depends is a cricket bat. No flash, imported object could convey its moral weight: an American baseball bat, let's say, or a Japanese tennis-racket. It had to be English.

Stoppard is famed for a variety of qualities which he certainly possesses – fizz, brains, verbal ingenuity – and since none of these qualities is exactly falling out of the trees these days, it seems ungracious to look for more. But what's the centre of the maze? Stoppard makes a clear distinction. Some of his plays – not many – have a polemical purpose: they deal, or dealt, with a specific human situation, generally in Central Europe. The rest write themselves, or that's the feeling: he starts with an idea which – once gone into, turned around and thought about and rummaged about in – draws its own internal map of opposites and correspondences.

There's an obsession with accuracy. It goes side by side with the knowledge that total accuracy can never be reached: that the world is so packed with crossed wires and faulty hearing-aids that ludicrous confusions are unavoidable. Misunderstandings are a running Stoppardian joke. From **Jumpers**:

BONES:	(*shrewdly*) You are the husband.
GEORGE:	Yes.
BONES:	Professor … Moore.
GEORGE:	Yes … (*lightening*) Yes, I'm something of a logician myself.
BONES:	Really? Sawing ladies in half, that sort of thing?
GEORGE:	Logician.

And the typical Stoppardian *tour-de-force* is the long and hilarious speech in which the search for precision is wrecked by its own punctiliousness. Again from **Jumpers**:

GEORGE: To begin at the beginning: is God? (*Pause.*) I prefer to put the question in this form because to ask, 'Does God exist?' appears to presuppose the existence of a God who may not, and I do not propose this late evening to follow my friend Russell, this evening to follow my late friend Russell, to follow my good friend the late Lord Russell, necrophiliac rubbish! To begin at the beginning: is God? (*He ponders a moment.*) To ask, 'Is God?' appears to presuppose a Being who perhaps isn't … and thus is open to the same objection as the question, 'Does God exist?' … but until the difficulty is pointed out it does not have the same propensity to confuse language with meaning and to conjure up a God who may have any number of predicates including omniscience, perfection and four-wheel-drive but not, as it happens, existence.

'I can't do plots and have no interest in plots,' he once said: this too is linked with a passion for getting things right, or saying no more than you know. Plot is where the playwright is forced to approximate: where the complexities that constitute the truth of the play are laid aside for the sake of some coarse and necessary action. Actors like plot and so, of course, do audiences, but when it comes to writing the wretched stuff even Shakespeare sounds bored. From *Twelfth Night*:

VIOLA: I'll serve this Duke:
Thou shalt present me as a eunuch to him:
It may be worth thy pains; for I can sing
And speak to him in many sorts of music
That will allow me very worth his service.
[At this point Shakespeare decides it's time for lunch.]
What else may hap, to time I will commit …

At the age of seventeen, Stoppard got a job reporting for a Bristol paper. An early chance to flex his imagination came when, unable to drive, he wrote the motoring column. Theatrical inspiration came from the local rep (where Peter O'Toole was the leading man for a season) and from local writers: both Charles Wood and Peter Nichols lived in Bristol. His first full-length play, written in 1960, **A Walk on the Water**, got him an agent, was shown on television and prompted a move to London. It's the quirky tale of a failed inventor, much influenced by Robert Bolt's **The Flowering Cherry** and Arthur Miller. ('My "Flowering Death of a Salesman" ', Stoppard called it later.) The RSC bought an option on **Rosencrantz and Guildenstern are Dead**, but let it lapse; an undergraduate production at the 1966 Edinburgh Festival caused a furore and the National Theatre bought it within the week:

> No! I am not Prince Hamlet, nor was meant to be;
> Am an attendant lord, one that will do
> To swell a progress, start a scene or two …

'Prufrock and Beckett,' Stoppard said (before anyone else got the chance to point this out) 'are the two syringes of my diet, my arterial system.' Asked about the Godot echo – two men pass the time in games and wordplay – he came up with a simile every writer will understand. 'It's as though you told the Customs that you'd nothing to declare. But when they open your suitcase, they discover a bottle of whisky, five hundred cigarettes and a stack of ten-pound notes. You don't remember packing them, but *there they are*!' Tynan pointed out a Czech connection: who else but Stoppard's compatriot Kafka had created a mysterious castle, scene of cryptic orders and fateful meetings? Echoes too (which Tynan missed) of twentieth-century terror, the world of Koestler and Solzhenitsyn.

> GUILDENSTERN: You can't act death. The fact of it is nothing to do with seeing it happen – it's not gasps and blood and falling about – that isn't what makes it death. It's just a man failing to reappear, that's all – now you see him, now you don't; that's the only thing that's real: here one minute and gone the next and never coming back – an exit …

Another play deserves a mention here. James Saunders' **Next Time I'll Sing to You**, written in 1962, is an ontological speculation about itself: an investigation, that is, into the nature of the play it would be if it ever began. In the process, the actors talk, pass the time, tell jokes … There's a speech, much admired by Stoppard, which is both beautiful and true. It's about a carp. It begins, 'There lies behind everything, and you can believe this or not as you wish, a certain quality which we may call grief.' Saunders' play,

307

Rosencrantz and Guildenstern are Dead.

successful though it was, was outside fashion even when first produced: it was avant-garde but decidedly not Royal Court, and therefore difficult to place.

Rosencrantz and Guildenstern took off like a rocket. Stoppard was now a celebrity and he entered the new decade radiating the golden aura of success that characterised the 1960s: a time when stardom had no dark side. This made him a figure of some suspicion among the new generation, and his politics clinched the matter. He was, he would claim, 'a supporter of Western liberal democracy, favouring an intellectual elite and a progressive middle class and based on an order derived from Christian absolutes'. Just as art – in Stoppard's view – is subject to absolute standards of good and bad, so are all political acts. 'There is a sense in which contradictory political movements are restatements of each other. For example, Leninism and fascism are restatements of totalitarianism.' It's hard to convey how much this cut across the orthodoxy of the times, according to which Lenin's beneficent vision had been cruelly betrayed by his successor. ('An absurd and foolish untruth' said Stoppard.) **Jumpers**, from the early '70s, breathes moral and intellectual isolation.

The play is distantly related to Robert Bolt's **The Tiger and the Horse** with its wracked philosopher, unstable wife and astronomical associations, but the comparison isn't useful. This is a farce, a laugh-machine with the stops pulled out, boasting a vast intellectual vocabulary, a dashing command of the stage, spiffing jokes and a vein of fantasy which feels more European than English: Bulgakov, say, or the Capek brothers.

At its heart is a quest. George, the bumbling, selfish don, struggles to prove, not that God exists – which would be intellectually presumptuous – but that a greater and more foolish form of presumptuousness is to assert that he doesn't. But George is on his own, surrounded by a bizarre and new-fangled breed of radicals: these are the 'jumpers', acting out the crass nature of their politics in none-too-graceful physical acrobatics. 'I belong to a school,' says George, 'which regards all sudden movements as ill-bred.' It's surprising how often this supposedly insouciant, distanced playwright says exactly what he thinks.

Different Stoppard plays have different levels of complexity: think of an animal-trainer holding out a bar for his charges to leap over. (The metaphor breaks down at the point where you realise that it's the playwright who's doing the leaping.) The height of the bar is sometimes middling, sometimes vertiginous. **Jumpers** is a high-bar play and **Travesties** is another. It's based on the fact that Lenin, James Joyce and Tristan Tzara, the noted surrealist, were all resident in Zurich in the fateful year of the Russian Revolution; so was an obscure British diplomat, Henry Carr, whose muddled recollections of an amateur performance of **The Importance of Being Earnest** give the play its fractured idiom. There are songs, parody and vaudeville: the play is if anything more demanding than **Jumpers** but the tone is broader. Tzara's view of art is nihilistic. Joyce, as Stoppard's spokesman, knocks him flat:

> JOYCE: An artist is the magician put among men to gratify – capriciously – their urge for immortality. The temples are built and brought down around him, continuously and contiguously, from Troy to the fields of Flanders. If there is any meaning in it, it is what survives as art, yes even in the celebration of tyrants, yes even in the celebration of nonentities … I would strongly advise you to try and acquire some genius and if possible some subtlety before the season is quite over. Top o' the morning, Mr Tzara!

Stoppard's interventions in the human-rights movement in Eastern Europe began in the mid-1970s. 'The climate was such that theatre seemed to exist for the specific purpose of commenting on our society directly,' he said later, with some irony. **Every Good Boy Deserves Favour** features a symphony orchestra; his TV play **Professional Foul** takes a professor of ethics on a morally educative trip to Prague. Neither of these two works is compromised in any way by the task of putting a message across. But in **Night and Day**, which turns its fire on the power of British trade unions (this was 1978, the year of widespread strikes, the Winter of Discontent) the polemic feels grafted on: it's of all his plays the only one you can imagine being written by somebody else.

For many years, his plays for radio had been regarded as impossible to put on stage: that was the point of them. 'As the front rank (of 1,800 marching men) reaches the bridge, the tramp-tramp of the march should start to ring hollow, progressively, as more and more leave terra firma and reach the bridge.' (**Albert's Bridge**.) 'A squadron of Cavalry gallops in quickly to occupy the foreground with a thunder of hooves; and recedes, leaving the men stunned and sobered.' (**Artist Descending a Staircase**.) **In the Native State**, broadcast in 1991, was something new. The use of sound is atmospheric rather than showy, and the filtering of the past through the eye of the present is done with a new delicacy. 'Character', till now, had never had much interest for Stoppard: he'd often joked that all the people in his plays must have been to school together, or why would they talk so alike? Here each voice has its own distinctive charm: the Fitzrovian new woman of the thirties, the elderly Indian matriarch of today. There must be something about writing about your childhood for radio in your early fifties: Stoppard's evocation of India is as rapt and sensuous as Beckett's Foxrock in **All That Fall**.

Paul Rhys,
Robert Portal and
Stephen Mapes in
The Invention
of Love.

The title of **Arcadia**, as every Elizabethan knew, has both Eden-like and deathly connotations: '*Et in Arcadia ego*', 'ego' being a skull. Death comes late in the play with the knowledge that Thomasina, the eighteenth-century mathematical genius, will burn to death on the eve of her seventeenth birthday. (Stoppard's heroines share a high mortality rate.) Her tutor Septimus, poet/intellectual, will spend the rest of his life trying to complete her calculations: they tell of the loss of heat, the sapping of earthly energy, the end of the world. In the twentieth century, such calculations can be done in a trice; what's harder, at least for Bernard the pompous modern critic, is to find the bedrock of these long-forgotten events. Who loved whom? Who killed whom in a duel? (And that's assuming a duel took place.) The past predicts the future while the present reconstructs the past. Nothing is known because nothing is stable. The end is a dream of consolation set against the reality of loss: it's heartbreaking. **The Invention of Love** is high-bar/low-bar: the grandest imaginable flights of intellectual daring pierced with simple darts of raw emotion.

Stoppard has, in later life, been much patted on the back for his 'new maturity': code for the fact that he's thought to have discovered a seam of human emotion and dropped the easy gags. The praise is doubtless kindly meant, but it always sounds a touch patronising, like the congratulations of the vicar who's just discovered that some notorious parish reprobate has finally given up the bottle. Having said which, what other playwright, after four fantastically productive decades, has entered mellow greatness? Painters do this and so do novelists and composers. Actors do it all the time. But most ageing playwrights join the paranoiacs' club: they write to the newspapers and shout at the television. The truth, almost certainly, is that too much success is good for you: stardom, sustained over year after year of hard work, gives you at least a partial invulnerability to the darts and dents of disappointment. Whatever the reason, no modern playwright since Ibsen has made such sense of late middle-age. This is Stoppard's gift to the next generation. Which isn't, in fact, much younger than him: not that it ever was.

6

Hare's rebuke to 1970s political playwrights applied with reasonable fairness both up and down the scale, but two wholly explicit political plays were beyond criticism.

In the 1960s, the South African playwright Athol Fugard (1932–) was approached for help by a black theatre group, Serpent Players, based in nearby Port Elizabeth. They had turned to theatre for the simple reason that every other way of saying what they wanted to say had been blocked by the state. Books could be censored, pamphlets seized, radio and film were out of bounds and television didn't exist. Plays were a last resort.

Fugard was already admired for his studies of South African white and so-called 'coloured' working-class life: **The Blood Knot, Hello and Goodbye** and **Boesman and Lena**. His collaboration with Serpent Players took his work on to a new level. Their first show was an adaptation of Gogol's short story 'The Coat'. The first of their shows to appear in London had a theme which Gogol would have been proud of: in an absurd society, fictitious people stand a better chance of survival than real ones.

Sizwe Bansi is Dead – created by Fugard, John Kani and Winston Ntshona – is such a profoundly moving play that it's easy not to notice how elegantly structured it is. The central image is something which both is and isn't a man: his photograph. Sizwe Bansi, a semi-literate hick, calls at a township-photographer's studio wanting a snap to send to his wife. He's quickly adorned in the props of prosperity: a hat, a pipe in his hand, a newspaper. The camera flash goes off: the play that follows is the letter that will accompany it home.

It tells, in flashback, the story of a second photograph. Sizwe finds a corpse in the road, in its pocket a passbook entitling the owner to look for work. The mugshots are swapped: Sizwe now has only to adopt the corpse's name to be eligible for a job in the city. He protests: the loss of his identity is too great a price to pay. But:

BUNTU:	Wasn't Sizwe Bansi a ghost?
SIZWE:	No!
BUNTU:	No? When the white man looked at you at the Labour Exchange, what did he see? A man with dignity or a bloody passbook with an N.I. number? Isn't that a ghost? When the white man sees you walk down the street and calls out 'Hey John! Come here!' ... to you, *Sizwe Bansi* ... isn't that a ghost? Or when his little boy calls you 'Boy' ... you, a man, circumcised, with a wife and four children ... isn't that a ghost? Stop fooling yourself. All I'm saying is be a real ghost, if that is what they want, if that is what they've turned us into. Spook them to hell, man!

*John Kani and Winston Ntshona in **Sizwe Bansi is Dead**.* Before it arrived in London, **Sizwe Bansi** had played in South Africa to huge popular audiences, in halls, squares, stadia: often in the open air. The result was a fierce explicitness in the playing, stark simplicity in the staging and buoyant wit. Kani and Ntshona are superb performers and Fugard a great director. Their next collaboration, **The Island,** was just as fine.

A persistent 1970s theme was sex. How could it not be? Sex in real life kept changing shape, like the digitally morphed monster in a modern sci-fi movie. The pill, a place of your own, gay liberation, feminism, and God knows what else seemed to be propelling it in all directions. You have to dip your toe into the '60s to find the play that defined this new, more liquid form of sexuality.

Joe Orton's **What the Butler Saw**, produced in 1969, sounds and works like farce: Dr Prentice undresses a young lady and before we know where we are the household is reduced to violence, transvestism and anarchy. But farce is built on shame and suffering. In Orton, shame is for suckers: everybody loves sex, nobody minds whether it's with a boy or a girl, and everybody knows this. The play isn't in fact a farce at all, but an example of that rare and difficult form, the burlesque: it parodies farce by using its mechanics but subverts them with the 'anything goes' sensibility of the '60s.

Orton had his first success, **Entertaining Mr Sloane**, in 1964, just as the sexual revolution was getting under way. After **Loot**, two years later, he was rich, fashionable and able to make the most of a city rippling with glamour, money and boys. He was attractive and had (he claimed) an enormous cock. Not since the great days of the blackout had sex been so easy. Never had the spirit of the times so smiled on it. For a working-class boy from Leicester, who thought that middle-class morality was humbug, this was delirium. And sexual delirium is what this curious, one-off parody is about.

Orton was killed by his lover, Kenneth Halliwell, after carelessly, or teasingly, leaving around a diary filled with baroque descriptions of his sex-life. When **What the Butler Saw** was posthumously produced, the spirit of parody was very unwisely extended to venue and casting. Sir Ralph Richardson, comparing the price of present-day rentboys with those of his youth, was a picture of uncomprehending misery. The gallery cried, 'Shame!' and it was all a disaster.

Orton died famous – 'the Oscar Wilde of the Welfare State' – but the comparison isn't a good one. Wilde was never a giggler. And there's something babyishly autocratic about the way that Orton forces his characters into his idiosyncratic design. 'You *will* do that! You *must*!' If you insist on finding parallels, his closest equivalent would be Ronald Firbank (1886–1926), author of that classic of high artifice **The Princess Zoubaroff**: long-forgotten and (ominously for Orton) never performed.

Sex got more explicit with the speed (it seemed at the time) of light. In the commercial sector, **Oh Calcutta!** was opportunistic trash. Attics and cellars produced the goods. Heathcote Williams' dazzling **AC/DC** had lingered on a pile of scripts in the Royal Court general office since pre-censorship days. It was set in a variety of typefaces, stuffed with pictures and bound in large, hard covers like a Victorian ledger: every summer, when the windows were open, the secretaries used it to stop papers blowing about. Was the problem the cluster-fuck in the photo-booth at the start of the play? Or the moment in Act Two when Sadie, the African-American diva of raised consciousness, disempowers the famous of the world by drenching their photographs in her vaginal juices? Finally produced at the Theatre Upstairs in 1970, it was applauded for its vision and Congrevian wit; the sex was seen for what it was, as part of the grander gesture.

The stakes got higher. After a noisy and excited playwrights' meeting at the Royal Court in 1971, David Hare proposed to those who were left that, rather than carry on grousing about the state of the theatre, they ought to do something practical, i.e. collaborate on a play. The result was **Lay By**, written by a historic line-up that included not only Hare himself but Howard Brenton, Brian Clark, Trevor Griffiths, Stephen Poliakoff and Snoo Wilson. In it, a naked young woman is wheeled in on a stretcher by two attendants. She has OD'd on heroin, as the stage direction makes clear. (*Dick looks up her arse. Pokes two fingers in. Takes out a screwed-up bit of baccy. Opens it and sniffs.*) They swing her about a bit. She dies. Further naked bodies are washed in blood, dumped in a bin, stirred up and turned into jam, which the attendants eat.

By this time a small and informal list existed of actors and actresses who were willing to take their clothes off for the sake of art: one tended to see the same faces, as it were, in play after play. When **What the Butler Saw** was revived at the Royal Court in 1975, no one was shocked at all.

The curious thing is that, for all the boldness of the decade, it was unerotic. There was plenty of sexual freedom ('good'), sexual degradation ('bad') and macho flashing ('very bad'), but it wasn't till 1979 that two important plays gave sex its moral and emotional value. In Martin Sherman's **Bent**, two gay men, forbidden to touch, make love in words: the dignity and sobriety of the scene made it a notable first. And Churchill's **Cloud Nine** had at its heart a middle-aged, middle-class woman's discovery of masturbation. It gives her something she's never before experienced: a sense of triumph.

Just as in any other revolutionary movement, the '70s new writers defined their radicalism in terms of the past. There was the past to follow and the past to reject. No one admitted to following Osborne – he was considered rich, right-wing and written-out – but the truth is that the coarse, enlivening impact of a leading character spouting his head off was a powerful influence. Anyone who tried to copy Samuel Beckett in terms of spectral abstractions was rightly thought an idiot, but his prose style was another matter: Pinter's influence was already profound. Bond was a powerful *éminence grise* and there were no Stoppardians. The greatest influence was Brecht.

The first British playwright to be called a Brechtian was John Arden (1930–). **Live Like Pigs**, written in 1958, was interspersed with earthy ballads, and **Serjeant Musgrave's Dance**, which followed, certainly had a Brechtian feel about it, but this was more on account of Jocelyn Herbert's spare and poetic design. This landmark play is more Utopian, more imbued with old-fashioned, Quakerish decency than anything Brecht could ever have come up with. A better candidate is Robert Bolt (1924–1995), surprisingly in a way, since by the time Bolt died he seemed a monumental middlebrow. But he was a searching writer and one of the mainstream theatre's few old-style ex-Reds.

A Man for All Seasons has the Common Man as commentator on the action and this wasn't just a way of keeping Binkie happy by keeping the cast-size down: it was a Brechtian message smuggled into Shaftesbury Avenue – even if at the heart of a rather clunking historical melodrama.

An interesting case is that of another comparative old-timer, Peter Shaffer (1926–), whose thumb on the public pulse was (and remains) sure and sensitive. In the late '50s he had a long West End run with **Five Finger Exercise**, a coded 'newcomer-upsets-the-household' drama along the lines of Turgenev's **A Month in the Country** or Pasolini's '60s movie *Teorema*. The locale is wealthy suburbia, the form of the play West-Endy. In **The Royal Hunt of the Sun**, Shaffer discovered epic scale, and his theme expanded accordingly. What before had been a minor domestic skirmish – inhibition versus sexuality – became the mythic war between Apollo and Dionysus; this would be Shaffer's theme in the years that followed, c.f. **The Battle of Shrivings**, **Equus**, **Amadeus**, and **The Gift of the Gorgon**.

The '70s writers followed Brecht in a way that was both more overt and more original. The big discovery was that the Brechtian epic had its roots in England: that Brecht's inspiration was the popular drama of the 1600s, that his ancestors were London playwright/poets, that the clue to the Brechtian style – for a British playwright – would be found, not far abroad, but in the family album.

So the version of Brecht that hit the 1970s stage had a highly Jacobean flavour to it. Lots of scenes, a sense of colour, noise and violence: it was all much more like Brecht's 'flaming cowpats' than anything Brecht himself had written after his early twenties. Soliloquies abounded; so did ghosts, heroic verse, flamboyant doubling, scenes in heaven, assaults on establishment heroes, song. The rediscovery of seventeenth-century vigour even extended to that long-neglected form, Jonsonian comedy: the breezy, biting satires of the Trinidad-born Mustapha Matura, **As Time Goes By** and **Play Mas**, were high-watermarks of the '70s.

In the early '70s, David Edgar (1948–) wrote many excellent plays on current issues – often as many as three or four a year – all of them rich in cheerful, irreverent, Brechtian devices. David Edgar has long been the champion and conscience of the socially concerned play, writing with extraordinary fluency and profusion about the significant social and political events of his time, most notably: **Mary Barnes** on schizophrenia as a psycho-social phenomenon; **Destiny**, an exploration of British fascism, exemplary in its immediacy and its depth of character, its seamless construction and its verve; **The Jail Diary of Albie Sachs**, an intensely moving indictment of apartheid; **Maydays**, a panoramic account of the politics of 1968; and two plays about the fall of Communism – **The Shape of the Table**, a dense description of the struggles involved in creating a new kind of politics in East Europe; and **Pentecost**, an epic depiction of the chaos engendered by the fragmentation of the Balkans. For many years he ran a course for theatre writing at Birmingham University, and has acted as a commentator on the state of the contemporary theatre: a polemicist of grave authority.

Howard Brenton (1942–) is the son of a policeman: a large, calm, gentle man, whose personality is in constant contradiction to his work. His plays have a sort of shaggy poetry: anarchic, full of arresting Francis Bacon-like images of pus and blood, sculpted lumpishly but vividly scarred with apocalyptic signs: **The Churchill Play**, written in 1974, foresaw a Britain where political dissidents were interned in concentration camps, and **Weapons of Happiness**, two years later, set the feebleness of English protest against the tragic passion of the East European dissidents. It was the first production to originate in the new National Theatre. **Romans in Britain** – also at the National Theatre – impacted the Roman army's invasion of Britain on the British army's occupation of Northern Ireland. It created a huge controversy for its sexual explicitness – male rape by Roman soldiers – but its political ideas, intended to shock and disturb, were absorbed by the audience in the Olivier Theatre with, for the writer, disappointing ease. His two partnerships with David Hare – **Brassneck** and **Pravda** – perfectly fused his flaming-cowpat-marksmanship with Hare's wit and lucidity; both plays were neo-Brechtian classics.

Howard Barker (1946–) stood in the Brechtian line, but took it further by giving sex the same naked energy that Brecht, accorded to money, war and power. **Stripwell**, from the mid-'70s, put middle-aged infatuation side by side with moral collapse and class revenge; **Claw** follows a working-class boy from class betrayal through to sex, political scandal and death at the hands of the Special Branch. In **Fair Slaughter**, the Russian Revolution lives on in the shape of a dismembered hand; **That Good Between Us** shows a (female) Labour Home Secretary becoming complicit in one after another repressive compromise: she ends up with a bullet in the brain. Labour compromise was the target again in **The Hang of the Gaol**, the prison an image of sunset Britain. **Victory**, written in 1983, found a metaphor for post-war betrayal in the defeat of the English Revolution, as in **Light Shining in Buckinghamshire**. In the scabrous climate of the Restoration, a Parliamentarian's widow carries about his disinterred remains: memento of a time when hopes were real … Barker's landscapes show you places you didn't expect, and his way of telling the story does the same: it's like riding a switchback over rocks.

It wasn't till the start of the '80s that the Brechtian legacy was explicitly criticised by one of the new-generation playwrights. 'Brecht always liked people to be aware that they were in a theatre,' says Horváth in **Tales from Hollywood** by Christopher Hampton (1946–). 'I said to him more than once, but Brecht, what makes you think they think they're anywhere else?'

The bouncy elegance is Hampton's hallmark. A paradox of his work is that so much of it, for all its civilised tone, celebrates the wilder sides of human nature: unorthodox love, or the artistic impulse or the life of a pre-industrial tribe on the banks of the Amazon or simple bad behaviour.

When Did You Last See My Mother?, written when Hampton was still an undergraduate, was a first play devised (like so many) to provide a stonking part for the author: a Schillerian anti-hero who provocatively seduces his best friend's mother. The part was played at the Royal Court by Victor Henry, a fiery working-class icon of the '60s; in Hampton's next salute to the romantic temperament, **Total Eclipse**, Henry was an unforgettable Rimbaud. (The part DiCaprio plays in the movie.) Hampton was by then considered a Royal Court writer, though his urbane style and literary interests meant a certain re-drawing of the definition. But the title page of **The Philanthropist**, describing the play as 'A Bourgeois Comedy', caused a tremor, and the play itself – a sparkling variation of Molière's **The Misanthrope**, set in the world of Oxford dons, boasting no social or political purpose whatsoever, did nothing to calm it. It was a huge success and made Hampton's reputation. **Savages** consolidated it: his only play to deal with contemporary political issues.

Throughout the 1970s, Hampton avoided succumbing to any of the crude categorisations of the day: political/non-political, serious/frivolous, left wing/right wing, etc. **Tales from Hollywood** is a homage to a playwright who was equally unaligned: the Austro-Hungarian Ödön von Horváth (1901–1938). Horváth, Brecht's contemporary, was in almost every way his opposite. He was a good listener rather than a good talker, he wasn't a Communist and he had a horror of spelling out the message. His death was unusual. Driven out of Austria by the Nazis, he was told by a fortune-teller in Amsterdam that the greatest adventure of his life awaited him in Paris. Horváth, who was deeply superstitious, at once left for Paris, where the prediction appeared to come true in the form of an invitation to meet the movie director Robert Siodmak in order to discuss a screen-writing job in Hollywood. The meeting took place; on his way back to his hotel, Horváth popped into a cinema to see *Snow White and the Seven Dwarfs* and then proceeded down the Champs-Elysées. A storm arose; he sheltered beneath a tree, was hit by a falling branch and died instantly.

Hampton's proposition is that the branch missed him: that Horváth sails to America, joins the West Coast *émigré* community and works in movies. In a crucial exchange with a mistress, he speaks for the playwright who, in **The Philanthropist**, wrote what Tom Stoppard once described as his favourite speech: 'My trouble is, I'm a man of no convictions. *(Longish pause.)* At least, I think I am.' From **Tales from Hollywood**:

HELEN:	No commitments, uh?
HORVÁTH:	Yes, maybe.
HELEN:	Feel the same about politics as you do about people?
HORVÁTH:	I like to keep … freedom of action, yes. Also I have very bad experiences with joinings. All kinds.
HELEN:	So you've given up. Too old, right?
HORVÁTH:	I think a writer must be always outside. You tell better the truth from standing looking in the window than from sitting at the table.

Late in the play, Brecht invites him to collaborate on a script. Delicately but firmly, Horváth turns him down. 'I knew we'd never be able to work together,' he tells us.

Hampton's Laclos adaptation, **Les Liaisons Dangereuses**, was a blissful hit with bittersweet results: the success of the movie meant that Hampton, who had worked for years on screenplays which remained unproduced, found himself massively bankable. Many movie-writing and movie-directing assignments followed, but only one play: the autobiographical charmer **White Chameleon**.

That the New Wave was overwhelmingly male will be obvious to anyone who has read this far. To this extent, the '70s were merely repeating the pattern of the past: when **Owners** opened in the Theatre Upstairs in 1971, Caryl Churchill was the first woman playwright to have her work produced in the main bill at the Royal Court since Ann Jellicoe, whose first play, **The Sport of My Mad Mother**, dated from 1956. The enfranchisement of women had a long way to go. There were, by the '70s, a few leading woman directors: one of them, Buzz Goodbody, revolutionised the RSC with a string of committed, small-scale classics before her tragically early death. There were many woman designers, though no woman lighting designers. Woman playwrights remained a small and often brusquely treated minority.

In 1976 Pam Gems' **Dusa, Fish, Stas and Vi** introduced a wise and powerful voice: her **Queen Christina** followed a year later, a deserved success at the RSC. Andrea Dunbar's **The Arbor** at the end of the '70s was a luminous, heartfelt growing-up play set on the Buttershaw estate in Bradford. It had been teased out of the teenage writer by one of her schoolteachers and was written in an exercise book, with large spaces left between the speeches. One scene – a fight in which half the estate gets involved, not to mention the police – seemed incomplete; Max Stafford-Clark, who directed the play, suggested that more speeches could be written to fill in the gaps. They were and the scene is now a classic of multiple action. But there were limits to what she could do. 'Perhaps the policeman can say something here,' suggested Stafford-Clark. 'No he can't, because he was round the corner and I couldn't hear him.' But too much talk about the help Dunbar was given is to obscure the point: she had a rare and honest talent. After **The Arbor**, she returned to the Buttershaw estate; she died of a brain haemorrhage in her local pub at the age of twenty-nine, leaving three children and three plays.

It wasn't till the 1980s that woman playwrights appeared in number: Louise Page: **Salonika**; Sarah Daniels: **Ripen Our Darkness, Neap Tide**, with a new perspective: raunchy, puritan, out-lesbian; Clare McIntyre, and Timberlake Wertenbaker, with a trio of timely and questioning works: **The Grace of Mary Traverse**, **Three Birds Alighting in a Field** and **Our Country's Good**, which ten years later proved to be a genuine stayer.

The marvel is that the movement hadn't gone further in the previous decade. But the achievements of the 1970s were not negligible: there was a new directness about political and social issues, and new theatres prospered – often small, poky, and unprepossessing but theatres nonetheless. There was also the opening of a large, grandiose and, from the perspective of the regional theatre, unnervingly expensive theatre complex: the new National Theatre on the South Bank: **This Theatre Is Yours**, said a poster to a hugely sceptical public.

A new generation of ambitious and assertive playwrights had taken on new forms, new kinds of staging, and used language, music, and design with a vivid inventiveness. And the spontaneous explosion was underwritten by an Arts Council which was able, financially and philosophically, to play the role of the unappreciated protector of the ungrateful young. The mood was ebullient. Bliss it was to be alive.

In the 1980s the theatre, as much as any other area of British life, became infected by the virus of opportunism. A kind of impatience grew. Actors who might previously have been content to do a year or two in a regional theatre looked anxiously for parts on TV, in films, or the national companies. Casting directors proliferated, talent brokers spotting actors at drama schools, prematurely promoting their talents and adding to their impatience with the previous *de facto* forms of apprenticeship.

The RSC expanded to mimic the new National Theatre, the resources to the regions and to small companies dwindled, and a generation of directors stayed at the two large national companies without ever running regional theatres. A new ethos emerged: younger directors seemed to lack the interest of the previous generation in nursing new writing, in running companies and in nurturing new acting talent. A haphazard empirical process was lost, and lost too was the unspoken sense of shared experience that used to exist between theatres in Newcastle, Nottingham, Exeter, Manchester, Liverpool, Glasgow and London. Soon the cocky optimism of the '70s seemed as remote as the Roaring '20s.

*Michael Gambon and Ian McDiarmid in **Tales from Hollywood**: 'But, Brecht, what makes you think they think they are anywhere else?'*

319

Popularity

'Surely the only thing that is not permissible these days is to lose the audience.'
TREVOR NUNN

1

Mass entertainment is an invention of our century. As to whether it's been a curse or a blessing, as Chou En-lai said of the French Revolution, it's too early to know. The ability to reproduce art and the invention of 'multimedia' has given countless millions of people the opportunity to experience and enjoy music, drama and the visual arts. It has also created, as a reaction, an avant-garde which has often taken refuge in obscurity and self-absorption, encouraging an audience to equate comprehensibility with vulgarity. Thus the peasants – the 'mass' – are locked out by the abbots, and peer through the monastery windows at the monks transcribing illuminated manuscripts in a scriptorium.

In the theatre, at one end of the spectrum, musicals have embraced a large audience on a broad social base and have been cloned all over the globe; at the other end, intimate confessional plays have been presented as sacramental offerings in small cellars. But even the most unambitious theatre has been chafed into self-examination about its physical conditions and the composition of its audience.

Whatever its form, the theatre will always provoke accusations of elitism: it's done by only a few gifted and skilful performers to an audience limited by the number of people who can sit in an auditorium at any one time, and that audience is usually drawn from a narrow social group. But to call theatre 'elitist' is only justified if the work seeks to obscure rather than illuminate, if the actors are reluctant to communicate, or if the theatre repels a potential audience through excessively high prices or a selectively exclusive attitude to the public.

Throughout the century efforts have been made to rid the British theatre of its 'elitist' tag: by Lilian Baylis at the Old Vic, by Joan Littlewood, by many if not most subsidised theatres, and by protagonists of 'popular theatre' – a definition that belongs to the musical leviathans produced by Cameron Mackintosh as well as to any number of shows produced by small politically evangelical companies.

No discussion of the aims of theatre can be divorced from a recognition of one of its inherent properties. To be blunt: size matters. The relationship between audience and actors is like a nuclear reactor – there has to be a critical mass of people in an auditorium for a 'state of theatre' to exist. The size of the critical mass varies with the size and shape of the auditorium; in the Olivier Theatre, which holds 1,160 people, a few hundred can feel as dismal as a convention of Druids on a wet summer solstice, whereas in the Royal Court the same number of people can create perfect conditions for theatrical detonation.

It is an equally invariable natural law that most plays that involve the audience in a conspiracy to accept the fourth wall do not thrive in large auditoriums – the nuances of vocal and facial expression vaporise in the vast void. Actors are always uneasy when they are obliged by the greed of theatre-owners and impresarios, or the need to satisfy the politics of government funding, to play on overlarge stages in inflated auditoriums.

It's a fair guess that Shakespeare's Globe was designed by actors, and it's a fair guess that, unlike the misproportioned re-creation by Southwark Bridge, there was a warm contact between the stage and the densely packed spectators, uninhibited by fire regulations or fears of intruding on a neighbour's 'space'.

In the candlelit proscenium theatres of the seventeenth and eighteenth centuries the intimacy between actors and audience (and audience members) was every bit as intense. A profusion of small playhouses flourished until the Theatres Act of 1737 created the 'legitimate' theatre by licensing the performance of spoken drama by only two companies, one in Covent Garden, the other in Drury Lane. Serious theatre in the US has continued to be known, quaintly, as 'legitimate' theatre.

The first Drury Lane theatre was built by Christopher Wren in 1674 for an audience of less than 1,000. Sheridan's **School for Scandal** and **The Rivals** were first performed there, and with their success Sheridan became rich enough to buy a majority share in the theatre. There was a greater appetite for plays than could be met by the two companies, and it was exasperating for playwright and managers to be unable to satisfy the demand, so both theatres were expanded in the 1790s – Covent Garden to 3,000 seats and Drury Lane to a capacity of 3,600. A contemporary playwright, Richard Chamberlain remarked:

> Since the stages of Drury Lane and Covent Garden had been so enlarged in their dimensions as to be henceforward theatres for spectators rather than playhouses for hearers, it is hardly to be wondered at if managers and directors encourage those representations to which their structure is best adapted.

His words were prophetic: the consequence of expanding the auditorium, apart from encouraging histrionic acting, forced vocal projection, spectacle and social event, was to deprive playwrights of a stage for plays that had any kind of intimacy, and that dealt with relationships with any complexity or ambiguity.

Sheridan, who had produced little since his earlier successes, having been diverted by politics and (largely unsuccessful) money-making ventures, staged a melodramatic spectacle incurring 'wonderful expense' in the new theatre in 1798. The play, called **Pizzaro**, was based on, or borrowed from, a German play called **The Spaniards in Peru**; like its successor in the Drury Lane theatre in the 1990s, **Miss Saigon**, it sought to assault the audience with spectacular visual effects, sensational staging – processions and Inca ceremonies – emotive music and declamatory acting. It was, 'More Sound than Sense – forced violent Situations, and everything brought forward to seize the imagination – Judgement has nothing to do in the business,' said the wife of the Lord Chamberlain's examiner of plays.

With the enlargement of the theatres the distinction between what was good for profit and what was good for art began to become more conspicuous. It was not until the next century, with the arrival of Shaw and Granville-Barker, that the priorities started to be reversed, and a large number of smaller theatres were built – although with the conception of the cavernous Olivier Theatre, it was clear that the lesson still hadn't been learned.

In 1809 the Drury Lane theatre burned down (to be replaced with an only slightly smaller theatre), watched from a nearby coffee-house by a philosophical, possibly mournful and probably drunk Sheridan, who wryly observed: 'A man may surely take a glass of wine by his own fireside.'

2

The term 'popular theatre' tends to be used proscriptively by its protagonists – be it producers of musicals in the West End of London or community shows in the Highlands of Scotland. Both categories of theatre could be said to be for people who don't go to the theatre and as such provide a rare bridge between high and low culture. That is all they have in common apart from mutual contempt: the theatre 'of the people' – meaning political theatre, meaning socialist theatre – being regarded by the one as *un*popular and inept, the theatre of 'pure entertainment' being regarded by the other much as a Michelin chef looks at a Big Mac.

Political theatre activists talk possessively of 'community theatre' as if by virtue of political commitment they had unique access to the hearts and minds of their audience – as it were 'the gay community', 'the Afro-Caribbean community', 'the working class', and so on. Except in the sense of a group of individuals becoming a community in the course of watching a successful piece of theatre, most people resist being categorised in this reductive manner.

However, if we were to apply this self-righteous jargon, Alan Ayckbourn (1938–) would have to be construed the most successful 'community playwright' in Britain. He was also incidentally the second most performed playwright in the world in the 1980s after Shakespeare. Ayckbourn serves his community as conscientiously as any self-proclaimed political playwright and within no less narrow (or no less wide) social parameters. His constituency is middle England – middle class, middlebrow – the heartland of British theatre audiences. He does not patronise his public, but then neither does he placate it, for his plays are often crammed with anxiety about social indignities and sexual dysfunction, full of lives of quiet misery and small ambition.

Ayckbourn's plays are staged all over Britain, North America, Europe East and West, and are filmed in French by Alain Resnais. Ayckbourn is director of a company in the Yorkshire seaside town of Scarborough, and each year he has teetered precipitously on the edge of catastrophe by finishing his plays sometimes only hours before the first rehearsal, driving round Scarborough at midnight to deliver scripts to anxious actors, having them snatched from his hand as he feeds them through the letterbox, like horses grabbing for carrots. For thirty years he has written and staged a new play – in a theatre-in-the-round – as part of his season, and almost invariably the following year that play has transferred to the West End (to a proscenium theatre).

The plays are about reclusive but not bloodless people who contain their emotions and fear confrontation – the sort of people that the French imagine the entire British nation is composed of. Ayckbourn's titles describe his social landscape: **Round and Round the Garden, Table Manners, Living Together, A Small Family Business, Relatively Speaking, How the Other Half Loves, Woman in Mind, Man of the Moment, Out of Mind, Absurd Person Singular, Just Between Ourselves, Time and Time Again** … and more. Fifty-seven of them.

Like many writers of light comedy – Flann O'Brien or P.G. Wodehouse, for instance – he presents an almost entirely hermetic world, in which events outside the play never intrude. There is an abstract quality to his work, on which audiences print their own sensations. On the page, the plays aren't witty, they're rarely touching, and are sometimes mechanistic, but in the theatre, playing to their constituency, they have an irrefutable potency.

The technique is dazzling, mathematically intricate plots of accidents, misunder-standings, and physical incompetencies woven into farcical extremity. Occasionally, as with all farce, the plays seem small-hearted or heartless; the plot logic unimpeachable, the emotional logic opaque.

Ayckbourn has the appetite and the ingenuity of an obsessional games player, a restless inventiveness with formal devices – sixteen alternative endings in **Intimate Exchanges**, three alternative endings in **Sisterly Feelings**, decided during the performance by a toss of a coin, simultaneous action in three bedrooms in **Bedroom Farce**, simultaneous action in two different *auditoriums* in **House** and **Garden** – one on a proscenium stage, the other in the round.

At his best and most characteristic – **The Norman Conquests** – he never lets the demands of farce over-ride the plausibility of events, consequently he never transgresses the binding laws of farce that insist that the characters must act within a doggedly consistent reality. Over three separate plays, each set in a different part of the house during the same period of time, he shows a group of people struggling frantically to preserve social niceties while despair creeps in like a spring tide. Like all farce it's about class and sex; it's funny and sad and, in its cool, mild-mannered way, a dyspeptic critique of family life.

Family life:
The Norman Conquests.

No one who saw **Small Family Business** in 1987 could claim that Ayckbourn was apolitical: the play was situated at the epicentre of the heartland of Thatcherism – a small family business – and offered an acerbic view of the social corrosion of the very people that Thatcher was alleged to be enriching. Ayckbourn is an observer, a social anthropologist, not a social emancipator, and few people now believe that society can be changed through theatre; it defies observed experience.

Ayckbourn's personality is hidden in his plays, Alan Bennett's is on show everywhere: there is no playwright who is so liked by the public, and so thought of as one of the family, and, like Coward, as quintessentially English.

'One hesitates to talk of Lawrence and his body,' says the Headmaster in **Forty Years On**, 'though the two were inseparable.' He's talking about T.E., the empire-building closet-masochist, rather than the D.H. who bared all in *Lady Chatterley's Lover*, so the joke is a sly, presumptuous one. It seems equally sly and presumptuous to mix up Alan Bennett the writer with Alan Bennett the man: what does it matter who wrote the plays, or the masterly TV films? The truth is that they're also inseparable: no playwright since Noël Coward has made his writing such a forceful, forthright channel for his own sensibility. It's true, as you'll discover if you read his marvellous diaries, that he's often to be found, notebook in hand, jotting down remarks he's heard on the bus or in the supermarket. It just so happens that everyone he overhears sounds exactly like a character in an Alan Bennett play; his reward is that everyone feels they know him.

He was born in Leeds in 1934. His father was a butcher, his mother (no doubt) the dearly loved, mildly exasperating figure whose complicated household routines, eye for class-giveaways and surrealistic leaps of logic inform so much of his writing. Later, she lost her mind: he would write about this, in one form and another, right up to the present day. He did National Service and then studied at Oxford, where he stayed on as a junior lecturer in Modern History until the revue **Beyond the Fringe** made him a comedy star, along with his collaborators Peter Cook, Jonathan Miller and Dudley Moore. His first play, **Forty Years On**, produced in 1968, was a direct continuation of the skits and sketches he performed in these early years. It comes in a host of rather similar middle- and upper-class voices: old-buffer-speak, literary mandarin-speak, don-speak, Bloomsbury-speak.

'Speaking properly', he calls it: the language of the metropolis, as opposed to the saltier, warm, demotic English that surrounded him as a child. His mastery of both languages is total but they seldom appear together. In fact they seldom even appear in the same medium: with only one exception, he writes for the stage in Southern English and reserves his Northern voice for television. That's one reason why, even in a book which is nominally about the theatre, his television work must be included. It's part of the jigsaw.

His career has an unusual shape. Most playwrights put a conceptual frame around each of their plays: if they've dealt with football (say) in play A, they'll probably avoid the subject in play B. Exceptions are the occasional grand diptych (**Angels in America**) and the trilogy (Hare, Wesker): generational milestones, all of them. Bennett works to a longer, slower clock than other playwrights. Once he's interested in something, he stays interested for many years and, throughout that time, whatever he writes will have at least some bearing on it. So reading his plays in sequence is like scanning the work of a painter who's moved, in no great hurry, from a favourite model to a favourite landscape to an interesting change of the light. 'There's that window again,' you think, moving from one canvas to the next. 'But now it's sunny outside. And there's that goldfish bowl.'

You notice it in small ways with the reappearance of minor characters: the anxious social worker, the vicar, the remote but courteous Asian. Props are recycled again and again: a lunch consisting only of an apple and a piece of cheese recurs over many years as code for a blinkered denial of the senses. (The persistence of hang-gliding, 'Pedro the Fisherman' and man-made fibres is harder to crack.) Hospitals are everywhere, not surprisingly given the omnipresence of senility and death.

Bennett was never thought of as a 1970s political playwright – he was far too funny and popular – so it's odd to discover him taking on two of the big political themes of the day before almost anyone else got to them. **Forty Years On** is a valedictory pageant of the Edwardian twilight very much in tune with the mood of 'Last orders on the Titanic', though written seven years earlier. He stuck with this theme in his first television film, **A Day Out** in 1972: it shows a working-class cycling trip on the eve of the First World War: the mood is summery, pastoral, doomed.

325

After this and for many years, he set his stories in the context of the modern Welfare State. Bennett's take on it was to show institutional care as deficient, not in funding or efficiency, but in heart. Life exists in family, love, sex, even in memory. 'Caring' may be needed, but it's sterile. **Me, I'm Afraid of Virginia Woolf** places a sexual flowering in the humdrum world of adult education. In **Intensive Care** the sexual flowering is prompted by the institutionalised death of a parent. **All Day on the Sands** introduces the core Bennett theme of living a lie. Young Colin, on holiday with his mum and dad, exposes their shameful secret: Dad is unemployed. **Marks** shows a sweet, not-very-bright boy falling through the DHSS safety-net: in the final shot we discover that he's become a rentboy.

In all these scripts, the story-telling takes its time, there's plenty of slack for enjoyable detour and the cast-lists are enormous, with many of the characters having only a line or two to say. So you never feel that the script's been 'knocked into shape' or had any of the other vile things done to it that scripts endure today. In those days, TV drama was generous and baggy; it suited Bennett down to the ground. His later, small-scale TV work – the **Talking Heads** cycle – is just as formally secure. Each time, a character tells their side of the story: through their words, or even in spite of them, we glimpse the truth.

In theatre, he's moved from form to form, never quite settling. His second play, **Getting On**, continued the theme of Labour disillusion. It looks and even sounds to the lazy ear like a conventional West End boulevard comedy, so it wasn't until the Brighton try-out that the star (Kenneth More) discovered that his character was in fact a selfish bastard. Hasty cuts and rewrites followed, to facilitate which the author was barred from the theatre. When the play was named 'Best Comedy of 1971', Bennett, who had never thought of it as a comedy at all, was taken aback: 'It's like entering a marrow for the vegetable-competition and being given the cucumber prize,' he announced, statuette in hand. In his next stage play, **Habeas Corpus**, he plumped for a style so bold and assertive that not even the thickest Garrick club member could misunderstand it. On an open stage, with three chairs for scenery, a fantasia of sexual awakening is enacted in seaside-postcard style. 'You've got it,' is the message, 'so you'd better use it.' In the words of Dr Wicksteed:

> Don't tell me you wouldn't, given the choice
> Old men with schoolgirls, ladies with boys
> If she's what I fancy you really can't quarrel
> 'Cos given the chance you'd be just as immoral.

It's the cleaner, Mrs Swabb, who points to the Arcadian skull:

> The smoothest cheek will wrinkle
> The proudest breast will fall.
> Some sooner go, some later
> But death will claim us all.

The woman-as-truth-teller is a persistent Bennett character. She's generally older than those around her, always capable both of wisdom and absurdity, always witty: comic understatement, knowing nuance, artfully structured sentences are in her blood. A comic sibyl.

In her original incarnation she was Northern, petit-bourgeois, morbidly obsessed with local transport and the state of her bowels. ('My stomach's on a knife-edge.') But over the years she's gone up in the world. (This progression is quite common amongst really great semi-fictional creations: Dame Edna Everage started life as a mild Australian housewife.) **A Woman of No Importance** found her shifting up the social scale to office-worker: she was much less fun this way. She returned in glory in **An Englishman Abroad** as the actress and wit, Coral Browne: glamorous, confident, smart, but nevertheless the moral touchstone, just as she always was. In **A Question of Attribution** she appears as no less a figure than Her Majesty the Queen. She could hardly go much higher, and indeed she didn't: **The Lady in the Van** finds her camping in Alan Bennett's driveway, filthy with excrement and quite insane, though with her vividness undimmed. Bennett's mam appears beside her. 'She should be in a home,' she comments. But Mam too is dotty by now, as Bennett the writer – or Bennett the son – is only too well aware:

> It's like a fairy-story, a parable in which the guilty is gulled into devising a sentence for someone innocent, only to find it is their own doom they have pronounced. Because my mother is much closer to being put in a home than Miss Shepherd.

Nigel Hawthorne in **The Madness of George III**.

The royal family had been one of Alan Bennett's recurring themes ever since his early TV plays, so it was bound to bump into his other preoccupations sooner or later. No member of the Windsor clan has yet had tea in a Lyons Corner House with Franz Kafka, even though Bennett has written about this enigmatic writer twice, in **Kafka's Dick** and **The Insurance Man**. But royalty and another Bennett theme – insanity – met up triumphantly in his international hit, **The Madness of George III**.

In some ways it's an untypical play. Bennett's quirkiness is subdued, his liking for parody is reined in hard, the oddities of detail are suppressed. The play's great strength is that it rests on a highly theatrical calculation. Everyone knows that George III went mad. What nobody knows is that he went mad more than once: not just at the end of his life, but in the middle of it. And it's this mid-life episode that forms the action.

So Bennett delivers a stunning surprise. We expect the King's decline to lead to a wretched death. Instead, halfway through the second act, his mind clears, he dismisses his brutal, arrogant doctors (a scene which never fails to produce a 'whoosh!' of delight from the audience) and the play ends happily. Madness will follow, and so will death. But not just yet.

King George is bluff, transparent, guileless. At the opposite end of Bennett's spectrum is a figure whose guilelessness is all guile, whose transparency is an optical illusion, whose bluffness is merely a bluff. He's the spy.

We meet him in disguised form in play after play: the night-school teacher of **Me, I'm Afraid of Virginia Woolf**, conducting a perfectly effective affair with his robust girlfriend while moving, amoeba-like, into the arms of an attractive male student; in the countless sons of formidable mothers, never quite saying what's on their mind; wherever passivity equals deception. Overtly, we meet him in three major works: **The Old Country**, **An Englishman Abroad** (about Guy Burgess) and **A Question of Attribution** (about Anthony Blunt).

The Old Country opens with 'a very English scene': a verandah overflowing with books, a middle-aged man dozing in a rocking-chair, an Elgar record playing in an adjoining room. But it's a fake: we're in the Soviet Union. Hilary is about to be taken back to Britain, there to face the music for his espionage activities. In a marvellous passage, he describes the routine of spying: how, in order to meet his contact, he would travel to obscure, end-of-the-tube-line suburbs which, as a Foreign Office official, he would normally never dream of visiting. It was the very ordinariness of these locales, he says, that made them so exotic:

> A little man on the loose. Past the ideal homes and Green Line bus stops. Factory sportsfields lined with poplars. I was so *happy*. Is it still unloved, that landscape? I loved it. Boarding kennels, down-at-heel riding schools, damp bungalows in wizened orchards. The metropolis trailing off into those forlorn enterprises. Had my superiors been blessed with irony I might have thought the setting deliberately chosen to point up the folly of individual endeavour. As it was I grew fond of it. And just as well. Shacks, allotments, dead ground.

The disjunction between where you are and who you are, or who you are and what you appear to be, is what lies at the heart of Bennett's writing. There's a striking entry in his diaries:

> Sunderland. An old-fashioned shoe-shop. High ladders and shelves piled with shoeboxes. Feeling this is what a genuine writer would do, I make a note of the labels.

Alan Bennett.

A *genuine* writer? He was already famous. Nevertheless, he's not quite sure. He feels he may be who he claims to be, or he may be a fake. Or is it the world around him that is fake, like the phoney English verandah in the heart of the Soviet Union, or the little terraced family home of **Enjoy**, doomed to double up as a heritage-museum of Northern life? Or the Oxford colleges which Bennett, from a totally different background, found so strangely unreal:

> I somehow regarded the nightly experience of dining in hall as a kind of theatre, a theatre in which the undergraduates were the audience and the actors were the dons … Exeter was still in the age of the proscenium arch, with the dons entering left in single file … while at Magdalen they entered through the body of the hall as if directed by Ariane Mnouchkine or some fashionable young man from the RSC.

329

The spy exists with equal authenticity in two opposing worlds, while feeling authentic in neither. He moves back and forth, observing, recording, seeing without being seen. He can even (as Burgess was constantly doing) reveal his secret from time to time, knowing that no one will take it entirely seriously.

In Bennett's only Northern stage play, **Enjoy**, the echoes of spying are all-pervasive. A long-lost son returns to the home of his elderly parents in the role of social worker. He wears convincing drag and doesn't speak in their presence. Left alone in the parlour, he/she describes the objects on the mantelpiece:

> One clock in light oak, presented to Mam's father after forty years with Greenwood and Batley. Stopped; the key lost. A wooden candlestick that's never seen a candle. A tube of ointment for a skin complaint that cleared up after one application. An airmail letter, two years old, announcing the death of a cousin in Perth, Western Australia, the stamp torn off. Two half-crowns not cashed at decimalisation because Mam read in the *Evening News* that one day they would be priceless. Four old halfpennies kept on the same principle. A dry Biro.

And so on: the speech is one of the most felt and beautiful things Bennett has ever written. In his notes on the play, he deals sharply with the critic James Fenton for referring to the social worker as 'the writer'. (As though 'I cherished a shamefaced longing to climb into twinset and pearls'.) But the gender-swap has a meaning, even if not the obvious one.

Silent and in disguise, the son can return to his childhood home without being recognised. It's like those childhood fantasies of being invisible: free to prowl the house, open drawers, read letters. It's also like those grown-up fantasies in which emotions are no longer burdensome. The son can listen, watch, observe the people he loves, or used to, safe in the knowledge that nobody knows he's there. And that he will soon escape.

Success in the commercial theatre depends on a cast of middle-class characters, a low intellectual level and a generally agreeable tone of voice. That's the conventional view: it harks back to some dim recollection of the West End of the 1950s and persists into the present day. Nothing seems to dent this nonsensical notion, not even the hugely successful dramatisation of *Trainspotting*. So it's not surprising that it survived those challenging playwrights who invaded Shaftesbury Avenue theatre in the 1960s and '70s.

No one could call Peter Nichols (1927–) an agreeable writer. He's a prodigiously entertaining one, with a bagful of excellent jokes. But the jokes are irritants: like the itchy powder that schoolboys used to buy by mail-order, they bring up a rash. His autobiography, *Feeling You're Behind*, evokes his father, a Bristol salesman of grocery sundries, whose showy addiction to puns, gags and comic ditties was the despair of all around him. Perhaps this is what robbed the son's comedic genius of its innocence.

Whatever the reason, the funnier Nichols is, the more he conveys disillusion, frustration and guilt. **A Day in the Death of Joe Egg**, in vaudeville style, reveals the murderous impatience of the parents of a disabled child. Charm and pathos are firmly excluded from this 1967 semi-autobiography, just as they are from his Bristol memoir **Forget-Me-Not Lane**, and his studies of wracked marriage **Chez Nous** and **Passion Play**. **Privates on Parade**, based on his National Service days in a song-and-dance unit, links horny youth, unsettling camp and national decline: it forms a bridge between his private plays and his large-scale public ones. These include **The National Health** and **The Freeway**, as well as **Poppy**, a fierce attack on Britain's Opium Wars, set in the world of Victorian panto. The mix, in 1983, was seen as uneasy or just plain wrong. What has a vile imperial war to do with principal boys and songsheets? But comedy of discomfort had been Nichols' style ever since **Joe Egg**: if the laughs get under your skin, it's because they're *meant* to.

The fact that Peter Nichols and Michael Frayn (1933–) look so alike – indeed, are often mistaken for each other – is a visual gag which you can imagine appearing in a play by either. In Nichols, it would be a comic routine with a sting in its tail: credit withheld or blame unjustly given. In Frayn, it would have the effect of reducing personality to something both more concentrated and more typical of itself: since all playwrights do the same job, perhaps they *all* look identical.

Frayn's great hit of the early eighties, **Noises Off**, is that rare thing, a classic farce guaranteed to reduce the audience to a helpless jelly in any language, any city of the world and any production, just as long as the stage-directions are adhered to. But it's a highly intellectual construct. The off-stage actors and their on-stage alter egos are as artificial as each other, their world is as self-referential as higher maths and the disasters into which they walk are neither the messy accidents of life, nor the primitive farce mechanics that Frayn is parodying: they're as carefully orchestrated as twelve-tone music.

Copenhagen, produced in 1998, is a close relation. The physicist Heisenberg is working for Hitler, either to build a Nazi nuclear bomb or (as he claims) to delay it. Visiting his old tutor Niels Bohr, he produces a formulation as graceful, and as abstract, as anything in his own equations – or in **Noises Off**.

> Now Bohr's an electron. He's wandering about the city somewhere in the darkness, no one knows where. He's here, he's there, he's everywhere and nowhere. Up in Faelled Park, down at Carlsberg. Passing City Hall, out by the harbour. I'm a photon. A quantum of light. I'm dispatched into the darkness to find Bohr. And I succeed, because I manage to collide with him … But what's happened? Look – he's been slowed down, he's been deflected! He's no longer doing exactly what he was so maddeningly doing when I walked into him!

Of course he isn't. Heisenberg's theory of uncertainty – as the play so elegantly explains – dictates that anything under observation will change its course as a direct result of being observed. If that's the case, can *anything* be observed with any accuracy, be it the movement of particles or the interplay of human motive? A parallel question: is there a popular audience willing to ponder such difficult questions? A hit at the National Theatre, **Copenhagen** moved seamlessly to the West End, for a successful run.

Simon Gray (1936–) is of all living playwrights the one whose work is invariably likeable. It's a paradox, because his tone is sharp, his politics unregenerate, his central characters often rumpled wrecks whose alcohol intake is auto-destructive and whose nicotine consumption is probably poisoning half the street. Gray's canon is enormous; behind it lies a kind of ghost-play, the cast of which appears in one play after another, swapping roles, suits and moustaches like an over-worked repertory company. There are, or appear to be, two leading men, one a flamboyant, clever, sexually exploitative show-off. He exasperates his wife, he disappoints his mistresses, he skives at work. There's an opposite figure, at times a diligent family man, more often an obvious loser. He's sometimes a brother, sometimes a childhood friend. Homosexuality is a constant theme, but it never erupts between the louche authorial figure and the prissy one. More to the point is the awkward closeness between two heterosexual Englishmen whose friendship is based on the fact that they were lovers as boys. Teachers are a different matter. Can they keep their hands off their attractive charges? Well, just about.

His early plays, **Wise Child** and **Dutch Uncle**, were grotesques in the Orton manner: this wasn't Gray's style. In **Butley**, which appeared in 1971, he seemed to be playing by the West End rules: the setting was academia, the plot adulterous, the dialogue breezily erudite. What was different, though nobody noticed it at the time, was the way in which Gray had appropriated the classicism of Racine. We see a character in a room: doors open, people enter and leave, and by a remorseless accumulation of incident, that character's doom is sealed. Nothing could be more perfect, or so you'd think. But **Otherwise Engaged** is even better: the basic proposition, which is that the selfish hero merely wants to listen undisturbed to *Parsifal*, is more insolently trivial, the tragedy is more understated, the violence kept more firmly off-stage in the classical style. **Quartermaine's Terms** takes classicism to extremes by placing the violence – adultery, murder, blackmail – *entirely* off-stage. Before us, through the eyes of a mild, good-humoured, unsuccessful tutor of English, nothing happens at all. It's strange that a playwright whose home subject is emotional dishevelment should write his masterpieces within the confines of a puritanical form. But there it is: emotion is nothing without restraint.

3

Many people in Britain in the post-war period have used the theatre to rehearse for social change if not to bring it about; none have achieved the synthesis of theory and practice of the Brazilian director Augusto Boal, through many have tried to emulate him. He was born in Brazil in 1931 and trained as a chemical engineer. He ran a theatre in São Paulo for fifteen years until he fell foul of the military government, was dismissed and then developed his 'Newspaper Theatre', which distilled news into theatre on a daily basis. He was imprisoned and tortured, exiled to Argentina then to Peru.

In Argentina, under another dictatorship, Boal conceived 'Invisible Theatre' in order to avoid detection by the police: plays were rehearsed in secret and presented in public places – markets, restaurants, trains – to people unaware that they were an audience. In Peru, Boal developed a theatre for the people in which the people were genuine participants.

Theatre divides into the few who do and the many who watch; it serves as a model for political power – few do and many are done to. With his 'poetics of the oppressed', Boal gave power to the audience, offering them the possibility of changing the outcome of a play by suggesting endings that the actors would then improvise – actors and audience participating in a model of democratic debate. 'While some people make theatre,' he said, 'we all are theatre.'

Which is exactly what Joan Littlewood was trying to create in the 1960s, with her project for a kind of giant tent dedicated to the culture of the people, 'a space where everybody might learn and play; where there could be every kind of entertainment, classical and ad lib, arty and scientific; where you could dabble in paint or clay; attend scientific lectures and demonstrations; argue; show off; or watch the world go by. It should be by a river.' She called it a Fun Palace; its muted progeny on a site by the Thames in Greenwich – called the Millennium Dome – mocks her memory.

Littlewood was still trying in 1973 to convince a tenant's association in Greenwich that they needed the Fun Palace:

> 'I've nothing against culture,' said the rough oldie, 'so long as you don't touch our bowling green.' I gave him my word and talked on, simply and directly, telling them about my fears for the next generation. 'Popular education is declining and so is government planning. We cannot afford to waste human talent. There is unexplored talent in each child. Let's get our priorities straight.' I appealed to them as citizens of a land where once untaught artisans had challenged the state and won …

Anxiety about 'wasting human talent' was in the wind and the water in the 1970s. There was no shortage of actors, writers and directors who, as George Devine urged, chose their theatres as they would choose their religion – or their politics. The names of their companies are like battle pennants flapping in the wind: Belt and Braces, Monstrous Regiment, Broadside, Red Ladder, Borderline, Northwest Spanner, 7:84 England, 7:84 Scotland, all committed to the notion of creating popular audiences for political theatre.

Of all these groups the most enduring – and exemplary – was 7:84 Scotland. The Scottish company was preceded by the English one, a product of the cell division that infects all political theatre. Its title was based on a 1971 statistic: 7 per cent of the population of the country own 84 per cent of the wealth, which translated into a frequently heard but apocryphal joke: Volvo Estate sporting 7:84 sticker pulls up at a garage; attendant asks driver what the sticker is for. Driver: '7 per cent of the country own 84 per cent of the wealth.' Attendant: 'Well, there's no need to rub it in.'

The company was started by John McGrath (1936–) a theatre, television and film writer who, with Troy Kennedy Martin, had originated the TV series *Z Cars* and watched it decline from a picaresque account of working-class life to a police procedural soap. He and his actress wife, both descendants of Irish and Scottish peasants, both socialists, both Oxford-educated – the one a son of teachers from Birkenhead, the other the daughter of Glasgow doctors – decided to abandon careers, to rediscover purpose in their work and lives and after years of living a de-racinated London life, reclaim a sense of belonging to somewhere.

Unusually for a left-wing playwright, McGrath graduated from a theatre of doubt and ambiguity to the certainties of polemic and direct address. Most writers do it the other way round. **Events While Guarding the Bofors Gun** opened at the Hampstead Theatre Club in 1966 and was subsequently made into a film; it was a fine play about conscription and the folly of nuclear defence. It dramatised the dilemma of the impotence of the liberal: a university-educated corporal fails to deal with a soldier's mutiny, goaded by a bitterly cold night and the futility of guarding an outdated weapon in West Germany to keep out the Russian hordes. It was prescient about McGrath's own frustrations, which he resolved by acting on the conviction that, if you believe in a political ideal, it's not enough to state it, you have to live it.

His company was founded on the belief that 'excellence' was not an objective conceit and that it didn't reside exclusively in institutions such as the National Theatre or the RSC; that the theatre establishment had excluded the working-class audience and working-class culture; that all art (and all funding of art) is political; that art can change the world; and that there is such a thing as society.

The form that McGrath adopted was derived from, or inspired by, Joan Littlewood: speaking to the audience in the language of working-class entertainment. Significantly that 'language' – live, spontaneous, musical, highly regionalised, direct in address and in content – was starting to dissolve in the face of the juggernaut of television, special effects and virtual reality.

The defining work of the company was their first show: **The Cheviot, The Stag and the Black, Black Oil**. McGrath developed the play from a commission from the Royal Lyceum Theatre in Edinburgh to write a play about the Highland Clearances and the dissolution of the Upper Clyde shipyards. The show McGrath wrote was indeed about the Highlands – from the Clearances to the oil boom – and with its mixture of sketches and songs, borrowed its form from the traditional Highland entertainment: the *ceilidh*. It played in towns and villages throughout the Highlands and Islands, and everywhere it went the audience had their fears and experience corroborated of being robbed of the ability to own their own lives.

Even if the audiences in the Highlands resisted social categories – were they working class? – the show was an utterly convincing vindication of the aims of the company. There were other successful shows during the life of the company played by many gifted actors and musicians, but none had the breath-taking vigour and mordant wit of **The Cheviot**, or seemed so comprehensively to address the concerns of its audience.

*7.84: **The Cheviot, the Stag and the Black, Black Oil**.*

Any company that depends so heavily on its founder (and his wife as principal actress) to write, direct and manage the productions must wilt in time. Only Eduardo de Filippo (1900–1985) in Italy seems to have resisted decline, becoming an actor in his father's company in Naples at fourteen, writing his first play at twenty-six, and starting his own company (with his brother – who he then fell out with – and sister) in 1931, which he ran until his death. Although he toured round Italy, he remained based in Naples, acting, directing and writing, sometimes in Italian, sometimes – with a strong socialist undertow – in the working-class Neopolitan dialect:

> I use dialect as a means of expression, nothing more. Just as I use standard Italian. The content of the play is what matters, not the words. Devoid of content all we're left with is a mass of inanimate sounds, and if they were in dialect it would just be so much folklore, which I detest.

The later years of 7:84's life, when the company's grant was cut, and the work started to look less self-confident, illuminate the precariousness and the essential contradiction of all political theatre. Is it the duty of the state to subsidise those who are advocating its overthrow? How objective are the standards of assessment of quality? Whose 'quality' is it?

One of the achievements of the company was in reviving a forgotten play called **Men Should Weep** by Ena Lamont Stewart, written for the Unity Theatre in 1947. About a group of working-class women in the Gorbals, it's a terrific play and anticipates (and exceeds) the 'Royal Court' plays of the late 1950s and early '60s. Its neglect speaks loudly of the ignorance of Scottish theatre in London and, as Stewart said, 'Men select the plays that are put on. They are more likely to put on a play by a man than a woman. Male chauvinism is rife in Scottish theatres. Scotsmen are the last to come out of their sties.'

7:84 was part of a movement that sought to reclaim Scottish culture from the synthetic *haut bourgeois* culture of the Lowlands, with its Lallens, its recycling of Scottish history, its constant invocation of the Age of Enlightenment and of the Jacobite Rebellion, of John Knox and Queen Mary, of Jamie the Saxth, of Walter Scott, of the Saltire Society, of the plays of James Bridie and Robert Kemp and Robert McLellan, of the poetry of Hugh McDiarmid (Communist though he was), of folk songs, of the White Heather Club on TV, of the Broons cartoon strip, of Edinburgh rock and Dundee shortbread. And this world borders on the tartan, haggis and bagpipe culture that annexes Burns as its patron saint and buries at least as great a writer, James Hogg; which packages Scotland as a seamless theme park, which in turn sharpens the working-class culture, which is self-mocking, wild, satiric, anarchic, energetic, sometimes self-pitying, often despairing – the novels of James Kelman, Alasdair Gray and Irvine Welsh, for instance, the films of Peter McDougall, the comedy of Billy Connolly – and much of the poetry, fiction, and drama (in theatre, film and TV) that emerged from Scotland and in the late 1970s and '80s.

For a decade from the mid-1970s to the '80s there were countless small companies that represented special issues – theatrical, political, sexual, racial, social, educational – Field Day, Joint Stock, Foco Novo, Paines Plough, Shared Experience, Hesitate and Demonstrate, Wildcat, Druid, Red Shift, Women's Theatre Group, Women-in-Theatre, Cunning Stunts, Scarlet Harlots, Gay Sweatshop, Black Theatre Co-Op, Tara Arts, Clean Break, Age Exchange, Bedside Manners, Chicken Shed, Graeae, Strathcona, Theatre Foundry, Bubble Theatre, Theatre In Education, and community theatres like Ann Jellicoe's Conway Theatre Trust in Dorset.

The country was dotted with sunbursts of activity, little islands of dissent. 'It is in the archipelago of dissenting islands,' said E.P. Thompson, 'that the only forces are mustered which may at some time liberate the mainland.' They didn't.

But surely it's important for a healthy society that there's an opportunity to speak to an audience directly; in short, that there are small theatre companies, underwritten by subsidy, whose success is not necessarily quantified at the box-office. It's a small price to pay to make a dent in the carapace of our homogenised culture, to make us, as Littlewood said, 'citizens of a land where once untaught artisans had challenged the state and won'.

'I think there's a huge misconception about what political theatre ought to be,' said Tony Kushner:

> Social good is incalculable. People use the phrase 'preaching to the converted', but I think that's who I want to address. I'm not going to change the minds of Jesse Helms or Margaret Thatcher. The people I can speak to are those who, like me, believe that society is transformable – although there are different views of how to go about it. What a seventy-year-old Communist Party member thinks is very different to what a twenty-five-year-old drag queen would believe … I think people are excited by any theatre that's speaking about social issues: even Beckett gives you hope by saying life is hopeless. The real hopelessness is silence. That's when the crazies take over.

The last word on this subject should be Auden's:

> In our age the mere making of a work of art is political. So long as artists exist, making what they please and think they ought to make, even if it's not terribly good, even if it only appeals to a handful of people, they remind the management of something managers need to be reminded of, namely, that the managed are people with faces, not anonymous numbers.

4

According to the Arts Council of England, 9,600,000 people went to the theatre in Britain in 1998. It's a fair assumption that most of them made only one visit, and a fairer assumption still that the visit was a penitential pilgrimage to the local pantomime. It would be little wonder if few cared to go inside a theatre ever again.

But pantomime has an astonishingly robust life. Year after year the form survives the parade of second-rate comics, self-revealing national bathroom habits, superannuated pop stars, has-been sportsmen, jokes about jokes about jokes about television marinated in the feeblest traditions of English variety and performed with the listlessness of a dead ritual. The painted gauzes and the transformation scenes are small compensation for the tyranny of audience participation, the witless slapstick, the graceless (and sexless) drag acts, the artless comic routines and the pretence that everyone is having a good time.

Pantomime derived from *commedia dell'arte* – the Italian form of rough but skilled knockabout comedy with crude plots about servants bettering masters, young love and lecherous old men. It was introduced to England in 1577 and a *commedia* company played in front of the Queen in 1602. The form didn't graft on to the English theatre, spoilt as it was with the sophistication of Shakespeare and restrained by the prohibition against women on stage. Perhaps pantomime's enthusiasm for cross-dressing retains a genetic imprint of that prohibition.

The first harlequinade or 'ballet-pantomime' in 1717 – **The Loves of Mars and Venus** by John Weaver – set off a string of imitations. By the mid-century the form was well established and George Colman (who collaborated with Garrick on **The Clandestine Marriage**) wrote in his magazine *The Connoisseur* that pantomimes should borrow their stories from folk-tales such as 'The Children in the Wood', 'Wolf', 'Little Red Riding Hood' and 'Puss in Boots'. Clearly his magazine was influential.

By the late eighteenth century Sheridan staged a version of **Robinson Crusoe** at Drury Lane in which he combined Defoe's story with a harlequinade, introducing the 'transformation scene' to the theatre, arguably as great a contribution (and as lasting) as his deathless comedies. Sheridan's 'transformation scene' turned the characters of the story into the characters from the harlequinade with a flourish of scenery and stage effects; this developed later into the traditional transformation – pumpkin into coach, mice into horses, black cat into coachman, kitchen into ballroom, Cinderella into ballgown, poverty into riches.

By 1850 and the repeal of the Theatres Act, dialogue was an essential ingredient of pantomime (rhyming couplets preferred), harlequinades became shorter, songs became more frequent, and by the end of the century the shows – ostensibly for children – were lasting up to four hours. The pantomime Dame – played by a man, the butch-er the better – started to appear at the end of the eighteenth century, but although there were 'breeches' roles in plays and operas, it was not until 1855 that a Madame (or possibly Mademoiselle) Celeste played the Principal Boy – in a costume that revealed as much of her breasts and legs as was legal. From this point on it became a 'family' entertainment: slapstick for the children, lavish costumes and songs for the mothers, mildly dirty jokes and scantily clothed women for the fathers.

Pantomimes became annual Christmas events and increasingly extravagant with spectacular scenery, huge casts, flying ballets, speciality acts, music-hall stars and comedy routines. In short, they became, with some notable exceptions (particularly in Scotland, particularly with Stanley Baxter and Ronnie Corbett), what we recognise now as 'panto': cynical, bland, homogenised, indigestible – the Kentucky Fried Chicken of theatre. Today only amateurs, in village halls all over the country, retain any sense of innocence and enthusiasm about the form.

Is it social ritual that draws people back to pantomime year after year? Or is it the audience participation? Or the warm company of strangers? Or the spectacular scenery? The costumes? The dancing? It can't be the jokes. Or is it the fact merely that the event is *live*, even if its life is a half-life? If pantomime makes an unconvincing argument for the virtue of the 'liveness' of theatre, set aside the most enduring monument to 'live' theatre – **The Mousetrap** – the most inert example looks like St Vitus's dance.

There have been nearly 20,000 performances of Agatha Christie's play since it opened in 1952 – starring Richard Attenborough – and it has played to more than 10 million people with more than 340 actors and actresses.

Dazzling statistics, and surely enduring evidence of the lure of the live theatre – if it weren't for the show itself, which is like a minor shrine attended not by the faithful hoping for a miracle cure or sign of divine affirmation, but by tourists dutifully following an entry in the guide book.

The play is set in an improbable guest house run by an improbable couple of indeterminate ages who occasionally peck each other on the cheek like budgerigars scouring for millet. Their baronial guest house would suggest a castle in Scotland, were it not for the fact that it suggests nothing more than the stage of the St Martin's Theatre. The plot (a murder the previous day in London) demands that the guest house is placed within an hour of the scene of the crime, but has to be as isolated as an island in a hurricane. The solution: set the play in Berkshire, during a snowstorm, sometime in the second Ice Age – although the furniture suggests a period sometime between late Marshall and Snelgrove and early IKEA, and the costumes mid-period C & A.

The characters are produced on stage, one by one, as if they were being announced for a formal dinner. Their entrance is heralded by a fanfare from a traditional wind machine (the *original*, we learn from the programme) which sounds like, well, a traditional wind machine, which sounds as much like wind as a comb covered with toilet paper sounds like a trumpet. It is turned with ferocious energy whenever the off-stage front door is opened and another character is introduced to us, covered with snowflakes the size of feathers, looking as though they'd been rolling on the floor in a hen house.

The young men jump up from contact with furniture and other human beings as if their trousers were on fire, while the other characters boom in monotonous, uninflected sentences that dribble purposelessly off the stage like ping-pong balls falling on a wet carpet. The behaviour of the characters has no more resemblance to real life than the characters in a Kabuki play. Each character has a sexual abnormality and is therefore a murder suspect: a screaming queen (stripy coloured jumper), a young dyke (man's suit, white shirt and tie) who is also a socialist – 'not red, pale pink', an old dyke (sensible shoes, deep voice, big strides), a dubious major (on loan from Rattigan's **Separate Tables**), and a camp foreigner dressed like Noël Coward, who wears make-up (rouge). Suspicions of cross-dressing can be banished; he is merely Italian.

The audience infers the homosexuality of the younger characters from their 'arty' and hysterical behaviour; the older ones – the mannish spinster and the foreigner – are less explicit. The major (in spite of his seediness) and the married couple who run the guest house are not portrayed as sexually abnormal and are therefore not plausible suspects. In Patrick Hamilton's **Rope** the connection between homosexuality and criminal tendencies was made unambiguously: gay = murderer.

There are jokes – 'Funny people, the English' – which cause a ripple among the audience who, given the evidence in front of them, can only agree. The highlight of the first act is the arrival of a skiing policeman outside the mullioned window. The highlight of the second act is the unmasking of the … The highlight of the curtain call is the request to 'lock the play's secret in your hearts'. During the first act the telephone lines are cut. A character picks up the handset, stares at it as if it were a dead rat, and says, 'This telephone's dead.' So is the play, but it has the innocence and familiarity of a fairy-tale. The audience watch it with good-humoured attention and curiosity, as if they were watching morris dancing or cheese-rolling. Funny people, the English.

The Mousetrap has much in common with J.B. Priestley's **An Inspector Calls**, a play with which there is at least a superficial similarity: every character nurses a hidden secret which emerges like a maimed bird dropped by a dog at his master's feet. So perhaps it's not an entirely bizarre coincidence that **The Mousetrap**'s rival in the West End is Stephen Daldry's production of **An Inspector Calls**. Daldry staged the play originally at the Royal National Theatre with a breathtaking bravura and passion; it didn't disguise the play's creaking mechanism but, like **Les Misérables**, it offered a rare and seductive mixture of visual spectacular and moral homily.

5

Twenty years ago there was a wide gap between straight plays and musicals, between 'boulevard' theatre and 'subsidised' theatre, but with the subsidised theatres taking musicals into their repertoire in an attempt to widen the constituency of their audience, there's been a convergence of the West End and the South Bank. It's been born partly out of a political need to justify subsidy (paid by all taxpayers but benefiting a narrow social segment) and partly out of a desire to argue that some, a few – well, eight or nine – musicals dissolve any divisions of 'low art' and 'high art'.

Those musicals are, of course, all American – with the conspicuous exception of the most successful musical ever, **Les Misérables**, which had its première in 1985 at the RSC's Barbican Theatre. Shortly after its opening, its director, Trevor Nunn, mused in the *Guardian*: 'Surely the only thing that is not permissible these days is to lose the audience.'

While American musical theatre was reinventing the wheel during the 1940s and '50s, the British musical remained locked in the horse-and-cart stage, wrapped in cosy parochialism. Until the 1980s the three most successful British musicals were an insipid romance involving a magic piano and several Oxbridge undergraduates, a modest pastiche of the flapper era, and a conventional adaptation of a Dickens novel – **Salad Days**, **The Boyfriend** and **Oliver!**. That these shows had charm is undeniable, but in spite of a number of gifted composers, performers, and lyricists, the British, after the days of Ivor Novello's soupy operettas, struggled to give the British musical an indigenous identity.

Willy Russell created a wry, demotic, and apparently eternally popular, play with music – a sort of folk musical for which he wrote the songs – in his adaptation of Boucicault's **Corsican Brothers**, called **Blood Brothers**. It's the story of twins being brought up separately in different class settings. In all his plays he writes about class: with what happens when class barriers are broken, usually when an aspirant working-class woman moves beyond the role and the culture assigned to her. His most popular plays,

Educating Rita and **Shirley Valentine**, have warmth, wit, and never patronise their characters. They're often on the cusp of sentimentality but have a direct truthfulness and guilelessness that is all too rare in successful popular theatre.

Notwithstanding **Blood Brothers,** and in spite of numerous attempts – **Billy Liar, A Hired Man, Mr and Mrs, I and Albert, The Good Companions** – the British have seemed unable to evolve a musical theatre in their own voice.

Which, in a sense, is still the case. Andrew Lloyd Webber's musicals have had a global success precisely because their 'voice' can't be identified as British: it's universal, an Esperanto spoken by cats in **Cats,** trains in **Starlight Express,** Argentinians in **Evita,** French people in **Phantom of the Opera,** film-folk in **Sunset Boulevard.** Or as Tim Rice put it: '99.9 per cent of the people on this ghastly planet want to see huge mega-musicals and couldn't give a stuff what language they're in.'

Michael Crawford in **Phantom of the Opera***.*

In the light of the enduring success of **Cats** – still going strong all over the world – a cynic might well accuse Lloyd Webber of opportunistically using the language of dumb animals to cross international boundaries, but even the most prescient cynic in 1981 could not have regarded turning T.S. Eliot's *Book of Practical Cats* into a musical as anything but a quirky folly. Eliot's poems ('Drivel', according to the poet James Fenton) are the sort of verse that adults think will charm children because written by a distinguished poet, but children find suspect because written by a distinguished poet. In turning the poems into a musical Lloyd Webber found and filled a perfect niche: the show you could take your children to, the show you could take your parents to – and return laden with CDs, brochures, T-shirts, mugs, watches, badges, bookmarks, baseball caps, key rings and musical boxes stamped with the ubiquitous logo of the cats' eyes with dancers floating in the pupils.

The show has an ingenious staging, no story, no jokes, one hit song, and is saturated with whimsical anthropomorphism. In Tony Kushner's **Angels in America** the monstrous lawyer, Roy Cohn, is dispensing largesse to his clients, juggling three phone calls:

> So, Baby-doll, what? *Cats?* Ugh. (*Button.*) *Cats!* It's about cats. Singing cats, you'll love it. Eight o'clock, the theatre's always at eight. (*Button.*) Fucking tourists …

Who, we learn, have been 35 per cent of the **Cats** audience in London, but that still leaves millions of British people – NOW AND FOREVER as the slogan has it – who have unquestionably been charmed by the antics of actors dressed in lycra body-stockings and leg-warmers pretending to be Bombalurina, Growltiger, Rum Tum Tugger, Mungojerrie, Rumpleteazer, Skimbleshanks, Bustopher Jones, Mistoffelees, Macavity, Munkustrap, Grizabella, Old Deuteronomy and, of course, Gus the theatre cat.

Which is not to deny the remarkable melodic gift of Lloyd Webber and – in **Phantom of the Opera** – the beguiling impact of a modern sensibility on the world of Offenbach. Or to fail to admire theatre that genuinely belongs to a popular culture. But that is no reason not to lament the death of a popular culture that – in **West Side Story** – could embrace the skills of Leonard Bernstein, Stephen Sondheim, Arthur Laurents, Jerome Robbins and William Shakespeare.

With Lloyd Webber we have returned to the form of operetta – with cursory characterisation and storyline, sung throughout, driven forward by the music rather than character, urged on by a generalised demand to FEEL and LOVE. We always know the outcome of Lloyd Webber's stories, based as they are on myths or fairy-tales: **Phantom of the Opera** is Beauty and the Beast, **Joseph and His Technicolour Dreamcoat**, **Evita** and **Jesus Christ Superstar** are Cinderella stories. With Jesus, Eva Peron, and Norma Desmond (**Sunset Boulevard**), the quest for stardom is their *via dolorosa*; the mirror for life is show business. Only in **Aspects of Love** do the ambiguities of real relationships intrude.

Lloyd Webber's pre-eminent position has been shared with two Frenchmen, the lyricist Alain Boubil and the composer Claude-Michel Schönberg, the authors of the eternally successful **Les Misérables** and **Miss Saigon**. Schönberg is a distant cousin of the atonal Arnold who, when asked if he was the composer, replied, 'Someone had to be.'

Les Misérables had to be, because Alain Boubil saw **Oliver!** in London and the sight of the Artful Dodger invoked the image of another urchin, Gavroche, in Victor Hugo's novel, *Les Misérables*. It's the winsome face of Gavroche (drawn by Victor Hugo) that now stares balefully out of a million theatre posters. The novel was knowingly written for a mass readership (which it achieved). 'I do not know whether it will be read *by* everyone,' said Hugo, 'but it is meant *for* everyone.' It anticipated the modern historical novel – history from the point of view of the scapegoat.

Boubil conscripted his collaborator Schönberg to create a 'concept album' which was then staged in a sports stadium in Paris. This came to the notice of the man who has been both the Prospero and the Pied Piper of the British musical theatre of the last twenty years – Cameron Mackintosh – who recruited an English lyricist, assembled a production team, which included his **Cats** collaborators Trevor Nunn and designer, John Napier, and agreed to stage the show as a co-production with the RSC.

The show was far from universally well received and it's not the least of Mackintosh's virtues that he doggedly persevered with it, transferred it to the Palace Theatre, marketed it with demonic flair, and watched as the show's success flouted its critics. It was done with unimpeachable good faith and staged with great skill by Trevor Nunn and John Caird, who imported the techniques of **Nicholas Nickeleby** into a dazzling fusion of classical and experimental theatre and unrestrained (and un-English) showmanship.

The producer – the person responsible for putting the elements of a production together, for financing it, for taking care of its run and for selling it – is a misunderstood and unappreciated role in British theatre, at least until Cameron Mackintosh, who is probably the most effective and certainly the best publicised, came on the scene. He understood that to take care of a show once it has opened is every bit as important as assembling the right ingredients, and if **Cats, Phantom of the Opera, Les Misérables**, and **Miss Saigon** continue to occupy theatres all over the world it's because of the systematic approach to looking after them and a meticulous attention to detail.

Mackintosh recruited a team of resident assistant directors and choreographers to keep the performances up to standard, and created a brand image – the 'Cameron Mackintosh musical' – which offered a guarantee of quality: the show you see in Sydney or Tel Aviv is essentially the same as in Los Angeles or on tour. Only the actors are different, only the actors change the specific gravity of a performance, only the actors remind you that what you are watching is live theatre – even if it is vulnerable to nothing but an accident or a power cut.

Above all Cameron Mackintosh showed a conviction – more or less unique in British theatre when he started – that marketing was an essential tool rather than an optional

343

extra. His spiritual ancestor is Florenz Ziegfeld, whose 'Follies' were synonymous with his name, and whose shows were replicated for tour while still playing on Broadway, where they were cloned on occasion in adjoining theatres. And with Ziegfeld, as with Cameron Mackintosh, there were only two stars – the show and the producer.

The ascendancy of the British musical has been the most significant theatre phenomenon in the world over the last twenty years, and has given the British theatre far more than a financial boost. You can't argue with the success of these shows; and such is their near-universal popularity and the power of cultural relativism, that it must seem churlish to observe that the shows are simply not as *good* as, for instance, **Oklahoma!, South Pacific, Carousel, Pal Joey, Guys and Dolls, Gypsy, West Side Story, My Fair Lady, Kiss Me Kate, On the Town, Annie Get Your Gun, The Pyjama Game, Brigadoon, Paint Your Wagon, The King and I** and **Sweeney Todd**.

Les Misérables and **Miss Saigon** advance on their audiences laden with weighty subject matter, portentous thin-framed machines for giving you generalised rather than particularised feeling, unmitigated by irony. They give the impression, rather than the reality, of feeling, like Victorians scattering water on letters to look as if they'd been written in tears.

An audience leaves **Les Misérables** ennobled by the saintly Valjean, disgusted by the villanous Javert, and with a faint but guiltless sense of unease about the world's dispossessed. Hugo wrote the novel as a specific indictment of the society served by the policeman Javert, a 'savage in the service of civilisation', and intended the novel to be a weapon of happiness, a moral panacea, a bible of popular optimism, proclaiming faith in progress and an end to misery. It is often said that the musical traduces the novel; this is not so, but the effect of the musical – removed from its period and softened by its music – is inevitably closer to this advertisement which was on the frontispiece of the cheap English edition of 1887:

> WHAT HIGHER AIM CAN MAN ATTAIN
> THAN CONQUEST OVER HUMAN PAIN?
> DON'T BE WITHOUT A BOTTLE OF ENO'S FRUIT SALT

Les Misérables would not have been a huge popular success as a musical if it had retained Hugo's pitch of moral indignation. His specific political scourge has been translated into a generalised message of goodness and God. As its book-writer said, 'The universal aspect of **Les Misérables** has less to do with political upheaval or revolution than with the eternal truths about human nature and our beliefs in God.' Nevertheless, it is remarkable that the world's most popular musical is not a monument to glitz and glitter, but something that has a conspicuous moral scheme – albeit a sentimental one.

D.H. Lawrence put his finger on the difference between the real and the simulated in art:

> Sentimentalism is the working off on yourself of feelings you haven't really got. We all *want* to have certain feelings: feelings of love, of passionate sex, of kindliness, and so forth. Very few people really feel love, or sex passion, or kindliness, or anything else that goes at all deep. So the mass just fake these feelings inside themselves. Faked feelings! The world is all gummy with them. They are better than real feelings, because you can spit them out when you brush your teeth; and then tomorrow you can fake them afresh.

But can we legislate as to whether people's feelings are real or not? When we see thousands of people, wracked with grief, mourning for Princess Diana, should we assume that the grief is fake? The tears are real enough. DIANA, FAIRY GODMOTHER OF THE NEEDY COLOMBIANS IN MOURNING, said one placard outside Buckingham Palace. If you're grieving like this for someone you've never met, what do you reserve for your own family?

    Les Misérables has played successfully all over the world except, with a poetic irony, in Paris.

Les Misérables: '*What higher aim can man attain than conquest over human pain?*'

France has also, until recently, resisted the Disneyfication of the world. The Disneyland theme park that opened in 1992 near Paris was regarded as a blight on French culture, until it started to relax the Aryan severity of its staff dress code, and introduced wine into its restaurants.

Disney is unaccustomed to failure and is impelled by the remorseless exigencies of business to expand its activities into every territory and every area of entertainment. In which spirit the Mighty Mouse has decided to invade the theatre. This is a logical strategy: their core product is film – feature-length cartoons. A great deal of cash has to be spent marketing these films and on the back of that effort a great deal of merchandise – toys, clothes, books – can be sold. It is a small step to including theatre as part of the merchandising effort, replicating the cartoons not with expensive animatronics but the often frail but essentially cheap human variety – actors.

For Disney's entry into the theatre, Times Square was purged of its porn shops and prostitutes, and $38m was spent on making the New Amsterdam Theatre (a Ziegfeld theatre) a site fit for its theatrical version of a cartoon film which had taken $700m at the box office. The surprise was that in **The Lion King**, an (almost) three-dimensional version of the cartoon – brilliantly directed by Julie Taymor – Disney produced a piece of originality and charm. Taymor's use of puppets and masks and theatre magic is entirely beguiling, even if the sheer relentless anthropomorphism is wearing – you long for a human being among the animals, and its parable of male supremacy is tiresome. **Beauty and the Beast** is another matter, and not heartening evidence of the popular theatre of the future. It is beyond category, a *tableau mort*, with all the liveliness of a wax museum and the charm of a yawning grave. 'A perpetual holiday,' said Shaw, 'is a good definition of hell.' He hadn't seen **Beauty and the Beast**.

Purity

'If theatre is to affect life, it must be stronger, more intense than ordinary life. That is the law of gravity.'
FRANZ KAFKA

1

In some ways Chekhov – along with Kafka – was the most prescient writer of the twentieth century, even though he died in 1904. In **The Cherry Orchard** he offers a model to any writer attempting to write about private lives and public ideas that is humane, spare, poetic, polemical, and unsentimental. It's the best play of the century. Chekhov was not a revolutionary, in fact despised absolutism even if he understood its motives, but he foresaw the demand for revolution in society in **The Cherry Orchard**, and for theatre in **The Seagull**. In that play, the young would-be writer, Konstantin, is prophesying the theatre of the future. He is usually played, absurdly, as if he was a member of the Flat Earth Society:

> KONSTANTIN: When I see a stage with an over-lit room and three walls, that we're supposed to think is real, and watch these famous and successful people, these high priests of the sacred art of theatre trying to show us how people eat and drink and dress and move and make love ... well, I just have to run away ...
> SORIN: We can't do without theatre ...
> KONSTANTIN: But we need new forms! We need new ways of doing theatre! If we can't find them, then we might as well have nothing at all.

By a wonderfully satisfying coincidence the part of Konstantin in the first production (directed by Stanislavsky) was played by a young actor called Vsevolod Meyerhold, who later – with Antonin Artaud – became one of the century's twin guiding lights of experimental theatre. Like Konstantin, both men were trying to achieve a synthesis of speech, music, and movement. Meyerhold's concern was with exhibiting the outer man, Artaud's with mining the inner man. Both men were autocrats, prototypes for the director as maestro.

Meyerhold (1874–1940) became a director and developed a style of acting in which theatre rhetoric was replaced with a 'light and unforced' delivery – 'the exterior calm that conceals volcanic emotions' – and by mime and improvisation; character and relationships were established not by words alone but by 'gestures, poses, glances and silences', with speech and movement not necessarily coinciding. It was a style derived ultimately from *commedia dell'arte*.

He developed a discipline for training actors that he called 'biomechanics', a system of highly stylised body exercises, which was as external as Stanislavsky's was internal. He was concerned with the actor's 'excitability', manifested externally in movement and speech; he scorned Stanislavsky's preoccupation with 'feeling', with the baggage of psychological reality. Like David Mamet, his interest was not in what the actor might *feel*, but in what the actor could *show*.

Vsevolod Meyerhold: the director as maestro.

For a while his actors, habituated to the realist tradition, couldn't translate his ideas on to the stage. But Stanislavsky had the same problem: the actors exposed to his 'method' were equally unresponsive to systematising their ways of working. Actors are invariably empiricists, but to be fair to Stanislavsky, he was trying to produce a concordance of common sense, rather than a rigid doctrine. Meyerhold wanted acting instruments: performers who were good at music, acrobatics, mime, and improvisation, had great verbal dexterity and considerable knowledge of other art forms – requirements that are now regarded as commonplace.

Many of his productions took a long time to develop, five years in the case of **Masquerade**, prompting a colleague to remark tartly that he 'built the production like a Pharaoh his pyramid'. After the Russian Revolution his productions became increasingly propagandist, using caricatured characterisation, slogans on screens, and pantomimic interludes. He introduced a device for the actor to indicate his attitude to his character and the story, which he called 'pre-acting'. It involved lifting a mask, literally or metaphorically, and it 'pre-acted' Brecht's theory of alienation.

Meyerhold always described himself as 'the author of the production'. His most celebrated creation (though not necessarily his best) was strictly speaking Gogol's **The Government Inspector**. The play was (and is) at the heart of the canon of Russian classical theatre, and Meyerhold's production is the archetype of productions based on the

Meyerhold's **The Government Inspector**: *concept production.*

'directorial conceit' – in both senses of the word. He re-wrote some of the text and relocated the play from the remote provinces to the capital; the production was wayward, innovative, sinister, rarely comic, occasionally tragic and it provoked a debate about how to present the classics which, within a year, engendered hundreds of articles and three books.

Meyerhold's approach to the classics – at its most extreme in his deconstructed **The Government Inspector** – had an epigrammatic clarity: he called it 'denuding the theatre'. It led to 'simplicity, schematisation, intensity, dynamism of action and ability to capture the rhythm of the epoch', and, it should be added, frequently denuded the theatre of the writer's intentions. In his desire to impose his will on a play, to 'create' the theatrical language of the event by introducing a controlling scheme, many (or most) directors have, at times, imitated him. But however dictatorial, Meyerhold was not a monster: 'He built a production as they build a house. And we were happy to be even a doorknob in this house,' said one of his actors.

Meyerhold's company continued for another eleven years in increasing difficulty. While his actors may have accepted Meyerhold's axiom: 'Freedom is in subordination,' he was unable to continue to submit to a political tyranny. His company was liquidated in 1938, and a year later he was arrested, and disappeared, but no one knew his exact fate until his file was opened in 1991, revealing that he had been executed and his cremated remains cast into an unmarked grave. He was effectively canonised by a generation in Eastern Europe during the Cold War, who equated Stanislavsky and the Moscow Art Theatre with Stalinist socialist realism, and exemplified Meyerhold as the revolutionary who had died for his art.

Which is true, albeit at his own hand, of Antonin Artaud (1897–1948) – a French actor, director, theorist, magus, madman and drug addict. 'In practical terms,' Artaud said, 'I want to resuscitate an idea of total spectacle, where the theatre will know how to take back from the cinema, the musical-hall, the circus and from life itself, all that has always belonged to it.'

Total theatre! The perfectibility of man! The war to end wars! The final solution! The end of history! The age of absolutism, fascism, socialism – the age of isms! – with modernism arching over art with the isms of expressionism, constructivism, futurism, cubism, Dadaism, surrealism – all growing up in opposition to naturalism, all attempts to open doors of perception, to reflect and understand an increasingly confusing world.

Modernism argues that the arts progress rather than evolve, that art forms become 'wrong' or 'irrelevant', that the representation of the human figure and human relationships become 'outdated', to be replaced by abstractions. Outdated humans? Outdated buildings? Outdated forms? 'Putting on new plays feels about as astute as using a horse and cart for haulage, or having an operation without an anaesthetic,' said a 1999 British newspaper article. Against this deterministic onslaught the theatre has often struggled to converge with other twentieth-century art forms by subverting or rejecting its conventions.

*Artaud in **The Passion of Joan of Arc**, directed by Carl Dreyer.*

'But first,' Artaud said, 'this theatre must exist.' It never did in his lifetime, but there's been no experiment in theatre in the last forty years that hasn't, knowingly or not, owed something to Artaud's catechism:

What space? Theatre, said Artaud, takes place in yesterday's buildings; the audience are detached, socially divided into strata, a line drawn between them and the actors, the stage locked within a picture-frame. Artaud wanted bare, undecorated buildings, uninfected with theatre of the past – in today's language 'new spaces' for 'site-specific work'. Artaud wanted the audience in the centre of the action, physical contact with the actors, 'direct communication', and total emotional involvement: 'Just as there are to be no empty spatial areas, there must be no let-up, no vacuum in the audience's mind or sensitivity.'

What text? Artaud saw narrative and text as a prison, the performer a prisoner of the pen. 'We shall renounce the theatrical superstition of the text and the dictatorship of the writer ... we rejoin the ancient popular drama, sensed and experienced directly by the mind without deformation of language and the barrier of speech.' He wanted a dialogue of written *theatre*, with the director as the auteur of the event, 'a kind of unique creator'.

What acting? Artaud wanted an actor to become as one with the role, in effect not to be an actor, exploring the inner world, often uttering visceral sounds, wordless sentences, above all living in the moment: 'Let's recognise that what has been said does not need to be said again: that an expression is worth nothing the second time ... that every spoken word is dead, and is crucial only at the moment it is spoken – a theatre in a constant state of self-destruction and re-creation, idealised, Utopian even:

> Theatre
> is the condition
> the place,
> the point,
> where the human anatomy can be seized
> and used to heal and direct life.

What design? What should be put on the stage? How much is it necessary to put on a stage? Nothing representational, everything for maximum expression, everything poetic – light used as 'arrows of fire', sound (he initiated the use of stereo in the theatre) loud and convulsive.

Who pays? He despised any sort of commercialism, anything that reduced the theatre

*Max Wall and Jack Shepherd in **Ubu Roi** at the Royal Court, designed by David Hockney.*

to a commodity. Courage, risk, danger, adventure (and madness) would inspire a theatre that 'shakes off stifling material dullness which even overcomes the senses' clearest testimony, and collectively reveals their dark powers and hidden strength to men'.

Artaud embraced the surrealist movement in his early twenties but shortly after was expelled from it: he always thought himself too surrealist for the surrealists. He had been inspired by Alfred Jarry, who in 1893 at the age of twenty burst on the Paris literary scene 'like a wild animal entering a ring' with his plays (developed from plays he'd written as a schoolboy): **Ubu Roi, Ubu Cocu** and **Ubu Enchainé**, which were violent, farcical, anarchic, blasphemous, scatological social satires.

The public dress-rehearsal of **Ubu Roi** caused a riot, not because of objections to the opening word – SHIT! (that happened on the second night and the leading actor countered the objections with a motor-horn), but because the director of the Théâtre Libre, André Antoine – in the vanguard of naturalism – objected to an actor simulating the opening of a door in Ubu's castle rather than using a real one.

The play was a fart in the face of naturalism – the main characters wore masks, the minor characters were represented by forty life-size tailor's dummies, and Ubu rode a life-size horse. Yeats was in the audience with Synge:

> The players are supposed to be dolls, toys, marionettes, and now they are all hopping like wooden frogs, and I can see for myself that the chief personage, who is some kind of king, carries for a sceptre a brush of the kind that we use to clean a closet. Jarry's intention was to confound every expectation that the audience might bring to the theatre; he wanted to offend their sense of theatrical propriety. He expressed the full implications of an irrational and destructive existence in a form that was equally irrational and destructive.

Jarry influenced Wedekind, Schnitzler and Strindberg but was forgotten in France until the surrealists re-discovered him in 1916, and in 1926 Artaud and two friends formed the Alfred Jarry Theatre. 'We ask our audiences to join with us, inwardly, deeply,' he said, and added as a superbly superfluous understatement, 'Discussion is not in our line.'

It was a sort of anti-theatre theatre, spontaneity guaranteed by the lack of rehearsals, money and organisation. The few performances were confrontational, full of wild exclamations, brutal humour, hallucinatory actions. The public and the critics were indifferent to it and the Alfred Jarry Theatre ceased to exist.

Artaud spent the next six years writing the manifestos, essays and letters that make up *The Theatre and its Double*, which was published in 1938. 'I have a thing about me to which I cannot give a name/Unless it be compassion,' says the dying Flamineo in one of Artaud's favourite plays, **The White Devil**. The thing that Artaud had about him was 'the whirlwind of life that eats up darkness … that pain which is ineluctably necessary to the continuation of life' to which he gave the name 'cruelty', and like many others in the twentieth century, he chose to pursue a kind of absolutism in order to dispel his despair. His idea of a 'Theatre of Cruelty' seems, with hindsight, all too apt for an age that saw Stalin's purges and the Holocaust.

It took Artaud until 1935 to secure the backing for his long-projected Theatre of Cruelty, which he received from a rich Russian woman who gave money on condition she could play a leading part. He chose to stage Shelley's verse tragedy **The Cenci**, based on the tale of a sixteenth-century atheistic Italian count – the Cenci – imprisoned for sodomy and incest and murdered at the behest of his daughter by two men sticking nails in his eyes and throat. 'There isn't *anything* that won't be attacked among the antique notions of Society, Order, Justice, Religion, Family and Country,' he said. He thought the play was commercial.

It was an odd choice. The intractable text was directly at odds with his theories – 'the difference between the roaring of a waterfall and its image' – but his aim was to overwhelm the audience with a massive accumulation of effects: the sound of tolling bells, screeching machines, echoing footsteps, thunder and lightning, an oscillating metronome, whispering voices in counterpoint, deafening fanfares, ringing anvils from loudspeakers placed at the four corners of the auditorium, and synchronised with lighting changes, sometimes blinding in their intensity.

The sets were designed by the painter Balthus: scaffolding for the palace like a giant ladder against the sky, red curtains hanging like clots of congealed blood, arches broken off in space. Artaud's benefactress, playing the Cenci's daughter, Beatrice, got more than she'd bargained for: she had to hang by her hair from the torturer's wheel, her head supported by a concealed rostrum, which Artaud was suspected of wanting to remove to make it more truthful.

His actors failed to understand his theories, and the seventeen performances, in a proscenium-arch music-hall, were not well received. Far from being 'plunged in fire' as

Artaud had hoped, the audience were at best confused and condescending, at worst apathetic and hostile. 'I believe that in order to make these people understand something, I would have to kill them.'

The production of **The Cenci** left Artaud in financial ruin, discredited, and exhausted. When he was in his twenties he wrote his longest poem; it was called *Fragments of a Journal from Hell*. Hell was not a metaphor for him; it was wherever he was. You can see Artaud on film as Marat in Abel Gance's *Napoleon*. His face as he lies dead in the bath, gaunt as a ghost, drained of the power of paroxysm, is a sight that haunts one for a lifetime.

When he turned away from the theatre, he travelled to Mexico and Ireland (including to Inishmaan in the footsteps of Synge), lost the tatters of his sanity and died – probably by an overdose of chloral – in 1948. These were his last words about theatre:

> A theatre of blood,
> a theatre where at each performance
> something
> will be won
> *physically* ...
> In reality, the theatre is the *birth* of creation.
> That will happen.

It happened, at least in homage, in 1964 when Peter Brook mounted a season in London of work-in-progress in a tiny theatre with a small group of actors at the culmination of a period of experiment, christened the 'Theatre of Cruelty'. The aim was characteristic of all Brook's work: to push the actors (and the imagination of the director) into finding a form of expression in the theatre that transcended its current conventions and artistic ambitions.

The experiment involved exercises that included a variety of improvisations, using sounds and rhythms rather than words to communicate, acting with nonsense texts, as well as acting with formal scenes – the wooing scene between Richard and Lady Anne from **Richard III** performed in mine, and a playlet called **The Public Bath** (performed by Glenda Jackson), investigating fame and voyeurism through a celebrated courtesan of the time, Christine Keeler, being persecuted for having sex with a cabinet minister, mutating into Jackie Kennedy grieving at the side of her husband's coffin.

The centrepiece of the 'Theatre of Cruelty' season was a brilliantly articulated production of **The Screens** by Jean Genet, a play about the reality of colonialism – the war for Algerian independence from France – wreathed in fantasy.

Genet (1910–1986) was Artaud's theatrical child; he was a French playwright and thief, who spent much of the first thirty years of his life in reform schools and jails. His plays, written with a limpid beauty in classical French, were about vice and violence, Catholicism, gay sex, crime, colonialism and moral decay. He teased the prejudices of his audience, using the whores and criminals of his world to hold up a smoky and distorted mirror to the corruption of conventional society. They fulfilled Artaud's definition of 'cruelty' and his longing for intensity, gushing with words and images, masturbatory fantasies, violent diatribes, mediated by elegant language and often surprising moments of tenderness. Brook thought – at the time – that Genet's plays were 'the most prophetic theatre in the twentieth century'.

Brook's experimental season was a means to an end: it gave confidence and knowledge to the actors (and the director) that led later that year to his production of Peter Weiss's animated debate about the nature of man and madness, society and the individual, revolution, violence and control: **The Persecution and Murder of Marat as Performed by the Inmates of the Asylum of Charenton under the Direction of the Marquis de Sade.** The play's title was as clumsy as the writing, but Brook's production, in an act of alchemy as rare in the theatre as in science, transformed the play not only into a tumultuous spectacle, but into something disturbing, touching, illuminating and often beautiful, marred only by occasional sententiousness and the pious gesture of the actors (still 'in character') mocking the applause of the audience at the end.

Brook used the patients in the insane asylum much as Joan Littlewood used the pierrots in **Oh, What a Lovely War!** (which was playing in the West End at the same time), as a metaphorical device for dealing with large subjects, harnessing the full armament of theatrical expression. Ironically, both productions, coming from wholly different starting points, achieved Artaud's wish that the theatre take back from 'the cinema, the musical-hall, the circus and from life itself, all that has always belonged to it'. At the same time they demonstrated that Brecht and Artaud were not irreconcilable: it is possible to watch a theatre performance and be both objective and involved.

Peter Brook was born in 1925 in West London, the child of Latvian *émigrés*. He had a comfortable upbringing playing with toy theatres, staging conjuring shows for his parents, an educated childhood: books, music, theatre and films. He became a dauntingly precocious Oxford undergraduate who thought nothing of approaching 'The Great Beast' – the black magician Alasteir Crowley – to ask for his help in raising spirits in **Doctor Faustus.** He wanted more than anything to be a film director, and because he thought he'd have to serve an intolerably long apprenticeship, he slipped into the theatre, where it's often enough to say you're a director to convince someone to allow you to become one.

At the age of twenty he was directing Paul Scofield at Birmingham Repertory Theatre. When he was twenty-one he was directing **Love's Labour's Lost** at Stratford and had become a phenomenon. Enfant terrible! Wunderkind! He became Director of Productions at the Royal Opera House at the age of twenty-two and, in a wilfully self-destructive mood, invited Salvador Dali to design a production of **Salomé.** Sadly this was never staged: the design required the Thames to be diverted so that an ocean liner could burst through the back wall of the Covent Garden stage.

Brook at work.

For many years he was a prodigiously busy and (mostly) successful freelance director in London, New York and Paris: new plays by Grahame Greene, Arthur Miller, Tennessee Williams, Jean Anouilh, Jean-Paul Sartre, and John Whiting; opera at Covent Garden and at the Met in New York; **Measure for Measure, Titus Andronicus, The Winter's Tale, Hamlet, The Tempest** in Stratford and London; and musicals – the delightful **Irma La Douce**, the sensationally unsuccessful **The Perils of Scobie Prilt** about a gossip columnist, the scarcely more successful **House of Flowers** by Truman Capote.

In 1960 he filmed Marguerite Duras' novel, *Moderato Cantabile* with Jeanne Moreau, and in the following year William Golding's *Lord of the Flies*. When he returned to the theatre after an absence of two years to direct **King Lear** at Stratford it seemed that he'd done with the 'train set' side of theatre – what he described as the 'quincaillerie' (the ironmongery) of stage production – which had so fascinated him as a child and an absurdly young and confident director of theatre and opera.

With his elemental production of **King Lear**, it was clear that he was embarked on a different course, one that took him over the next eight years into an exploration of Artaud, into **The Marat/Sade**, into a politically engaged show about the Vietnam War, **Tell Me Lies**, an awkward and ill-fated production of Seneca's **Oedipus**, and then in 1970 into his glorious production of **A Midsummer Night's Dream**, which for once earned that over-exercised adjective: celebratory.

The Marat/Sade.

Then he went. At the age of forty-five he left the world of first nights at Stratford, or London, New York or Paris – escaped the infection of self-doubt, the vagaries of fashion, the attrition of parochial sniping, the weariness of careerism. He exempted himself from the mid-life crisis that affects most theatre directors (not always in mid-life), which comes from repetition, from constant barter and compromise, from a frustration at not being an 'auteur' and an inability to re-invent the medium.

With hindsight, his self-exile from British theatre seems unsurprising: he had spent most of his professional life in flight from what one of his actors caricatured as 'the bloody British theatre' – insular, class-bound, text-bound, earth-bound. And there was then (and is now) an engrossing cosiness, a repressive tolerance and reassurance in the British theatre (or British culture in general), that often goes hand in hand with being pragmatic to a fault, that has made exiles out of Joan Littlewood, Granville-Barker, and Gordon Craig, and a recluse out of Edward Bond. 'England destroys artists,' said Brook. 'Their edge is rapidly knocked off … No one presses them to do anything – all they do is create a climate in which the artist will only too readily castrate himself.'

On the other hand it is precisely the rough empiricism that has been part of the continuing strength of British theatre – its eagerness to absorb theatre from other cultures and its willingness to adapt to existing resources of talent and money. By eschewing that pragmatism, Brook has sometimes subverted his work by turning seriousness into

357

solemnity, leading to impenetrable gnomic thinking – 'The enigma of tradition and the mystery of transmission cannot change, but the great set of keys is always there' – and opaque work such as his production of **Oedipus** at the National Theatre and **The Ik** at the Round House.

Brook withdrew from British theatre and set up a Centre for Theatre Research (CIRT) in Paris, funded by an American corporate foundation, and two years later took over a disused music-hall – the Bouffes du Nord – and made it his theatrical home. His work became an explicit search for meaning, a spiritual quest. Spiritual enlightenment is either the search for an inner world or it's a flight from the outer one; theatre is a re-creation of another world, even more intense, distilled, meaningful and real than the 'real' one. When he was the same age as Brook, Stanislavsky wrote this to Meyerhold: 'I have utterly lost faith in everything that serves the eye and ear on stage, I only trust feeling and most of all, nature herself. It is wiser and more subtle than we are.'

Brook embarked with his theatre family – a group of fifteen actors – on a succession of journeys, explorations of the nature of theatre and the nature of nature: to Iran (funded by the Shah of Iran) to perform a play written by Ted Hughes in an invented dramatic language, a fusion of Greek, Latin, Spanish, speech and chant and song, which was mystical, ritualistic, and obscure, but deeply moving according to those few people who shared the experience on a mountain top in the small hours of the morning – 'a great precious thing beyond words', said Hughes; to West Africa to re-invent theatre from scratch, playing stories on a carpet laid out on sand to audiences who shared no language or social or artistic conventions with the actors; to California, to perform improvised sketches for strikers with El Teatro Campesino, a politically committed theatre group led by Luis Valdez, and to Colorado, Minnesota and Brooklyn to perform versions of a Sufi poem, **The Conference of the Birds**.

'Exploring life beyond the clichés' was what Brook said they were doing. Life and theatre merged seamlessly. They risked privation, physical and mental exhaustion, foolishness, self-delusion, and even emptiness. What did it lead to? Eventually, in 1985, to **The Mahabharata**, adapted from the world's longest narrative poem, the core of Hindu culture: a trilogy of plays, adapted by Jean-Claude Carrière, first performed in a quarry in Avignon. It told the story of two warring families, a society on the edge of collapse, and ended with a vision of Paradise – peace, harmony, forgiveness – as the first light of dawn broke over the cliff's edge.

The production was at heart a story told to a small boy for a small group of spectators, and in spite of its size and its sophistication, it never lost its simplicity. It was performed by twenty actors and musicians with a few simple props and exquisite emblematic costumes on a floor of red earth. It made a patchwork of different theatre styles and traditions, different nationalities, races and accents; it held stage magic, ritual, and psychological reality within a Shakespearian span, arching over private and public lives – vast sweeping battles following moments of intense intimacy.

A snake of flame twisted out of the dark, pulling a dancer in its wake, a torch-lit battle ended with a nuclear flare; arrows appeared to fly across the stage, horses to gallop; the elements of the production were the elements of life – earth, fire, air and water. The staging had the flair, brilliance and bravura that could have been attention-seeking were it not so obviously the consequence of trying to find the most expressive way of telling the story. *The Mahabharata.*

The Mahabharata achieved what Artaud craved when he saw Balinese dancers in Paris in 1928, a theatre that 'has its origins in the *dance*. The means of expression employed in the dance are equally the natural means of expression for the actor, the difference being merely one of *range*'. For Brook it was the culmination of years of persistently asking questions of his actors and himself. From **The Conference of the Birds**:

HERMIT: Why are you laughing?
DOVE: I'm laughing because I know why.
HERMIT: Why what?
DOVE: Why you haven't found the answer.
HERMIT: And why haven't I found the answer?
DOVE: Because you don't think about your question.
HERMIT: What do you mean? I think of nothing else!
DOVE: You're wrong. You only think about your beard.

359

For all that his work bears his unmistakable imprint, Brook's shows confer authority on the performer rather than celebrate the director. His effects are achieved through speech and movement, utterly pragmatically. 'Rehearsing,' he says, 'is thinking aloud with others ... nothing in a theatre performance is more important than the people of whom it is composed.'

That thought was exemplified in his lucid productions at the Bouffes du Nord of **The Cherry Orchard** and **The Tempest**, and of **Carmen** and **Peléas et Mélisande**, where he succeeded in making fresh theatre out of the most intractable and least demotic of forms: opera. His work in Paris has had a sense of resolution, conspicuous after a lifetime of febrile search for peace in theatre, and in film as a flight from theatre, and in travel as a flight from both film and theatre, and in Paris as a flight from London.

Brook has been more like a writer than a director: his productions have developed, one from another, like a writer pursuing a theme. His theatrical experiments seem to have been attempts to square the circle of the genius he has for directing and the desire he has to be the author of the event. He has thus triumphed over the endemic frustration of directors, stuck with the role of mediator, suspended between the writer's need to impel the play forward, and the actor's desire to stand still and create a character.

In **The Man Who,** the director and 'author' became indivisibly linked. The show was based on Oliver Sacks' clinical accounts of dealing with several varieties of neural and mental dysfunction, such as aphasia, ataxia, aphonia, aphemia, aphelia, Tourette's syndrome – terms which amount to describing the wires of the brain getting crossed. Sacks' book was called *The Man Who Mistook His Wife For A Hat*. Brook's show, set on an almost bare white platform, using only the odd institutional metal chair and table, showed a series of scenes illuminating the function of the brain, implicitly reflecting on the questions: 'How do we think?' and 'What is a man?'.

Like Brecht, like Stanislavsky, like Granville-Barker, Brook argues that for the theatre to be expressive it must be, above all, simple and unaffected: a distillation of language, of gesture, of action, of design, where meaning is the essence:

> I take an empty space and call it a bare stage. A man walks across this empty space while someone else is watching him, and that is all that is needed for an act of theatre to be engaged.

2

There is no one working in the British theatre who explains his ideas with such clarity, and lack of dogma, as Peter Brook. His *The Empty Space*, based on four lectures he gave in 1968, is one of only a handful of indispensable books about the theatre. Brook describes four categories of theatre: 'deadly theatre' – inert, trapped in conventions and clichés (far from always being in the commercial sector); 'rough theatre' – vulgar, eclectic, populist; immediate theatre – the theatre of 'the vital spark' (Brook's theatre);

and 'holy theatre' – compulsive, communitarian, a search for secular rituals to replace spiritual vacuums.

'Holy theatre' represents a desire to turn water into wine, to transform the act of making theatre from entertainment into communion, from professional collaboration into a communal family, from art into religion. The theatre will always be inclined to a form of Utopianism – social, political or aesthetic. It's a necessary part of the process: you work to create something in which everyone has a purpose, contributes to the success of the whole, and shares in the achievement or the failure.

'Holy theatre' wholly defined the theatre of Jerzy Grotowski (1933–1999), who started as a director in a small experimental theatre company in a provincial town near Auschwitz in Poland. Like Artaud, Grotowski was fascinated by oriental theatre, which he'd seen in his student years, but, unlike Artaud, he regarded Stanislavsky as his 'spiritual father', sharing his obsession with examining the processes that lead to an actor's performance. He rejected Stanislavsky's system in favour of discovering a means of 'eliminating from the actor's psyche all that blocked the path towards the transgression of self'. It was a search for Artaud's holy grail: the 'total act of theatre'.

He became less and less interested in performance and more and more in research, starting the Laboratory Theatre, subsidised, somewhat reluctantly, by the state. He rejected the superficial elements of performance: sets, lighting, props, sound. 'Poor theatre', he called it. 'The core of theatre art,' said Grotowski, 'is the actor-spectator relationship.' The actors were pushed in rehearsal to a state of exhaustion – to trances – through which they transcended 'the limits we impose upon ourselves that block the creative process'. An actor playing Christ on the cross would sweat near-blood from his crown of thorns. Acting was an entirely personal process, a spiritual autobiography: 'It is a question of giving oneself. One must give totally in one's deepest intimacy, with confidence, as when one gives oneself in love.' It was a commitment to a way of life as complete as entering a religious order, which of course, in a sense, it was.

Consequently Grotowski only wanted an audience who was prepared to worship, open to the prospect of exploring their spiritual selves; mere theatrical tourists need not apply. The audience members were thus cast as conspirators, participants or communicants. After years of experiment he faced the fact of the inevitable passivity of the audience, and decided that his future research would concern itself with the 'creativity of the spectator' rather than that of the actor. Which meant, in short, that he abandoned theatre – in the sense of performance – for a form of collective activity that he called 'paratheatre'.

'We are not seeking to create characters as in a play. We are ourselves. Is this theatre? Or is it something else?' The 'something else' could only be seen by private arrangement in small rooms to which the audience would be taken by bus. It was an attempt to create a genuine encounter between individuals who meet as complete strangers and, through contact with the 'actors', share in a sense of ritual and ceremony. In a sense it's what every theatre performance aspires to, in some modest form, taken to the power of infinity and of futility: 'total theatre'. In 1984, the Laboratory Theatre dissolved, its journey complete, performance dissolved into solipsism.

Grotowski's work was never very popular in Poland, where the conventional theatre had a power conferred on it by state censorship, and the problems of navigating through Communism hardly gave an allure to living in a collective. In the Western world however, Grotowski had a messianic appeal, and in the US he corroborated the work of the Living Theatre, which was led by a husband and wife, Julian Beck and Judith Malina: he was bald, pale, scholarly-looking; she was dark, wild, joyful; both were natural anarchists.

They were adventurers in the search for 'authenticity' – of feeling, that is. They became part of a 'New Left', a loose, quasi-political movement characterised by support for the civil-rights movement, opposition to the escalating Vietnam War, and belief in the transforming power of sexual love. Politics became eroticised and sex – MAKE LOVE NOT WAR! – was used to challenge the prevailing deities of hypocrisy, commercialism and militarism.

In 1958 Beck and Malina read an advance copy of the first American translation of Artaud's work and it delivered them from dependence on the articles of faith of their medium – character, narrative, dialogue – into imagining a new theatre for a new society. Their work in the early '60s – Jack Gelber's **The Connection** and Kenneth H. Brown's **The Brig** – were productions that tested the extremities of naturalistic acting, and challenged the expectations of the audience. Drug-addicts waiting eternally for a fix, prisoners in a violently sadistic Marine Corps prison, both offered worlds that had 'rules' which parodied the social norm, and intended to provoke a visceral response in the audience – and society. For which they were rewarded with being harassed by the Internal Revenue Service for back taxes.

They accumulated a 'family' of about thirty actors and became intermittent voluntary exiles, touring Europe like a nomadic tribe with a production based on the works of Artaud, **Mysteries**, followed by a production of Genet's **The Maids**, then a communal spectacle, **Frankenstein**, in which ritual, dream, myth were the ingredients of a reflection on man's capacity for self-destruction. In **Paradise Now**, which they based on the work of the Jewish existentialist philosopher Martin Buber, they called for a revolution NOW! The audience were invited to come on stage, smoke dope, have sex, change the world through an anarchy of the senses. In practice – as in the Round House in 1968 – their strategy of exposing the repressions of society was often subverted by the audience: 'I am not allowed to smoke marijuana,' said an actor to a member of the audience who was quite conspicuously smoking a large joint. 'I am not allowed to take my clothes off,' provoked an outburst of undressing.

What the Living Theatre had in common with many American theatres was that they lived to act, and they acted to live, and they questioned the role of the audience as much as the role of the actor, the form of society as much as the form of drama. They followed the Group Theatre and the Provincetown Players in establishing a model of communitarian living that served as a template for their social ideas. The Open Theatre, for example, led by an actor from **The Connection**, Joseph Chaikin, was set up to try to develop a style of acting that went beyond naturalism, and an acting ensemble that would demonstrate that, in a disintegrating world, theatre offered a model society: 'a point where we are brought together'.

The Open Theatre was the one American theatre group that gained the respect of Grotowski. They were rigorously disciplined, worked with writers – Megan Terry with **Viet Rock**, Jean Claude van Itallie with **America Hurrah** among others – and were constantly engaged in debate about theatrical and political change. Similarly the Performance Group, led by Richard Schechner, demonstrated in **Dionysus 69** a desire to elevate the ensemble above the individual actor. The Performance Group were liberationists – freedom from text, from character, from naturalism, from Stanislavsky, from illusion, from repression, from clothing: nudity was presented as if it put the actors in a state of primal innocence, rather than the audience in a state of terminal voyeurism. The company failed to discover a mythic element, or rituals which had anything but an anecdotal resonance, and self-deluded, imprisoned by the dogma of '60s psycho-babble, they disintegrated, to re-emerge from the splinters as the Wooster Group.

Ostensibly these companies were as free as the society that they were intended to engender. In truth, the authority of the writer had been replaced by the authority of the director, and the communities, for all their castigation of society for its repressive mores, were invariably inward-looking: they were cults. The concern to free themselves from text, to re-invent the mystical, to release the sensations, to make the body speak, became evasions, strategies to avoid moral or political responsibility.

They make a stark contrast to the work of companies like the Bread and Puppet Theatre who also lived, in near-poverty, as a collective – a wildly inventive group who used puppets of all sizes from glove puppets to twenty-foot giants. They performed expressionist parables, often on the streets, Bosch-like fables, using dance and mime and masks with a wild and irresistible charm and energy. Their visit to London in 1968 was one of those invasions of the imagination, like Ariane Mnouchkine's promenade production of her show about the French revolution, **1789**, at the Round House in 1974, that changed the way a whole generation of British writers, actors and directors thought about their work.

If all these companies did nothing else, they offered a chiding example to the British (and American) theatre of the importance of acting from the neck down as well as up. As Grotowski said: 'The body is your instrument.'

1789: Ariane Mnouchkine's French Revolution.

The late '60s was a time of unshackling and abandonment to the joys of Dionysus and the exploration of the senses. The well-made play with its limited confines and its stressed and forced dialogues had no magic for the new apostles of the theatre. I was tutored by the blazing experiments of the early Living Theatre.

That was Steven Berkoff, who has made his mark on the British theatre as an actor/writer/director with a nagging, strident, iconoclastic, voice – a 'kvetch that keeps you awake and drives you crazy' as he said of his play **Kvetch**.

He was born in Stepney in 1937, became an actor, and like so many English actors since, trained in Paris with the remarkable teacher of physical acting and story-telling, Jacques Lecoq (who also taught Ariane Mnouchkine and Simon McBurney). Frustrated by his failure to be offered the parts that he wanted, he started in the 1970s to write and perform his own work, relying on his voice, body, and face to create a 'poor theatre' in which 'a set should be able to melt in an instant and never represent a real heavy piece of pseudo-reality'. Berkoff turned to Kafka, creating adaptations of **In the Penal Colony**, **Metamorphosis**, and **The Trial**, and the Berkoffian style – a sort of bullying minimalism – has remained largely unchanged ever since: highly mannered, even ritualised, movement married to highly artificial vocal technique, the whole underwritten by a latent, and sometimes explicit, violence.

East offered a retrospective slap at the sloth of his childhood; **Decadence** poured acid scorn on the British upper classes, **Brighton Beach Scumbags** on the working classes; **Sink the Belgrano!** gave Thatcher a going-over for the Falklands War, while **Greek** ransacked the classical myths; in his production of Wilde's **Salomé**, by staging the whole play in grave slow-motion, he gave an authority to Wilde's incense-laden poetry. He directed and starred in **Hamlet**, provoking a self-effacing book on the experience, *I am Hamlet*, and created a one-man show based upon Shakespeare's villains, **Villain!**. He's the last Victorian actor-manager.

3

There are those who regard the desire for collective living and the lure of the united response as inherently corrupting. The playwright Howard Barker, for instance: 'We must overcome the desire to do things in unison … the baying of the audience in pursuit of unity is a sound of despair.' It's rare to find this in a playwright, but after the exuberant gush of exhortation in the 1960s to DO IT! and COME TOGETHER! it was increasingly common in the '70s and '80s to find the audience placed in the role of the passive spectator, as if at an art exhibition. The avant-garde theatre moved closer to the art gallery, the art gallery closer to the theatre; a piece of art revealed itself in time and space – performance art, living sculpture.

By far the most successful exponent of this form of theatre was a Pole who was a one-time teacher of Grotowski: Tadeusz Kantor (1915–1990). During the Nazi occupation he started an underground theatre. He found himself frustrated by theatrical illusion and by conventions of space, character, text, and time, and in 1956 he began to work with a group of visual artists, creating a theatre in which actors were used as props and sculpture and the text existed merely as a part of the texture of the production.

The first time British audiences saw his work was in 1970 when **The Water Hen** visited the Edinburgh festival, playing in a scarred warehouse off the Royal Mile. It was like taking a journey through a war-torn foreign country, and a journey was at the centre of the performance – Father and Son, like Pozzo and Lucky laden with cases, tramped through a landscape peopled by black- and dun-coloured figures sowing chaos like Brueghel's *Dulle Griet*.

In the beginning vodka was served to the audience by obsequious, black-tail-coated waiters: the Old World. This disintegrated into a cycle of revolution, anarchy, order through force, misery, chaos, and revolution, in a wild profusion of images: two businessmen – financial wizards, capitalists, bureaucrats, what-you-will – organised themselves, operated sewing machines, shaved themselves, and ostentatiously displayed their cunning in survival and command; a frenzied girl hammered a typewriter to feed the media appetite; a drag queen vamped the audience; a bourgeois lady shouted, 'Has it started yet?'; a rotund enveloping plastic-pink lady sat above the action like an umpire; hands snatched food from an immaculate white tablecloth; huge bundles of papers cascaded like a civil servant's nightmare; the Waterhen, a plump, attractive, fashion-conscious woman, was shot by her lover; a sentimental psychopath stabbed his dummy dancing partner; the Waterhen was resuscitated in a warm bath; a body was stretched in torture twenty feet or more. And through it all, the tall heron-like figure of Kantor stalked like a spectral conductor …

Kantor: the language of modern theatre.

Towards the end the entire company, the whole catalogue of society, was crammed inside a corral, jumbled, piled like meat, guarded by soldiers in field-grey, even their faces. The audience were invited in: some came, wandering nervously, shy, confused, like uncomprehending tourists in an East European country. Then revolution broke out and the corral broke up. The Son shot himself, the Father played cards. 'The world,' he said (in English), 'is breaking apart.'

Kantor's work was theatre and painting and poetry, and his company was composed of actors, painters, critics, gallery directors, and poets. **The Water Hen**, though improvised, though devoid of linear logic, though working in images, though mostly in Polish, was astonishingly clear and specific and quite free of sensationalism. It had the force of Joseph Beuys' 'social sculpture' without his metaphorical vagueness and gallery-installation portentousness. If there is a language of modern 'ritual' theatre, then Kantor invented the syntax.

Kantor has had a considerable influence on 'physical theatre' in Europe – Pina Bausch's company, for instance – and in this country. Théâtre de Complicité's production (with the National Theatre) of **The Street of Crocodiles,** based on the stories of the Polish Jewish writer Bruno Schultz, drew extensively on imagery from Kantor's work, although it was certainly at second or third hand – the company were young and the last time a production of Kantor's was seen in this country was in 1992 when **Today Is My Birthday** played at the Edinburgh Festival. Kantor died during rehearsals, after an argument with

The Street of Crocodiles: physical theatre.

the cast; as a mark of respect, they continued to play it after his death, his 'role' played by an actor and the audience and cast fogged with tears.

Théâtre de Complicité was founded in 1986 as a collective, but although many of the company have remained, the actor/director Simon McBurney has emerged as their defining talent. They combine movement, text, and design in the service of maximum expression of meaning, and achieve a genuine synthesis that dignifies the awkward neologism, 'theatre-making', which is invoked with religious piety by those who hold that 'text-based theatre' is inevitably inert and outdated.

The patron saint of the anti-text zealots is the American director, Robert Wilson (1941–), although ironically his work is ferociously dependent on what Tom Wolfe called 'the painted word' – literary references and codes that refer to other art forms. Wilson's work is elusive, almost inaccessible; it requires the complicity of the knowing spectator, the membership of the club – but then in the US it's hard to find a middle way between oppressive populism and the avant-garde. As one of his collaborators said, 'When Bob's theatre is popular, it's getting near to kitsch and that's a danger.' And it *is* often near to kitsch – rich, empty, exquisite images executed with great finesse that would be the stuff

367

of Broadway musicals were they not subverted by stretching time – his **Overture to Mountain** lasted twenty-four hours – by slowing down movement, repeating actions or simply allowing real time, rather than theatre time, to flow.

Wilson rejects narrative, plot and character, finding language too specific and gestures more expressive than words. The work resists a single interpretation: it's a defiance of meaning. His work has been described as 'autistic' – a private world peopled by subjective imagery, detached, cool and unreachable. He's a theatre animal in the sense that he collaborates with performers (often amateur), writers and composers – Philip Glass, for instance, in the case of **Einstein on the Beach**. Nevertheless, he's the undiluted autocrat and *auteur*, barely crediting his writers – except for his brain-damaged friend Christopher – and using designers as mere marionettes to execute his designs.

Much of Wilson's imagery is musical, conceived and composed and 'played' with an appeal not to observable truth in human behaviour but to dream, illusion and sensation. 'I make silent operas – images which are composed in structured space and time.' The images are consistently set within a proscenium frame. In spite of their authority and beauty, they seem etiolated, drained of resonance and life, like nineteenth-century academic paintings. 'Go like you would to a museum,' he suggests, 'like you would look at a painting. Appreciate the colour of the dress, the line of the apple, the glow of the light … ' A work of art, in Wilson's work, is not about something: it's the thing itself without a response to society or to politics.

He now does opera productions of great elegance in international opera houses; he says it brings together all the arts, but as Peter Brook says, 'You don't call soup great cuisine because you put everything into it.' Wilson is the artist of our times *par excellence*, part visionary, part businessman, part shaman, part charlatan.

4

Is all experiment over? Is there no adventure, no ambition, no courage, no politics, no spirituality? Does career triumph over vocation, celebrity over achievement? We claim that the theatre flourishes, but is that self-serving propaganda?

It's hard to be pessimistic about an art form which at the moment harbours such a singular talent as the director, Robert Lepage. Robert Lepage was born in Quebec City to a French Canadian family in 1957. His father was a bilingual taxi driver, from whom he unquestionably inherited his passion and facility for story-telling. For a few years he worked as an actor, a comedian, in a puppet theatre, in opera, and developed his habit of juggling projects simultaneously like a Chinese acrobat – in recent years skimming from theatre productions in London, Tokyo, Stockholm, Munich and Quebec, and finding time to direct two films and several operas.

He founded Théâtre Repère with friends and over a period of many years developed his most distinctive work – and also his best to date – **The Dragon's Trilogy**. While it was devised collectively, the tone was unique to Lepage. It was seen in its entirety at the

Riverside Studios in 1992; it could be said that at six hours the show was too short.

Upturned suitcases became the Hong Kong skyline; a streetlight was transformed into a comet; an art-exhibit – skeins of tiny lights – became Vancouver seen from the sky at night. An ancient English shoe-salesman, addresses us from his wheelchair – simultaneously as middle-aged man and child; when he dies in a plane crash the wheelchair becomes the rickshaw of his youth, then bursts into flames.

His shoes are his merchandise, but are also the people who wear them; kicked around the sandpit-stage they become the victims of war. Later we see the pilot – the one who will crash the plane – hurl himself at an airport gift shop: lights flash, the soundtrack roars, while the half-Japanese salesgirl cowers inside. Hiroshima?

Two childhood friends, Jeanne and Françoise, spend their adult lives linked by distance: the instructions of Françoise's typewriting course mesh with the diagnosis of Jeanne's cancer, the 'ping' of her typewriter with the bell on Jeanne's boyfriend's bike. Jeanne is married to a Chinese laundryman, who has won her in a game of poker; on a stage stripped of colour, the bright copper hair of daughter and natural father stand out like flames. A garrulous nun (never more so than when standing bolt upright on the luggage-basket of a fast-moving bike) arrives to take the brain-damaged daughter to an institution: the daughter is nowhere to be seen until, in a stunning *coup-de-théâtre*, the nun turns into her.

Characteristically, that scene emerged entirely pragmatically – the actress playing the nun was also playing the daughter and didn't have the time to change costumes between a scene with the mother and a scene in the mental hospital. So the girl's mother undressed the nun, one piece at a time, and put each piece of clothing in her daughter's suitcase; the nun became the daughter, and the dialogue, a sort of ritualistic catechism, was invented to accompany the transformation.

Behind every image there lurked a second. Behind the second, a third and a fourth. The invisible linking threads joined up, then formed a pattern: then the pattern itself gained meaning. It was as though, bit by bit, the secret paths of chance and destiny were being revealed.

Lepage doesn't scorn text as a tyranny to be liberated by gesture and imagery. It's more that it's a part, but not the core part, of a blend of art and architecture, music, dance, light, dialogue and movement. The writing – and the meaning – is in the whole event. If there's a motto that could be attached to Lepage's work it would be 'Only connect': Europe and America, Cocteau and Miles Davis in **Needles and Opium**, Venice and Jim Morrison in **Tectonic Plates**, Gurdjieff and Frank Lloyd Wright in **The Geometry of Miracles**. His productions of Shakespeare – **Macbeth, The Tempest, A Midsummer Night's Dream** – have been more successful in Québécois French than in English; his National Theatre production of **A Midsummer Night's Dream** in 1992 presented a flawlessly imaginative visual reading of the play, turning the Olivier stage into a giant pool in which the dream became a muddy nightmare. It gave a new visual syntax to the play, even if it rarely gave an equivalent power to the language.

Lepage is as undaunted by large subjects as by iconic classics. His last major show, **The Seven Streams of the River Ota**, was created with his own company Ex Machina (the 'Deus' tactically left out). It embraced Hiroshima, the Holocaust and AIDS, and contrived to do so with humane wit and beguiling grace. An amazing number of theatrical and filmic devices were combined alchemically with no sense of ostentation; the stylistic vocabulary of film, video, ballet, sitcom, Shakespeare and Japanese theatre made a syntax accessible to a generation weaned on the remote control, the rock video and TV naturalism, but was always at the service of telling the story.

The openness and eclecticism was liberating. In the middle of **Seven Streams**, following a succession of scenes where the space and the time seamlessly expanded and contracted, there was a scene in a room in Amsterdam played in real time, entirely naturalistically: the euthanasia of a man infected with AIDS. It was immensely simple, immensely touching, and was no less 'theatrical' than the cascade of visual images and surrealistic scenes that preceded it.

Lepage's work is often compared to Peter Brook's. There's the same perfect taste and unruffled tempo, but Brook's attachment to story-telling is philosophical: he's a maker of parables, whereas for Lepage the story is the key to a wilderness of realities, some near to hand, some remote, some buried beneath our feet like the Chinatown (and, still further down, the China) under the car-park in which **The Dragon's Trilogy** begins and ends.

Lepage is confident of creating theatre that can have meaning for a new generation, and if he is pessimistic about an art form, it is film rather than theatre. He said this recently:

> In the next four or five years we'll be amazed how theatre and film will have to live together, because film cannot continue in the form it is, in the way it's presented. People want direct life, three-dimensional interaction, and that's something that belongs to the theatre. Our field of work is telling stories and if we want to be exciting theatre story-tellers we have to be interested in film, television, and novels, because those forms of story-telling are changing how we tell stories. You have to have the humility to say, 'This subject deserves this, or this,' not try to imprison it or stifle it because you have a style, a way of doing things.

Robert Lepage's work is similar in many respects to that of another North American who exploded like a sunburst into the British theatre of the 1990s: Tony Kushner. Like Lepage, Kushner is eclectic, inventive, and stylistically daring. Both have a style that is always determined not by cross-referencing to fashion or to other art forms, but by the stories they want to tell. They're not 'avant-garde' or 'experimental', but neither are they mainstream or conservative. They simply attempt, like the best art, to make sense of the world.

Tony Kushner, instructively, came to light from the supposed dustbowl of the American regional theatre. He emerged for British audiences at the British National Theatre in 1992 with a two-part, seven-hour play about the American Right, McCarthyism,

*'People want direct life, three-dimensional interaction, and that's something that belongs to the theatre': Lepage's **Seven Streams of the River Ota**.*

Mormonism, Marxism, the Millennium, homosexuality, AIDS, zealotry, faith, God and angels. 'I just started writing something about America in the '80s, which was transparently not going to be short.'

Born in Manhattan in 1957 – the same year as Robert Lepage – and brought up in Louisiana, the son of musician parents, Kushner was steeped in the theatre before he started writing. He never lacked for boldness: his first play in 1985, **A Bright Room Called Day**, linked the last days of the Weimar Republic with the days of Reagan and Thatcher, and was performed in London at the Bush Theatre. His next play began life in 1987 as a commission for San Francisco's Eureka Theatre, was presented there in May 1990, dropped on the desk of the Director of the National Theatre in London in the following year, and was presented there in 1992. Only after its success there did it find its way to New York, a depressing indictment on the sloth or cautiousness of supposedly fiercely opportunistic producers. The second part simultaneously opened in London and New York.

The title of the play gives a sense of Kushner's uninhibited ambition – and of his drollery: **Angels in America (A Gay Fantasia on National Themes)**. To call it a 'gay play' is as accurate as calling **King Lear** an 'issue play'.

The centrifugal fragmentation of America heading for the end of the century is mirrored in the making of the plays, which shuffle locations with the deftness of a card sharp – heaven, Salt Lake City, San Francisco, New York, Antarctica – offering a vertiginous ride between naturalism and surrealism and expressionism, fact and fantasy, epic and soap opera. 'Theatre has always been about popular entertainment and the plays have a serial story … I have no argument with that. I can be cheap,' says Kushner.

A brief description of the plays can give a taste of their idiom, but only a bare fragment of their exuberance and the sense that they aspire to be about EVERYTHING that's happening NOW! – a dashing refutation of O'Neill's comment in 1946 on why he had set **The Iceman Cometh** in the past:

> I do not think that you can write anything of value or understanding about the present. You can only write about life if it is far enough in the past. The present is too mixed up with superficial values; you can't know which thing is important and which is not.

But Kushner proves him wrong by writing about the lurking fascism in US politics, the effects of the death of Communism, the rise of fundamentalist religions, the spread of AIDS, the cancer of racism: death, hope, fear, and love written in unpredictable stage poetry which slaloms between visionary wit and ardent polemic, and acute pain rubs shoulders with genial farce.

Part One is called **Millennium Approaches**, Part Two **Perestroika** – the first title is a factual description, the second an affirmation: the first play analyses America, the second argues that the USA must change as radically as the Soviet Union:

When I first called the play **Perestroika** it was 1988, when Gorbachev made the announcement at the Party Congress … Overnight everything was going to be different … I really think Perestroika is a beautiful model for political and human change; it is completely terrifying and ugly and chaotic and deeply unpleasant to go through because you don't know what's coming. Optimism doesn't come into it.

In an America that is 'terminal, mean, crazy', finding cures for society is as important as finding cures for AIDS; healing personal relationships is as important as healing bodies. But to cure relationships you must cure yourself, examine who you are and admit it to yourself. It takes courage to make a choice: I am this person and this is how I live. It's a defiant affirmation for an age of doubt and despair, crawling towards the Millennium unarmed with God or ideology. With an arsenal of wit, intellect, rhetoric, knowledge and dizzying theatrical invention, Kushner argues unsentimentally and irresistibly for common humanity and community enterprise, that the power of the whole – a couple, a group, a society – is greater than that of a diaspora of individuals.

Arthur Miller has said he feels fearful for Tony Kushner because he can never follow the success of **Angels in America**. That's possibly true, and it's several years since he received a joint commission from the New York Public Theatre and the Royal National Theatre to write a play – **Henry Box Brown** – about slavery. But it's hard to doubt the resolve and sangfroid of a man who, in his playwrighting course at New York University, insists that his students must first read Marx in order that they should know what it is that they're demonising.

Kushner's passionate democratic socialism is a paradox in a country that plays host to countless religious cults and right-wing political zealots; it marks him out as a political anomaly and an eccentric visionary. Either way, he lies in that seam of American Utopian thinking that connects directly with the first emigrants from England in search of the 'new commonwealth'. In the theatre at least the new commonwealth is always an alluring and achievable model, even if on the political stage it has scarred the history of the twentieth century and cost countless millions of lives.

Theatre is often regarded in Britain as the cricket of the performing arts – meaning archaic, quaint, thinly attended, and not done as well as it used to be. It's true that after a century of unparalleled vigour and invention in the British theatre, it now seems subdued: a landscape of uncertainty under a cloud of anxiety. It's true, too, that the body of British theatre – that anatomy made up from theatres up and down the country – has atrophied through lack of financial support, inducing a lack of confidence and ambition.

But everything in the world obeys the motion of a wave: what goes up, comes down, what comes down, goes up. Looking back on the theatre of this century, it is clear that we have been here before and what's more, today's news is far from all bad: at the start of the twenty-first century, tourists flock to London to see 'our wonderful theatre', British writers and actors dominate Broadway, British directors are fêted in Hollywood and on the international jet-set circuit, German dramaturgs ransack British studio theatres for poets of dystopian disillusion, as though they had none of their own. Established actors, writers, directors and designers continue to produce occasional stabs of thrilling theatre and are challenged by a new generation of gifted writers – Patrick Marber, Sarah Kane, Mark Ravenhill, Martin McDonagh, and Jonathan Harvey, to name a few, and directors – Nicholas Hytner, Stephen Daldry, Deborah Warner, Declan Donnellan, Simon McBurney, Sam Mendes, Matthew Warchus, and Katie Mitchell, to name a few more.

One of the themes of this book is the extent to which, over the course of a century, the British theatre has managed to free itself from the baggage of the past. The purpose of our trips back into history has been to show how some of this baggage originated; the milestones we have celebrated are the points where one or another cumbersome parcel has been dropped, or shaken a little looser than it was before.

Censorship is rare and barely enforceable. Britain no longer depends on Ireland for its genius, and Ireland has a vigorous drama of its own. Theatre of moral or intellectual muscle isn't seen as a dour eccentricity, while interventions into contemporary politics are positively welcomed. The political realm itself has split and diversified: the politics of sex and gender have equal status with those of class and economics, if not higher. The epic form, glory of the Jacobean theatre, has been brought into the theatrical mainstream after centuries of exile, and gay writers don't any longer have to function in disguise.

One result of all this is that the styles and themes and forms available to young playwrights are almost infinite. The only limiting factor is the imagination. This is why, when anyone asks what the style of the day is amongst younger writers – what subjects appeal to them, what the shared aesthetic is – all one can say is that they're writing *much less like each other* than ever before: that Patrick Marber's **Closer** and Mark Ravenhill's **Shopping and Fucking** are indeed both modern, smart, sexy and set in London, but that the cool, acerbic pain of the one shares neither style nor sensibility with the nightmare wit of the other; that Phyllis Nagy and Martin Crimp are indeed both cracking the old theatrical templates, but are doing so in different ways.

Sarah Kane was a profoundly original playwright who, in her tragically brief writing life, rewrote the theatrical map. **Blasted** starts with an abusive sexual relationship between father and daughter and expands it into the world of war and atrocity. Public and private violence stand as metaphors for each other. Hideous actions follow: the father is raped, his eyes are sucked out, he eats a dead baby. Finally, redemption comes in the form of rain.

Blasted was first produced at the Theatre Upstairs, which had recently knocked up an outstanding run of plays by other new writers: Joe Penhall, Judy Upton, Nick Grosso. The word was out that new writing was exciting again, that it might even be news, so the critical turnout on the first night consisted not only of those loyal faithfuls who regularly reviewed plays on the fringe, but more middlebrow critics who hadn't been

following form. They couldn't believe their eyes. Hurried conferences took place on the pavement outside and the following day a vast shock-horror story erupted. Kane was doorstopped and went into hiding; Pinter and Bond came out in support. Most inflammatory, as far as the press was concerned, was the fact that Kane was a well-mannered and attractive young woman. When even nice gels talk dirty (ran the message) what hope is there for civilisation?

What's easy to miss about Kane's work is how classic it is. **Phaedra's Love,** her version of **Hippolytos,** seems on the face of it an irreverent work, but it's entirely in keeping with the tart perversity of Euripides' original. Her technique of setting the play within a dream-landscape, consistent with its own internal logic but no other, is the method of Maeterlinck, the *fin de siècle* avant-gardist who above all other playwrights was the inspiration for Yeats. And her subject – suffering – has been a central theme of English drama since the mystery plays.

Crave is set at the focal point of unbearable pressures. 'Depression's inadequate,' says the young woman at their centre. 'A full-scale emotional collapse is the minimum required to justify letting everyone down.' One year later, Kane took her life: her death at the end of the second Millennium seemed iconic.

Suffering has stood at the heart of British drama since it began. In the mystery plays, Christ's suffering on the cross stands at the hub of a vast wheel of echo and implication. Birth, mortality, sin, revenge, love and redemption all have their place, but all relate to the agony at the centre: the forsaken cry of the man/god whose life, for a single despairing moment, seems stripped of meaning. It's no accident that our common test of greatness in a play, to this day, is the extent to which it conveys the complexity of suffering; or that the plays that give us the most delight are that handful of Arcadian masterpieces which posit a world without it – **The Importance** or **Guys and Dolls**; or that plays that dodge around the subject of suffering in a dishonest way seem guilty pleasures at best.

Afterword

For the last twenty years neither matter nor space nor time has been what it was since civilisation began. 'Virtual reality' has now become as much a description of many people's lives as a technological device. Our age has become at best sceptical and at worst cynical of any sort of public social obligation or ceremony.

We have been handed the weapons of dissent – the video recorder and the remote control – and we use them without conscience or remorse, becoming habituated to byte-sized, time-shifted fragments. We've become hanging judges, impatient with any idea that takes more than a few minutes to develop, intolerant of space between words, of stillness and silence. All of which conspires to make the survival of the theatre more remarkable – and more desirable.

When television began in the 1950s, there was a justifiable fear that the theatre would evaporate, leaving a few wisps of nostalgia above the battlefield. Many theatres died under the weight of their own inertia, those that remained were forced to make the medium more intense, more concerned with the hell or heaven of real life. Hence the prodigal profusion of playwrights, the foundation of the National Theatre and the Royal Shakespeare Company, and the cocky buoyancy of a generation who, regarding 'text-based theatre' as inert and old-fashioned, achieved a genuine synthesis of movement, text, design in the service of maximum expression of meaning.

In the theatre we have to use what is necessary to say what we want to say: there should be no hierarchy of form. A two-and-a-half-hour naturalistic play set in real time in one location can be as potent as a seven-hour play that moves from Hiroshima to New York and from wartime to the present day. Both can use the theatre to tell stories that have power, resonance and relevance to the way we live our lives. As long as the theatre has the desire and ability to do that we shouldn't mourn for its decline, or feel that we are failing to solve the question: what direction does the theatre go in?

From looking at the theatre of the past in Britain, a few things are clear about its future:

1. Theatre is a medium that lives in the present tense; if it is to survive it must reflect the heartbeat of its time. We must remember George Devine's maxim: 'Treat new plays like classics, and classics like new plays'. The classics are our genetic link with the past and our means of decoding the present. We find in them not the past throwing a shadow on the present, but a distorted image of ourselves.

2. All theatre is dead that isn't newly made. What's new in the theatre lies as much in the subject matter as in the intensification of forms that are already in existence. But any view of art that insists on locating its meanings in its power *merely* to do what hasn't been done before narrows its doors of perception rather than opens them. 'The common symptom of immaturity,' said Edith Wharton, 'is the dread of doing what has been done before.' And as long as the attention is locked only on to form, the results will be purely formal. Salvation will never come from technological innovation.

3. Theatre companies have a finite lifespan; few manage to sustain artistic ardour beyond seven years. While theatre will remain inextinguishable, its survival won't depend on the institutions that have been established for the needs and aspirations of different generations. Buildings can be changed and replaced; institutions can evolve. The large theatre companies – the RSC and NT – which emerged from a particular time and imperative must adapt. Any theatre will dwindle that does not allow for the luck of genius and possess the will to accommodate it.

4. Money is required to make ticket prices accessible to all, to secure buildings, to provide continuity for theatre companies, and to underwrite risk-taking; the power to engender *real* access will only be achieved by the efforts of the arts *and* educational organisations to abolish the sense of apartheid that exists between those who benefit from subsidy to the arts and those who feel excluded from them. This will never be achieved without the enthusiastic support of the state.

5. Money alone never produced any art worth having. 'Writers can't be forced like rhubarb,' said Gorky. You can't legislate for talent, it's inequitable and unpredictable. What money can do to help is allow talent to breathe, to be educated, trained, exercised, recognised and enjoyed.

6. The case for the survival of theatre can only be made through the art itself. It has to exploit its unreproducible elements: to proclaim the virtues of its liveness and its uniqueness; to ravish the eyes and ears and enchant the soul; to assert its unique dependence on the human form and voice; to exploit our ability to tell stories and our willingness to listen to them.

7. Nothing can live in the theatre that is not conceived out of passion, nurtured on obsession, and educated in enthusiasm.

Brecht asked this question in Germany after the First World War: 'What is the purpose of these theatres?' Artaud gave him an answer:

The human face carries a kind of perpetual death on it and it is up to the painter himself to save it with his strokes by giving it back its rightful features.

Calendar of Notable Events
1900–1999*

1900 Ben Greet stages first productions in Regent's Park. Granville-Barker plays Marchbanks in Shaw's **Candida**. Paris: death of Oscar Wilde. Sarah Bernhardt in Rostand's **L'Aiglon**. Stockholm: Strindberg's **Easter** and **The Dance of Death**. USA: Belasco's **Madame Butterfly**.

1901 J.M. Barrie: **Quality Street**. William Poel directs **Everyman**. Barker's **The Marrying of Anne Leete**. Wedekind's **Spring Awakening** privately performed by the Stage Society. Stockholm: Strindberg's **A Dream Play**. At the Moscow Art Theatre: Chekhov's **Three Sisters**.

1902 J.M. Barrie's **The Admirable Crichton**. Berlin: Strindberg's **Dream Play**. Première of Büchner's **Danton's Death** (written 1835). Moscow Art Theatre: Stanislavsky directs Gorky's **The Lower Depths**.

1903 Edward Gordon Craig designs Ibsen's **The Vikings**. Thomas Hardy's **The Dynasts** published in three parts between 1903 and 1908.

1904 First Barker/Vedrenne season at Court Theatre. Shaw's **John Bull's Other Island**. J.M. Barrie's **Peter Pan**. Herbert Beerbohm Tree founds RADA. The Abbey Theatre opens in Dublin; Synge's **Riders to the Sea**. Russia: Gorky's **Summerfolk**, Chekhov's **The Cherry Orchard**. Death of Chekhov.

1905 Barker's **The Voysey Inheritance** and Shaw's **Man and Superman**, both at the Court. Charles Chaplin plays Billie the Page in William Gillette's **Sherlock Holmes**. Edward Gordon Craig: *On the Art of the Theatre*. Sir Henry Irving dies playing **Beckett** in Bradford. Norway: Ibsen dies. Vienna: Wedekind's **Pandora's Box**. Berlin: Max Reinhardt directs **A Midsummer Night's Dream**. USA: Belasco's **The Girl of the Golden West**.

1906 Ellen Terry as Hermione: her last new Shakespearian role. Also Lady Cecily Waynfleete in Shaw's **Captain Brassbound's Conversion**. Court Theatre: Galsworthy's **The Silver Box**. Paris: André Antoine appointed director of the Odéon.

1907 Elizabeth Robins' **Votes for Women!** Barker and William Archer publish *A National Theatre*. Desmond MacCarthy: *The Court Theatre*. Annie Horniman takes over the Gaiety Theatre, Manchester. J.M. Synge's **The Playboy of the Western World**. Stockholm: Strindberg's **The Ghost Sonata**.

1908 Society of West End Theatre Managers (SWET) formed. Ellen Terry: *The Story of My Life*.

1909 John Galsworthy's **Strife**. **The Seagull** first performed in English at the Glasgow Repertory Theatre. Stockholm: Strindberg's last play, **The Great Highway**. Moscow Art: Stanislavsky directs Maeterlinck's **The Blue Bird**.

1910 J.M. Barrie: **The Twelve-Pound Look**.

1911 Barker's **The Madras House**. D.H. Lawrence writes **The Daughter-in-Law**. Reinhardt's **The Miracle** in London, starring Lady Diana Manners.

1912 Githa Sowerby's **Rutherford and Son**. Stanley Houghton's **Hindle Wakes**. Granville-Barker directs **Twelfth Night** and **The Winter's Tale** at the Savoy Theatre. The Stage Society presents the British première of **The Cherry Orchard**. Lilian Baylis takes over the Old Vic from her aunt, Emma Cons. Edith Evans in William Poel's **Troilus and Cressida**. Paris: Paul Claudel's **L'Annonce faite à Marie**, dir. Lugné-Poe. Moscow: Craig designs **Hamlet** for Stanislavsky. Budapest: première of Schnitzler's **Reigen** (aka **La Ronde**).

1913 Barry Jackson opens the Birmingham Repertory Theatre. Paris: Copeau founds a theatre company in the Vieux Colombier on the Left Bank. Munich: première of Büchner's **Woyzeck** (written 1837).

1914 Beerbohm Tree and Mrs Patrick Campbell in Shaw's **Pygmalion**. Granville-Barker's **A Midsummer Night's Dream**.

1915 Harold Brighouse's **Hobson's Choice** at the Gaiety, Manchester.

1916 **Chu Chin Chow** begins five-year run. Rome: Luigi Chiarelli's **The Mask and the Face**. Russia: Meyerhold directs Lermontov's **Masquerade**. USA: Susan Glaspell's **Trifles**. Founding of Provincetown Players.

1917 Maugham's **Our Betters**. Germany: Georg Kaiser's **From Morn to Midnight**.

1918 Nigel Playfair takes over the Lyric, Hammersmith: over the next fourteen years he will put on plays by Sheridan, Dryden, Congreve, Molière, Wilde, Pirandello. USA: the Theatre Guild is formed to present 'the best of European and US drama'. Also first Pulitzer Prize awarded. In the USSR: Meyerhold directs Mayakovsky's **Mystery-Bouffe**. Munich: Brecht writes *Baal*.

1919 George Pierce Baker: *Dramatic Technique*.

1920 Shaw's **Heartbreak House**. Nigel Playfair directs **The Beggar's Opera** at the Lyric Hammersmith, with Lovat Fraser designs. The American monologuist Ruth Draper makes her debut at the Aeolian Hall, London.

1921 Vienna: Hofmannsthal's **The Difficult Man**. New York: the Theatre Guild presents Molnar's **Liliom**. Rome: Pirandello's **Six Characters in Search of an Author**. Prague: the Čapek brothers' **RUR**.

1922 Laurence Olivier makes first stage appearance in school production of **The Taming of the Shrew**. ('The boy who played Katherine is already a great actor': Ellen Terry.) Birmingham: Shaw's **Back to Methuselah**. New York: the Theatre Guild presents Andreyev's **He Who Gets Slapped**. John Barrymore's **Hamlet**. Italy: Pirandello's **Henry IV**. Germany: Toller's **The Machine Wreckers**. Prague: the Čapek brothers' **The Insect Play**. In the USSR: Vakhtangov directs **The Dybbuk** for the Habimah.

1923 Sybil Thorndike in Shaw's **Saint Joan**. The Phoenix Society set up to revive neglected playwrights: Farquhar, Congreve, Vanbrugh, etc. Death of Sarah Bernhardt. Dublin: O'Casey's **Shadow of a Gunman**. France: Louise Jouvet in Jules Romains' **Dr Knock**. USA: Elmer Rice's **The Adding Machine**. Munich: Brecht's **In the Jungle of Cities**.

1924 Noël Coward's **The Vortex**. Edith Evans as Millament at the Lyric Hammersmith. John Gielgud/Gwen Ffrangcon-Davies as **Romeo and Juliet**. Dublin: O'Casey's **Juno and the Paycock**. USA: Paul Robeson in O'Neill's **All God's Chillun Got Wings**. Eleonora Duse dies in Pittsburgh. USSR: Tairov's constructivist **The Man Who Was Thursday** at the Kamerny.

1925 Coward's **Hay Fever**. J.R. Ackerley's **Prisoners of War**. Barry Jackson's 'plus-fours' **Hamlet**. Berlin: Piscator directs **Despite All!**: documentary revue.

1926 Ben Travers' **Rookery Nook**. Edgar Wallace's **The Ringer**. Stanislavsky's *An Actor*

Prepares is translated into English. Dublin: O'Casey's **The Plough and the Stars**. In Germany: Ferdinand Bruckner's **The Pains of Youth**. Hungary: Molnar's **The Play's the Thing**. USSR: Meyerhold directs **The Government Inspector**. Bulgakov's **Days of the Turbins** gets thumbs-up from Stalin.

1927 Gladys Cooper produces and stars in Somerset Maugham's **The Letter**. Cambridge: Terence Gray directs **Henry VIII**. 1927–1946: Granville-Barker's *Prefaces to Shakespeare*. Berlin: Piscator founds the Piscatorbühne. In the USA: Kern/Hammerstein's **Showboat**. In the USSR: Bulgakov's **Flight** banned.

1928 R.C. Sherriff's **Journey's End**, dir. James Whale. Brecht visits London and sees T.S. Eliot's **Sweeney Agonistes**. Dublin: the Abbey rejects **The Silver Tassie**; Micheál Macliammóir and Hilton Edwards open the Gate Theatre. In the USA: Hecht/MacArthur's **The Front Page**. Sophie Treadwell's **Machinal**. O'Neill's **Strange Interlude**. Berlin: Piscator/Brecht **The Good Soldier Schweik**. Brecht/Weill/Hauptmann's **The Threepenny Opera**.

1929 A.A. Milne/Kenneth Grahame **Toad of Toad Hall**. British Actors' Equity founded. Dublin: Denis Johnston's **The Old Lady Says 'No!'**. Berlin: Marieluise Fleisser's **Pioneers in Ingolstadt**. Piscator publishes *The Political Theatre*. Moscow: Meyerhold directs Mayakovsky's **The Bedbug**.

1930 Coward's **Private Lives**. Paul Robeson/Peggy Ashcroft in **Othello**. France: Michel Saint-Denis directs the Compagnie des Quinze in Obey's **Noah**. USA: Kaufman/Hart's **Once in a Lifetime**. USSR: Erdman's **The Suicide** banned. Bulgakov's **Molière** banned.

1931 Coward's **Cavalcade**. Wilde's **Salome**, written in 1891, gets its first production in England. Dublin: Orson Welles, aged sixteen, joins the Gate as actor. Germany: Brecht/Eisler's **The Measures Taken**. Horváth's **Tales from the Vienna Woods**. USA: Harold Clurman founds the Group Theatre.

1932 Nigel Playfair gives up the Lyric, Hammersmith. George Devine (President of OUDS) invites Gielgud to direct **Romeo and Juliet**. Terence Rattigan has one-line role. Moscow: Stanislavsky/Bulgakov **Dead Souls**. USA: Hecht/MacArthur **Twentieth Century**.

1933 Noël Coward's **Design for Living**. Maugham's last play: **Sheppey**. Tyrone Guthrie becomes Director of the Old Vic. Laughton in **Measure for Measure**. Germany: Brecht flees to Denmark. Spain: Lorca's **Blood Wedding**. USSR: Tairov directs Vishnevsky's **An Optimistic Tragedy**.

1934 Gielgud as romantic **Hamlet**: it runs for 155 performances. Gow/Greenwood **Love on the Dole**. USA: Lillian Hellman's **The Children's Hour**. Moscow: Soviet Writers' Congress imposes socialist realism.

1935 Gielgud, Olivier, Peggy Ashcroft and Edith Evans in Motley-designed **Romeo and Juliet**. T.S. Eliot's **Murder in the Cathedral**. Auden/Isherwood's **The Dog Beneath the Skin**. Saint-Denis directs Gielgud as Obey's **Noah**. In France: Antonin Artaud directs **The Cenci**. USA: **Porgy and Bess**. Elia Kazan directs Odets' **Waiting for Lefty**. In the USSR: Isaac Babel's **Marya** banned.

1936 Old Vic: Tyrone Guthrie directs Ruth Gordon in **The Country Wife**. Rattigan's **French Without Tears**. Komisarjevsky directs Gielgud, Ashcroft, Evans in **The Seagull**. Ivor Novello's **Careless Rapture**. Unity Theatre formed. Bulgakov writes his satire on the Moscow Art Theatre and censorship: *Black Snow*. USA: Orson Welles directs **Macbeth** with an all-African-American cast. Eugene O'Neill receives Nobel Prize.

1937 Old Vic: Guthrie directs Olivier in uncut **Hamlet**. Redgrave/Evans in **As You Like It**. Saint-Denis/Olivier **Macbeth** at the Old Vic. Death of Lilian Baylis. John Gielgud's season at the Queens. New York: Welles directs modern-dress **Julius Caesar** for his and John Houseman's company Mercury Theatre. Marc Blitzstein: **The Cradle Will Rock**.

1938 Old Vic: Guthrie directs Alec Guinness in modern-dress **Hamlet**. Michel Saint-Denis directs **Three Sisters** in Gielgud season. Saint-Denis directs Ashcroft/Redgrave in Bulgakov's **The White Guard**, adaptor Rodney Ackland. Patrick Hamilton's **Gaslight**. USA: Thornton Wilder's **Our Town**. France: Artaud publishes *The Theatre and its Double*. Horváth killed in Paris. Denmark: Brecht writes **Life of Galileo**. USSR: Meyerhold disappears into the Gulag.

1939 T.S. Eliot's **The Family Reunion**. Ivor Novello's **The Dancing Years**. Gielgud, Evans, Ashcroft, Margaret Rutherford in 'black-and-white' **Importance**. The Stage Society presents **Blood Wedding**: its last production. Death of W.B. Yeats. USA: Philip Barry: **The Philadelphia Story**. Eugene O'Neill's **The Iceman Cometh**. William Saroyan's **The Time of Your Life**. Finland: Brecht writes **Mother Courage and her Children**.

1940 Founding of the Council for the Encouragement of Music and the Arts: precursor of Arts Council. USA: Gene Kelly in Rodgers/Hart **Pal Joey**. In the USSR: Bulgakov dies of natural causes.

1941 Margaret Rutherford as Madame Arcati in Coward's **Blithe Spirit**. Brecht reaches the United States; his collaborator Margarete Steffin dies in Moscow. In the USSR: Isaac Babel dies in prison camp. USA: Lillian Hellman's **Watch on the Rhine**.

1942 Samuel Beckett arrives in Roussillon.

1943 In the USA: Rodgers and Hammerstein's **Oklahoma!**, choreography: Agnes de Mille.

1944 Start of the Olivier/Richardson Old Vic season's at the New Theatre. USA: Bernstein/Comden/Green/Robbins's **On the Town**. USSR: Evgeny Shvarts' **The Dragon** is banned.

1945 Joan Littlewood and others start Theatre Workshop. Paris: Giraudoux's **The Madwoman of Chaillot**, director Louis Jouvet, designer Christian Bérard. Gérard Philipe in Camus' **Caligula**. USA: Tennessee Williams' **The Glass Menagerie**.

1946 Peter Brook directs **Love's Labour's Lost** at Stratford-upon-Avon. Max Wall appears for the first time as Professor Walloffski. Founding of the Arts Council of Great Britain. Michel Saint-Denis, George Devine and Glen Byam Shaw start the Old Vic School. Founding of the Bristol Old Vic. Naples: De Filippo's **Filumena Maturano**. USA: Irving Berlin's **Annie Get Your Gun**.

1947 Richardson, Guinness in **The Alchemist**. William Douglas Home's **The Chiltern Hundreds**. Ena Lamont Stewart's **Men Should Weep**. Priestley's **The Linden Tree**. Milan: Giorgio Strehler co-founds the Teatro Piccolo and directs first of several productions of Goldoni's **The Servant of Two Masters**. France: Louis Jouvet directs Genet's **The Maids**. Jean Vilar founds the Avignon Festival. In the USA: Brando in **A Streetcar Named Desire**, directed by Kazan. Laughton plays Galileo. Brecht outwits HUAC and leaves for East Berlin. Elia Kazan and others found the Actors' Studio.

1948 Christopher Fry's **The Lady's Not for Burning**. Paris: Barrault directs Edwige Feuillière in Claudel's **Partage de Midi** (' … the play which for text, production and performance was the best I have ever seen, either in France or anywhere else': Harold Hobson). Prague: Josef Svoboda becomes head designer of the Czech National Theatre.

1949 Ivor Novello's **King's Rhapsody**. T.S. Eliot's **The Cocktail Party**. Ashcroft/Richardson in Goetz's **The Heiress**. **Buoyant Billions**: Shaw's last play. The Old Vic Governors fire Olivier, Richardson and their associate John Burrell. In New York: Kazan directs Arthur Miller's **Death of a Salesman**. East Berlin: Brecht and Weigel found the Berliner Ensemble; Brecht's *An Organum for the Theatre*.

1950 Brook directs Paul Scofield, Claire Bloom and Margaret Rutherford in Anouilh/ Fry **Ring Round the Moon** designed by Oliver Messel. Ashcroft/Gielgud in **Much Ado About Nothing**. Brian Rix in **Reluctant Heroes** at the Whitehall. Kenneth Tynan: *He That Plays the King*. Paris: Ionesco's **The Bald Prima Donna**. New York: Frank Loesser's **Guys and Dolls**.

1951 Olivier/Vivien Leigh in **Antony and Cleopatra** and **Caesar and Cleopatra**. Guthrie directs Donald Wolfit as **Tamburlaine**. Peter Ustinov's **The Love of Four Colonels**. Paris: Jean Vilar appointed head of the Théâtre National Populaire. Avignon: Gérard Philipe as **Le Cid**. New York: Lee Strasberg becomes Artistic Director of the Actors' Studio.

1952 Rattigan's **The Deep Blue Sea**. Rodney Ackland's **The Pink Room**. **An Evening with Beatrice Lillie**. The Old Vic Governors close down the Old Vic School. **The Mousetrap** opens. Paris: Ionesco's **The Chairs**. Agnes de Mille: *Dance to the Piper*.

1953 At the Old Vic, Richard Burton and John Neville alternate as **Hamlet**. Michael Benthall embarks on five-year plan to present the whole of the Shakespeare canon. At Stratford: Redgrave and Ashcroft in **Antony and Cleopatra**. Gielgud/Scofield in Brook's **Venice Preserv'd** at the Lyric, Hammersmith. N.C. Hunter's **A Day by the Sea**. Sandy Wilson's **The Boyfriend**. Theatre Workshop takes over the Theatre Royal, Stratford East. Rattigan invents 'Aunt Edna'. Radio: Dylan Thomas's **Under Milk Wood**. Paris: Beckett's **En attendant Godot**. USA: Arthur Miller's **The Crucible**. Bernstein/ Comden/Green's **Wonderful Town**. Death of Eugene O'Neill. Canada: First Festival at Stratford, Ontario: Guthrie develops the thrust stage, prototype for Chichester, Olivier Theatre, etc.

1954 Rattigan's **Separate Tables**. Peggy Ashcroft as **Hedda Gabler**. John Chapman: **Dry Rot**. Tynan joins the *Observer*. Margaret Ramsay founds literary agency. The Berliner Ensemble triumphs at the Théâtre des Nations in Paris. USA: Joseph Papp founds the New York Shakespeare Festival. James Baldwin: **The Amen Corner**.

1955 Olivier/Brook **Titus Andronicus**. Peter Hall directs **Waiting for Godot** at the Arts. Orson Welles' **Moby Dick**. Joan Littlewood directs and plays **Mother Courage**. Evans/Ashcroft in Enid Bagnold's **The Chalk Garden**. Gielgud in **King Lear**, designed by Noguchi. **Joyce Grenfell Requests the Pleasure**. USA: Williams' **Cat on a Hot Tin Roof**. Miller's **A View from the Bridge**.

1956 Brecht dies. Berliner Ensemble visits London. George Devine starts the English Stage Company at the Royal Court. Osborne's **Look Back in Anger**. 'Angry Young Men'. Behan's **The Quare Fellow** at Stratford East. New York: **Long Day's Journey into Night**.

Rex Harrison in Lerner and Loewe's **My Fair Lady**, costumes by Cecil Beaton. Paris: Jacques Lecoq sets up his international mime school. GDR: Brecht dies.

1957 N.F. Simpson's **A Resounding Tinkle**. Maggie Smith/Kenneth Williams in **Share My Lettuce**. Olivier in Osborne's **The Entertainer**. Richard Pilbrow founds Theatre Projects: redefinition of lighting design in Britain. Paris: Beckett's **Fin de Partie**. Lyons: Roger Planchon takes over the Théâtre de la Cité in Villeurbanne. USA: Bernstein/Laurents/Sondheim/Robbins **West Side Story**.

1958 Behan's **The Hostage** and Shelagh Delaney's **A Taste of Honey**, both at Stratford East. Ann Jellicoe's **The Sport of My Mad Mother**. John Arden's **Live Like Pigs**. The Lunts in Dürrenmatt's **The Visit**, dir. Brook. Gielgud: **The Ages of Man**. New York: opening of Caffe Cino: first 'Off-Off-Broadway' venue.

1959 Arden's **Serjeant Musgrave's Dance**. Wesker's **Roots** and **The Kitchen**, dir. John Dexter. Peter O'Toole London debut in Willis Hall's **The Long and the Short and the Tall**. Stratford East: Frank Norman/Lionel Bart's **Fings Ain't Wot They Used T'Be**. Stratford-upon-Avon: Olivier as **Coriolanus**, Charles Laughton as **Lear** and in Peter Hall's **A Midsummer Night's Dream**, Zoe Caldwell in Guthrie's **All's Well That Ends Well**, Robeson's last **Othello**. Opening of first British post-war theatre: the Belgrade, Coventry. In Ireland: J.B. Keane's **Sive**. In Paris: Jean-Louis Barrault appointed Director of the Odéon. USA: Rodgers/Hammerstein's **The Sound of Music**, Ethel Merman in Styne/Laurents/Sondheim/Robbins **Gypsy**. Albee's **Zoo Story**. Lorraine Hansberry's **A Raisin in the Sun**.

1960 Zeffirelli directs **Romeo and Juliet** at the Old Vic. Pinter's **The Caretaker**. Welles directs Olivier in Ionesco's **Rhinoceros**. Finney in Waterhouse/Hall **Billy Liar**. Robert Bolt's **A Man for All Seasons**. Lionel Bart's **Oliver!** with Sean Kenny designs. **Beyond the Fringe**. Under Peter Hall, the Shakespeare Memorial Theatre establishes a London base at the Aldwych Theatre. O'Toole/Ashcroft in **The Taming of the Shrew**, O'Toole as Shylock. Michel Saint-Denis' *Theatre: A Rediscovery of Style*. Dublin: Micheál Maclíammoír's **The Importance of Being Oscar**. Paris: Brook directs Genet's **The Balcony**. New York: An Evening with Mike Nichols and Elaine May.

1961 At the Royal Court: Beckett's **Happy Days**. Ann Jellicoe's **The Knack**. Finney in Osborne's **Luther**, designed by Jocelyn Herbert. Peter Hall transforms the Shakespeare Memorial Theatre into the Royal Shakespeare Company. Vanessa Redgrave's Rosalind in **As You Like It**, dir. Michael Elliott. John Whiting's **The Devils**. **The Hollow Crown**, devised John Barton. Tom Murphy's **A Whistle in the Dark** at Stratford East. Arnold Wesker starts Centre 42. New York: Peter Schumann starts the Bread and Puppet Theatre. South Africa: Athol Fugard's **The Blood Knot**.

1962 Lenny Bruce in London. Olivier's first Chichester season: Redgrave/Olivier **Uncle Vanya**. RSC: Scofield, Irene Worth, McCowen, Alan Webb in Brook's **Lear**. Wesker's **Chips With Everything**. James Saunders' **Next Time I'll Sing to You**. Bond's **The Pope's Wedding**. The RSC presents an experimental season at the Arts, inc. Rudkin's **Afore Night Come**. Joe Orton and Kenneth Halliwell imprisoned for defacing library books. In Stoke-on-Trent, Stephen Joseph founds Britain's first theatre-in-the-round. In Edinburgh, Jim Haynes founds the Traverse Theatre. In Germany: Piscator appointed Director of the West Berlin Volksbühne. USA: Ellen Stewart founds Café La Mama. Uta Hagen in **Who's Afraid of Virgina Woolf?** Zero Mostel in **A Funny Thing Happened on the Way to the Forum**: lyrics and music by Sondheim.

1963 Hall/Barton's **The Wars of the Roses** at the RSC, designed by John Bury. National Theatre opens at the Old Vic, under Laurence Olivier with O'Toole in **Hamlet**; Kenneth Tynan joins as Literary Adviser. Gaskill directs Maggie Smith and Robert Stephens in **The Recruiting Officer**. Joan Littlewood/Theatre Workshop **Oh, What a Lovely War!**. James Saunders' **Next Time I'll Sing to You**. Edinburgh sees early 'happening': naked lady appears on trolley during theatre conference. In New York: Joseph Chaikin founds the Open Theatre. Mike Nichols directs Neil Simon's **Barefoot in the Park**.

1964 Devine directs Beckett's **Play** at the National Theatre. Olivier's **Othello** with Frank Finlay, Maggie Smith. Coward directs **Hay Fever**. John Dexter directs Peter Shaffer's **The Royal Hunt of the Sun**. Peter Daubeny's first World Theatre Season. Brook's Theatre of Cruelty season and **Marat/Sade**. Nicol Williamson in Osborne's **Inadmissible Evidence**. Osborne's **A Patriot For Me** staged in 'Club' conditions. Dublin: Brian Friel's **Philadelphia, Here I Come!** In Paris: Ariane Mnouchkine founds Théâtre du Soleil. USA: LeRoi Jones' **Dutchman**, Adrienne Kennedy's **Funnyhouse of a Negro**. USSR: Yuri Lyubimov takes over the Taganka Theatre.

1965 Zeffirelli directs Smith/Stephens in **Much Ado**. Bond's **Saved** and subsequent trial. Orton's **Loot**. Berliner Ensemble's second visit to London: **Arturo Ui, Coriolanus, The Days of the Commune**. Trevor Nunn joins the RSC. Hall directs **The Homecoming**; also David Warner as dissident student-Hamlet. David Halliwell's **Little Malcolm and his Struggle Against the Eunuchs**. Death of George Devine. Helen Mirren's first Cleopatra for the National Youth Theatre. World Theatre Season includes the Actors' Studio in **Three Sisters** and Anna Magnani in Verga's **La Lupa**; also the first London sighting of Josef Svoboda's stage designs. First Theatre-in-Education programme at the Belgrade Theatre, Coventry. Jan Kott's *Shakespeare Our Contemporary*. Ritsaert Ten Cate founds the Mickery Theatre in Amsterdam: hot stop on the British fringe circuit. Poland: Jerzy Grotowski establishes research centre in Wroclaw. Czechoslovakia: Václav Havel's **The Memorandum**. USA: Luis Valdez forms El Teatro Campesino, to support Filipino and

Mexican-American strikers against California grape farmers.

1966 RSC: First **Revenger's Tragedy** in England for 300 years, dir. Trevor Nunn. Hockney designs **Ubu Roi**. Stoppard's **Rosencrantz and Guildenstern are Dead** on Edinburgh fringe. Peter Handke's **Offending the Audience**. Paris: Maria Casares in Genet's **The Screens**, dir. Roger Blin. Germany: Gunter Grass's **The Plebeians Rehearse the Uprising**. USA: Chaikin/van Itallie **America Hurrah!** Neil Simon has four shows running on Broadway.

1967 Peter Nichols' **A Day in the Death of Joe Egg**. Joe Orton's **What the Butler Saw**. Peter Terson's **Zigger Zagger**. Charles Wood's **Dingo** banned. Richard Burton/Elizabeth Taylor in Oxford **Dr Faustus**. Roland Muldoon and the Cartoon Archetypical Slogan Theatre present **Mr Oligarchy's Circus**. Joe Orton is murdered. New York: Richard Schechner founds the Performance Group. Rado/Ragni's **Hair**. Gay bad-taste breakthrough in first Theatre of the Ridiculous production: dir. John Vaccaro, starring Charles Ludlam. Nigeria: Wole Soyinka detained without trial.

1968 Abolition of Lord Chamberlain's powers of theatre censorship. **Hair** in London: first multiple on-stage nudity. Osborne's **Hotel in Amsterdam**. Peter Gill directs D.H. Lawrence trilogy at Royal Court. Christopher Hampton's **Total Eclipse**. Peter Barnes' **The Ruling Class**. RSC: Peggy Ashcroft in Marguerite Duras' **Days in the Trees**. Terry Hands' **Merry Wives of Windsor**. Royal Court: Bond's **Early Morning** performed in semi-secret. Judi Dench in **Cabaret**. The Living Theatre's **Paradise Now** in London. Jim Haynes opens the Drury Lane Arts Lab: it stays open for eighteen months. Ed Berman starts Inter-Action: inner-city community arts centre. John Fox forms Welfare State International: carnivals, processions and outdoor spectaculars. *Time Out* starts fringe listings. Grotowski's *Towards a Poor Theatre*. Peter Brook's *The Empty Space*. Paris: Barrault is fired from the Odéon after student occupation; then stages **Rabelais** in a Montmartre wrestling hall. Italy: Luca Ronconi directs **Orlando Furioso**. Poland: Tadeusz Kantor's **The Water Hen**.

1969 Peter Nichols' **The National Health**. Storey's **In Celebration** and **The Contractor**. Pinter: **Landscape** and **Silence**. Howard Brenton's **Gum and Goo** and **The Education of Skinny Spew. Oh Calcutta!**. The Royal Court opens the Theatre Upstairs. Elizabeth Sweeting's *Theatre Administration*: the first book on the subject. In Amsterdam, young actors institute 'Aktie Tomaat' by throwing tomatoes at actors thought to be giving reactionary performances.

1970 Maggie Smith as **Hedda Gabler**, dir. Ingmar Bergman. Brook directs **A Midsummer Night's Dream**. Gielgud/Richardson together again in David Storey's **Home**. Trevor Griffiths' **Occupations**. Hampton's **The Philanthropist**. David Mercer's **After Haggerty**.

Heathcote Williams' **AC/DC**. Howard Brenton: **Christie in Love**. The **Come Together** festival at the Royal Court: showcase for radical theatre. Frank Dunlop founds the Young Vic, under the auspices of the National Theatre. Olivier becomes first actor to become a life peer: Baron Olivier of Brighton. In Glasgow: Giles Havergal, Philip Prowse and Robert David MacDonald set the Citizens' Theatre on path of theatrical flamboyance to great approval from the surrounding tenements. In Paris: Brook directs **Timon of Athens** at the Bouffes du Nord: first show of his self-exile. In New York: the Performance Group is re-formed as the Wooster Group. Lee Breuer, Joanne Akalaitis form Mabou Mines. Sondheim: **Company**.

1971 Olivier in **Long Day's Journey into Night** and **The Dance of Death**. Mnouchkine's **1789**. RSC: Hall directs Pinter's **Old Times**. Simon Gray's **Butley**. David Storey's **The Changing Room**. Peter Gill deconstructs **The Duchess of Malfi**. Nuria Espert visit to World Theatre Season with **The Maids**. Brook/Ted Hughes **Orghast** at Persepolis. West Berlin: Peter Stein's **Peer Gynt**, with four different Peers, at the Schaubühne.

1972 RSC: Boucicault's **London Assurance**. Stoppard's **Jumpers**. John Arden and Margarette D'Arcy picket the RSC's production of their play **The Island of the Mighty**. E.A. Whitehead's **Alpha Beta**. Gielgud in Charles Wood's **Veterans**. Smith/Stephens in **Private Lives**. Portable Theatre's **England's Ireland**. Sam Shepard's **The Tooth of Crime** at the Open Space. The Half Moon opens with Brecht's **In the Jungle of the Cities**. The Bush Theatre opens: plays by Poliakoff, Edgar, Robert Holman, Snoo Wilson. West Berlin: Stein directs Vishnevsky's **An Optimistic Tragedy** and Kleist's **Prince Frederick of Homburg** at the Schaubühne.

1973 Dexter/Harrison **Misanthrope** at the National Theatre. Olivier's last stage appearance in Trevor Griffiths' **The Party**. Peter Hall takes over as Director of the National Theatre. Dexter directs Shaffer's **Equus**. West End: Guinness in Alan Bennett's **Habeas Corpus**. Alan Ayckbourn's **The Norman Conquests**. Royal Court: two Bonds: **The Sea** and **Bingo**, and Jim Sharman directs Richard O'Brien's **The Rocky Horror Show**. Fugard/Kani/Ntshona's **Sizwe Bansi is Dead**. Brenton's **Magnificence**. 7:84's **The Cheviot, the Stag and the Black, Black Oil**. Binkie Beaumont dies. Richard Eyre takes over Nottingham Playhouse: Brenton/Hare **Brassneck**. New York: the Open Theatre dissolved. Sondheim's **A Little Night Music**. Uta Hagen: *Respect for Acting*.

1974 Fugard/Kani/Ntshona's **The Island** at the Royal Court. At the instigation of Buzz Goodbody, the RSC opens The Other Place in Stratford. Joint Stock founded. Brenton's **The Churchill Play** and Ken Campbell's **Bendigo** at Nottingham Playhouse. Lindsay Kemp's **Flowers**.

1975 Griffiths' **Comedians** at Nottingham Playhouse. Stoppard's **Travesties** at the RSC. Berkoff's **East**. Pip Simmons' **An Die Musik**. Joint Stock presents Hare/Hinton **Fanshen**. Hare's **Teeth 'n' Smiles**. Gielgud/Richardson in Pinter's **No Man's Land**. Ben Travers' **The Bed Before Yesterday**. Robert Patrick's **Kennedy's Children** at the Arts. Simon Gray's **Otherwise Engaged**. Riverside Studios opens under the direction of Peter Gill. Paris: Brook's **The Ik**. West Berlin: Stein directs Gorky's **Summerfolk** at the Schaubühne. In USA: Mamet's **American Buffalo**. Michael Bennett's **A Chorus Line**.

1976 The National Theatre moves into Lasdun's building on the South Bank. Hare directs Brenton's **Weapons of Happiness**. At the RSC: Trevor Nunn directs musical version of **A Comedy of Errors**; also Ian McKellen and Judi Dench in studio-sized **Macbeth**. Edward Bond's **The Fool**. Pam Gems' **Dusa, Fish, Stas and Vi**. David Edgar's **Destiny**. Monstrous Regiment in Caryl Churchill's **Vinegar Tom**. Peter Gill's **Small Change**. Tadeusz Kantor's **The Dead Class** at Riverside Studios. The TNP visits the National Theatre with **Tartuffe**, dir. Roger Planchon and **La Dispute**, dir. Patrice Chéreau. Manchester: Royal Exchange opens. USA: Hal Prince directs Lloyd Webber's **Evita**. Steppenwolf founded in Chicago. Ntozake Shange's **for coloured girls who have considered suicide when the rainbow is enuf**. South Africa: Barney Simon and Mannie Manim found the Market Theatre in Johannesburg.

1977 Hampton/von Horváth **Tales from the Vienna Woods** at the National. The Cottesloe Theatre opens with Ken Campbell's **Illuminatus**. **The Passion**: first instalment of Bryden/Harrison **Mysteries**. Mike Leigh's **Abigail's Party**. Bill Morrison's **Flying Blind**. Barrie Keeffe's **Gimme Shelter**. Peter Stein's **Summerfolk** visits London. The RSC opens a Studio venue: the Warehouse in Covent Garden. Nunn directs Donald Sinden as **King Lear**. Berlin: Peter Stein's **As You Like It** at the Schaubühne. USA: Andrei Serban directs Irene Worth in **The Cherry Orchard** at the Lincoln Center.

1978 Hare's **Plenty**. Pinter's **Betrayal**. Ayckbourn's **Bedroom Farce**. Neil Oram's/Ken Campbell's twenty-hour epic **The Warp**. Peter Nichols' **Privates on Parade**. James Saunders' **Bodies**. Stephen Lowe's **Touched** at Nottingham Playhouse. Peter Gill directs **The Cherry Orchard** at Riverside Studios.

1979 Martin Sherman's **Bent**. Hall directs Shaffer's **Amadeus**. Caryl Churchill's **Cloud Nine**. Mike Leigh's **Ecstasy**. David Edgar's **Mary Barnes**. Friel's **The Faith Healer**. Pam Gems' **Piaf**. Julie Walters in Willy Russell's **Educating Rita**. Augusto Boal's *Theater of the Oppressed*. Czechoslovakia: Václav Havel imprisoned. USA: Sondheim's **Sweeney Todd**.

1980 David Edgar/Trevor Nunn/John Caird **Nicholas Nickleby**. Brenton's **The Romans in Britain** is prosecuted. Gambon in **Life of Galileo**, directed by Dexter, designed by

Jocelyn Herbert. Fo's **Accidental Death of an Anarchist**. Richard Eyre directs Jonathan Pryce as **Hamlet** at the Royal Court. Ronald Harwood's **The Dresser**. Brian Friel/Stephen Rea start Field Day Theatre Company with Friel's **Translations**. Andrea Dunbar's **The Arbor**. Pam Gems' **Piaf**. RSC: John Barton's **The Greeks**. Peter O'Toole **Macbeth** at the Old Vic. Florence: Kantor creates **Wielopole, Wielopole**. USA: Sam Shepard's **True West** at the Magic Theatre, San Francisco.

1981 Simon Gray's **Quartermaine's Terms**. C.P. Taylor's **Good**. Eliot/Lloyd Webber/ Nunn **Cats**. Aeschylus/Tony Harrison **Oresteia**, directed by Hall, designed by Jocelyn Herbert. RSC: Ashcroft in **All's Well That Ends Well**, directed by Nunn. Nell Dunn's **Steaming**. USA: Sondheim's **Merrily We Roll Along**.

1982 Churchill's **Top Girls**. Frayn's **Noises Off**. Terry Johnson's **Insignificance**. Stoppard's **The Real Thing**. John Byrne's **Slab Boys** trilogy completed. Willie Russell's **Educating Rita**. National Theatre **Guys and Dolls** and **The Beggar's Opera** directed by Richard Eyre. The RSC moves its London base to the Barbican.

1983 Mamet's **Glengarry Glen Ross**. Hampton's **Tales From Hollywood**. David Hare: **A Map of the World**. Howard Barker's **Victory**. Sarah Daniels' **Masterpieces**. Willy Russell's musical **Blood Brothers**. Dublin: Tom Murphy's **The Gigli Concert**. Paris: Giorgio Strehler becomes head of the newly formed Théâtre de l'Europe, with headquarters at the Odéon. USA: Sondheim's **Sunday in the Park with George**. Sam Shepard's **Fool for Love** at San Francisco's Magic Theatre.

1984 Antony Sher as **Richard III**. National Theatre Studio founded. Arts Council's *The Glory of the Garden* report recommends devolvement to regions. USA: Martha Clarke's **The Garden of Earthly Delights**. William Ball's *A Sense of Direction*. Simon Callow's *Being an Actor*. USA: August Wilson's **Ma Rainey's Black Bottom**. USSR: Yuri Lyubimov is fired from the Taganka and stripped of Soviet citizenship.

1985 Brenton/Hare's **Pravda**. The Harrison/Bryden **Mysteries**: complete cycle. Timberlake Wertenbaker's **The Grace of Mary Traverse**. Frank McGuinness's **Observe the Sons of Ulster Marching Towards the Somme**. John Godber's **Bouncers**. Lyubimov's **The Possessed** in London. The RSC presents **Les Misérables**, dir. Nunn and John Caird. Avignon: Brook's **Mahabharata**. Vienna: Havel's **Largo Desolato**. Larry Kramer's **The Normal Heart**. South Africa: Mbongemi Ngema's **Asinamali!**

1986 Jim Cartwright's **Road**. Nick Dear's **The Art of Success**. Lloyd Webber's **Phantom of the Opera**. Yvonne Brewster founds the all-black Talawa Theatre Company. The RSC unveils the Swan Theatre. Howard Davies directs Christopher Hampton's **Les Liaisons**

393

Dangereuses: the cast includes Juliet Stevenson, Alan Rickman, Lindsay Duncan, Fiona Shaw. USA: August Wilson's **Fences**. Washington: Peter Sellars directs Sophocles' **Ajax**. Australia: Baz Luhrmann writes and directs a new play: **Strictly Ballroom**.

1987 Judi Dench/Anthony Hopkins in **Antony and Cleopatra** dir. Peter Hall. Maggie Smith in Shaffer's **Lettice and Lovage**. Peter Stein's production of O'Neill's **The Hairy Ape**. Ninagawa's **Medea**. Royal Court: Caryl Churchill's **Serious Money**. Jim Allen's **Perdition** cancelled after political protests. RSC: Nicholas Hytner directs **Measure for Measure**. Opening of British Theatre Museum. Paris: Patrice Chéreau directs Bernard-Marie Koltès' **In the Solitude of the Cotton Fields**. Canada: Lepage's **The Dragon's Trilogy**.

1988 Deborah Warner directs **Titus Andronicus**. Timberlake Wertenbaker's **Our Country's Good**. David Hare's **The Secret Rapture**. Nicholas Wright's **Mrs Klein**. Ken Campbell's **Recollections of a Furtive Nudist**. RSC: Adrian Noble directs **The Plantagenets**. Greenwich: Tim Albery directs Fiona Shaw as **Mary Stuart**. Richard Eyre takes over as Director of the National Theatre.

1989 Declan Donnellan directs Lope de Vega's **Fuenteovejuna**. Winsome Pinnock's **A Hero's Welcome**. Steppenwolf's **The Grapes of Wrath**, dir. Frank Gelati. Steven Berkoff directs **Molière** at the Gate, Dublin.

1990 Brian Friel's **Dancing at Lughnasa**, National Theatre. Lepage's **Tectonic Plates** visits the National. Adrian Noble becomes director of the RSC. **Five Guys Named Mo**. Jonathan Kent and Ian McDiarmid take over the Almeida Theatre in Islington. Richard Eyre directs Hare's **Racing Demon** and Ian McKellen as **Richard III**. Howard Barker's **Scenes from an Execution**. David Lan's **Desire**. Stephen Daldry takes over the Gate Theatre, Notting Hill. Glasgow: Bill Bryden's **The Ship**. Berlin: Peter Stein directs Koltès' **Roberto Zucco** at the Schaubühne. Milan: Strehler directs de Filippo's **La Grande Magia**.

1991 Nigel Hawthorne in Bennett's **The Madness of George III**. Christopher Hampton's **White Chameleon**. Wallace Shawn's **The Fever**. Hare's **Murmuring Judges**. Théâtre de Complicité's **The Visit**. Daldry directs Tirso de Molina's **Damned for Despair**. RSC: Noble directs Sophocles/Wertenbaker's **The Thebans**. John Godber's **Happy Families** is performed by fifty amateur companies throughout Britain. Dublin: Deborah Warner directs Fiona Shaw as **Hedda Gabler**. Paris, Théâtre du Soleil: Ariane Mnouchkine's **Les Atrides**.

1992 At the National Theatre: Théâtre de Complicité's **Street of Crocodiles**, Tony Kushner's **Angels in America**, dir. Declan Donnellan. Stephen Daldry directs Priestley's **An Inspector Calls**. Lepage's **A Midsummer Night's Dream**. Hytner directs

Rodgers/Hammerstein **Carousel.** Eyre directs **Night of the Iguana.** RSC: Adrian Noble directs Branagh's **Hamlet** and Terry Hands directs Antony Sher as Tamburlaine. Royal Court: Phyllis Nagy's **Weldon Rising.** The Warehouse is re-formed as an independent off-West End theatre under the direction of Sam Mendes. Václav Havel becomes President of Czechoslovakia. Milan: Strehler directs Goldoni's **La baruffe chiozzotte.** USA: Mamet's **Oleanna.**

1993 The Wooster Group's **Brace Up!** in London. Sophie Treadwell's **Machinal,** dir. Daldry. Stoppard's **Arcadia.** Hare trilogy at National Theatre: **Racing Demon, Murmuring Judges, The Absence of War,** dir. Eyre. Lloyd Webber/Hampton/Don Black/Nunn **Sunset Boulevard.** Pinter's **Moonlight** at the Almeida.

1994 Complicité's **The Three Lives of Lucie Cabrol.** Caryl Churchill's **The Skriker.** Joe Penhall's **Some Voices.** Nick Grosso's **Peaches.** Patrick Marber's **Dealer's Choice;** Tennessee Williams' **Sweet Bird of Youth** at the National Theatre. Jonathan Kent directs **The Life of Galileo** at the Almeida. Brook's **The Man Who** visits the National Theatre. New York: Shepard directs his **Simpatico** at the Public Theatre.

1995 Declan Donnellan/Cheek by Jowl all-male **As You Like It.** Sarah Kane's **Blasted.** Jez Butterworth's **Mojo.** Hare's **Skylight.** Ralph Fiennes in Almeida **Hamlet** at the Hackney Empire. Sebastian Barry's **The Steward of Christendom.** The Arts Council of England gives first capital grant from the National Lottery Fund.

1996 Lepage's **The Seven Streams of the River Ota.** Paul Scofield, Vanessa Redgrave and Eileen Atkins in **John Gabriel Borkman** dir. Eyre. Martin McDonagh's **The Beauty Queen of Leenane.** Out of Joint: Mark Ravenhill's **Shopping and Fucking.** Ayub Khan-Din's **East is East.**

1997 Patrick Marber's **Closer.** Conor McPherson's **The Weir.** Judi Dench in Hare's **Amy's View.** Richard Eyre directs Ian Holm as **King Lear** and Tom Stoppard's **The Invention of Love** with John Wood. Peter Gill's **Cardiff East.** Phelim McDermott's **Struwwelpeter.** Chekhov/Hare/Kent/Fiennes **Ivanov.** Martin Crimp's **Attempts on Her Life.** Caryl Churchill's **Blue Heart.** Trevor Nunn takes over as Director of the National Theatre. Opening of Shakespeare's Globe.

1998 Almeida **Phèdre** and **Britannicus** in the West End. Nicole Kidman in Hare/Schnitzler **The Blue Room.** David Hare's **Via Dolorosa** and *Acting Up.* USA: Disney/Taymor **The Lion King.** Warner/Shaw **The Waste Land.**

1999 Trevor Nunn directs **Summerfolk** and **The Merchant of Venice** at the National

Theatre. **Cloud Street** visits London, dir. Neil Armfield. **Spend, Spend, Spend.** A fatwa is declared on Terrence McNally's **Corpus Christi**. **The Dispute**, dir. Neil Bartlett. Death of Sarah Kane. Maggie Smith in Bennett's **The Lady in the Van**. Tricycle Theatre: **The Colour of Justice.**

*Production in UK unless otherwise stated.

Picture Credits

Every effort has been made to seek permission for the use of these photographs. Grateful acknowledgement is made to the following for the use of their photographs:

Mary Evans Picture Library, p.17; The Raymond Mander and Joe Mitchenson Theatre Collection, pp.28, 35, 36, 42, 48 (top right), 99, 103, 113, 119, 122, 199, 228, 268, 356; SCR Photo Library, pp.31, 34; Shakespeare Centre Library, Stratford-upon-Avon, pp.37, 48 (left), 50, 56 (top left); Michael Boys and Weidenfeld & Nicolson Archives, p.39; V&A Picture Library, pp.40, 86, 219, 239, 308; Sir Barry Jackson Trust Department of Leisure and Community Services, Birmingham Libraries, p.48 (bottom right); John Haynes, frontispiece, pp.49, 56 (bottom), 132, 163, 175 (bottom), 216, 222 (bottom left), 247, 255, 256, 292, 301, 310; Zoë Dominic, pp.51, 116, 151, 223 (bottom right), 237, 244, 253, 352; Donald Cooper/Photo*stage*, Milton Keynes, pp.54, 56 (top right), 57, 87, 90, 92, 97, 128, 161, 191, 274, 283, 297, 298, 312, 319, 364, 366; Archive Photos, pp.65 (left), 179; National Portrait Gallery, London, pp.65 (top right), 65 (bottom right); Hulton Getty Picture Collection, pp.69, 74, 115, 196, 350; Hugh Lane Municipal Gallery of Modern Art, Dublin, p.70; the Director and University Librarian, the John Rylands University Library of Manchester, p.71; Robbie Jack, pp.75, 146; Charles Deering McCormick Library of Special Collections, Northwestern University, Evanston, Illinois, p.79; Douglas H. Jeffrey, pp.96, 109; Catherine Ashmore, pp.125, 171, 327; © Bettmann/Corbis, pp.137, 156; Museum of the City of New York: Gift of Mrs Meta Solotaroff Goldin, p.139, Gift of Max Haas, p.145, Gift of the Burns Mantle Estate, 158, Gift of Harold Friedlander, 194, Gift of Jeffrey Richards, 195, The Lucas-Monroe Collection, p.209; Museum of the City of New York, pp.155, 159, 166, 175 (top), 188; Yale Collection of American Literature, Beinecke Rare Book & Manuscript Library, p.143; © Eileen Darby, pp.185, 186; Münchner Stadtmuseum, p.204; Bildarchiv Preussicher Kulturbesitz, Berlin, pp.201, 206; Stiftung Archiv der Akademie der Künste, Bertolt Brecht Archive, pp.202, 212; © Lewis Morley/Akehurst Bureau, p.213; AKG London/Erich Lessing, p.220; Harold Pinter private collection p.226; John Bretton & Co., p.227; Nobby Clark, pp.231, 233, 235, 279, 291, 304, 341, 367; Sandra Lousada, pp.243, 249; © *Guardian*/Kenneth Saunders, p.252; Theatre Royal, Stratford East, pp.260, 265; Bobbie Hanvey, Downpatrick, Co. Down, p.272; Richard Mildenhall/Arena Images, p.275; Chris Davies, p.286; Ivan Kynel, p.289; © *Guardian*/David Sillitoe, p.295; © James Blair/Corbis, p.300 (top); © Estate of Roger Perry, p.300 (bottom); © DERRY Moore, p.329; © Barry Jones, p.335; Michael Le Poer Trench/Arena Images, p.345; from *Russian and Soviet Theatre* by Konstantin Rudnitsky (Thames & Hudson, London and New York, 2000), pp.348, 349; Morris Newcombe/Arena Images, p.357; Giles Abegg, Paris, p.359; Henrietta Butler/Arena Images, pp.370, 375; the Rodgers and Hammerstein Organization, pp.165, 169, 172.

Index